Russian Foreign Policy

Eric Shiraev and Konstantin Khudoley

Russian Foreign Policy

First published 2019 by
RED GLOBE PRESS

Red Globe Press in the UK is an imprint of Springer Nature Limited,
registered in England, company number 785998, of 4 Crinan Street,
London N1 9XW.

Red Globe Press® is a registered trademark in the United States,
the United Kingdom, Europe and other countries.

ISBN: 978-0-230-37098-2 hardback
ISBN: 978-0-230-37097-5 paperback

This book is printed on paper suitable for recycling and made from fully
managed and sustained forest sources. Logging, pulping and manufacturing
processes are expected to conform to the environmental regulations of the
country of origin.

A catalogue record for this book is available from the British Library.

A catalog record for this book is available from the Library of Congress.

Contents

List of Figures, Maps and Tables

Figures

Maps

Tables

Preface

Few countries in history have changed as swiftly and dramatically as Russia has done over the past thirty years. These three decades saw a relentless process of searching, reinventing, rebuilding, and restructuring. This process was very difficult. Not everything went smoothly. In fact, many developments were real challenges for Russia. Reinvention is never easy, and Russia was reinventing itself in every sense of the word. Since the year 2000 Russia turned to playing an increasingly important role in regional and global affairs as an economic and military power. Today, Russia's international behavior attracts global attention. It also causes serious concerns, especially in the West and among western allies. What is Russia's ultimate goal? Why does Russia see the West as an adversary? Will Russia remain a threat? Are these fears exaggerated? If not, what should be done to address them? Which regions are available to cooperate with Russia? For those who study Russia, grasping these developments and answering these questions remains a constant contest.

Why do these tasks remain so challenging? Upon further review, almost everything in Russia is a "work in progress" marked by sudden accelerations, slowdowns, turnarounds, and contradictions. To illustrate, in the context of international politics:

> Russia insists on a new type of relationship among the states based on their mutual respect of sovereignty and territorial integrity; by contrast, Russia was involved in military conflicts with Georgia in 2008 and, according to the view accepted in the West, annexed a territory of a sovereign state (Ukraine) in 2014. Russia disputes these interpretations.

> Russia aspires to become a global economic power and a dependable trade partner, yet it relies mostly on its natural resources such as oil and gas. Except for weapons and a few other manufactured products, Russia so far has had little to offer to the world.

> Russia is calling for global cooperation among countries. Yet Russia has very few allies, and most of them are in the developing world. In 2014 Russia was suspended from G-7, an international platform for the world's most dominant countries.

> Russia is convinced that the West deliberately misrepresents its position and undermines its policies. The West disagrees, pointing to Russia's own actions as a source of international concerns and, as a result, counteractions.

> Russian people tend to be suspicious of the West and its policies, but at the same time many of them tend to admire Western culture, economic prosperity, and social institutions.

> Russia wants to project its power globally. Yet the "brain drain" from the country continues: many of the most educated and the most skilled leave Russia for good, trying to start new lives elsewhere.

When you study Russia, you constantly encounter these inconsistencies and contradictions. This book reflects on these and many others challenges and paradoxes that refer to Russian foreign policy.

A distinct feature of the book is its structure.

- After the introductory chapter there is a chapter covering the history of Russia's foreign policy.
- The next chapter describes the institutions of foreign policy.
- The discussion then turns to key players, sources, and internal political aspects of foreign policy.
- Following that, the book discusses the key principles and strategies of Russia's international behavior.
- Chapters 6–11 cover the key global and regional directions of foreign policy. A concluding chapter then discusses general assessments and predictions of Russia's foreign policy.

Russian Foreign Policy incorporates and emphasizes a critical thinking approach. This emphasis should encourage the reader to be an informed skeptic and help to distinguish facts from opinions. The book also brings together various facts and theories from the fields of Political Science, International Relations, History, Sociology, and Political Psychology.

This book incorporates several pedagogical devices designed for classroom use and homework assignments. Each chapter begins with an opening quotation, contains a brief prologue, and ends with a conclusion and review questions. In every chapter you will find several boxed features including visual aids and tables. A test bank and lecture slides are available for teachers.

The book has a dedicated website, which contains the most recent updates, factual data, interviews, editorials, and opinion polls related to current developments in Russia. The website also contains specially selected links for readers who are either studying or are already proficient in the Russian language. In addition, practice examination questions for students are posted on the companion site.

No project of this scale could have been realized without the invaluable contributions, assistance, and support of many individuals. We have benefited from the insightful feedback and advice of colleagues and reviewers in the United States, Russia, Poland, Germany, Norway, Kyrgyzstan, and the United Kingdom; from the thorough efforts of research assistants; and from the patience and understanding of coworkers and friends on several continents.

As authors, we live on opposite sides of the planet. Yet our cooperation, mutual visits, discussions, and creative agreements on almost everything we have been working on shows that good will and mutual friendship are always the key to success in any international enterprise.

We wrote this book with a new generation of young people who were born mostly after the end of the Cold War in mind. We hope that those readers who lived through the Cold War era will also find this text useful. Many things in Russia might change while you are reading these pages. Russia will remain a fascinating work in progress.

Acknowledgments

This book could not have been realized without the invaluable contributions and support of scores of individuals. It has benefited from the insightful feedback and advice of colleagues and reviewers, from the diligent efforts of research assistants, and from the patience and understanding of our family members and friends. In particular we wish to acknowledge Marlene Laruelle, Henry Hale, Renée Lerner, and Henry Nau (George Washington University); James Goldgeier (The American University); Phil Tetlock (University of Pennsylvania); Dimitri Simes and Paul Saunders (Center for the National Interest); Robert Dudley, Sergei Samoilenko, Mark Katz, Eric McGlinchey, Peter Mandaville, Fred Bemak, Nelson Lund, Craig Lerner, and Mark Rozell (George Mason University); Jason Smart (International Republican Institute); Martijn Icks (University of Amsterdam); Jennifer Keohane (University of Baltimore); Ursula Jakubowska (Polish Academy of Sciences); Cheryl Koopman (Stanford University); Jonathan Aronson (USC); Tom Farer (University of Denver); Vendulka Kubalkova (University of Miami); Jakub Zajączkowski (University of Warsaw); and Bojko Bucar and Anton Bebler (University of Ljubljana). Our special thanks to Sergei Tsytsarev, David Levy, Andrey Khudoley, Dmitry Shiraev, Dennis Shiraev, and Nicole Shiraev.

We received tremendous help from our colleagues and friends in Russia, including Nikolai Skvortsov, Stanislav Eremeev, Dmitry Mezentsev, Stanislav Tkachenko, Olga Deineka, Leonid Ivanov, Olga Makhovskaya, Andrei Agapov, Vladimir Gritskov, Anton Galitsky, Irina Novikova, Vladislav Sobolev, Igor Gretsky, Evgeny Treshchenkov, Tatiana Romanova, Dmitry Lanko, Konstantin Golubev, Natalia Zaslavskaya, Nikolay Gudalov, Alexander Izotov, Natalia Tsvetkova, Ivan Tsvetkov, Niyazi Niyazov, Konstantin Meshcheryakov, Yana Leksyutina, Natalia Markushina, Yury Akimov, Nikolay Vlasov, Andrey Pavlov, Sergey Nabok, Dmitriy Tulupov, Grigory Yarygin, Ruslan Kostiuk, Victor Jeifets, Lazar Jeifets, Konstantin Pantserev, Yuri Kuzmin, Philipp Khanin, Natalia Ryazantseva, Olga Tserpitskaya, Kirill Likhachev, Andrey Kovsh, Irina Lantsova, Dmitry Levi, Maria Soldatenkova, and Irina Chigireva.

We would also like to thank the book's reviewers for their insightful comments.

A special word of appreciation is due to the administrations, faculty, staff, and students at George Mason University, St. Petersburg University, George Washington University, and other academic institutions where we have consistently been provided with incredible research opportunities. We also would like to take this opportunity to acknowledge the tremendous support we received at every stage of this project's development from the team at Red Globe Press, in particular, Stephen Wenham (who initiated this project), Tuur Driesser, Lloyd Langman, and Elizabeth Holmes (who patiently navigated us). Additional thanks go to the management and staff at Integra, particularly Sangeetha Sathiamurthy for her help in the production process.

A special word of gratitude to our parents Boris, Nina, and Margarita: We can never thank them enough. Last, also on a personal note, we wish to express our feelings of thankfulness to Vladislav Zubok (London School of Economics), our colleague and friend, for his continuous inspiration and support.

Our voyage continues.

Washington, DC – St. Petersburg

Chapter 1
Introduction to Russia's Foreign Policy

*We are not surrounded by enemies and we will not end up in that position. This is
absolutely out of the question. We have good, friendly relations with most countries.*

Vladimir Putin, Russian President 2016
Direct Line with Vladimir Putin

Learning objectives

- Describe the importance of studying Russia as a country and Russia's policies.
- Discuss why Russian foreign policy mattered yesterday and still matters today.
- Explain and critically examine the key methods used to study Russian foreign policy.
- Outline ways to interpret and predict Russia's future actions.

Russia today

Introducing Russia

Russia, officially known as the Russian Federation, is the world's largest country.
It is one of the top fifteen biggest economies in the world. It has a mixed economic system with both private and state ownership. It possesses nuclear weapons,
a capable army, the air force, and the navy. It has a stable yet evolving political
system. Russia has an educated population and a trained workforce. Russia's contribution to the world's culture is noticeable. The country plays a meaningful role in

1

global economic and political affairs. Overall, Russia's ability to influence international developments makes it a major player today.

However, Russia's actions during the first two decades of the twenty-first century have caused serious concerns. Difficult questions have arisen about the meaning of Russia's strategic long-term goals and specific short-term plans. What does Russia want as an international player? Is Russia a partner or a foe to the West? Do people – in the United States, Canada, the United Kingdom, and elsewhere – have to resolutely oppose Russia in international affairs, or should they remain neutral or even supportive sometimes? Is cooperation with Russia a better alternative to competition? To answer these and many other questions, one needs to better understand Russia's rich history, better know its current potentials and weaknesses, and better analyze its policies and decisions. Our understanding of Russian foreign policy should help in developing effective bilateral relations between Russia and other countries, especially the United States, Canada, the United Kingdom, China, South Korea, and with the European Union. Knowing more about Russian foreign policy should also facilitate the effectiveness of many international organizations and nongovernment groups. This should help in preserving and building a more secure, stable, and prosperous world.

Before we begin the study of Russia's foreign policy, let's first review some basic facts about Russia as a country and then turn to its political and economic systems. This background will be important when we discuss particular events and specific policies (Map 1.1).

Map 1.1 Russia

Russia as a country

The Russian Federation stretches over 6.5 million square miles (more than 17 million square kilometers – Russia, as do most countries in the world, uses the metric system). It is almost twice the size of the United States, Canada, or China. Russia has ten time zones extended across Eurasia. When you arrive at midday in Kaliningrad, Russia's most western seaport in Europe, it is 1 pm in Moscow, Russia's capital, and already 10 pm in Petropavlovsk, the city on the Kamchatka Peninsula in Russia's far east. Russia borders the Baltic Sea in the west, the Black and the Caspian Seas in the south, the Arctic Ocean in the north, and the Pacific Ocean in the east.

Russia is among the top ten most populous countries in the world. Its 144 million citizens live on one-eighth of the planet's inhabitable area. About 80 percent of Russia's citizens identify as ethnic Russians. As a group, Russians share common Slavic ancestral roots (including cultural and linguistic) with many peoples of Eastern and Central Europe such as Belarusians, Ukrainians, Slovaks, Czechs, Serbs, Poles, Bulgarians, and Montenegrins. There are also about 30 million people in Russia who are not ethnic Russians and identify with about 70 different ethnic groups. They are called "nationalities" in Russia, which is a rather unusual label. Nationality – in legal terms – refers to a person's formal identification with a group of a people who share common geographical origin, history, and language and are unified as a political entity – an independent or sovereign state recognized by other countries. In Russia, however, "nationality" refers mostly to an ethnic or cultural group. Some of these cultural groups, or nationalities, are concentrated within twenty-six separate administrative units, but there are no official restrictions on where any Russian citizen may live in Russia. Among the largest ethnic minorities are Tatars, Ukrainians, Belarusians, Chuvash, Bashkir, Armenians, Chechens, and Mordovans. Tens of thousands of Russian citizens identify with German or Jewish origins (these are also called "nationalities"), but their numbers have declined over the past twenty-five years as a result of massive emigration of people from these groups to Israel or Germany and other Western countries. The overwhelming majority of people in ethnic groups speak fluent Russian (which is the only official language in the country), and in most interethnic marriages Russian is the first language (Rosstat, 2017).

It is estimated that Russia has approximately 7 million legal migrants who have obtained short-term status as temporary workers. In addition (there are no exact numbers), there are approximately 3 to 4 million undocumented migrants. This number has been changing over the past ten to fifteen years due to several factors, including the conditions of Russia's economy, the exchange rates of the ruble (the official Russian currency), the implementation of various residency laws, ongoing regional conflicts (such as the one in Ukraine that started in 2014), the severity of anti-immigrant sentiment within Russia, and, of course, a few other reasons.

Russia officially recognizes four major (or "traditional," as they are referred to in official documents) religions: Russian Orthodox Christian, Muslim, Jewish, and

Buddhist. More than 70 percent of people in Russia identify in opinion polls as Orthodox Christians. Approximately 10 percent of Russians identify as Muslims (mostly Turkic groups living across the country). These estimates do not include temporary migrants, most of whom are laborers from the post-Soviet states who tend to identify as Muslims. There are between 1 and 2 million Protestants, about seven hundred thousand Buddhists, and about two hundred thousand Jews (these estimates vary). Despite considering themselves believers, most Russians do not practice religion or maintain firm religious beliefs. For example, only 30 percent of Russians stated, according to polls, that religion plays either a "very important" or an "important" role in their lives. For various personal or political reasons (Levada, 2012, 2015), many people, including Muslims and Christians, do not openly acknowledge their religious identity.

Introducing some key definitions

What makes Russia important in today's global world? Have Russian policies made the world a more stable, safer place? How should the United States and its allies treat Russia and respond to its policies? Is Russia destined to be a constant adversary of the West, or will it find a path to cooperation? To answer these and many other questions, we need to critically assess Russia's foreign policy in the context of its domestic developments and international relations.

On International Relations

As a discipline, **International Relations (IR)** studies interactions among states and the international activities of nonstate organizations (Shiraev and Zubok, 2016). These interactions take several forms. They may be negotiations about territories, borders, military threats, migration of people, economic agreements, environmental cooperation, educational exchanges, and so on. International Relations is an academic discipline in which scholars discuss their ideas, arguments, and theories. It is also an applied field because it proposes solutions to the world's many problems. Even a short list of the issues related to IR is vast. Several topics remain prominent: (1) international politics, (2) international political economy, and (3) international law. International politics is the analysis of how states interact and pursue and protect their interests. International political economy investigates how politics among states influence their economic relations and how global markets affect the international system. International law studies mutually agreed formal rules and regulations concerning interactions among states, institutions, organizations, and individuals involved in international relations.

The field of International Relations differs from **Comparative Politics**, which focuses more on comparing domestic politics, political institutions, and systems rather than on how they interact. Yet the interests of both disciplines frequently overlap. The study of foreign policy is inseparable from International Relations and Comparative Politics and has become increasingly multidisciplinary. Professionals working in this field should know the basics of fields such as government, economics, history, sociology, cultural studies, psychology, and military studies, to name a few.

On foreign policy

In general terms, **foreign policy** involves sovereign states' interactions – including official decisions and communications, public and secret – with other state governments, nongovernmental organizations, corporations, international institutions, and individual decision-makers. A country's foreign policy is typically directed through embassies or other official offices overseas. Their main activities involve diplomacy.

Diplomacy is the practice of managing international relations by means of negotiations. The content of foreign policy ranges from peace treaties to threats of force; from trade agreements to trade sanctions; from scientific, technical, and cultural exchange programs to visa and immigration restrictions. Countries' governments usually prefer diplomatic means of interaction, but violence or a threat of it frequently backs diplomatic moves. In today's developed democratic states all three branches of government commonly participate in foreign policy, although their roles differ. Within the executive branch top government institutions dealing with international relations usually include a ministry or department of foreign affairs. The legislative branch passes laws about the direction, financing, and handling of foreign policy. In democratic countries parliaments commonly ratify (or approve) international agreements signed by state executive leaders. The judicial branch is involved in foreign policy in several ways. For example, courts can make assessments about the applicability of certain international laws or agreements about the territory of the country. The courts also decide on claims submitted by foreign countries, including businesses and private individuals.

Countries differ in terms of the involvement of the three branches in foreign policy. In some countries, such as the Netherlands or the United Kingdom, their legislative branches have more say in foreign policy than the legislature in countries such as Russia. Differences between foreign policy executed by democratic and nondemocratic governments are also important. In democratic countries political parties, nongovernmental organizations, the media, and public opinion play a more important role in foreign policy than in nondemocracies (Shiraev and Sobel, 2006, 2019).

The importance of specific definitions

In the English language the word "Russian" refers to something or somebody associated with Russia. However, if you translate this word into the Russian language you have to be careful, because there are two different meanings for this term. One refers to "Russian" as an ethnic category ("Roos-ski"). The other adjective

("Rossiy-ski") refers to something or somebody belonging to or associated with the Russian Federation as a sovereign state. The latter is a civic, not an ethnic, category. Both these adjectives are translated in English as Russian, which sometimes creates confusion. For example, some people belonging to various ethnic groups living in Russia will likely disagree if you apply the term "Russian" to them. They might have been born and raised in Russia and hold Russian citizenship but ethnically not be Russians (Sakwa, 1993: 116). If you speak Russian, you can avoid this confusion by using the right adjective when referring to Russia or Russians. In English, you have to provide additional qualifying explanations of the word "Russian" as referring to either (a) an ethnic group or (b) statehood or citizenship.

Russia's past 125 years: A snapshot

In Chapter 2, in which we outline Russia's foreign policy, we also provide a somewhat detailed review of several historical developments that affected Russia, its policies as a state, and its actions as an international power. Here we will review Russia's rich past focusing on only a few major developments of its recent history.

Imperial Russia

Russia, the biggest world state and a multiethnic empire, was already a powerful international actor early in the twentieth century. Of the more than 125 million people who lived in Russia during the reign of Emperor Nicholas II (1868–1918), about 65 percent were native Russian speakers. Russia was rapidly developing its economy and infrastructure. However, the first two decades of the past century were perhaps the most turbulent in Russia's history. In a twelve-year period the country endured three revolutions. These were the historic political changes of 1905–1907 (the first revolution) and later the fundamental and violent political transformations in February and then October 1917 (the second and third revolutions). The second revolution marked the end of the monarchy. A brief transitional period followed, which ended with the creation of a communist state.

What is known as the October 1917 Revolution was an extraordinary and traumatic event for the entire country. It sparked a devastating civil war that lasted until 1922. The war had several interconnected causes. Because of the revolution and new confiscatory policies imposed by the Communist Party (known in Russia as the Bolshevik party, or the Bolsheviks), all people lost their property, possessions, and monetary savings. Peasants by law had to surrender large portions of their harvests and stock to specially appointed representatives of the government. Several millions had died on World War I and the civil war battlefields, lost their lives due to starvation and diseases, or emigrated over the five-year period after 1914. The exact estimates of the population loss vary. Production levels had plummeted by 80 percent and agricultural output had dropped 40 percent compared with the pre–World War I period. Millions of people became unemployed. Inflation and food shortages were constant for several years (Erlichman, 2004). Nevertheless, by the early 1920s a functional centralized government had finally established control over the vast territory of the former Russian Empire.

The core ideology of the new communist government was Marxism, which was a set of theoretical principles formulated by the German philosopher and economist Karl Marx (1818–1883). Applied to politics, Marxism claimed that capitalism was a fundamentally unjust form of production reinforced by an oppressive political regime. Working people, according to Marxism, are the main producers of value (a measure of quantity and quality of products and services). Therefore, working people should become the true owners of resources; they must seize political power, abolish private property, and then establish a new political and social system of universal equality called communism (Lenin, 1917). For many decades Marxism remained a major ideological foundation for communist, socialist, and social-democratic movements around the world. It remains a formidable ideology today in Russia and elsewhere.

Vladimir Lenin, the leader of the Bolshevik party and head of the new government of Soviet Russia, a lawyer by education, was a Marxist. He believed in the inevitable death of capitalism in the West and globally (Lenin, 1916/1969). By liberating the oppressed, he wrote, the world's working class, called the proletariat, would abolish private property, thus simultaneously destroying the roots of injustice and war. As a result, a new international community would emerge through revolutionary violence against the oppressive social classes. Lenin justified dictatorship of one party (which would rule on behalf of the working class) as a tool to overcome domestic resistance and then build a new society.

The Bolshevik party assumed the role of the only self-proclaimed representative of the working class and peasantry. The party adopted a hammer and sickle as its motif on the red flag and coat of arms of the new state. All symbols of the old regime, including the Russian traditional tricolor flag established early in the eighteenth century, were abolished. (Russia restored the tricolor as the national flag in 1991.) In 1918 the Bolshevik government issued the first constitution of Soviet Russia, legitimizing the dictatorship of the "city and rural proletariat and poor peasantry" with the goal of eliminating capitalism in the country. Thus the ruling party established an early legal precedent for its unlimited power, which it maintained until 1991. Under these conditions, the State of the Soviet Union was officially formed on December 30, 1922. It lasted for nearly seventy years.

The Soviet years

By the 1930s the Soviet Union was an industrialized state with an increasingly educated multiethnic population. Russia, as a republic itself, dominated the union. The legal foundation of the government was a one-party political system. The new constitution of 1924 declared the Union of Soviet Socialist Republics (USSR) a federation of republics. On paper, each of the republics had the right to leave the federation and to conduct its own educational, social welfare, and labor policies. In reality, Moscow controlled practically all the republics' institutions and their policies.

The government in Moscow implemented a policy of rapid and massive industrialization. According to the communist doctrine, the strength of a state is determined by the size and quality of its heavy industries. Therefore, Soviet leaders in the 1920s and later focused on steel production and the manufacturing of machinery. The Communist Party also wanted all peasants to be organized into collective farms whose members shared property and land. As a result, individual ownership of land was abolished. The government introduced mandatory quotas for harvests and established extremely low prices for collective farms' agricultural products. The government exercised almost total political control over the peasantry. The compulsory collectivization was the foundation of Soviet agriculture for many years to come. This policy, unfortunately, among many other negative impacts, significantly reduced the peasants' incentive to produce (Conquest, 1986).

Both industrialization and collectivization required massive support from the state. The government in Moscow needed to develop a coercive bureaucratic system capable of functioning in a new social and economic environment. It did so and put the Communist Party at the center of it. The party played a major role in all areas of economic and political life in the Soviet Union: factories and plants became part of a sophisticated network administered by a centralized system of planning, production, distribution, and management. From the 1920s until the late 1980s, in big cities and small towns, a centralized bureaucratic structure was in charge of every aspect of economic planning and social development (Ruble, 1990).

The Soviet Union defeated Germany in World War II (1939–1945). Yet the victory was very costly. On the one hand, the Soviet Union became a major player in international affairs; many communist, pro-Soviet states have emerged in Europe and Asia. On the other hand, the Soviet Union was substantially weakened economically: the country lost more than 26 million people dead, and its infrastructure was devastated. Despite these difficulties, the Soviet Union emerged from the war as a proud nation unified around its autocratic and charismatic ruler Joseph Stalin (1878–1953). Although the leaders in Moscow, Washington, and London had established very productive contacts during the war, after 1945 they failed to create the conditions for lasting good relations. The difficult period of international tensions from the late 1940s to the late 1980s is known as the Cold War (we will return to this topic in Chapter 2 as well as in other chapters).

Most Soviet people for many years showed support for the government and its leadership, no matter who occupied the highest offices in the Kremlin. In the 1970s, however, the prestige of the official communist ideology diminished. In most places labor ethics were in decline. Mass cynicism (a mixture of skepticism and fake enthusiasm) spread. The period from the late 1970s to the middle of the 1980s was a time of widespread political apathy in the Soviet Union. The political ascendance of the new Soviet leader Mikhail Gorbachev (b. 1931), who became General Secretary of the Communist Party in 1985, changed the country forever. Gorbachev introduced a series of massive reforms that shook the country and had global consequences (Glad and Shiraev, 1999).

On the plus side, in the course of these reforms the people of the Soviet Union had obtained political freedom by the late 1980s. Censorship was gradually eliminated and freedom of speech guaranteed. The one-party political system was gone. Limited private property became legal, and small private businesses grew. The Cold War was seemingly over, and the Soviet Union called for a normalization of relations with the West. Moscow and Washington agreed to destroy thousands of nuclear warheads and the means to deliver them. People could finally travel overseas with their own foreign currency and without **exit visas** (which were difficult-to-obtain government permits that for decades allowed only limited foreign travel for the vast majority of Soviet citizens). The reforms of the 1980s, however, caused a profound crisis in all spheres of life. Sharp social inequality and polarization emerged. Inflation skyrocketed. Food shortages became common by the end of the 1980s. Crime flourished. Lawlessness was rampant. In many ethnic regions violence broke out, taking thousands of lives and bringing destruction and despair to hundreds of thousands of people. In 1991 the Soviet Union collapsed. Russia and fourteen former Soviet republics became independent. Except in Latvia, Estonia, and Lithuania, democracy was struggling in the former Soviet republics. Central Asian states turned to authoritarianism.

The transformation of 1985–1991 was full of contradictions, uncertainties, and disputed outcomes. Many contemporary Russian policies, as we will examine later in this book, took root in the processes that started in the 1980s and continued through the 1990s and later.

Russia after 1991: Major transitions

From a historical viewpoint, the period from the early 1990s to today was very short. Yet these years were filled with dramatic events that have few parallels in Russian or even world history. Over just two-and-a-half decades Russia had to be reassembled in every sense: it had to build a legitimate government, regain economic and military might, maintain a multiethnic state, and attempt to build democracy. The challenges were daunting. Privation and lawlessness in the 1990s, several economic crises, terrorist attacks, and scores of social problems slowed down the development of a new civil society. On paper, the political restructuring in Russia was a transition to a democracy. Yet the type of democracy existing in Russia today is unique and full of contradictions. According to the Constitution, Russia has three independent branches of government. The executive power is disproportionately strong, and it has been getting ever stronger since the early 2000s. Russia has an increasingly personal form of political rule, which is a source of uncertainty in domestic and international policies. Yet Russia as an international player has become more confident and predictable even in the ways in which it was developing tensions with its close and distant neighbors.

Russia's political and economic systems today

Russia's political system

Russia is a presidential, federal republic, organized according to Russia's basic law or Constitution, which was adopted in 1993. The term republic means that supreme power in the country belongs to the people and their elected representatives. The term "federal" means that Russia, as a sovereign state, consists of several subdivisions or units that can initiate and exercise certain policies and make particular independent decisions. Article 10 of the Constitution of the Russian Federation states that the power of the state in Russia is divided among three independent branches of government: the executive, legislative, and judiciary. The article also guarantees a separation of powers (see Figure 1.1).

Based on the Constitution, the president of Russia is head of state. Presidents are elected by popular vote once every six years (they were elected to four-year terms

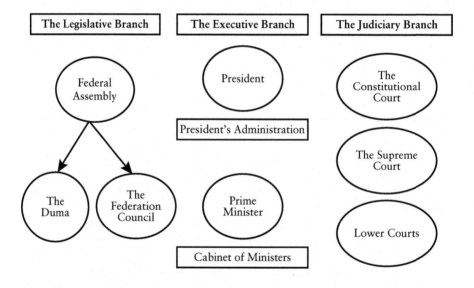

Figure 1.1 Russian government's structure

before a recent amendment to the Constitution). The country's executive power is also in the hands of the prime minister who chairs the Russian Council of Ministers. The prime minister is appointed by the president and must be approved by the State Duma. After 1990, there have been three Russian presidents: Boris Yeltsin (1931–2007), who was elected in 1991 and 1996; Vladimir Putin (b. 1953), who was elected in 2000, 2004, 2012, and 2018 for his fourth term; and Dmitry Medvedev, who was elected president in 2008 for only one four-year term.

The highest legislative body of the Russian Federation, according to the Constitution, is a parliament called the Federal Assembly. It consists of two chambers, the Federation Council and the State Duma. The members of each chamber are elected by means of a complicated system, the details of which have frequently changed. However, over a period of a little more than two decades, Russia has produced a stable legislative system based on democratic principles. It is somewhat different from the legislative systems in the United States, the United Kingdom, Japan, and many other democracies. One substantial difference is that the Russian legislature today tends to approve most of the bills introduced by the powerful executive branch. The influence of the legislature on the executive branch is relatively minor.

The Constitution is also the principal source of law in Russia. The Constitution states that only *law courts* administer justice in Russia. As in other countries, a court of law in Russia is supposed to establish the legality or otherwise of a certain action (which could be the behavior of an individual, a decision of an institution, or a government decree, for example) and then pass a ruling. Judiciary power is exercised in four major areas: constitutional, civil, administrative, and criminal. The law courts in Russia constitute a hierarchy, with the higher courts having the right to overrule decisions of lower courts. The Constitution identifies two federal legal bodies and outlines their basic responsibilities: the Constitutional Court of the Russian Federation and the Supreme Court of the Russian Federation. Despite gradual changes that have taken place in the judiciary since the 1990s, it has not achieved full independence from the executive branch. The justice system – Russia's leaders admit this openly – suffers from inefficiency, bureaucratic delays, and corruption.

According to the Constitution (Article 65), the Russian Federation consists of republics, regions (known as *oblasts*), special regions (known as *kraj*), three cities with special federal status (Moscow, St. Petersburg, and Sevastopol after 2014), and autonomous regions. All of these are the subjects of the Russian Federation or specially recognized territorial units within the federal state. The definitions of these units are fairly complicated, and the exact number of the subjects of the Russian Federation has changed several times and may be changing in the future.

To reiterate, the executive branch of government in today's Russia is the paramount power and is in almost full control in most areas of life. In comparison, in some other countries that, like Russia, underwent democratic transition in the 1990s, more powerful parliamentary systems emerged (for example, in Slovakia, Hungary, and Estonia) with relatively weaker executive branches. Moreover, in the past fifteen years Russia has introduced specific legal reforms as constitutional amendments that have further consolidated the executive power in the president's hands and increased the power of the federal (central) government in Russia's capital, Moscow, where the vast majority of federal institutions are located.

Russia's economic system

Russia is an economically developed country. The country's **Gross Domestic Product** (GDP or the value of all goods and services produced over a specific period), is one of the world's twenty largest. Russia's economy, relative to its size, is behind those of the United States, China, the European Union, Canada, and India, among a few others. It is ahead of South Korea, Mexico, and Spain. Russia has a functional economy with both private and state control of major industries (IMF, 2016) (see Figure 1.2).

Russia entered the 1990s as a decayed, centralized yet disorganized, economy, which was transformed within ten years (Shleifer and Treisman, 2004). Russian exports (mostly oil and gas) and fiscal austerity have generated a steady economic growth in the early 2000s (McFaul and Stoner-Weiss, 2008). Russia's economic policy-making, based on free-market principles coupled with significant government

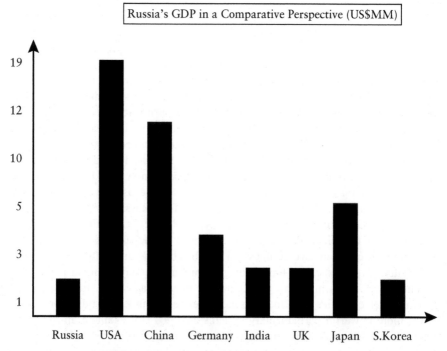

Figure 1.2 Russia's GDP in comparative perspective
Source: Created using IMF (2018)

regulation of key industries, has worked well during the period of high prices for energy resources, as the Russian leaders acknowledged themselves (Putin, 2012c). In addition, capital gains and personal income taxes remained low in order to attract new foreign investments and stimulate foreign business. By the early 2010s Russia had achieved financial stability and a budget surplus. Inflation remained modest, and the Russian economy grew at a steady pace of around 6–7 percent annually. Wages on average went up 350 percent, compared to the late 1990s (Strategy, 2012). These were major characteristics indicative of Russia's economic success early in the 2000s.

Yet several global and local developments have negatively affected Russia's economy. The global financial crisis that began in 2008, plummeting global oil prices, and the serious structural problems of Russia's economy have contributed to Russia's slower economic growth and the economic stagnation that began in 2014. In the area of international relations, Russia's actions in Georgia in 2008 and in Ukraine in 2014 and after (we will return to the latter case several times in the following chapters) prompted a very negative reaction in the European Union, the United States, the United Kingdom, Canada, and many other countries. Russia had to deal with economic and political sanctions, to which it has responded with its own counter-sanctions. In part as a result of these developments, scores of foreign investors pulled out of the country's markets.

Overall, Russia is highly dependent on its oil and gas revenues. This reliance on its natural resources affects Russia's policy choices. The leadership was long aware that Russia needed to modernize its economy, develop manufacturing, and make itself less dependent on exports of its natural resources (Strategy, 2012). Yet in simple terms, Russia so far has been interested in prolonging the world's dependency on imported fossil fuels, thus keeping the global oil and gas prices high.

Assessing Russia's political and economic system

Traditionally, the assessments of the Russian political and economic system have differed: most homegrown experts in Russia have tended to see it in a positive, mostly uncritical light, while most Western experts have taken a critical view (Isaev and Baranov, 2009; Shleifer and Treisman, 2004; Shlapentokh, Shiraev, and Carroll, 2008). According to a popular view from Russia, the country's political system is rooted in Russia's unique historic and cultural experiences. Russia is a sovereign country pursuing its own national interests and conducting policies that are no different from those of most other countries, including the United States. From a regime of the early 1980s, allowing one party and no private property, the country turned to a multiparty democracy. What used to be a planned economy has been reshaped into a market one. Supporters of this view also maintain that political censorship has gone for good. Russia's economic and political systems are far from perfect, yet they are the best option in the current economic and political conditions. The view that Russia's political system is unique and different from Western models finds support among many Russian experts (Dubin, 2012).

Experts in the West tend to disagree with these generalizations. Every country's political system, not only Russia's, has unique elements; yet every country can be evaluated according to some common criteria. For example, Russia resembles a "hybrid" state combining or mixing both democratic and authoritarian features (Hale, 2011). **Authoritarianism** refers to a political system in which individual freedom is subordinate to the power or authority of the state – meaning an individual or a small group such as a political party. Authoritarian leaders rely on a small inner circle and impose their decisions on their country's population. The country thus lacks at least three main institutions of accountability: viable opposition parties, independent media, and an independent court system (McFaul and Stoner-Weiss, 2008: 83). Elections are held, but they are not necessarily democratic because of the government's control of the media and interference in the electoral process. In Russia important political decisions belong to one person (the president) or very few individuals; their actions can be criticized but are not commonly scrutinized or rejected by opposing political forces, who remain, in most cases, either quiet or powerless. Russia has established a free market but did not develop the political freedoms common in the West. The legal protection of private property is rather weak. Although the people have more individual liberties than in Soviet times, such guarantees have not been fully implemented yet. The government limits people's major civil rights in exchange for providing them with social stability and economic security (or at least promises of stability and security). The leader's individual characteristics play a more significant role in decision-making than in democratic (nonauthoritarian) political countries. In the context of international relations and foreign policy, governments of democratic countries often see authoritarian leaders as less cooperative than they were expected to be (King, 2008). Indeed, Russia in the 2000s has been on an increasingly confrontational course with the United States and most European countries (Sestanovich, 2008: 28; Shlapentokh, 2015). In sum, as most critics maintain, Russia during the past fifteen years or so has developed a highly centralized and powerful government within a weak civil society lacking democratic traditions.

In this book we shall be introducing these and other points of view and assessments of Russia's foreign policy. It will be up to you to decide which of these views better reflect historical realities as well as unfolding events.

After we have examined several major definitions and reviewed several key points in Russia's history, let's discuss why we should spend more time studying Russia. What is Russia's role today in global affairs?

Five reasons why Russian foreign policy matters

Geopolitics

In the context of foreign policy, **geopolitics** refers to countries' power in relation to geographic space. The space that Russia occupies affects its foreign policy. Russia shares land borders with five NATO countries (Norway, Estonia, Latvia, Lithuania, and Poland), faces others (Turkey, Romania, and Bulgaria) across the Black Sea, and is separated only by the fifty-three-mile-wide Bering Strait from the United States, which is another NATO member. Overall, Russia borders sixteen internationally recognized sovereign states. The facts of Russia's location are an important geopolitical factor affecting policy: anything that happens on Eurasian territories stretching from Central Europe to the Sea of Japan can appear critical to Russia and cause it to react. All these and other factors point to Russia's important role as a regional power. In addition, Russian leaders increasingly often emphasize Russia's significant role in global affairs. As an example, Russia participates in several UN peacekeeping operations in various parts of the world. Russia remains active in the Middle East. Russia is reaching out to several Latin American countries. Therefore, it is important to understand and anticipate Russia's reactions in many regions that are close to Russia's borders.

Differences in policies

From Russia's perspective, its strategic interests do not generally correspond with the strategic interests of the United States, Japan, the United Kingdom, and their allies. As a result, Russia tends to conduct policies that challenge the foreign policies of most Western countries. For example, despite Russia's unenthusiastic view of North Korea's military posturing, especially in recent years, Moscow has for decades maintained its economic and political ties with the government of that country. By contrast, the West has mostly cut its relations with the government in North Korea. Russia has also maintained friendly relations with the government of Iran despite this country's nuclear ambitions and support of international terrorism (based on Washington's point of view). Russia has been building multistate economic and political coalitions with nearby countries, including major international players such as China, India, and Iran. Russia also claims its own "privileged interests" in the so-called post-Soviet territories (Putin, 2012a).

Russia's relations with most Western powers during the past fifteen years have been, at best, lukewarm and, sometimes, unfriendly. Relations between the United States and the United Kingdom and Russia have rapidly deteriorated since 2008. Although the White House attempted to "reset" United States–Russia relations after 2009, this effort has failed (see Chapter 7 on US-Russian relations). In light of these and many other problems that have surfaced in the past twenty years in the relations between Russia and the West, several important tasks for foreign policy, defense, and security decision-makers in the West will likely remain as follows:

- monitoring Russia's international actions;
- assessing Russia's economic capabilities and its global energy policies;
- assessing Russia's military capabilities;
- checking Russia's ambitions and actions in various regions; and
- finding ways for productive cooperation in several key areas, including conflict resolution, nuclear security, and counterterrorism.

Energy politics

In the twenty-first century Russia has become one of the biggest world energy suppliers and competitors in the global market. Further, it has confirmed vast reserves of natural gas and oil on its territory, which should be available for exploration and extraction in ten or fifteen years (if this proves to be necessary). These assets include Arctic gas and oil reserves, a large, unexplored source of hydrocarbons. Moscow claims that they must belong to Russia; other countries disagree. Such international disagreements may cause significant tensions in the future. Because of its size and economic infrastructure, Russia remains one of the biggest contributors to greenhouse gases: it is just behind the United States, China, and the European Union as a global polluter. Russia is aware of these facts as well as its role as an important decision-maker in global energy environmental policies. The drop in oil and gas prices after 2013 has brought new, long-term, and difficult challenges to Russia. Therefore, its actions in the area of energy policies should be monitored and properly addressed.

Nuclear power

Russia remains a very strong military state with immense nuclear capabilities. Having strong military capacities has always been the highest priority of Russian and Soviet leaders in the past (Pipes, 1984). Russia successfully tested nuclear weapons in 1949 and reached nuclear parity with the United States by the 1970s. In the twenty-first century Russia maintains a nuclear arsenal and delivery systems (such as missiles and bombers) generally comparable with the arsenal of the United States (Legvold, 2009). It is important to make sure that Russia continues its policies of nuclear nonproliferation, which mean that no other country or political force should gain access to nuclear weapons as well as to nuclear materials. It is important that Russia, together with the United States and other nuclear powers, continues policies aimed at reducing the risk of nuclear war. These policies, however, receive different assessments and interpretations. We will return to these discussions in later chapters such as Chapter 7 on US-Russian relations.

Soft power

Natural resources, technologies, and deadly weapons are not the only sources of power in international relations. Countries can influence other countries as well as international politics by means of example, persuasion, and reputation. This is called **soft power**. The liberal tradition of international relations emphasizes the importance of economic and cultural factors (such as economic aid, fashion, sports, music, role models) in making a country's foreign policy effective. Russia's soft power – to some degree – is rooted in its rich culture. Russians tend to consider their culture as part of Western civilization. In the field of art, Russia has given the world many celebrated musical composers, such as Tchaikovsky, Glinka, and Rachmaninoff. Russian writers including Tolstoy, Dostoevsky, Nabokov, and Chekhov (to name a few) are known worldwide. Russian ballet, with its unique choreography and performance, remains among the best in the world. Several Russian cities, St. Petersburg in particular (designed by top European architects), are among the world's most desirable tourist attractions. The art collections in Russian museums, such as the Hermitage in St. Petersburg, are priceless. Cultural and educational programs between Russia and other countries, including student exchanges, have continued for years.

Today, Russian youth listen to Western rock and hip-hop, follow British and American singers on Twitter, dress very much like their peers in London or Boston, and watch European soccer tournaments and NBA games on television. Yet, as we will see later, despite Russia's pro-Western cultural orientation, the country overall maintains a very ambiguous love-hate relationship with the West. Nationalism has been on the rise for years. Understanding Russian cultural values, identities, and their inconsistencies as well as their impact on Russian domestic policies and foreign policy is a very important yet challenging task.

How we study foreign policy

The study of foreign policy includes three basic kinds of interconnected activities. The first is informational: you have to search for and gather facts. You describe events, decisions of political leaders, the media's commentaries, and other developments. The second is interpretive: you have to analyze and explain the facts that you have gathered. The third activity is critical thinking: you look critically at the facts, the ways they were gathered, compare the different views, and the ways in which others have interpreted them.

Official reports

All government organizations in Russia issue official reports and publications related, directly or not, to foreign policy. Political parties regularly upload official statements and publish their leaders' interviews and press conferences. Every government office at the federal and regional level has its own website containing updates, policy statements, and statistical information. Big agencies often make these reports available in English. How reliable are such documents? When working with Russian as well as other foreign sources, always keep in mind that their accuracy and objectivity are related to the professional prestige of the sources, political ties with the government, the quality of previous reports, or competition from other sources of information. Government institutions (and this of course refers not only to the Russian government) can deliberately distort facts in official reports. History provides examples. In the Soviet Union before the 1980s, for example, many government organizations knowingly falsified their official printed statements to cover up existing problems or generate a false impression of success. Most of the published official statistics about crime in the former Soviet Union, for example, provided deliberately lowered numbers. Thus, it was next to impossible for a scholar or reporter to know the frequency of violent crimes or the number of prison inmates in the Soviet Union. Today the vast majority of published official reports in Russia are reliable. In many cases there are no deliberate government interventions to distort statistical information or other facts. However, some facts can be easily overlooked, while others are purposely exaggerated for political or other reasons. In the book, we will learn about many cases in which the Russian government's version of certain international events differs substantially from the views of the United Kingdom, France, Germany, the United States and many other countries.

Statements, letters, and communiqués

Official statements provide evidence on how the government communicates with other states and international institutions. A communiqué, which is an official report, provides information about the intentions, expectations, or actions of political leaders or government agencies. Historians and political scientists view correspondence between state leaders as an important source of information. For example, official letters exchanged between US President Franklin D. Roosevelt and Soviet leader Joseph Stalin during World War II show detailed evidence of the difficult bargaining process in strategic decisions affecting millions of lives. However, most government documents including letters remain classified for years: Russian officials are no different from public officials in other countries who are interested in keeping communications away from the public for as long as possible. Today Russian public officials, including the president and prime minister, frequently use televised interviews, press conferences, and live Internet chats to convey the government's vision of policies and events. Of course, official lines of communication can be used to distort the facts or mislead the public, as has happened in the past (Pearson, 1987). However, with the spread of social networks, the number of independent reporters representing various views has also grown dramatically. Keep in mind though that not all web-based sources are reliable. You have to check and verify their reports using multiple sources including eyewitness accounts.

Eyewitness sources

An eyewitness account is a description of an event or a chain of events provided by an individual who observed them directly. In some cases eyewitness accounts are the only available source of knowledge. Personal testimonies tend to provide valuable facts and important details that are not always necessarily supplied by the official institutions or independent media. Former ambassadors often publish their own accounts of important events they witnessed, such as private negotiations with top state officials, as the former US ambassador to Russia Jack Matlock did in his influential book on US-Russian relations (Matlock, 2005). Personal translators to political leaders such as Pavel Palazhchenko (1997) and family members of top diplomats such as Naomi Collins (2007), bring valuable observations and add important details to official publications related to diplomacy.

Biographical studies of Russian leaders can be helpful too. Biographical research often provides a comprehensive picture of how a leader's policies were initiated and executed. For instance, books such as *The Man without a Face* (Gessen, 2012), *The Strongman* (Roxburgh, 2012), or *Wladimir Putin: Der "Deutsche" im Kreml* (Rahr, 2000) provide factual information about the Russian president's ascendance to power and discuss the individual motivation behind his policies. Still, we need to understand that biographers' personal views may affect their discussion of facts, especially in relation to politics.

Political memoirs often include details previously unavailable even to experts. Some Russian officials, like most other countries' politicians, usually after retiring from active politics, choose to write memoirs and provide valuable information about their past policies and decisions (Gorbachev, 2006; Yeltsin, 1994, 2000; Yakunin, 2018). Beware, though: most leaders do not necessarily write memoirs in order to describe their foreign policy mistakes. In most cases they want to show off their achievements. Even when witnesses try to describe facts candidly, they almost inevitably put their spin on them. *Investigative journalism* has brought a new dimension to eyewitness accounts: a reporter specifically pursues cover-ups or looks for facts unavailable to most people. In many countries, including Russia, this type of journalism is especially effective in dealing with government schemes, corruption, or political censorship. Unfortunately, investigative journalism frequently meets with resistance from Russian authorities (though they routinely deny this), and many reporters face mistreatment from the government simply because they try to provide truthful information about serious problems.

One useful research technique, used for the quantitative examination of reports, is content analysis. This systematically organizes and summarizes both the manifest (what was actually said or written) and latent (the meaning of what was said and written) content of information. A researcher, for example, can analyze official documents, including transcripts of speeches. As an illustration, Former President Medvedev in his first annual address to the Federal Assembly (parliament) in 2008 mentioned the United States ten times but only two times in the three subsequent years of his presidency. President Putin after 2012 began to mention America in his speeches significantly more often (Green, 2015). Does this suggest anything important about Russia's priorities in foreign policy? Perhaps yes. Most official statements of Russian leaders as well as government documents published between 2006 and 2019 suggested Russia's reorientation in its foreign policy, which was becoming more confrontational toward the West. Researchers do not limit their focus to official speeches and statements; they also examine the content of television or radio programs, posted comments, and printed articles. As an example, Shlapentokh, Woods, and Shiraev (2005) examined how Russian newspapers reacted to the events of September 11, 2001, in the United States, describing the common tendencies and the overall tone of the reports: although papers expressed their concerns about the tragedy, most reports in Russia indicated that America itself and its policies were partially to blame for the attack.

Intelligence reports

In a general sense, **intelligence** is information about the interests, intentions, capabilities, and actions of foreign countries, including government officials, political parties, the functioning of their economies, activities of nongovernmental organizations, and the behavior of private individuals. Intelligence can be electronic or human. The term is often used to refer specifically to the output of state intelligence agencies. Today most intelligence information about foreign countries comes from open sources such as official reports, press releases, opinion polls, and interviews with government officials. Specially trained intelligence professionals gather and interpret "open source" information. State leaders can use intelligence information effectively, but they also can manipulate and misuse it. It is customary for many political leaders to "push" their intelligence agencies to produce information (or "leak") that corroborates their own views of foreign policy. In 1982 the head of the Soviet security forces (the KGB) and soon-to-be top Soviet leader Yuri Andropov pushed intelligence professionals to generate evidence of US preparations to launch a surprise attack against Russia (Zubok, 2007). In the United States there were periodic scares produced by the military and intelligence establishment that the Soviet Union was getting ahead in the nuclear arms race. Although the Soviets were not necessarily getting ahead, the US Congress sometimes voted for huge military appropriations to retain American strategic superiority.

On the other hand, political leaders often believe that they are better judges of international relations and foreign policy than intelligence and national security professionals. Thus, they often ignore the intelligence gathered – and may even suspect that it is misinformation "planted" by the other side. Infamously, Joseph Stalin ignored a number of signals from Soviet intelligence before Nazi Germany's surprise attack on the Soviet Union on June 22, 1941. In retrospect, some intelligence failures are in reality the personal failure of the leadership to recognize foreign threats.

Media reports

In the days of the Soviet Union the government controlled the press, and any truthful information coming from the media about the real state of affairs in the country was extremely difficult to gather for both inside and outside observers. Experts studying the Soviet Union often exchanged anecdotes about the "tricks" they used to unravel facts from the media accounts and published collective photographs of Soviet leaders, such as figuring out the actual status of top party officials by the order of their appearance onstage for an official ceremony. Today researchers on Russia use open media sources – most of them on the web – to find valuable information about a wide range of events in the country and about its foreign policy. There are hundreds of professionals working for their governments and nongovernmental organizations in countries such as the United States, Germany, and the United Kingdom who translate and analyze websites, blogs, Twitter, Instagram, and Facebook accounts, newspaper articles, individual statements, informal interviews, and other reports related to Russia. Government agencies, research institutions, and marketing firms hire seasoned professionals as well as college graduates for this job. It is important to know that as the diversity of media sources increases, so do the chances that the information will become biased, inaccurate, or both. It is worth repeating that you must learn more about the media sources you are using, as well as about their owners, political affiliations, and sources of their facts. This book's website provides a sample of relatively reliable sites that deal with Russia, its policies, and its people (in English or Russian).

Polls and surveys

Polls or surveys are investigative methods in which large groups of people answer questions on a certain topic. Two types of survey are most valuable: opinion polls and expert surveys. In the following chapters, you will see the results of many surveys. They will illustrate certain tendencies in Russia's politics or provide additional illustrative examples. Today's Russian polling companies are highly reputable professional organizations. Many Russian researchers studied polling at schools in Western Europe or North America. They use advanced techniques of information gathering and publish their results immediately after taking a poll. In general, national surveys are difficult to design and expensive to administer. Therefore, most organizations that conduct surveys these days are relatively big commercial enterprises.

If legitimate professional groups conduct them, opinion polls can give an instant assessment of people's perception of specific events or government policies. For example, more than 70 percent of Russians viewed the role of the United States in global affairs negatively. More than 60 percent had negative feelings toward Europe after 2014 (Levada, 2015, 2016). Where do people get most of their information about foreign countries? Russians, compared to Americans, use the Internet significantly less and watch the television significantly more (Levada, 2016a). Other survey-type assessment methods are less expensive than full national surveys. Many researchers use small-scale, personalized surveys to study tendencies in people's opinions on a variety of topics related to their daily lives (Carnaghan, 2008). Focus group methodology is used, for example, in foreign policy planning, conflict resolution analysis, and commercial or academic research. The typical focus group contains between seven and ten participants who discuss a particular situation or problem and express their opinions to the focus group moderator. Leading research centers use the focus group method (CSR, 2012). One of the principal advantages of this method is the opportunity to analyze specific foreign policy issues in an informal atmosphere where people can speak freely and are not necessarily constrained by the presence of authorities.

An expert survey is another popular method of research, where the respondents are experts in the subject rather than a cross-section of the wider population. Such surveys can reflect reliable professional opinions about Russia's domestic and international actions. For example, Freedom House in Washington DC, an internationally recognized non-government organization, publishes annual reports on the degree of democratic freedoms in most countries. Based on experts' evaluations, The Freedom in the World survey provides an annual rating of a country's treatment of its citizens' most basic liberties. These ratings determine whether a country is labeled free, partly free, or not free. Russia is consistently rated as "not free" (Freedom House, 2018). The validity and reliability of scientific survey methods used by Freedom House can be debated. However and undoubtedly, such critical evaluations from a leading NGO can affect Russia in a negative way: tourism, international business, educational exchanges, and trade may suffer as a result. That is why Russian officials are openly displeased with such assessments and call them either wrong or irrelevant.

Transparency International (TI) is another well-known nongovernmental organization (NGO) that uses survey methods to create the internationally recognized Corruption Perception Index. It asks international entrepreneurs and business analysts how corrupt they perceive various countries to be and then ranks the countries accordingly. Russia has consistently ranked very low on this list (meaning that corruption is perceived as a major problem): in 2017 it was in 131st place out of 175 countries examined (the United Kingdom was 10th and the United States was 17th). You can easily check the latest TI numbers online. Senior Russian government officials openly agreed with these and other critical assessments and considered corruption as one of the most serious domestic problems (Bastrykin, 2008; Medvedev, 2009; Putin, 2012c). However, we will also discuss the fact that many experts in Russia criticize Freedom House and Transparency International for being, they believe, biased *toward* Russia.

On the importance of theory

Knowledge of a country's foreign policy takes more than observation and measurement. *Analysis* is the breaking of something complex into smaller parts to understand their essential features and relations. This is difficult enough, but even more is needed. What makes a country change its foreign policy course? Which policies are more efficient than others? How would these policies evolve tomorrow? These and scores of other questions cannot be answered without looking into broader ideas about how foreign policy works in many contexts. The ancient Greeks called this knowledge "from above" theory (θεωρία). Theorizing about foreign policy requires strong empirical knowledge and a measure of imagination.

Many foreign policy debates ultimately rest on competing theoretical visions. Two approaches that have dominated the study of international relations at many universities in the United States, Canada, and the United Kingdom during the past half century are realism and liberalism (sometimes the latter is called international liberalism). Realism focuses on the power of states (sovereign countries), their interests, and their search for security. States can reasonably act on the world stage as they wish, without any authority above them. They defend their core interests, protect their resources, create alliances with other states, respond to outside threats, and, if necessary, impose their will on others. States, according to realism's followers, are constantly preoccupied with the *balance of power* and look for the best position within the international order. They also balance one another by trying to prevent any state from gaining a rapid and significant advantage over others. Among common instruments of this balancing are strategic alliances, armament increases, threats of using military force, and, ultimately, war (Shiraev and Zubok, 2016). One of the most important factors that affects a country's foreign policy is the distribution of power in regions as well as globally, which results in a certain *structure* of international relations. States conduct their policies according to an existing structure for an international system. Such structures can be unipolar (when only one country dominates globally), bipolar (when two countries dominate, as during the Cold War), or multipolar.

Liberalism is a different approach. It claims that international anarchy does not necessarily lead to conflicts and wars. It may result in cooperation among states. Liberalism emphasizes international collaboration, economic ties, international law, and shared values. It also sees international organizations and nonstate actors as influencing state choices and policies. Supporters of liberalism focus on states' cooperation. Some scholars show that the growth of economic dependence among sovereign countries has become increasingly complex and multilayered. This interdependence should hinder war. Others focus on the increasing influence of intergovernmental and nongovernmental organizations, as well as the emergence of a so-called international society where sovereign states voluntarily follow common norms of behavior to enhance their security and prosperity.

The dominant theories in the last sixty years were realism and liberalism. In the past several decades a theory of **constructivism** has gained attention. According to this view, states' actions and policies are based on how leaders, bureaucracies, and societies interpret or construct the information available to them. This does not mean that politicians manipulate realities and images of realities at will. Constructivism posits that power and security are socially created, within a cultural process where people's interests and identities are formed. For that reason specific foreign policies should have different meanings for different states. One state's (country's) action may be seen as a serious threat by some states but not others. Like individuals, states can exaggerate external threats, undervalue them, or completely overlook them. During the past twenty years constructivism became a third major theoretical approach to international relations.

There are other alternative theoretical approaches, including Marxism, feminism, world systems theory, and others (Walt, 2005). Political psychologists, for example, when studying foreign policy, focus on individual factors affecting leaders' decisions such as their ability to analyze information, emotional stability, past experiences, and so on. Different theories and approaches suggest different principles for the analysis of international relations. It is becoming increasingly common these days, when one analyzes a country's foreign policy, to take into consideration not one but several theoretical perspectives. We shall be doing this in our analysis of Russia's foreign policy.

Conclusion

The Russian Federation is a major global power with vast natural resources, a large nuclear arsenal, an educated population, and substantial economic capacities. A country with a rich history and traditions, Russia is now defining its new role in the twenty-first century. Its journey to potential prosperity and international stability has been difficult and contradictory. Russian people relish political freedom, but – in reality – this freedom is still limited. Russia embraces democracy in some areas of life yet turns to authoritarianism in others. Although Russia's relations with some countries remain effective, with many others its relations have significantly worsened. Russian leaders declare that they seek international peace and global stability, yet their actions often suggest otherwise in the eyes of Russia's critics. Russia today is a constant newsmaker. Some strategic decisions taken by its leaders domestically and internationally appear perplexing to an average Western observer. Other decisions appear clearly wrong. Yet other decisions are interpreted in the Western media in simplistic terms. Whose judgments are more accurate? In this book we shall maintain that behind Russia's foreign policy there is a complex strategy based on a comprehensive vision of today's world and Russia's role in it. Some elements of this strategy keep on changing, but the most essential ones are likely to remain the same for some time. For a future diplomat, journalist, entrepreneur, educator, officer, analyst, or policy-maker, it is essential to learn about, understand, and correctly interpret this "Russian strategy" and the resulting foreign policy.

After the Soviet Union as a sovereign country disappeared from the map in 1991, Russia, both weakened and isolated, became a less popular area of study than it had been before the 1990s. Many experts also believed that Russia was "done" as a leading world power. At least two scenarios were expected. First, and this was the *rosy* scenario, Russia would become an automatic and willing ally of the free world. In the *gloomy* scenario Russia would remain adversarial yet largely irrelevant as an economic and political power. Both of these scenarios were wrong. Today, Russia is "back" as a major power, an important player in international politics, a subject of study, and a source of new debates. Those who saw Russia as a sure ally have already reconsidered their view. Those who argued that Russia was "irrelevant" now realize their error, too. Russia is a formidable military, economic and political player. It has vast energy resources. It has a charismatic and powerful leader (for how long?). Its people are educated. Russia actively pursues its interests near its borders and around the world. It supports some but frequently challenges most other Western countries' policies.

However, it is wrong to believe that Russia is destined to be a constant adversary to the Western democratic world. Russia considers itself closer to the West (not to the East), culturally and historically. Yet it also remains a Eurasian power with interests and aspirations in both Europe and Asia that have to be recognized and acknowledged.

Russia's national symbol is a double-headed eagle looking both east and west. It will be a challenge to engage Russia in a mutually productive and reliable cooperation. But this challenge is worth pursuing.

Summary

- Russia is the world's biggest country; it is one of the top fifteen largest economies in the world. It has a mixed economy with both private and state ownership in important areas. It possesses nuclear weapons, a capable army, an air force, and a navy. About 80 percent of Russia's citizens identify as ethnic Russians.
- The transformation of 1985–1991 was full of contradictions, uncertainties, and disputed outcomes. Many contemporary Russian policies took root in the processes started in the 1980s and continued through the 1990s and later.
- Russia today is a presidential, federal republic, organized according to Russia's basic law or Constitution, which was adopted in 1993. The executive branch of government over today's Russia is the paramount power and has almost full control over most areas of life.
- Russia's economy is based on the free market; the state controls many industries. The country is heavily dependent on its oil and gas revenues, which affects Russia's policy choices.
- Russia's foreign policy should be understood in the context of International Relations theory.
- At least five reasons exist to justify why we are studying Russian foreign policy matters: geopolitics, differences in policies between Russia and many other countries, energy politics, nuclear nonproliferation, and Russia's soft power.
- Many foreign policy debates ultimately rest on competing theoretical visions. The two approaches that dominated the study of international relations at the universities of the United States and Great Britain during the past sixty years are realism and liberalism (sometimes called international liberalism). Most recently, a theory of constructivism has begun to gain attention.

Glossary

Authoritarianism refers to a political system in which individual freedom is subordinate to the power or authority of the state.

Comparative Politics as a discipline focuses on comparing domestic politics, political institutions, and systems rather than on how they interact.

Constructivism assumes that states' actions and policies are based on how leaders, bureaucracies, and societies interpret or construct the information available to them. Constructivism posits that power and security are socially created, within a cultural process where people's interests and identities are formed.

Diplomacy is the practice of managing international relations by means of negotiations.

Exit visas In the Soviet Union, these were government permits that for decades allowed only limited foreign travel for the vast majority of Soviet citizens.

Foreign policy involves sovereign states' actions including official decisions and communications, public and secret, with other state governments, nongovernmental organizations, corporations, international institutions, and individual decision-makers.

Geopolitics refers to countries' power in relation to geographic space.

Gross Domestic Product (GDP) is the value of all goods and services produced over a specific period.

Intelligence is information about the interests, intentions, capabilities, and actions of foreign countries, including government officials, political parties, the functioning of their economies, activities of nongovernmental organizations, and the behavior of private individuals.

International Relations (IR) studies interactions among states and the international activities of nonstate organizations.

Liberalism claims that international anarchy does not necessarily lead to conflicts and wars. It may result in cooperation among states. Liberalism emphasizes international collaboration, economic ties, international law, and shared values. It also sees international organizations and nonstate actors as influencing state choices and policies.

Realism focuses on the power of states (sovereign countries), their interests, and their search for security. The states (sovereign countries) can act on the world stage as they want, without any authority above them. They defend their core interests, protect their resources, create alliances with other states, respond to outside threats, and, if necessary, impose their will on others. States are constantly preoccupied with *balance of power* and look for the best position within the international order.

Republic The term means that supreme power in a country belongs to the people of this country and their elected representatives.

Soft power The term means that countries can influence other countries as well as international relations by means of example, persuasion, and reputation.

Review questions

1. Summarize why Russia as a country matters in today's world.
2. There are two different meanings of the term "Russian" in the Russian language. Could you explain them? Why is it important to distinguish between these two meanings?
3. Why was the 1917 Revolution a significant and traumatic event for Russia?
4. What is soft power? How would you describe Russia's soft power these days, from your point of view?
5. Do you personally see Russia mainly as the West's foe or the West's partner? Maybe neither? Explain. Which areas of cooperation with Russia do you see as most important today in your country?

Chapter 2
The Evolution of Russian Foreign Policy

You, gentlemen are in need of great upheavals. We are in need of Great Russia.

Russian Prime Minister Pyotr Stolypin (1862–1911),
in a Duma speech May 24, 1907

Learning objectives

* Describe the key milestones and highlights of Russian foreign policy during the past few centuries and Soviet policies in the twentieth century.
* Discuss the transformations in Russia's foreign policy over the past thirty years.
* Explain and critically analyze the major events and challenges that have shaped Russia's foreign policy and highlight the similarities and differences between Russia and the West regarding several key international developments.

To understand any country's current foreign policy is first to learn about its history. We have alluded to this subject briefly in Chapter 1. Not everything in Russia's current foreign policy can be explained by the events that took place centuries, decades, or even years ago. Yet, if we apply our knowledge about past events judiciously and critically, history should teach us many valuable lessons. We can apply many of them today. With this general strategy in mind, in this chapter we shall look at the evolution of Russia's foreign policy. We shall first review Russia's foreign policy strategies, its institutions, and actors after Russia became an empire in the eighteenth and nineteenth centuries, and then we shall focus on the key developments of the twentieth century.

The growth of the Russian state: Milestones and highlights

The Russian people have their roots in eastern Slavic tribes who practiced agriculture and populated a vast territory in Europe roughly between the Baltic and the Black Seas. Russian rulers called *Knyazes* (translated as princes or dukes), despite unremitting internal disputes, expanded their lands and possessions through the eleventh century. The Byzantine Empire had a very strong influence on Russia's actions. In 988 Duke Vladimir accepted Christianity. Later Russians chose Orthodox Christianity, which was predominant in the Byzantine Empire, as the official state religion, which Russia maintains today.

In the thirteenth century Russian states lost their political independence to the khans – the rulers of the khanates, vast Eurasian territories (the Mongol world empire) east of Russian lands and in Central Asia and China. The western Muslim khanate, called the Golden Horde, gained political, economic, and military control over Russia after a series of invasions in the 1230s and 1240s. From the fourteenth through the fifteenth century the influence of **Mongol-Tatars** (the most common Russian name for the rulers of the Golden Horde) deteriorated. In 1480 Russian rulers proclaimed independence from the Mongol-Tatar power and then increasingly attacked and annexed the territories of several khanates located east and southeast of Moscow. At the same time, German and Swedish rulers persistently attacked Russian lands from the west.

The consolidation of Russian lands coincided with a period of strengthening of Moscow. Russian leaders refused a deal with the Catholic Church in Rome and preserved Russia's independent religion. After the Ottoman capture of Constantinople, the heart of the former Byzantine Empire, in 1453, Moscow unilaterally assumed the role of the center of Orthodox Christianity. From then on many Russian intellectuals (long ago and today) referred to Moscow as the Third Rome, emphasizing Russia's unique role as a cultural and religious center.

In the sixteenth and seventeenth centuries Russian rulers expanded Moscow's territorial possessions. Under Grand Duke Ivan IV (1530–1584), the Russian state continued to grow. Ivan IV, commonly known as Ivan the Terrible, was the first Russian to take the title of czar. That was a symbolic yet very important event. In acquiring this title Ivan IV stressed the importance of the Russian throne, whose occupants were no longer "dukes" but sovereigns equal to European kings. Among this czar's most important acquisitions were large areas of the Astrakhan and Kazan khanates, which expanded Moscow's possessions to the Volga River and beyond. Several strategic fortresses were built in the areas of the Ural Mountains and western Siberia. Less successful were Moscow's attempts to expand its territories westward, where Russia faced tough resistance.

From the late sixteenth to the early seventeenth century Russia experienced a difficult period of political and social instability worsened by constant foreign invasions. Historians call this period the Time of Troubles to indicate the dismal state of affairs in the country; these troubles included starvation, violence, and territorial losses to Lithuania, Sweden, and Poland. In Russian history the Time of Troubles is also associated with the popular movement led by Kuzma Minin and Dmitry Pozharsky, two charismatic leaders who mobilized and led a large army of volunteers against the ongoing Polish occupation of Moscow in 1611–1612. For many years and today Russian patriotic and nationalist forces use this popular uprising as an example of Russia's victorious struggle for independence.

New land acquisitions took place under Czar Alexis I (1629–1676). Russia continued its colonization of Siberia. Among the most significant events was a treaty of unification with Ukraine in 1654. Planned by the Ukrainian elites as a strategic union against Poland, the treaty resulted in the effective Russian rule over Ukraine. This event, as you can imagine, is interpreted quite differently today. While some experts claim that Ukraine never volunteered to lose its independence to Russia, others argue that the unification treaty established Ukraine as a legitimate and natural part of a greater Russia. The discussion goes on (see Map 2.1).

Foreign policy of the Russian Empire

Czar Peter (1672–1725), who was Alexis's son, remains one of the most prominent figures in Russian history. Peter initiated a significant transformation of Russia's government and the radical "Europeanization" of Russia's upper class and its culture (the masses were not affected by the imposed cultural transitions in fashion, cuisine, or music). He wanted to reform the Russian government based on the best examples of governance in Europe. In reforming these institutions, Peter generally pursued Western patterns of statehood. For example, following the Swedish model, he founded twelve government departments (called collegia, prototypes of ministries). Each department was responsible for a particular statewide activity, including foreign affairs, military affairs, and naval affairs. In other venues, being an authoritarian ruler, he followed his own designs. Peter moved the new Russian capital from Moscow to St. Petersburg, a brand-new city on the eastern coast of the Baltic Sea, which had been founded in 1703. (In 1918 the capital was moved back to Moscow by the communists.) Peter promoted a culture of patriotism and militarism amidst Russia's engagement in many military conflicts at that time.

Peter modernized the armed forces and mobilized vast state resources to build battleships for a brand-new, formidable navy. He introduced a new military draft system according to which one young peasant male from every twenty households was randomly chosen for military service. Formal military regulations established the responsibilities of officers, soldiers, and sailors. All male members of the nobility also had to serve in the armed forces. Newly established military schools educated and trained new generations of officers.

During Peter's reign Russia fought several wars. After defeating Sweden in 1721 following a twenty-one-year conflict, Russia acquired the lands of northern parts of contemporary Latvia and Estonia and the northwestern territories of the Baltic coast. In the south Russia fought, with mixed results, to gain access to the Azov Sea and the Caspian Sea. Territorial expansions continued in the east as well. Russia was building new fortresses in Omsk deep in Siberia and Semipalatinsk in today's eastern part of Kazakhstan. The Nordic War (1700–1721) against Sweden was the first one in which Russia participated in the conflict in a coalition among several European countries.

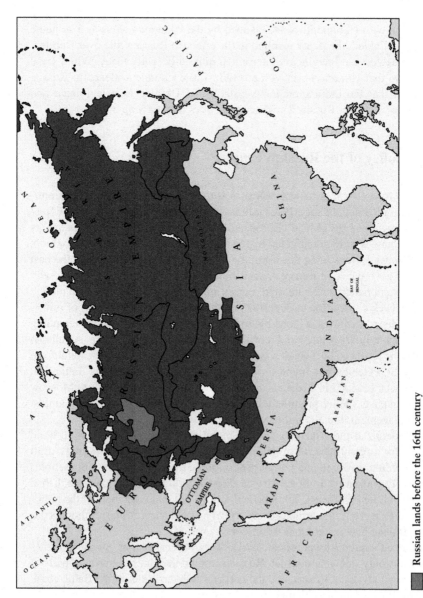

Map 2.1 The expansion of the Russian state, 1613–1914

▢ **Russian lands before the 16th century**

▢ **Russian expansion during the 16–19th centuries**

At home Peter strengthened his absolute power, and after the victorious war against Sweden he assumed the title of emperor. European monarchies gradually recognized this title. This recognition indicated that Russia was indeed becoming an empire – a vast, increasingly multiethnic, and centralized state. Russia was emerging as a legitimate and powerful player in European and Asian affairs.

Foreign policy in the eighteenth to nineteenth centuries

There were about 30 million people living in Russia by the end of Peter's reign in 1725 (this is roughly the population of Texas or Poland today). The first Russian census in 1897 estimated the number at 125 million. In the eighteenth and nineteenth centuries Russia continued its territorial expansions. Russia had acquired the territories of today's Lithuania, Latvia, and Estonia, Eastern and Central Poland, and southern and central parts of Ukraine. It also added to its possessions Finland, the Crimean Peninsula, the Caucasus states (today's Armenia, Georgia, and Azerbaijan), and Central Asian states (today's Kazakhstan, Turkmenistan, Tajikistan, Uzbekistan, and Kyrgyzstan). In the east Russia possessed Siberia and vast areas of the Eurasian continent north of China, spreading to the Bering Straits, which separate Russia from North America. In the first part of the nineteenth century Alaska and a few adjacent areas of North America were also under Russian control. Russia became a vast multiethnic state stretching from the Baltic Sea in the west to the Pacific Ocean in the east.

Any country's geographical location undoubtedly influences its foreign policy. For centuries sovereign states pursued territorial and geographic advantage. International Relations theory defines these actions as **geopolitics** – the theory and practice of using geography and territorial gains to seek security and achieve political power. Supporters of Realism (see Chapter 1) suggest that geopolitics is one of the most important features of many countries' foreign policy. This is because geographical position and size gave some countries clear advantage in security matters, while others remained vulnerable (Shiraev and Zubok, 2016). Keep in mind that one of the most distinctive characteristics of today's Russia's geopolitics is that Russia emerged as a big and powerful Eurasian state a few centuries ago. Its relations with foreign states have always been influenced by the interplay of "Western" (European) and "Eastern" (Asian) strategies. In terms of Realism, Russia's relentless territorial expansions have always affected the balance of power in adjacent regions and caused their neighbors to seek help from other states to respond to Russia's actions.

In dealing with foreign challenges, Russian leaders pursued several interconnected goals.

First, Russia needed favorable domestic and international conditions for its territorial advancement farther east from the Ural Mountains, through Siberia, to the Pacific Ocean. This eastward expansion continued during the eighteenth and nineteenth centuries.

Second, in Europe Russia attempted to secure its permanent access to the Baltic Sea and Black Sea. Therefore Russia needed an effective combination of diplomacy and military policies in the process of securing its borders in the west, south, and southwest.

Third, Russia needed security and stability in Central Asia, vast areas of which would fall under its control in the eighteenth and nineteenth centuries. During that period St. Petersburg explored possibilities for further expansion in Central and South Asia.

Fourth, to secure its possessions and guarantee security in the future, Russia had to build efficient relations with its most powerful neighbors, such as the Ottoman Empire and the Persian Empire in the south, Prussia and Austria in the west, and Japan in the east, as well as with distant powers including France and Great Britain among others.

Pursuing these goals, Russia took an active part in European and Eurasian affairs. Russia participated in three consecutive partitions of Poland late in the eighteenth century and later incorporated a substantial part of Poland into the Russian Empire. The Russian Emperor Pavel I (1754–1801) joined coalitions with Austria and Great Britain to contain the French Revolution, which was perceived as a threat to European monarchies. Thus Russia turned to military actions in Europe far away from its own borders. During the American War for Independence Russia proclaimed neutrality, but in practice its politics were supportive of the American revolutionaries.

Russia's active engagements in European affairs continued under Emperor Alexander I (1777–1825). In 1809 Russia and the United States established diplomatic relations, but Washington at that time stayed out of European wars. The French under the command of Emperor Napoleon invaded Russia in 1812 and captured Moscow. However, Napoleon had to retreat and suffered major casualties in the process. Russia joined a multistate coalition pursuing the defeat of French troops. Napoleon's expulsion from Russia and his final defeat and abdication in 1814 are viewed in Russia today as one of the most significant military and political triumphs in Russia's history.

St. Petersburg became a key player in European affairs. Aiming at protecting international stability, Alexander I, emperor of a predominantly Christian Orthodox state, and the sovereigns of Protestant Prussia and Catholic Austria signed a 1815 treaty establishing the so-called **Holy Alliance**, a military and political pact later joined by many other European states. Its official goal was to preserve, as it claimed, justice and peace, but in reality the alliance was to protect the existing dynastic principles of government and thus prevent popular uprisings and democratic revolutions in Europe. Russian Emperor Nicolas I saw the Revolution (1848–1849) in Europe as a dangerous development. Russia supported antidemocratic forces across Europe. St. Petersburg sent troops against the uprising in Hungary. Russia's foreign policies in Europe were increasingly seen as reactionary and aiming at preservation of oppressive monarchies.

In the south Russia expanded its possessions between the Caspian and the Black Seas. This was known as the Caucasian War (1817–1864). It resulted in the annexation of this multiethnic region, which would remain under Russian and then Soviet control until the 1990s. These developments stirred tensions and a constant tug of war not only with local rulers but also with the Persian and the Ottoman Empires.

Russia turned to its soft power (see Chapter 1) by pledging its defense of Christians living in the Holy Land (today's Israel and Palestine) and in other places such as Greece, Bulgaria, Macedonia, Serbia, Montenegro, and so on, which were controlled by the Ottoman Empire. These territorial expansions and geopolitical claims, as supporters of the Realist tradition would argue, threatened the power balance in the region. Diplomatic miscalculations intensified tensions between Russia, on the one hand, and Great Britain, France, and the Ottoman Empire, on the other. These countries declared war on Russia, which suffered a painful defeat in the Crimean War of 1853–1856. This war served as a valuable lesson to Russia: neighbors tend to frequently challenge rapid territorial expansion and growing political influence of Russia. One of the consequences of the war was the selling of Alaska to the United States and the evacuation of all Russian colonies from the Americas.

Meanwhile, in Asia Russia continued the strategic rivalry with Great Britain for new possessions and supremacy in Central and South Asia – the process that historians call the **Great Game**. While St. Petersburg expanded its influence in Asia, London resisted and considered Russia's action as a very serious threat to British interests in Afghanistan and India (Hopkirk, 1992).

Foreign policy in the early twentieth century

In the twentieth century Russia emerged as the biggest world state, a multiethnic empire, and a major international player. Emperor Nicholas II (1868–1918) continued the foreign policy of his predecessors and sought the expansion and strengthening of Russian interests in Eurasia. In 1905, however, Russia suffered a painful defeat in the Russo-Japanese war. Both countries were competing for territories, resources, and influence in the Eurasian Far East and both chose military conflict to resolve their differences. Russia lost that war. Not only did it cede significant territories to Japan, it also sustained almost fifty thousand casualties and accumulated a huge financial debt. Several European countries, especially France, later became Russia's key sponsors (MacMillan, 2013). Taxes went up to pay for the war, and the prestige of the monarchy in Russia reached its lowest ebb. Facing tough domestic challenges, Emperor Nicholas II in 1905 turned to political reforms: he proclaimed basic political liberties including freedom of speech, assembly, and conscience. The first national parliamentary elections took place in 1906. New laws eliminated political censorship. Political prisoners were freed.

In Europe Russia continued building coalitions to address its own security concerns. Alarmed by the rapid economic and military developments in Germany, Russia joined Great Britain and France to form a military bloc. Germany, in response, gathered its own powerful allies including the Austro-Hungarian and Ottoman Empires. World War I broke out in 1914. Many people in Russia, as elsewhere in Europe, initially supported the war out of patriotism. An anti-German mood swept the country. St. Petersburg, capital of Russia, was renamed with a Russian name, Petrograd. However, this nationalistic and militaristic elation soon diminished. For the most part, Russia fought the war on its own territory, and the Russian army suffered heavy casualties. The country mobilized more that 15 million people over the four years of the war. The official statistics of Russian losses were not gathered. However, modern researchers consider that nearly 2 million were killed and about 4 million were wounded (Krivosheev, 2010). By 1917 the country's socioeconomic conditions had worsened. The emperor and his government showed ineptness in handling both military and civil affairs. Nicholas II was forced to abdicate in March 1917. A new provisional government vowed to honor Russia's international obligations and sustain its war efforts. The government also called for a Constitutional Assembly – a nationally elected body to decide the future of Russia as a state.

However, the October revolt of 1917 (often called the October Revolution) brought dramatic changes to the country's foreign policy. The new government, run by the Communist Party with Vladimir Lenin (1870–1924) at its head, issued three decrees of historic significance. The Decree on Peace called on all the nations at war to start peace negotiations. The Decree on Land confiscated all private land and nationalized all natural resources in Russia. Finally, the Declaration of the Rights of the Peoples of Russia announced the right of ethnic regions to secede from Russia. All foreign debts and international agreements were annulled and repudiated. In 1918 the new government signed the Brest peace treaty with Germany and its allies. Russia surrendered huge territories and paid war reparations. The treaty was nullified later that year, however, after Germany exited the war. Meanwhile, Russia itself plunged into civil war. It lasted five years and caused millions of casualties. Almost 2 million people emigrated from Russia during that period (Sabennikova, 2002). At the end of the civil war, former Russian territories became independent states. Among them were Finland, Estonia, Latvia, Lithuania, and Poland (Bianchini, 2017). Neighboring countries occupied large portions of Ukraine, Belarus, Moldova, and Armenia.

Foreign policy of the Soviet Union

As discussed in Chapter 1, the Soviet Union as a state was formed in 1922. The new leadership that came to power after the devastating civil war focused primarily on domestic affairs. Gradually, a new foreign policy of the young state began taking shape.

Foreign policy in the 1920s–1930s

The key goal of Moscow's foreign policy was to guarantee the survival of the state. Other goals involved the promotion of communist ideology. Moscow sponsored the **Comintern**, an international communist organization (The Communist International). It was designed in 1919 to coordinate the activities of communist parties around the world, to facilitate the collapse of capitalist regimes, and to establish socialism as a form of government. In 1920 the Comintern called for a global civil war (commonly known as a "world revolution"), but after the defeat of communist revolts in Germany, Bulgaria, Poland (1923), and Estonia (1924) the Soviet leaders backed off. After Lenin's death in 1924 Joseph Stalin in the late 1920s and in the 1930s focused on the consolidation of his domestic powers, building a powerful bureaucratic machine and securing the state. These tasks required an assertive yet cautious, not reckless, foreign policy. Some Western academics believed that Stalin had made the decision to abandon the idea of the "world revolution." Others, including Russian scholars, suggest that he continued pursuing this idea but by less obvious, even covert, means (Zubok and Pleshakov, 1996; Khudoley, 2017).

In the late 1920s Stalin pursued an active role for his country in international relations. Moscow initially supported Germany, which tried to revise the Versailles treaty, signed in 1919, that seemed an unfair burden on the German people. However, after Adolf Hitler (1889–1945) and the Nazi party came to power, Moscow refocused on balancing its relations in Europe. The Soviet Union increasingly saw Germany as a threat. Moscow wanted to avoid a major conflict with Berlin and thus maintain the existing European order. From the position of Realism, as discussed in Chapter 1, it was a valid strategy. In 1935 Moscow signed security pacts with France (an opponent of German expansionism) and Czechoslovakia. In 1933 the Soviet Union and the United States established diplomatic relations. The Soviet Union also joined the League of Nations.

Gradually, the Kremlin's policies became more assertive. Moscow sent military personnel and sanctioned hundreds of Comintern volunteers to fight on the side of the left-wing government in Spain during the Spanish Civil War (1936–1939) and in China (1927–1936). Moscow was involved in several military confrontations with Japan in 1938–1939. While negotiating with France and Great Britain, Stalin secretly consulted with Nazi Germany and in 1939 reached a political agreement known as the Molotov-Ribbentrop Pact (named after the names of the countries' foreign ministers). In the wake of this treaty Soviet troops attacked Finland in 1939 and seized some of its southern territories. For this action the Soviet Union was expelled from the League of Nations. Moscow claimed that this annexation was necessary for security reasons. The Soviet Union soon moved its troops to Estonia, Lithuania, Latvia, and portions of western Belarus and Ukraine, which were Polish territories. Using support from friendly communist groups in the Baltic countries, the Soviet Union seized these regions. Supporters of these actions insisted for years that this was an act of "unification" based on mutual agreement between Moscow and the local political leaders. Critics, however, argued that these actions were illegal and immoral. Yet others maintained that although Soviet policies toward the Baltic States and Poland were questionable at best, they were necessary at that time to protect the Soviet Union's security. This view is common in official Russian sources today.

World War II

On June 22, 1941, Germany attacked the Soviet Union. Moscow came to this major military confrontation with Germany unprepared. Back in 1937 Stalin – due to his own ambitions and political struggles within his inner circles – had persecuted many top military commanders. This seemingly inexplicable political move seriously disrupted the country's defense policies and the process of modernization of the military. Although Stalin thought that a confrontation with Germany would be inevitable, he did not believe that it would start as early as the summer of 1941, when the Soviet military was still unprepared to fight a war of this magnitude. The German plan was for the Soviet Union to be occupied, broken into pieces, and converted into several vassal states. But the Soviet Union resisted bravely and fiercely. This was perhaps the most devastating war in the history of Russia.

By the end of 1941 the Soviet Union had mobilized more than 14 million people between the ages of eighteen and sixty-one. Despite the mobilization of all available Soviet resources to resist the aggression, German troops reached Moscow and St. Petersburg (which had been renamed Leningrad in 1924, although it resumed its original name in the 1991, the final year of the Soviet Union) in the early fall of 1941. The situation was grave, and some ministries of the central government as well as the US and British embassies had left Moscow and relocated in the east. Most other government offices prepared for evacuation. However, this never took place. The Soviet troops pushed the German armies back. Yet by the winter of 1941–1942 Leningrad had been encircled and remained under siege. The siege of the city lasted for more than two years, and cost more than 1.2 million Soviet people's lives, more than the combined total of British and US losses during World War II. In 1942 German troops pushed back into the southern part of Russia, captured several strategic regions in the Caucasus region, and reached Stalingrad, a major city in the region (which was renamed Volgograd in 1961). The Soviet Army defended the city in a historic battle. A full-scale Soviet counteroffensive began in 1943. In 1944 the Soviet military, aided by the British and American troops of the Second Front in Western Europe, began a final push. They ended the war in Europe in May 1945 by capturing Berlin.

The whole European region of the Soviet Union was ruined and the country's resources exhausted. The country lost about 26 million people, including about 11 million military casualties (Krivosheev, 2001). Yet World War II (the Great Patriotic War in Russia) is widely considered to be one of the most glorious events in Russian history. Russians, regardless of their political orientation, are proud of this victory. The many battles of the war are glorified in Russia's mass culture. In 2015 the seventieth World War II victory anniversary was marked by unprecedented mass government-sponsored as well as informal celebrations. Such celebrations continue these days on the ninth of May, which is an official holiday in Russia. Opinions vary today, however, about the role of Stalin in the victory against Germany. His decisive role is as undisputable as it is controversial. He is credited as the supreme commander but is criticized for making fatal mistakes, not just in the preparations (including the execution of military commanders) but also in the conduct of the war. According to pubic opinion, his recklessness and remorseless disregard for human life likely contributed to the very heavy casualties (Levada, 2018).

On the whole, most Soviet people felt that the victory over Germany was a triumph not only for Russia but also for the Soviet system. This is an important point in understanding Russian foreign policy and the motivations behind it. According to the constructivist view of international relations, to better understand a country's foreign policy one should focus on how that country perceives its role in international affairs. After the war Soviet leaders promoted the view that the country had acted as the defender of humankind against aggressors. This view was widely accepted in the Soviet Union and later in Russia. The war awakened Russia's national self-identity and nationalism (Grossman, 1970). Russians to this day are very sensitive about any evaluations of World War II that play down the role of the

Soviet Union in ending the Nazi regime in Germany. They tend to give less weight to Stalin's mistakes and the aggressive nature of the Soviet Union's foreign policy after 1945. For example, in a national poll, 77 percent of Russians considered the deployment of the Soviet Army in Central and East Europe by the end of the war as "liberation," and only 11 percent saw these actions as an act of "establishment of communist regimes" there (WCIOM, 2009b).

The Cold War

During World War II the Soviet Union joined an alliance with the United States and Great Britain against the Axis powers (Germany, Japan, and Italy). In the 1945 summits in Yalta and in Potsdam Stalin agreed on the postwar composition of Europe and globally. Yet Stalin treated his Western partners with deep mistrust. He never believed in a lasting cooperation between the communist Soviet Union and the capitalist powers; he wanted to expand Soviet territory, establish communist governments in several countries, and build a security "buffer zone" between the Soviet Union and the West. After 1945 the Soviet Union emerged as a substantially weakened yet victorious nation. Although the leaders in Moscow, Washington, and London had established very productive relations during the war, in 1945 they failed to create the conditions to make this last. The period from the end of the war to the late 1980s is known as the **Cold War**. This describes the global state of tension (though not outright warfare) between the Soviet Union and its closest allies, on the one hand, and the United States with its allies, on the other (Zubok and Pleshakov, 1996).

There were several causes of this global division that influenced international relations for more than forty years. The United States and the Soviet Union were examples of different types of political system, and both claimed that the opposite system was inhumane and dangerous. Soviet ideology maintained a belief in the inevitability of a conflict between communism and capitalism. Anticommunism was the official policy in Washington. By August 1949 the Soviet Union had become the second nuclear power after the United States. The emerging nuclear competition brought fear and distrust to both countries. Personal factors also contributed to the tension. Stalin, for example, became increasingly fearful about a nuclear conflict with the West (Zubok, 2007). In his last work, *Economic Problems of Socialism in the USSR* (1952), Stalin wrote that as long as capitalism (frequently called imperialism by Soviet sources) existed, war would be inevitable.

However, the new Soviet leader Nikita Khrushchev (1894–1971) proclaimed in 1956 that global war was preventable and that Soviet foreign policy would focus on the process of peaceful coexistence between the two antagonistic systems – communism and imperialism. Despite these statements, the Cold War continued.

For almost all of the second half of the twentieth century both countries engaged in continuous global competition. Mutual suspicions and fears drove the defense and security policies of both nations, and the buildup of weapons in the "arms race" significantly drained national resources. The **Warsaw Treaty Organization**, the Moscow-dominated security bloc of Eastern and central European communist states, emerged in 1955 in response to Washington dominated NATO. The Soviet Union became a major international player. It tried to challenge the United States and its allies, in almost every part of the world.

The Soviet Union joined China and North Korea in their fight against troops from South Korea, the United States, and the United Nations known as the Korean War, (1950–1953). Later, Moscow was sending instructors, antiaircraft missiles, weapons, food, and money to the Vietnamese forces fighting against the United States during the Vietnam War in the 1960s–1970s. The Soviet government sponsored and supported communist parties in countries in Central Europe. Moscow crushed anti-communist revolts in East Germany (1953), Hungary (1956), and a reformist movement in Czechoslovakia (1968). The Soviet pressure was the key factor of the state of emergency declared in Poland in December 1981 to suppress a popular grass-roots political movement, *Solidarity*. The Soviets openly supported Fidel Castro in Cuba and placed nuclear missiles there in 1962, causing one of the most dangerous nuclear crises in history. In 1979 the Soviet military invaded Afghanistan to support a friendly communist government there and remained there until February 1989. More than fifteen thousand Soviet people died and more than fifty thousand were seriously wounded in this conflict. During this period Moscow also provided supplies and either openly or covertly participated in local armed conflicts in Nicaragua, Palestine, Angola, Mozambique, Ethiopia, Yemen, and many other countries.

Foreign policy reconsidered

Many political changes that took place in the late 1980s also marked the beginning of serious changes in Soviet foreign policymaking (Dobrynin, 1997). Socialism, according to the official doctrine developed in the Soviet Union for decades, was supposed to be a system better than capitalism. According to official sources, an individual's life in the Soviet Union was expected to be prosperous, happy, and simply great. Most people, however, were ultimately unhappy with their economic conditions and political freedoms. They were increasingly critical of their government and its domestic policies. Many people were also critical of their country's foreign policy rooted in confrontation with the West.

The reasons for the changes

By the early 1980s, the whole of Soviet society had seemingly reached a point of economic and moral stagnation (Hosking, 1992). Most people were disappointed with the quality of their lives and disenchanted with socialism. There were several major sources of this dissatisfaction.

First, the country was experiencing serious economic problems. The Soviet economy struggled. The growth rate of GDP declined steadily through the Brezhnev years (1964–1982), from 4.7 percent per year in the middle of the 1960s to 2.0 percent in the early 1980s. The government in Moscow could not address many basic socioeconomic needs of the population (Gaidar, 2007).

Second, the increasing economic failure went hand-in-hand with massive social problems. Bureaucracy and corruption at all levels exemplified the enormous organizational inefficiency. Bribery became an everyday norm: people paid bribes to avoid a traffic ticket, obtain a pair of East German shoes, or fix a leaking faucet. Soviet society was turning into an undeclared caste system. On the one hand, there was a small but powerful circle of people with status, perks, and privileges. These were party bureaucrats, government officials, and those with direct access to the state-run and corrupt distribution of goods and services such as retail sales. On the other hand, the working poor had no assets and low incomes. In the middle, there was the majority: people with jobs – teachers, nurses, engineers, and so on – but with very little financial savings.

Third, social apathy was widespread. Political censorship suffocated new ideas. In the absence of real political competition within a one-party system, voting was mostly a theatrical act staged by the government. Most people for years silently accepted this (Bahry and Silver, 1990: 837–38). Yet more people in two successive generations began to recognize that, in reality, American, Swedish, and West German social systems were more humane, that their living standards were much higher, and that the economic gap between the Soviet Union and most Western countries was widening. Most people at that time believed that the wealth disparity between the Soviet Union and the West was because of the inefficiency of the socialist system. They also believed that the socialist economic and political system could be fixed if only the right people were to take charge of it (Gorbachev and Mlynar, 1994).

The Gorbachev reforms

In March 1985 the sixth General Secretary of the Communist Party, Mikhail Gorbachev, who was 54 then, took office. He had spent nearly thirty years in the ranks of the party bureaucracy, gradually moving to the highest position. His arrival there meant the beginning of a new and final stage of the Soviet Union (Kort, 2006). He wanted to change the system, make it more efficient and humane. Moreover, he believed in socialism and thought it could be reformed. Most people in the Soviet Union shared his point of view (Shlapentokh et al., 2008). Gorbachev won broad support among the elites and ordinary people alike. His support came largely from three groups. Party officials, factory managers, and military commanders saw Gorbachev as a leader who could revive the declining economy and consolidate more power in the institutions of the Communist Party. Most ordinary people saw him as an energetic and relatively young leader, who could punish thieves, fire bureaucrats, and quickly make the entire country work efficiently. Many critics of the communist regime hoped that Gorbachev would allow some long-awaited political changes in the country. The country needed massive reform in all areas of its political, social, and economic life. The deep and sweeping changes initiated by Gorbachev and his close supporters were labeled **perestroika and glasnost**.

Gorbachev called these initiatives in foreign policy **new thinking**. His policy questioned some of the basic assumptions of international relations in the nuclear age. In particular, Gorbachev raised three important points. First, he argued that the ongoing confrontation between the superpowers should stop immediately and without preconditions. Second, all nuclear countries, particularly the Soviet Union and the United States, should reduce their deadly arsenals to the minimum needed to guarantee mutual security and international stability. Third, the new world of the end of the twentieth century should stop ideological competition and turn to what were described as the universal values of peace and cooperation in international relations. This was perhaps Gorbachev's central point: world leaders should change the way they understood politics and global affairs (Gorbachev, 1985: 1). He was convinced that the world should and could function according to certain basic values of universal validity (Sheehy, 1990: 220).

The "new thinking" foreign policy led to progress in arms limitation talks with the United States. Top-level meetings between Gorbachev and US President Ronald Reagan in Geneva (1985), Reykjavik (1986), Washington (1987), and Moscow (1988) resulted in the signing of the Intermediate Range Nuclear Forces (INF) treaty. Major progress toward the limitation of intercontinental nuclear weapons was also achieved. Reagan and Gorbachev established direct and informal personal communications, which helped to develop mutual trust (Chernyaev, 2000). Both leaders soon began to talk about burying the Cold War for good. The dismantling of the confrontation between the superpowers proceeded apace, in 1989 and later, under George H. W. Bush's administration (1988–1992).

Gorbachev took unilateral steps to implement his vision of a new world. By 1989 the Soviet Union withdrew its troops from Afghanistan. Moscow stopped supporting procommunist insurgencies around the world. In 1989 communist regimes in East and Central Europe collapsed, while Soviet troops remained in their barracks. By 1991 the Warsaw Pact, the Soviet-led military and political coalition in Central Europe, was dissolved. East and West Germany were on the way toward unification (1990). The Kremlin no longer felt that it should deceive the West about the size of its military budget, and in May 1989 it revealed its "real" size. It was about four times larger than had previously been acknowledged (The State, 1989: 11).

Criticisms of foreign policy

The majority of people in the Soviet Union supported the ending of the unpopular war in Afghanistan and establishing productive relationships with the West. Yet the conservative communist opposition was generally unhappy with Gorbachev's foreign policy. They accused him and his advisers of making several fatal blunders. These arguments are especially popular today among Russian foreign policy elites. There were three main points of criticism.

First, the critics maintained that Moscow had lost its strategic positions in Eastern Europe. They saw the disintegration of the Soviet empire in Eastern Europe – as Poland, Hungary, Czechoslovakia, East Germany, Bulgaria, and Romania overthrew their communist governments – as a defeat in the Cold War. Following the fall of the Berlin Wall in November 1989, East Germany was officially reunited with West Germany, creating a country firmly in the Western camp, and the Warsaw Pact was disbanded. Yet the US-led rival NATO alliance remained intact. This situation, the critics believed, effectively put the Soviet Union in a very vulnerable strategic position.

Second, Gorbachev was accused of abandoning most of Moscow's long-term allies, such as Cuba, Nicaragua, Vietnam, Ethiopia, and Angola. Such a policy weakened Soviet geopolitical positions (Katz, 1991). Critics also maintained that Gorbachev was setting a dangerous precedent, which would move other countries further away politically from the Soviet Union (Dobrynin, 1995: 622–32).

Finally, it appeared that the ongoing negotiations with the United States had really taken the form of unilateral concessions to the West. The Soviet Union was about to lose its superpower status. Critics underlined that although the Cold War was ending, Moscow had had to pay an unfair price: the Soviets had lost their strategic allies around the world and accepted the global domination of the United States in the post–Cold War situation. Washington offered almost nothing in return.

The end of the Soviet Union

In a nutshell, perestroika and glasnost represented a political program aimed at reforming the institutional, economic, and political systems of the Soviet Union. In 1985 the leaders of the reforms wanted to make the economy more efficient, the political system less authoritarian, and foreign policy less confrontational. They did not envision (and were not ready for) the sweeping changes that would later engulf society and would lead to the collapse of the powerful state in 1991. The **Commonwealth of Independent States (CIS)** appeared in place of the defunct USSR. Eleven out of the fifteen former republics of the Soviet Union have joined. (Estonia, Lithuania, and Latvia did not join, and Georgia left in 2008.) The CIS remains mostly a formal association without real political power. We will return to this in Chapter 6.

The peaceful ending of the Soviet Union and the Cold War continues to present a considerable intellectual challenge to many experts working in the fields of political science, history, foreign policy, global affairs, and international security. Gorbachev's motivation and personal qualities were crucial in the course of the reforms (Brown, 1997). Of the greatest importance were (1) his belief that the Soviet system could be reformed and (2) his rejection of violence to achieve his ambitious political goals. Only a few times in history (US President Woodrow Wilson is an example of this) has the leader of a great power renounced the old rules of foreign policy in favor of a sweeping idealist agenda based on nonviolence, cooperation, and interdependence (Levesque, 1997). Some historians and political scientists believe that without Gorbachev, the Soviet Union would have likely existed today. Others disagree and emphasize the depth and scope of the Soviet Union's problems that would have inevitably caused the state's radical transformation (Zubok, 2007). Either way, the world would be different today if the Soviet Union had had a different political leader in the 1980s.

In search of a new foreign policy (1991–2000)

In essence, by the end of the 1980s the Soviet Union was disappearing as a political and social system. A new Russia, headed by its new leader, Boris Yeltsin (1931–2007), had to be remade as a world actor in a new, post–Cold War world, and forging domestic consensus on a new foreign policy was difficult. Russian foreign policy since 1991 has gone through at least three phases: accommodation, reorientation, and consolidation. During the early period of the young state Russia played its role in global affairs by trying to be a key and accommodating partner of the United States and major European countries. During the second period of reorientation, from 1996 to 2000, Russia began to reconsider its major foreign policy priorities. During this period Russian policy was mostly a reaction to international events. After 2000, when President Putin took office, Russia began to rearrange its foreign policy. It was a stage of "consolidation," as Russian commentators try to portray it today. They refer to Russia's increasingly consistent behavior: seeing and building itself as a new center of power, actively seeking new useful partners and alliances, strengthening the country's security, and challenging Western policies on issues that Russia believes important to its own interests (see Table 2.1).

President Boris Yeltsin and his close associates who came to power after 1991 faced a tough challenge. They inherited an incredibly large military infrastructure and the world's largest nuclear arsenal. However, Russia did not have enough resources and capabilities to maintain the military and security forces at full operational capability. Moreover, Russia had to rethink its old foreign policy commitment in a new international structure that was emerging after the implosion of the socialist bloc. When there was no pressing external enemy and there were mounting security problems, foreign policy did not seem to be the most important challenge facing Moscow's government.

The 1993 constitutional crisis rooted in a legal and political clash between Yeltsin and the parliament was the first serious test of the new government system. Yeltsin wanted more personal power and rapid reforms. The parliament objected. On October 3 and 4 sporadic but deadly violence paralyzed Moscow. Supporters of the parliament captured the Office of the Mayor and stormed the Central Television Center. Yeltsin turned to the military, which gained control over the city. After a military assault with tanks and machine guns on the parliament building

Table 2.1 Three stages of Russia's foreign policy after 1991

Accommodation	Reorientation	Consolidation
Approximately 1992–1995	Approximately 1995–2000	From 2000–the present
Dependent on the West, Russia tried to be a key and compliant partner of the West; this was seen by many as a "soft" foreign policy period.	Russia becomes more assertive and gradually turns away from generally pro-Western, accommodationist policies.	Russia starts looking for new useful alliances, strengthening the country's security and challenging Western policies on many issues. Confrontation grew.

(CNN broadcast this event live), the members of the parliament and its leaders were arrested. All those arrested were pardoned a few months later. The 1993 confrontation was a small-scale civil war with huge consequences. It gave Yeltsin and his supporters a chance to design a new Russian Constitution, which granted the executive branch and especially the President vast powers. The Constitutional Referendum was held in December of that year. Some in the West questioned the referendum's legitimacy referring to the violent confrontations that had taken place weeks earlier.

During the early period of the young state, Russia played its role in global affairs by trying to be a key and accommodating partner of the United States and major European countries. As it turned out, however, many people among Russian political elites provided only lukewarm support for the Yeltsin administration's Western-oriented policies. Moreover, this support gradually waned (Malcolm, 1995: 26–28). Before presidential elections in 1996 Yeltsin decided to appease some of his communist and nationalist critics and finally removed Foreign Minister Andrei Kozyrev. He replaced him with a reliable and seemingly "tough" individual and foreign policy expert, Evgeny Primakov (1929–2015) – a move cheered by the antiliberal opposition. It was really the turning point in Russia's foreign policy. Kozyrev's fall also signaled a new age in Russian policy, which began to be shaped primarily by elite power struggles and the search for a new post–Cold War identity for Russia. The new leaders were turning away from the pro-Western and cooperative policies of the early 1990s (Shiraev and Zubok, 2000).

During the second period of reorientation, from 1996 to 2000, Russia began to reconsider its major foreign policy priorities. However, during this period Russian policy was mostly a reaction to international events. In essence, Russia had to be remade as a world actor in a new, post–Cold War world, and forging consensus on a new foreign policy was difficult. Not only was the domestic political context highly contentious, post-Soviet Russia was greatly weakened economically and militarily. Its leaders had to contend constantly with the fact that their country was no longer one of the world's superpowers.

Foreign policy after 2000

After 2000, when President Putin took office, Russia was already rearranging its foreign policy. It was a stage of "consolidation," as Russian commentators try to portray it retrospectively. They refer to Russia's consistent patterns of international behavior after 2000: looking for new useful alliances, strengthening the country's security, and challenging Western policies on many key issues (Morozov, 2004).

Significant changes took place in Russia's defense and security policies as well. The concept that foreign enemies threatened Russia was brought back and became a central theme justifying the strengthening of Russia's defense and security, which certainly reflected the country's foreign policy. Essentially similar policies largely continued during the presidency of Dmitry Medvedev (2008–2012), despite his modest attempts to establish better relations with the West. The increasingly large resources available to the government during the economic boom of the early 2000s and high oil prices at that time gave the Kremlin an opportunity and the money to invest in defense and security. However, the economic crisis of 2008–2009 and the economic slowdown that followed forced the government to make adjustments and corrections.

To better understand the dynamics of Russia's foreign policy in the end of the twentieth century and the beginning of the twenty-first century, we will look at several events and Russia's interpretation of these events and its policy actions.

Foreign policy: Events and challenges

Several specific international developments affected Russia's foreign policy. Among these were the conflicts in the Balkans, the expansion of the North Atlantic Treaty Organization (NATO), the conflict around the Caucasus region, the struggle against international terrorism, the wars in Iraq and Afghanistan, the Arab Spring (the political turmoil in several Arab countries that started in 2011), the war in Syria, the tragic events in Ukraine, the diplomatic "showdown" after 2017, and the status of treaties related to nuclear weapons. The way that Russia responded to these problems reflected the evolution of its foreign policy over the previous twenty-five years. We will briefly review these developments and then will return to a more detailed analysis in the following chapters.

The war in Bosnia and the Kosovo conflict

The civil war in the republics of the former Yugoslavia in the 1990s, and the Western response, provided the first serious point of disagreement between Russia and its Western partners. Russia considered Western pressure against Serbia and Serbian forces in Bosnia as unfair and a direct insult to Russia, a historical ally of the Serbian people. Polls showed that a majority of Russians, along with many Russian senior officials, perceived Western military intervention in Bosnia as an attempt to unfairly punish Serbia and establish American control over the Balkans (Shiraev and Terrio, 2003). The NATO bombing of Serbia (1999) for its belligerent actions in Kosovo also met with a very critical reaction in Moscow. Prime Minister Sergei Stepashin even warned dramatically that Moscow could be the next target of the West. These criticisms found support among Russia's elites as well as ordinary people. Russians were especially irritated by what they called the aggressive and irresponsible actions of the Western powers against a sovereign country in the heart of Europe. This powerful anti-Western and anti-American sentiment crossed party lines. Even moderate politicians issued statements against American and NATO policies in the region. Some believed that the Kosovo precedent could be used to pressure Moscow to give sovereignty to several Muslim regions in Russia, such as Chechnya. In the wake of the war in Serbia, by the end of the 1990s opinion polls yielded a steady 60 percent national average of anti-Western attitudes, which doubled the ten-year average for anti-Western sentiment (Shiraev and Zubok, 2000).

The NATO expansion

After 1991 relations between Russia and the former socialist countries of Central Europe and the Baltic states remained stable yet uneasy. The former Soviet satellites wanted to be part of a new, united Europe, defended by American and NATO power. In 1996–1999 Poland, the Czech Republic, and Hungary gained NATO membership. Washington supported the expansion of the alliance (Goldgeier, 1999). In 2004 Estonia, Latvia, Lithuania, Slovenia, Slovakia, Bulgaria, and Romania acquired full membership, too. Russia, however, viewed NATO's eastward expansion very critically. While Washington saw the NATO enlargement as a response to the desire of several European countries guarantee their security, Russia saw it as an open challenge and a demonstration of disrespect to Russia's own security concerns. Two attempts (1991 and 2001) to negotiate Russia's membership in NATO were rejected by the West. Although the NATO-Russia Council appeared in 2002 to coordinate policies, this was rather a symbolic institution. Russia accused the United States of deliberately attempting to undermine the post–Cold War strategic balance in Europe. Russian leaders did not understand why NATO forces should be introduced into countries from which Russia had removed its troops in the 1990s. Today the Kremlin considers any further expansion of NATO (which may include Ukraine and Georgia) as a threat to Russia's national security.

Counter-terrorism and the Caucasus region

In the 1990s Russia had its first series of tragic encounters with domestic terrorism. Several separatist groups from the Chechen Republic launched a wave of deadly attacks against the civilian population and some neighboring territories, which all lie in the Caucasus region in the southern part of Russia. The Chechen rebels (Russians commonly call them terrorists) claimed that their attacks were a response to Russia's brutal crackdown on the independence movement. Russia, by contrast, considered Chechnya an inseparable part of Russia and viewed the terrorist groups as a direct threat to Russia's security (see Chapter 7). Moreover, Russia claimed that some foreign organizations and groups, intentionally or not, had supported the Chechen and other regional rebels in an attempt to create an Islamic state in the Caucasus region. This assertion by the Kremlin effectively framed the terrorist acts within Russia as an international problem, not a purely domestic one.

September 11, 2001

The tragic events of September 11, 2001, moved both Russia and the United States closer together in terms of their shared attitude to and policies against international terrorism. It was one of only a few international issues over which both capitals have agreed. Both Moscow and Washington began to consider many violent forms of Islamic fundamentalism and jihadist tactics as dangerous threats to Russia's national and international security. Both countries agreed to collaborate in a range of antiterrorist policies. American policy-makers began to evaluate Moscow's policies in the Caucasus region and elsewhere in the context of Russia's struggle against international terrorism (Shlapentokh, Woods, and Shiraev, 2005).

The US wars in Afghanistan and Iraq

Russia's response to the United States' invasion of Afghanistan in 2001 was both emotional and pragmatic. Although President Putin first quickly confirmed his country's strong support for the United States, high-ranking officials in the Kremlin soon articulated the conditions under which Russia would participate in any international actions to support the United States. They clearly signaled that Russia was not giving the United States complete discretion in its actions. Moscow indicated that it would support Washington, but not on all occasions. The Kremlin ruled out the idea of direct military action in Afghanistan. However, Russia cooperated with the United States on intelligence issues and did not object to America's pursuit of temporary military bases in Central Asia (in Uzbekistan and Kyrgyzstan). Moscow was also displeased with Washington's reluctance to include Russia in any discussions about broader political aspects of the Afghan problem and other strategic issues.

Russia was very critical of the 2003 US invasion of Iraq. Moscow resisted US initiatives targeting Iraq in the United Nations prior to the invasion and even appealed directly to France, Germany, and several NATO countries in an attempt to prevent the imminent war. Russia at that time saw itself as an important member of the antiterrorist coalition of states and felt itself excluded from strategic international decision-making. Moscow continued to be one of the most vocal opponents of the Iraq war. It considered the conflict as a source of instability in the region. It also viewed the United States' presence in the region as a form of aggression, expansionism, and neocolonialism.

Nuclear arms talks

Negotiations between Russia and the United States concerning nuclear weapons have impacted Russia's foreign policy. Washington's decision in 2001 to walk away from the Anti-Ballistic Missile Treaty, the agreement that limited the ability of both countries to expand the arms race, was criticized in Russia. Although the strategic reasons for the US decision were understandable to a few experts (the treaty restricted the ability to develop and deploy defensive systems), the government and the media in Russia considered President Bush's move unwise and dangerous. In April 2010 Russia and the United States reached a new agreement called *Measures for the Further Reduction and Limitation of Strategic Offensive Arms*, projected to last until 2021. However, many old Cold War concerns and rhetoric reemerged more recently. These concerns were caused in part by US plans to build early warning antimissile defense systems in Europe. Washington insisted such systems would protect against a possible attack from Iran or other rogue states. Moscow believed the United States was seeking unilateral advantages at the expense of Russia, which would be forced to match them by escalating the arms race or by other measures. After 2010, however, almost all new US-Russian nuclear arms negotiations have stalled. In 2018 Russian President Vladimir Putin claimed that Moscow had developed a new type of nuclear weapons and means to deliver them that could defeat any country's missile defence system (Putin, 2018). The Kremlin insisted that this was a defensive measure. The West considered this announcement as an escalation of international tensions.

The 2008 Georgia Conflict

Georgia, with its capital in Tbilisi, is a former republic of the Soviet Union that is now an independent state. Unfortunately tensions between Georgia and Russia increased in the 1990s and grew into open hostility in the first decade of the twenty-first century. From Russia's standpoint, Georgia has always attempted to distance itself from its northern neighbor. Moscow accused Tbilisi of deliberate attempts to turn to the European Union, NATO, and the United States, to the detriment of Russia. The Kremlin used Georgia's own problems with two areas with large ethnic populations – South Ossetia and Abkhazia – as a source of pressure: Russia began to support ethnic separatists in these areas. Russian troops, using an international peacekeeping mandate, moved into Abkhazia and South Ossetia. Many people in these regions became Russian citizens (Moscow initiated this move), which gave Georgia another reason to accuse Russia of anti-Georgian policies. The conflict culminated in summer 2008 in open war between Georgia and Russia. Russia declared its support for the independence of South Ossetia and Abkhazia. Several agreements on integration (especially in the fields of army, security, police, and some social services) were signed later between Russia and South Ossetia and Abkhazia.

One of the most remarkable issues related to the conflict is the substantial difference between the way the conflict was portrayed by the Russian media and in the West. Russia categorically refused to call itself an aggressor and accused Georgia of war crimes in South Ossetia. However, most countries condemned the Russian attack on Georgia and did not recognize the independence of the two new proclaimed states. The Kremlin tended to read this as if the rest of the world was failing to support Russia's actions simply because Russia had acted independently (Lavrov, 2008). The events in Georgia, as well as many other international developments, provide evidence about the pattern of Russian reactions, the evolution of its foreign policy methods, and the Kremlin's responses to other countries' decisions. The conflict in Georgia was the first after the end of the Cold War in which Russia was a direct participant and the West supported the opposite side. Back in 2008 NATO leaders inclined to secure membership for Georgia (and Ukraine) but backed off – in part because of Russia's opposition – from granting the former Soviet republics Membership Action Plan (MAP) status, which would have accelerated their membership. A decade later, however, Moscow's strategic goal to prevent Georgia from getting aligned with the West and from making plans of joining NATO has not been reached (Sajalia, 2018).

The "Arab Spring" and the conflict in Syria

Political turmoil in many Arab countries (often called the Arab Spring) started in 2011 and resulted in sweeping political reforms in Tunisia and protracted instability and violence in Libya, Egypt, Yemen, Syria, and some other countries. These events evoked different evaluations and responses in Russia from the reactions in most Western capitals. Although Moscow acknowledged the necessity of political reforms in the Middle East and North Africa, it disagreed with the scope and methods of such reforms. Russia feared that the sweeping political changes in the region (in the name of democracy) would bring violence and instability rather than peace and security. Many Russian politicians considered the Arab Spring as a kind of revolution, organized by the United States, in preparation for a regime change in other countries including Russia. Further, Moscow warned that the political forces that may come into power would not necessarily be democratic.

Russia has repeatedly stated that it does not want to see the rise of political Islam in the region. Moscow was also reluctant to lose some of its former "friendly dictators," such as President Assad in Syria. To restore its strategic presence in the Middle East (lost during the Cold War) and to fill the political vacuum resulting from US and Western policies in the region in the 2000s, Russia escalated its support of the regime in Syria and started military operations there in 2015. Russia's massive bombings of the rebel forces in Syria in 2016 and later (Russia was also accused of bombing civilians) have provided a relief for the government of President Assad and helped his regime reclaim almost two-thirds of the lost territory in 2018. Moscow established an airbase and a naval seaport in Syria. Iran also agreed to coordinate its military actions together with Russia. Thus Russia's military and political presence in the Middle East has been established. How far could Russia reach in the Middle East? What is the reaction of Arab countries to Russia's policies? We will examine these and other developments in Chapter 10.

The events in and around Ukraine

In March 2014 Russian president Vladimir Putin signed a law to admit the republic of Crimea and the city of Sevastopol into the Russian Federation. After the collapse of the Soviet Union in 1991, Crimea was a part of Ukraine, a sovereign state. Putin argued that he acted in response to the will of the people of Crimea, after they voted in a referendum. Putin also claimed that Russia protected the Russian-speaking population of Crimea against the Ukrainian nationalists who took power in Kiev following a violent coup.

Ukraine regarded this takeover as a blatant act of aggression and violation of Ukraine's sovereignty. The United States, all members of the European Union, and the majority of UN members also considered Russia's move an annexation and a gross violation of international norms. The danger of a larger-scale war in Eastern Europe became real. The Kremlin inspired and backed armed separatists in

Donbass, an industrial region in southeast Ukraine with a mixed Russian-Ukrainian population. The Ukrainian government launched an "antiterrorist operation" against the separatists. The government also accused the Russian military of violating Ukraine's sovereignty and escalating a military confrontation in Donbass. Russia denied its direct involvement.

This conflict created a profound sense of insecurity in Eastern Europe and beyond. NATO returned to action. The United States and the United Kingdom sent military equipment and troops to the Baltic countries and Poland to reassure them of support. In addition, the United States and the European Union imposed a series of economic and financial sanctions on Russia in an attempt to deter further aggression. Putin, however, viewed the conflict in Ukraine as a local conflict, denied Russia's involvement in it, and organized a retaliatory response to the sanctions.

Did this conflict mark a new period of increased insecurity not only in Europe but also globally? On the one hand, Russia by its actions in Ukraine has challenged the regional and global order (Freedman, 2018). What if other states begin annexing territories and supporting separatists overseas, citing ethnic and religious "solidarity" as the reason for aggression? On the other hand, one can also argue that Russia acted from a position of weakness and used force to reestablish its security interests in Eurasia. It was an opportunistic action, a powerful signal to NATO and the United States that Russian interests should be acknowledged. Nevertheless, 2014 marked the end of the post–Cold War period in Europe, when peace and stability were taken almost for granted. Washington claimed that Russia's actions challenged American power, influence, and interests (Beinart, 2018). The situation around Crimea and in eastern Ukraine is likely to remain difficult and unstable for years.

The diplomatic war after 2017

After the 2016 US presidential elections when Donald Trump was elected president, there has been a relentless discussion in the media and in many political offices in Washington DC about whether Russia had interfered in the elections by persuading the American public (one way or another) to vote for Trump or not to vote for Hillary Clinton. Some political opponents of Trump accused the Trump administration of "colluding" with Moscow. A heated debate about Russia's involvement continued in the United States for a very long period (we shall return to this subject in Chapter 7). Meanwhile, Russian-American relations have deteriorated. Washington has broadened sanctions against Russia for its involvement in the conflict in Ukraine as well as for Moscow's interference with the 2016 US elections. In 2018 Washington has expanded its sanctions targeting Moscow's top business moguls. Russia denied any electoral interference and condemned the sanctions. Both countries, accusing each other of unfair political actions, began cutting each other's diplomatic personnel in the embassies and other diplomatic offices. The United Kingdom's relations with Russia too reached their lowest level since the 1980s. London accused Moscow of secretly using chemical weapons to settle scores with former Russian citizens residing in the United Kingdom (we shall cover this subject in Chapter 8). Many business, professional, educational, cultural, and business contracts and programs between Moscow on the one hand, and London and Washington, on the other, have been suspended. The term "a new Cold War" has entered the vocabulary of foreign policy experts (Freedman, 2018).

Conclusion

At the beginning of the twenty-first century Russian foreign policy strategists generally rejected the accommodationist approach and focused on an independent, often confrontational course with the West. Russia claims that its foreign policy is nonideological. Quite often, however, ideological arguments are used to justify Russia's behavior in global affairs. Several factors, both domestic and international, have shaped this policy and continue to influence it.

The first group of factors is related to the foreign policy of other states. Russia chose to overlook many positive developments in its relations with the West during the 1990s (Rivera and Rivera, 2009) and focused on problems instead. For example, the continuing NATO expansion has been an issue of major concern to Moscow. The civil war in Bosnia in the early 1990s and the conflict in Kosovo were seen differently in Moscow from how they were perceived in Paris, London, and Washington. Moscow presented the conflict in the former Yugoslavia as for the most part a coordinated Western aggression against Serbia. When US-led coalition forces invaded Iraq in 2003 Russian-American relations reached one of their lowest points since the Cold War. The Western support of Georgia in 2008 and Ukraine in 2014 and later convinced many Russians that Moscow's foreign policy actions were simply not welcome in the West. International sanctions followed. Russia challenged the West in the conflict in Syria.

The second group of factors is related to Russia's domestic situation. Russia has learned that it can act independently and decisively against threats such as separatism in Chechnya or instability in Syria. In the wake of terrorist attacks on Russian soil, such as suicide bombings in Moscow, airplane crashes, and the killing of hundreds of people including children, most Russians showed their support for the federal authorities in their pledge of worldwide unilateral actions against terrorism. Nevertheless, many Russian officials maintain that their country is unfairly criticized for its actions in Chechnya and Syria in particular (Moscow argued that it was fighting against international terrorism). Russian leaders believe that the West applies one set of rules to its own policies and another set to Russia's.

The third factor was cultural-psychological. Washington's crucial error back in the 1990s was probably a habit of treating post-Soviet Russia as a defeated opponent. The United States and the West might have "won" the Cold War, but this did not mean defeat for Russia (Simes, 2007: 36). Russia constantly reminded its Western neighbors that it is a formidable power to reckon with (Legvold, 2009). For a decade Russians have been repeating the arguments about the world's multipolarity (or *policentricity*, as they prefer to say it in Russia) with Russia as another power center, like the United States. An increasing number of Russians, including the elites, have come to doubt that American and Western economic models, the principles of free market capitalism, and civil liberties could take root in Russia (Trenin, 2017). We will discuss further whether this approach was a crucial error of Moscow's elites.

Summary

- The Russian people have their roots in eastern Slavic tribes.
- After the Ottoman capture of Constantinople, the heart of the former Byzantine Empire, in 1453 Moscow unilaterally assumed the role of the center of Orthodox Christianity.
- Czar Peter (1672–1725) initiated a significant transformation of Russia's government and the radical "Europeanization" of Russia's upper-class culture.
- In the eighteenth and nineteenth centuries Russia continued its territorial expansions. Russia became a vast multiethnic state stretching from the Baltic Sea in the west to the Pacific Ocean in the east.
- The October revolt of 1917 (often called the October Revolution) brought dramatic changes to the country's foreign policy. The newly formed Soviet Union for decades conducted an ideology-driven foreign policy.
- In the 1920s and 1930s Stalin turned to a more active role in international politics. In 1933 the Soviet Union and the United States established diplomatic relations.
- During World War II the Soviet Union joined an alliance with the United States and Great Britain against the Axis powers (Germany, Japan, and Italy). In the 1945 summits in Yalta and in Potsdam Stalin agreed on the postwar composition of Europe.
- Although the leaders in Moscow, Washington, and London had established very productive relations during the war, in 1945 they failed to create lasting conditions of cooperation. The period from the end of the war to the late 1980s is known as the Cold War.
- The Warsaw Treaty Organization, the Moscow-dominated security bloc of Eastern and Central European communist states, emerged in 1955 in response to Washington-dominated NATO. The Soviet Union became a major international player and tried to challenge the United States and its allies in almost every part of the world.
- In the mid-1980s Mikhail Gorbachev initiated a new foreign policy called "new thinking."
- By the end of the 1980s the Soviet Union was disappearing as a political and social system. A new Russia, headed by its new leader, Boris Yeltsin (1931–2007), had to be remade as a world actor in a new, post–Cold War world, and forging domestic consensus on a new foreign policy was difficult. Russian foreign policy since 1991 has developed in roughly three phases: accommodation, reorientation, and consolidation.

- After 2000, when President Vladimir Putin took office, Russia was rearranging its foreign policy. It was a stage of "consolidation."
- Several specific international developments affected Russia's foreign policy. Among these were the conflicts in the Balkans, the expansion of the North Atlantic Treaty Organization (NATO), the conflict around the Caucasus region, the struggle against international terrorism, the wars in Iraq and Afghanistan, the Arab Spring or political turmoil in several Arab countries that started in 2011, the war in Syria, the events in Ukraine, and the status of treaties related to nuclear weapons. The way Russia responded to these problems reflects the evolution of its foreign policy over the past twenty-five years.

Glossary

Cold War A state of geopolitical tension (from the late 1940s to the late 1980s) between powers in the Eastern Bloc (supported by the Soviet Union) and powers in the Western Bloc (supported by the United States, its NATO allies, and other countries).

Comintern Also known as the Communist International, this was an international organization designed in 1919 to coordinate the activities of communist parties around the world, to facilitate the collapse of capitalist regimes, and to establish socialism as a form of government.

Commonwealth of Independent States (CIS) An international organization formally created in place of the defunct USSR. Eleven out of the fifteen former republics of the Soviet Union have joined. Estonia, Lithuania, and Latvia did not join, and Georgia left in 2008. CIS remains mostly a formal association without real political power.

Geopolitics The theory and practice of using geography and territorial gains to seek security and achieve political power.

Great Game The strategic rivalry between Russia and Great Britain for new possessions and supremacy in Central and South Asia (referring mostly to the nineteenth century).

Holy Alliance A military and political pact of the nineteenth century later joined by many other European states. Its official goal was to preserve justice and peace, but in reality the alliance was to protect the existing dynastic principles of government and thus prevent democratic revolutions in Europe.

Mongol-Tatars The most common Russian name for the rulers of the Golden Horde.

New Thinking The policy initiated by Gorbachev to ease international tensions and create conditions for cooperation and peace in the nuclear age.

Perestroika and Glasnost The deep and sweeping changes initiated by Gorbachev and his close supporters in the 1980s. This was a massive reform in all areas of the Soviet Union's political, social, and economic life.

Warsaw Treaty Organization The Moscow-dominated security bloc of Eastern
and Central European communist states that emerged in 1955 in response to
Washington-dominated NATO.

Review questions

1. Why do we have to study Russia's history to analyze today's Russian foreign
   policy?
2. Which countries' geographical positions and sizes gave them, in your view,
   (a) clear advantage and (b) disadvantage? In terms of Russia's geography,
   which advantages and disadvantages seem significant to you? Think of natural
   resources, access to the sea, border protection, and so on.
3. Explain key ideas of Gorbachev's "new thinking" strategies in international relations and foreign policy.
4. Why did Russia occupy portions of Georgian territory in 2008 and declare its
   support for the independence of two ethnic regions?
5. What were the reasons for the "new Cold War"? What would you do as president
   to prevent the future escalation of tensions between the West and Russia?

Chapter 3
Institutions and Decision-Makers in Russian Foreign Policy

We are polite people. We don't visit someone without an invitation.

Sergei Lavrov, Russian Foreign Minister

Learning objectives

- Describe the roots of current Russian institutions of foreign policy.
- Describe the structure and functioning of the current foreign policy institutions in Russia.
- Explain the role of the Kremlin and the president in making foreign policy.
- Outline the interactions between the executive and other branches of the Russian government responsible for foreign policy.

Foreign policy institutions of the Russian government have been evolving for centuries. The most drastic changes took place about three hundred years ago when the Russian Empire emerged in the early 1700s and when the basic institutional foundation of Russian diplomacy was shaped. The next substantial change took place in 1917, when a new communist state was established. The dissolution of the Soviet Union, however, has brought only minor changes to Russia's foreign policy institutions. We will discuss these historical events briefly and then focus on more contemporary developments.

Historical background

The Russian Empire

The Emperor Peter I created a new centralized system of administration of the Russian Empire in the early eighteenth century. He established twelve departments called *collegia* subordinated to the ruling Senate (see Chapter 2). From the beginning the key roles in foreign affairs were assigned to the foreign office, the war ministry, and the admiralty responsible for the navy. Heads of these three collegia were typically members of the Senate (unlike some heads of other collegia) and in effect were directly reporting to the emperor. The Senate regularly decided on matters related to foreign trade and some other foreign policy issues.

In 1802 Emperor Alexander I abrogated the old collegia and set up institutions called ministries, including the foreign ministry. The Minister for Foreign Affairs reported directly to the emperor. At that time the Senate gradually lost its administrative power and key governing functions. In 1857 a Council of Ministers was formed. It performed only a consultative role for the emperor, who was responsible for most executive decisions.

In October 1905 Nicholas II reformed the country's political system. The Council of Ministers was then formally transformed into the Government Cabinet and its chair for the first time in Russia's history was given significant executive powers. A new legislative body elected by popular vote was also established. This was Russia's national parliament called the **State Duma**. These changes, however, did not alter the mechanisms of foreign policy-making. The *Fundamental Laws of the Russian Empire* (1906), for example, clearly identified the emperor "as the supreme authority for all the external relations of the Russian state with foreign powers." The emperor's exclusive prerogatives included matters involving declaring war and peace, as well as signing treaties with foreign states (Article 13). Before World War I it became customary to include foreign policy issues in the agenda of the Council of Ministers' discussions. In practice, however, the emperor acted unilaterally through his foreign minister.

In sum, Russia had an authoritarian, heavily centralized institutional system of decision making in foreign affairs. The emperor possessed almost unlimited powers and sought advice from other government institutions only when he deemed it necessary.

The Soviet Union

The Revolution of 1917 brought the Bolshevik government into power. The government pursued at least two interconnected foreign policy strategies. The first was a push for the **world revolution**, or a global and prompt transformation of political power to replace capitalism. The other was a continuation – with certain modifications – of the imperial foreign policy of the Czarist regime (see Chapter 2). Foreign policy institutions and basic decisions were made in accordance with these two general strategies. The world revolution strategy was soon abandoned, yet the goal of global transformation based on the Communist doctrine remained (a new term, "the world's revolutionary process," replaced the old term, "the world revolution"). The Communist Party of the Soviet Union maintained close relations with communist and leftist parties of many other countries. The Party was influencing (or attempting to influence) their governments, domestic policies, and international behavior. Financial, military, and political assistance was also provided to most nationalist, anticolonial parties in Asia and Africa.

The Communist Party's Central Committee, the leading institution of the Party responsible for most important decisions, its top office consisting of just several people, the Politburo, and, ultimately, the General Secretary, were the key decision-makers in foreign policy. All other institutions of power in the Soviet Union were essentially rubber-stamping the rulings of the party. Two historic examples should illustrate the patterns of such decision-making. In 1939 the Supreme Soviet, the top legislative body in the country, ratified, without even opening a debate, the treaty between the Soviet Union and Nazi Germany (the Molotov-Ribbentrop Pact). The members of the Supreme Soviet were not informed of the infamous secret protocol appended to the agreement, which divided parts of Europe into German and Soviet "spheres of influence." The second example is the 1979 invasion of Afghanistan. A few top party officials made this major decision. Not until the late 1980s, the time of the disintegration of the Soviet Union, did foreign policy debates become more transparent.

The Bolsheviks created the People's Commissariat of Foreign Affairs in 1917. Nearly all diplomats and other officials working for the former government were sacked. Communist Party members, who obediently carried out the instructions of the party leaders, staffed the vacant positions. The Commissariat's top officials (called People's Commissars) were members of the Communist Party Central Committee and at times members of its top body, the Politburo. Only the People's Commissariat for Foreign Trade had the right to negotiate and sign contracts with foreign states and private companies. In the 1920s–1940s the role of secret security institutions (precursors of the KGB [Committee for State Security]) and military intelligence grew in prominence. In some cases the government used these institutions – rather than official diplomatic channels – in important international negotiations.

An important role in Soviet foreign policy was played by the Communist International (1919–1943) or Comintern (see Chapter 2). It was a centralized international organization of communist parties. The Comintern's leaders were usually the members of the Politburo of the Communist Party of the Soviet Union (such as Grigory Zinoviev and Nikolai Bukharin) or foreign communists closely linked to Soviet leadership (such as Georgi Dimitrov in Bulgaria). Most of the Comintern's activities were sponsored by the Soviet Union. The Comintern participated in election campaigns in many countries and was involved in the violent uprisings in Germany and Bulgaria in 1923 and Estonia in 1924, in China's civil war, and in other world events. It also directed global communist propaganda operations including the organization of political campaigns in support of the Soviet Union and the gathering of political, economic, and military information abroad for the Soviet leadership. Over the years, however, the role of the Comintern in Soviet foreign policy decreased. Stalin, after numerous political setbacks in foreign countries, became increasingly skeptical about this organization's effectiveness.

In 1944 the Kremlin established foreign ministries in all the republics of the Soviet Union. Stalin sought admission of all these republics, as supposedly sovereign states, in the future United Nations. This strategy would have secured him seventeen votes (sixteen republics at that time plus the Soviet Union) in the UN, but membership was granted to Ukraine and Belorussia only. The foreign ministries in the republics remained but generally played a only formal role, for Moscow was making almost all key decisions. By contrast, the role of security services in foreign policy decision-making was increasing (except during the period when Nikita Khrushchev headed the Communist Party in the late 1950s and the early 1960s).

Though the Comintern was dissolved in 1943, the Communist Party of the Soviet Union remained the leader of the world communist movement. After World War II it helped communist parties take power in countries of Eastern and Central Europe as well as in China, North Korea, and North Vietnam. However, the process of integration of the world's communist forces suffered serious problems. In 1948 Yugoslav communists proclaimed their independence from Stalin; in the early 1960s the communist parties of China and Albania broke their ties with Moscow. Several other parties did not dare to confront Moscow yet sought more independence from it. These unexpected challenges in the world communist movement affected the structure of the Central Committee of the Communist Party of the Soviet Union. Now it had two new departments responsible for international relations. The first one dealt with the ruling communist parties loyal to Moscow (called the "world's socialist commonwealth"). The second was responsible for the relations with "other" communist parties, including some leftist, anticolonial, and nationalist parties and movements. The first department was, in fact, in many ways more politically powerful than the Ministry of Foreign Affairs. The role of the second was somewhat limited.

The years of *perestroika* (the word means "restructuring" in Russian; see Chapter 2), which began in 1985, was a time of a gradual diminishing of the power of the Communist Party over the institutions of foreign policy of the Soviet Union. In addition to these changes, the emerging new states (especially those of the Baltic republics including Estonia, Latvia, and Lithuania) were forming their own foreign ministries, independent from Moscow. The reaction of Western countries to these developments was generally neutral because, legally, the Soviet Union was a sovereign country still and Western governments did not want to antagonize increasingly friendlier leaders in Moscow. However, *de facto*, the United States and its Western allies were supportive of the new foreign policy institutions in the republics that were gradually distancing themselves from the Soviet Union.

Present day: Foreign policy management

After the disintegration of the USSR in 1991 Russia entered a period of transition to democracy and market economy. As we have mentioned in Chapter 1, modern Russia's political system and its institutions, the foundations of which were shaped mainly during the turbulent period between 1991 and 1993, are changing, even today. However, the structure and functioning of the key institutions of foreign policy as well as the decision-making process remain, probably, the least transformed and the most stable among all government institutions in Russia. The importance of the legacy and tradition of diplomacy of the Soviet period (or even of the Russian imperial period) appears obvious. This legacy is not necessarily rooted in the old symbols of Soviet power: many Russian embassies' buildings today still have the official coat of arms of the Soviet Union on their façades. The management of foreign policy historically has been and still remains highly centralized. Likewise legislative influence in foreign policy remains insignificant. Although Russia's foreign policy today is more transparent than in the days of the Soviet Union, it still is far less transparent in comparison to foreign policies of many other democratic states such as Canada or the United Kingdom. A prominent feature of Russia's policy offices (as well as other state institutions) is that their functioning is largely dependent on the personality of their institutional leader.

The President and the Kremlin

The president of the Russian Federation and president's administration occupy the key position in the political system of the Russian Federation. The president's authority, in fact, legally exceeds that of other institutions, including the legislative and judicial branches. It is common to see this system, as we mentioned in Chapter 1, as a **vertical of power**, which is the subordination of policies of all government institutions to the president and his administration. Although government officials are only seldom using this term, the subordination of policies has become a reality. This assessment is relevant to Russia's foreign policy today.

The President of the Russian Federation

The 1993 Constitution endowed the Russian president with substantial powers, including those in the sphere of foreign policy. These presidential powers can be explained from several angles.

First, the president directs Russia's foreign policy. Specifically, Article 86 of the Constitution states that the Russian Federation president

- is responsible for the management of the Russian Federation's foreign policy;
- conducts talks and signs international treaties on behalf of the Russian Federation;
- signs international treaties and the ratification letters; and
- accepts letters of credence of diplomatic representatives in Russia (such letters establish the diplomatic status of foreign representatives).

The president also sends his annual memorandums or statements on the directions of the state's domestic and foreign policy to the Federal Assembly (although both chambers only seldom gather for joint meetings).

Next, the president makes key personnel decisions. According to the Constitution (Article 83), the president forms the Presidential Administration and the Security

Council. The president also appoints members of key ministries, top commanders of the armed forces, and diplomatic envoys to foreign countries and international organizations. The State Duma should approve or reject the president's choice of prime minister. Although consultations with the respective committees of the Federal Assembly regarding the appointment of diplomatic representatives to foreign countries and international organizations are required, they are (unlike in many democratic countries) for the most part purely formalities.

Third, the president holds other powers related to foreign policy. The control over the implementation of international treaties signed by the Russian Federation is one of them. Thus, in accordance with the Constitution (Article 85), the president may suspend any executive or legislative act of any Russian region (the regions are called Subjects of the Federation) if this act conflicts with the Russian Federation's international commitments. The president also controls citizenship and asylum policies (Article 89).

A specific characteristic of Russia's political system development in the period following the country's Constitution coming into force in 1993 was the adoption of laws that significantly widened the president's powers. Thus, Boris Yeltsin received 165 specific new powers during his tenure (1991–1999); Vladimir Putin's first two terms (2000–2008) gave him 226; and between 2008 and 2012 Dmitry Medvedev gained 111 (*Novaya Gazeta*, 2012). After Putin returned to the Kremlin as president for his third (2012) and fourth (2018) terms, this trend continued. What are these "powers"? For example, according to the Constitution, the official military doctrine of Russia must be approved by a presidential decree; this applies also to the official doctrines related to national security and foreign policy. We will return to these doctrines in the following chapters. The president also must approve candidacies to the Minister of Foreign Affairs and many other officials responsible for the implementation of foreign and security policies. And he does. In May 2018 the Federal Assembly gave Russia's president special powers to introduce "anti-sanctions" against the United States and other countries that had imposed or might impose their sanctions on Russia. It is likely that presidential powers are continuing to expand as you read these pages.

The president's style

Studies in political psychology suggest that the top leader's individual style matters in any country's foreign affairs. It matters in Russia, too. According to International Relations theory, in transparent political systems foreign policy is supposed to be **institutional**, which means that it is mostly based on established institutional practices and identifiable political interests that do not shift unexpectedly. Foreign policy can also be mostly **personalized**: that is, it is based on the immediate or long-term interests and choices, rational or not, of the leader and the most powerful political elites. These choices remain generally unknown to the public. Russia's foreign policy is likely to be more personalized than institutional. Consider the following examples.

Mikhail Gorbachev was a politician with a strong international reputation, experience, and influence, which he gained in the 1980s. The world was optimistic about his foreign policy. He frequently travelled abroad. Most world leaders embraced him as a reforming politician. His openness and excellent communication skills were helpful in promoting his ideas of peace and cooperation in international relations (Brown, 1997). By contrast, before becoming president, Boris Yeltsin had had very little experience in international affairs. He appeared unpredictable, flamboyant, awkward, and at times vulgar. His international reputation deteriorated in the 1990s, to some extent as a result of his personal style.

Before 2000 Vladimir Putin had gained some experience in international affairs: he served as a Soviet intelligence agent in East Germany, and he worked as a deputy mayor in St. Petersburg, where he was responsible for international affairs. When he moved to Moscow, he was in charge of Russia's property abroad in the Presidential Administration. He headed the Federal Security Service (FSB). During his first two terms in office as president he established good personal relations with many leaders including George W. Bush (the United States), Tony Blair (the United Kingdom), Gerhard Schroeder (Germany), and Silvio Berlusconi (Italy). He appeared straightforward, decisive, and strong as a leader. It certainly helped in rebuilding a positive attitude toward Russia and its policies in the early 2000s.

Yet Putin adopted a more confrontational attitude later, especially after he took the office again in 2012. Putin's message to the Russian people has been that their old enemies in the West wanted to keep their country under siege and that resisting this requires national unity and a readiness to sacrifice (Freedman, 2018). His international reputation has deteriorated as has that of Russia and its policies: Russia's international image remains more negative than positive. Critical opinions of Russia are strong in the United States and Europe, and they are mixed in the Asia, the Middle East, Sub-Saharan Africa and Latin America. Europeans are particularly critical of Putin, with a median in Europe of 78% expressing low confidence in him. In the United States and Canada three times as many people dislike Putin as like him (Vice, 2017). His propensity to appear (on official photos) athletic, tough, and engaged in various risky activities has evoked critical and sarcastic reactions from the foreign media, especially in the West. After returning to presidency in 2012 Vladimir Putin's style changed again; he appeared more straightforward and brisk than ever before. Bear in mind, though, that perceptions of political leaders differ from country to country (Mearsheimer, 2014). What Western commentators saw as Putin's confrontational style, most Russian insiders labeled as Putin's assertiveness and toughness.

The Presidential Administration

The Presidential Administration plays a key role in the executive branch. The head of the Administration is informally regarded as the third most important person within the executive branch after the president and the prime minister. The role of the Presidential Administration in shaping the country's foreign policy has varied

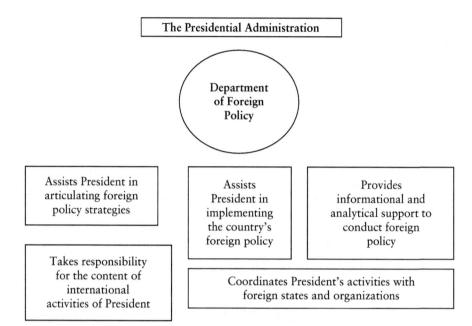

Figure 3.1 The functions of the Department of Foreign Policy in the Presidential Administration

over the past two decades, but its importance has increased. A special department within the Administration is in charge of foreign policy. There is also a special unit responsible for relations with post-Soviet states. It has several general functions.

First, the Administration is in charge of relations with the countries of the former Soviet Union. Russian ambassadors to these states often served as the president's special "envoys" there. For example, Victor Chernomyrdin (1938–2010), who was the Russian ambassador to Ukraine, served simultaneously as the president's special representative responsible for oil and natural gas policies.

There are other, more important, reasons why the Presidential Administration is in charge of policies related to the countries of the former Soviet Union. One of the key tasks of the Administration is the control and regulation of many venues of political life in Russia. In the 1990s Russian domestic political developments were closely linked to those in the former Soviet republics, which maintained significant ties with Russia. Russia's business and political elites considered these countries as their "backyard," or a legitimate zone of Russia's interests, where they have the right and the opportunity to conduct business.

The Administration is also in charge of policies related to the so-called unrecognized states in the post-Soviet space. Two of these are Abkhazia and South Ossetia, formally recognized only by Moscow and a few countries. A special position of Assistant to the President has been established to coordinate these policies. The fact that the Administration is focusing on the post-Soviet space can be viewed, to a degree, as a continuation of the old Soviet-era policies. Moscow's policies toward socialist countries during the Soviet period were under the direct control of the Central Committee of the Communist Party rather than the Ministry of Foreign Affairs.

Assistants to the President responsible for international affairs were "old-timers" of Russian politics. Three of these old-timers were Dmitri Riurikov (served from 1991 to 1997), Sergei Prikhodko (from 1997 to 2012), and Yuri Ushakov (after 2012). All three were career diplomats for years. Yuri Ushakov, for instance, served as ambassador to the United States from 1998 to 2008. In general terms, the Foreign Policy Directorate of the Administration is responsible for major strategic foreign policy decisions, and the Ministry of Foreign Affairs determines the tactics to implement such decisions.

Russian presidents (like US presidents) have a practice of appointing special representatives or envoys to deal with certain international issues. In some cases this is done to strengthen the negotiating position, to build up the envoy's status, or to underline attention to a particular problem. For example, Mikhail Margelov, then Chairman of the Federation Council's Committee for International Affairs (2001–2014), was appointed as a special envoy responsible for the issues of peaceful settlement in the Sudan (Decree of the President of Russian Federation No. 1731, 2008) and subsequently as an envoy in charge of Russia's cooperation with Africa (Decree of the President of Russian Federation No. 329, 2011). The vast network of special envoys and representatives enables the Presidential Administration to directly steer Russia's foreign policy and avoid bureaucratic delays.

The Security Council

The Russian Federation's Security Council (RFSC) plays a special role in the country's foreign policy. Article 83 of the Constitution gives the president the power to direct the activities of the Council, which is made up of permanent and non-permanent members. The former are the Security Council Secretary, the Chairman of the Government, the head of the Presidential Administration, the chairs of the Federation Council and the State Duma, the ministers of Foreign Affairs and Defense, directors of the Federal Security Service and the Foreign Intelligence Service, and a few others. The Security Council Secretary directs several commissions. Although full-membership sessions of the Security Council are convened infrequently, the president regularly holds individual meetings with the permanent members of the Council.

The Security Council members discuss Russia's foreign policy strategies such as the National Security Doctrine, the Military Doctrine, and the Foreign Policy Concept. They deal with the most current issues in foreign policy such as international conflicts, nonproliferation of the weapons of mass destruction, international terrorism, drug trafficking, organized crime, activities of the Collective Security Treaty Organization (CSTO), and Russia's relations with NATO countries. Resolutions of the Security Council are often formalized by presidential decrees. The Security Council maintains working relations with similar structures in other countries. Among the most influential holders of the top Security Council's position have been Vladimir Putin (from 1998 to 1999); Sergei Ivanov (from 1999 to 2001), who has been one of Putin's closest allies for many years; and Nikolai Patrushev (appointed Secretary of the Security Council in 2008).

Other executive institutions

The Government (Cabinet of Ministers)

According to the Constitution (Article 110), the government of the Russian Federation consists of the government chairperson (prime minister), deputy premiers, and federal ministers. Article 114 of the Constitution requires the government to be responsible for Russia's defense, security, and the implementation of its foreign policy.

In practice, the government has been for the most part subordinate to the president who appoints its members and has the right of chairing its meetings, issuing instructions, and retracting the government's rulings. An exception to this practice was noticeable between 2008 and 2012, when Vladimir Putin was prime minister. Although he avoided making public statements on foreign policy, his influence on its direction was considerable. Putin appointed a deputy chief-of-staff (Yuri Ushakov) for international affairs. In 2012, when Putin became president, Ushakov joined the Presidential Administration.

The government chair (prime minister) does not usually participate in international summits and other events involving heads of states. At the same time, the prime minister plays an important role in developing international economic relations. Deputies of the prime minister and federal ministers usually direct intergovernmental economic affairs with other states and international organizations.

The 1997 federal law identifies several ministries that report directly to the president, not to the prime minister. These ministries include defense, security, internal affairs, justice, foreign affairs, and emergency situations. Just as during the times of the Russian Empire and the Soviet Union, today's foreign policy is under direct presidential control.

The Ministry of Foreign Affairs

The Russian Federation's Ministry of Foreign Affairs was formed in December 1991 on the basis of the defunct Soviet ministry. There were no serious structural changes during the transition process, and most senior officials retained their positions. Unfortunately, major financial difficulties immediately affected the ministry's work Its budget was slashed. Salaries plummeted as a result of rampant inflation in the country. The social status of the diplomat was seriously weakened. Scores of professionals resigned from the foreign ministry, and many sought jobs in private business or elsewhere. The ministry could not quickly replace them with new specialists and remained understaffed and underfunded for years.

Andrei Kozyrev, the new foreign minister of Russia, had to manage the ministry under these difficult circumstances. Kozyrev, one of the most prominent Russian politicians of the 1990s, was actively involved not only in international affairs but also in the internal political struggle in Russia. As one of the most consistent supporters of radical market reforms and the integration of Russia into the community of developed democratic states, he was a convenient political target of the communists and nationalists who wanted to see Russia playing a different role in international affairs. They saw Russia's policy as weak. They accused Kozyrev of not doing enough during the crisis in Yugoslavia in the 1990s and of allowing NATO's eastward expansion. Boris Yeltsin saw Kozyrev as a political liability and replaced him in 1996.

From 1996 to 1998 Dr. Evgeny Primakov (1929–2015), a prominent scholar and expert on the Middle East, led the foreign ministry. In the 1980s Primakov was part of the segment of the Soviet elites who understood the necessity of social and economic changes in the country. Mikhail Gorbachev appointed him to several top government positions. In the fall of 1991 Primakov became chief of the Foreign Intelligence Service. Later, as a foreign minister, he carried out a number of important changes: he boosted the ministry's efficiency, reorganized its bureaucracy, improved diplomats' working conditions, and increased their salaries. It appeared to many that the prestige of the diplomatic profession was back.

In 1996 Yeltsin gave the foreign ministry the authority to coordinate the international activities of the other government ministries and agencies, including those on the regional level (Decree of the President of Russian Federation No. 375, March 12, 1996). This gradually strengthened the role of the ministry in all government affairs. Primakov's personal role in policy-making was significant. He returned to foreign policy strategies that would assign Russia a more affirmative role in global affairs (the role that many believed had been lost under Kozyrev). During Primakov's tenure phrases such as "a multipolar world," "spheres of influence," and "the red line" (i.e., the last line of defense) came into use. In the second half of the 1990s Primakov, according to opinion polls, appeared to be one of the most influential public figures in Russia (Levada, 2000). For openly declaring that he was putting Russia's interest first, he enjoyed support from various political forces in the country. He later chaired the Cabinet of Ministers from 1998 to 1999. After Primakov's departure, his deputy Igor Ivanov became minister of Foreign Affairs (1998–2004), followed by Sergei Lavrov. Both Ivanov and Lavrov were highly competent diplomats. They generally avoided participating in the internal political struggles in Moscow.

In 2002 President Putin acknowledged the significance of the diplomatic profession by establishing a special professional holiday, the Diplomat's Day. More people now are choosing diplomatic careers. Moscow's Institute of International Relations, St. Petersburg University's School of International Relations, and a few other universities have become key educational institutions to educate future diplomats and civil servants. Today the Ministry of Foreign Affairs employs many professionals knowledgeable in international relations, history, comparative politics, political science, economics, and humanities. Almost all of them are proficient in at least one foreign language. By contrast, many diplomats-the young and the seasoned—have retained or learned the old way of thinking, the one that often resembles a mixture of Marxist attitudes and assessments from the time of the Cold War. Such "old" and "new" schools of thinking are probably common in every foreign ministry and in every country. In Russia, however, such differences appear more consequential, because of the complicated international situation and Russia's role in global politics.

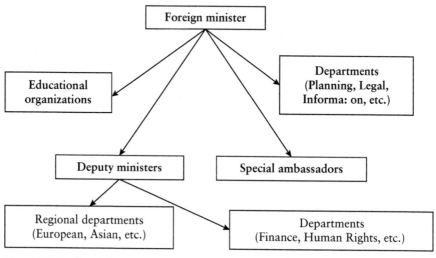

Figure 3.2 Structure of the Ministry of Foreign Affairs

The structure of the Ministry of Foreign Affairs has undergone some alterations over the past twenty years, but no radical changes have been carried out. Most of its departments are organized geographically. The number of departments responsible for the world's regions is more often determined by the ministry's internal considerations rather than by the importance of a particular region. Thus, for example, it has four departments to deal with the Commonwealth of the Independent States, which is a regional organization whose participating countries are some former Soviet Republics. Five other departments deal with Europe, and there is just one department for North America. The Ministry of Foreign Affairs also pays little attention to economic relations, such as Russia's ascendance and participation in the World Trade Organization (WTO). In addition to its centralized structure, the Ministry of Foreign Affairs maintains offices in different regions of the Russian Federation and assists them in developing their own international ties, mostly in education, trade, and so on (see Figure 3.2).

The Ministry of Defense

A principal role in the shaping of Russia's foreign policy belongs to the Ministry of Defense. In the 1990s its activities were almost exclusively focused on military issues. This changed in 2001 when Sergei Ivanov, at that time one of Putin's closest confidants, was appointed defense minister. From the beginning of his tenure he was actively engaged in a wide range of foreign policy issues, such as relations with other countries and antiterrorist policies.

His successors, including Anatoly Serdukov and then Sergei Shoigu (appointed in 2012), were allowed to expand their responsibilities to include more foreign policy issues on the list. In 2011, the position of Deputy Defense Minister for International Affairs was established. The leadership clearly wanted to make their defense policies global. For example, Anatoly Antonov, a career diplomat and former First Deputy Defense Minister for International Affairs became Russian Ambassador to the United States in 2017.

The Federal Security Service

The **Federal Security Service** (in English, commonly abbreviated as FSB) of the Russian Federation is the centralized system of federal services performing security-related tasks. The FSB was created in 1995 under President Boris Yeltsin. According to federal law, the president is directly in charge of the FSB (Federal Law No. 40 FZ, April 3, 1995). Over the years this institution has undergone several structural reorganizations to improve its efficiency. As an example, in 2003 President Putin moved Russian border patrol operations under the control of the FSB. The Service performs other functions. One is counterintelligence or, simply put, antispying activities. The FSB has the right to investigate, prevent, or interrupt any activity by the intelligence services of other countries, as well as acts of individuals who are considered a threat to the security of the Russian Federation. The law allows FSB to conduct preventive or retaliatory measures against individual terrorists and terrorist organizations regardless of their whereabouts (Golz, 2007).

Intelligence gathering is another function of the FSB. It is also responsible for preventing people and goods from entering Russia illegally. This role also involves protection of the country's economic interests within the zone of Russia's continental shelf, as well as protection of fish resources. The FSB also organizes informational security related to the transmission of sensitive or secret information within Russia and overseas. In 1991 the Foreign Intelligence Service (SVR) became a separate government structure. Matters of foreign intelligence are also the responsibility of the Main Intelligence Directorate of the General Staff of the military (Federal Law No. 5-FZ, January 9, 1996).

A distinctive feature of the Soviet period was the powerful role of the government's special agencies on decision-making in international affairs. In the Soviet Union the functions of political police, state security, and external intelligence were typically executed by one government institution (the KGB was the latest). Today several special agencies associated with intelligence play a key role in Russia's daily functioning. Their role in the shaping of Russia's foreign policy is important, but it is seldom emphasized in official reports. We will discuss the role of special agencies in Chapter 4.

The Finance Ministry

The role of this ministry in foreign affairs is considerable. First, in the 1990s, Russia's federal budget was strongly dependent on borrowing abroad, which certainly impacted the country's foreign policy. After the devastating financial crisis of 1998 the Kremlin pursued the policy of reducing Russia's dependency on foreign institutions in the financial sphere. Oil and natural gas exports became the principal source of the country's revenue. The Ministry of Finance is responsible for saving and spending policies.

Next, Russia's participation in the Group of Eight (G8), Group of Twenty (G20), and other international organizations also facilitated the role of the Ministry of Finance and, especially, its regulatory power during the 2008–2011 global financial crisis.

Finally, the Ministry of Finance evaluates funding requests by the Ministry of Foreign Affairs and other government offices working with foreign governments and organizations. From 2000 to 2011 Alexei Kudrin, an economist by education and a close friend of Putin's, headed the Ministry of Finance. Kudrin resigned from his government position partly because of his disagreement with Russia's sharp increase in military expenditures. He remains an authoritative expert and an influential figure in Russian political life. In 2018 he became chair of the Accounts Chamber of the Russian Federation, the institution that exercises financial control in the country. Check his professional position today, because it is likely to change.

Other government institutions

The Ministry of Economic Development is responsible, among many things, for Russia's international economic cooperation. Out of its twenty-nine departments, at least six deal directly with international affairs; they coordinate policies in America, Europe, Asia, and Africa. The ministry also promotes economic cooperation with CIS countries. One of the ministry's assignments was the preparation for Russia's entry into the World Trade Organization (WTO). Russia became the 156th member of the WTO in 2012 (WTO, 2012).

The Ministry of Industry and Trade's responsibilities are primarily in the economic field. In particular, it was involved in the creation and development of the Eurasian Economic Union (EEU, which involves Russia, Belarus, Kazakhstan, Armenia, and Kyrgyzstan). The EEU coordinates the free movement of goods, capital, services, and individuals across its members. The organization also oversees common agriculture, transportation, and energy policies and is involved in Russia-WTO relations, as well as interactions with the European Union and other international economic organizations.

The Ministry of Justice's role in Russia's foreign policy may appear somewhat limited. The ministry's activities include the interpretations of the rulings of international courts involving Russia and its interests. The ministry also provides expert assessments of international treaties' drafts before they are signed. Such activities, however, do not necessarily influence the process of political decision-making; rather, they provide legal "groundwork" for the Ministry of Foreign Affairs and the Kremlin.

There is a separate institution called the Federal Agency for CIS Affairs, Compatriots Residing Abroad, and International Humanitarian Cooperation, which was established in 2008. It reports directly to the Ministry of Foreign Affairs. In 2016 it had representations in eighty countries. This agency's tasks involve the promotion of Russia's cultural heritage, educational exchanges, science, and technology. It supports teaching the Russian language in foreign countries, selects foreign students to study in Russian universities, and promotes educational exchange programs, and international collaborative research.

The legislative branch

The highest legislative body of the Russian Federation, as you may remember, is a parliament called the Federal Assembly. It consists of two chambers, the Federation Council and the State Duma. In theory the legislative branch of the government is quite powerful, but in reality the current legislature has little political power compared to the executive. This is important to keep in mind when we study how Russia's foreign policy works.

Article 106 of the Constitution formally identifies three areas in which the Federal Assembly should render support of or opposition to the executive branch: the Russian Federation's international treaties; the Russian Federation's borders; and decisions associated with declaration of war and peace. In the past only a few legislative battles took place over agreements signed by the Kremlin. For example, when President Yeltsin and German Chancellor Helmut Kohl agreed in 1998 on the restitution (return) of cultural treasures captured by the Soviet Union during World War II, the Duma and the Federation Council blocked the agreement and overrode the president's veto. Overall, however, unlike in the United States, the legislative branch has not been a key institution in the process of approving or rejecting international agreements. Parliamentary procedural delays have been rare, and when they did take place they were almost always discussed with the Kremlin. In terms of political support, Putin and Medvedev, the two Russian presidents in the twenty-first century, have always had a significant supporting majority in the Federal Assembly.

One of the important venues of the Federal Assembly's international activities is the creation and upkeep of so-called interparliamentary links or direct contacts with foreign countries' parliaments. The Federation Council and the State Duma maintain membership in various interparliamentary associations such as the Parliamentary Assembly of the Council of Europe, the Interparliamentary Assembly of CIS Countries, and many others.

The Federation Council

The Federation Council, which is one of the two chambers of the parliament, should include, according to the Constitution, two members from each subject of the Russian Federation. Typically, individuals with strong connections in the federal government as well as popular local politicians are picked for the Federation Council. The procedures by which the Council is formed have been changed several times, and new procedures may be in place as you read these pages.

The Federation Council has two committees directly engaged in foreign policy matters: one deals with international affairs and the other's activities focus on CIS countries. Formally, the Federation Council (unlike the Duma) has no official party factions. However, nearly all the members of the Council belong to United Russia, the leading progovernment political party in Russia. For this and other reasons, the Federation Council commonly represents the interests of the federal government and not necessarily its local constituencies. For example, the Council members from the Khabarovsk region (2005) voted for the ratification of the border treaty with China; yet the population of their region was overwhelmingly against several provisions of the treaty containing Russia's territorial concessions to China (for example, according to the treaty, some popular holiday destinations frequented by Russians were given to China).

The Federation Council has the legal authority to authorize the use of armed forces abroad. In August 2008, for example, President Medvedev ordered a military action against Georgia using the formal consent of the Federation Council to deploy the CIS peacekeeping military units in South Ossetia and Abkhazia. A federal law passed later gave even more powers to the president to make urgent decisions regarding the use of armed forces outside Russia's borders. These powers may be used to repel attacks on the Russian military, to prevent aggression against Russia, to defend Russian citizens abroad, to fight piracy, and to secure the safety of shipments (Federal Laws No. 61-FZ, 1996 and No. 252-FZ, 2009). This law expanded the president's authority to act without approval of the Federation Council. In March 2014 the Federation Council unanimously adopted a resolution authorizing President Putin's use of armed forces on the territory of Ukraine.

The State Duma

The Constitution stipulates that the State Duma of the Russian Federation should have 450 deputies (members). Since the constitutional amendments of 2008 the members of the Duma have been elected for five-year terms. In most recent years only four parties have been represented in the State Duma (see Chapter 6). On most major issues related to foreign policy and security these parties have maintained relatively similar positions. As we will see later in this book, these parties' political platforms have reflected anti-Western (and particularly anti-American) sentiments.

The State Duma has many committees, of which at least two deal directly with foreign policy: the International Affairs Committee (chaired usually by the member of the leading party, which is United Russia) and the CIS Affairs Committee. In the 1990s there was a Duma committee on geopolitics, which was headed by a member of the LDPR (one of the most nationalist and anti-Western parties). After this committee was abolished, LDPR members commonly chaired the committee on CIS affairs. After the 2016 Duma elections the chairmanship of the International Affairs Committee for the first time was given to the Liberal Democratic Party. The Communist Party (also known for its anti-Western position) appoints its representative to chair the CIS Affairs Committee. These decisions were likely to give so-called hard-liners more power in the legislative process related to foreign affairs.

Although visits by foreign ministers to the Duma are very few and far between, the Duma frequently debates foreign policy and international relations during its regular sessions and regularly makes official statements about international affairs. In most cases these statements require voting. They are passed with little opposition or quite often unanimously. Most statements are critical of Western and the US policies. The only significant exception was the statement of the State Duma *On the Katyn Tragedy and Its Victims*, which was passed in 2010. At that moment the Russian leadership was trying to improve relations with Poland and avoid the Polish veto on negotiations on a new agreement with the European Union. The recognition of the Soviet government's responsibility for the Katyn tragedy back in 1940 (see Chapter 8) was a significant attempt to change Polish public opinion in favor of Russia. Nevertheless, several influential political groups in Russia opposed this recognition. A compromise was found: the Duma resolution recognized the political responsibility of Stalin for the Katyn tragedy, but any legal remedies to compensate for Stalin's decisions were rejected. The practice of issuing foreign policy–related statements by the legislature is common in other countries.

All things considered, the activities of the Federal Assembly in the international sphere take place within the framework set by the Kremlin. The legislative influence on Russia's foreign policy and the decision-making process has been so far insignificant.

The judicial branch

There are two federal legal bodies, each carrying specific responsibilities: the Constitutional Court of the Russian Federation and the Supreme Court of the Russian Federation. These courts have the right of legislative initiative within their jurisdiction. Issues related to foreign policy are mainly the prerogative of the Constitutional Court, which should check and rule on the constitutionality of Russia's international treaties (no such precedents on the record so far).

The Constitutional Court does exert a certain influence on Russia's policy regarding its membership in the Council of Europe and Moscow's assumed obligations there. Russia became a member of the Council of Europe in 1996 after signing and ratifying the European Convention on Human Rights and then recognizing the jurisdiction of the European Court of Human Rights in Strasbourg (ECHR). That was a remarkable political move: for the first time in history Russia's citizens received the right to seek protection of their civil rights in an international organization.

However, views about Russia's membership in the Council of Europe have been debated for some time: many politicians, officials, and legal scholars tended to disagree about what the membership obliged Russia to do. The General Prosecutor's Office, for example, objected to the transfer of several of its powers to European courts, which Russia's membership in the Council of Europe demanded. At the same time, the number of legal cases coming from Russia to the ECHR rapidly grew. By 2010 Russia ranked first out of all ECHR participants in the number of lawsuits filed. Many such lawsuits were lost by the Russian authorities (meaning that the plaintiffs won), which further contributed to the anguish in Russia's judicial circles as well as among politicians. Some were convinced that the European human rights standards were inappropriately high. Others believed that the ECHR's decisions were politically biased against Russia. President Putin commented that the decisions of the ECHR could be accepted only if they did not contradict the Russian Constitution; otherwise, the Constitutional Court should block such decisions. In July 2015 the Constitutional Court officially declared its right to do so (*Rossijskaya Gazeta,* July 14, 2015).

Russia observes the international agreements it had entered into earlier. Therefore, the Kremlin continues to allow Russian citizens to file cases and appeals before the ECHR, despite the domestic political opposition to this practice. The opposing voices have been louder since Russia's participation in the Parliamentary Assembly of Council of Europe was suspended and the European Union imposed economic sanctions on Russia (for its actions in Ukraine) in 2014 and sustained them after that. We will discuss these developments later in the book. The role of the Supreme Court in matters of foreign policy is considerably less important than the role of the Constitutional Court.

In general, the judiciary, which is an independent branch of power, commonly aligns itself with the Kremlin, the executive branch, on key international issues.

Interactions between government and nongovernment structures

In democratic countries, government institutions commonly interact with nongovernment structures and citizens in managing foreign policy. Public opinion and the media often play a key role in this process. Certainly, the scope and depth of such interactions are determined by each country's history, political system, traditions, and many contextual factors.

The Civic Chamber of the Russian Federation has been designed as an institution to promote cooperation between citizens and the state. It also exercises public control over federal authorities. The chamber has three sections: the first consists of individuals directly appointed by the president; the second is made up of a few representatives of a few regional civic chambers; and the third consists of a diverse range of representatives of various public associations. In 2012 the Russian Public Council for International Cooperation and Public Diplomacy was created. The Council holds regular meetings to discuss current issues of foreign policy and international affairs. Similar public councils were set up within some ministries and departments, including the Ministry of Defense, Ministry of Internal Affairs, Federal Security Service, and others. The Foreign Ministry did not form a public council. Yet it works with several advisory and consultative agencies involving local and business leaders.

The Russian Council for International Affairs was created in 2010 on the president's instructions. The goal of this group was to serve as a link between the government, on the one hand, and the community of experts, business leaders, and ordinary citizens, on the other. This council organizes major international conferences and discussions on specific subjects involving international relations and Russia's foreign policy. It also publishes analytical reports on current international issues.

The National Committee for BRICS Studies (the abbreviation stands for Brazil, Russia, India, China, and South Africa) was created in 2011. The committee analyzes the role and position of BRICS countries in world politics and economy. It also coordinates efforts of Russian and international researchers, including sponsorship of conferences and preparation of analytical reports related to economic, business, education, and so on, and related to BRICS countries.

In 2003, after the summit involving President Putin, the French president Chirac, and the German chancellor Schroeder at the University of St. Petersburg, the leaders had an informal get-together with Russian and foreign researchers studying international affairs (one of the authors of this book was present). That meeting gave an impulse for the creation of the **Valdai International Discussion Club** (2004), which is an informal group of international scholars, political experts, as well as journalists who meet to discuss Russia, its domestic and foreign policy, and its role in the world. The Valdai Club holds annual sessions after which the participants usually meet with Vladimir Putin for an informal exchange of opinions on the most important issues. It is hard to judge whether Putin's foreign policy is in any way affected by his regular discussions with journalists and scientists. During these verbal exchanges he prefers to give his opinion of foreign events, brushes off criticisms, and always defends his policies. Nevertheless, the Valdai Club may be the only well-known regular and transparent event where the key Russian leaders meet informally with international scholars and journalists.

Conclusion

The institutional mechanisms of foreign policy decision-making in today's Russia are affected both by the country's historical legacy, especially from its imperial and the Soviet periods, and by the new trends evident in the last two decades since the collapse of the Soviet Union. The emerged and emerging institutions continuously evolve. However, the foreign policy decision-making system remains mostly under the control of the president.

The interaction between Russia's government and nongovernment structures involved in international activities is insignificant. On the one hand, the very precedent of such interaction is a relatively new phenomenon in Russian politics. On the other hand, critics maintain that twenty-five years is already a long period to build new and transparent forms of civic participation in foreign policy. What are the key reasons for a low level of civic engagement in Russia in foreign policy matters?

The first reason is rooted in to Russia's political culture: traditionally, many federal executives tend to treat nongovernment groups as unimportant (and even inconvenient) subordinates rather than partners, as mouthpieces of interest groups rather than advisers.

Second, Russian civic leaders, business community members, journalists, and scholars tend to disagree among themselves on key foreign policy issues, including whether public opinion could and should affect foreign policy. Personal or corporate interests often prevail.

Next, unlike in the Soviet Union, today's Russian leaders have already developed wide-ranging international connections. Yet these leaders' direct involvement in global processes remains, unfortunately, only skin deep. The Russian economy remains inward oriented, which affects the international position of Russian businesses. Russia's civic leaders are not well represented in global organizations and networks. The sanctions imposed on Russia after the 2014 crisis in Ukraine have negatively affected Russian experts' participation, at least for some time, in global nongovernmental organizations. The Kremlin also imposed several limitations on Russian government officials, including a ban on having foreign bank accounts and limits on international travel for law enforcement officials.

Finally, Russia's mass media, for the most part, are controlled by the state. Most journalists working for major media corporations tend to support the official line on foreign policy, whatever it is. They, as reporters and commentators, play an important role in forming public opinion in Russia. Government authorities regularly monitor opinion polls. However, except for some major international crises (such as in Kosovo in 1999, Georgia in 2008, or Ukraine in 2014 and after), foreign policy is seldom ranked among the top ten issues of greatest concern of the ordinary Russian citizen.

Summary

- The dissolution of the Soviet Union has brought only minor changes to Russia's foreign policy institutions, which have been developing for a few centuries.
- During the time of the Soviet Union the Communist Party's Central Committee, its top office the Politburo, and ultimately, the General Secretary were the key decision-makers in foreign policy. The years of perestroika that began in 1985 were a time of a gradual diminishing of the power of the Communist Party over the institutions of foreign policy of the Soviet Union.

- Russia's political system and its institutions, the foundations of which were shaped mainly during the turbulent period between 1991 and 1993, are changing still.
- According to International Relations theory, in transparent political systems foreign policy is supposed to be institutional, which means it is mostly based on established institutional practices and identifiable political interests that do not shift unexpectedly. In other countries, including Russia, foreign policy is mostly personalized: it is based on the immediate interests and choices, rational or not, of the leader and the most powerful political elites.
- The Presidential Administration plays a key role in the executive branch.
- The structure of the Ministry of Foreign Affairs has undergone certain alterations over the past twenty years, yet no radical changes have been carried out. Most of its departments are organized geographically. The number of departments responsible for the world's regions is more often determined by the ministry's internal considerations rather than by the importance of a particular region.
- A principal role in the shaping of Russia's foreign policy belongs to the Ministry of Defense, the Federal Security Service, and a few other top government institutions.
- The Federation Council has two committees directly engaged in foreign policy matters: one deals with international affairs and the other's activities focus on CIS countries.
- The State Duma has many committees, of which at least two deal directly with foreign policy: the International Affairs Committee (chaired usually by the member of the leading party, which is United Russia) and the CIS Affairs Committee.
- In general, the judiciary, which is an independent branch of power, commonly aligns itself with the Kremlin, the executive branch, on key international issues.
- In Russia government institutions commonly interact with nongovernment structures and citizens in managing foreign policy. Public opinion and the media sometimes play a role in this process. The scope and depth of such interactions are insignificant, however.

Glossary

Federal Security Service of the Russian Federation (in English, commonly abbreviated as FSB) is the centralized system of federal services performing security-related tasks.

Institutional foreign policy Established institutional practices and identifiable political interests that do not shift unexpectedly.

Personalized foreign policy Policy based on the immediate interests and choices, rational or not, of the leader and the most powerful political elites.

State Duma The legislative body elected by popular vote (Russia's national parliament).

Valdai International Discussion Club An informal group of international scholars, political experts, and journalists who discuss Russia, its domestic and foreign policy, and its role in the world. The Valdai Club holds annual sessions after which the participants usually meet with Vladimir Putin for an informal exchange of opinions on the most important issues.

Vertical of power The subordination of policies of all government institutions to the president and his administration.

World revolution The communist concept of the global and rapid transformation of political power to replace capitalism.

Review questions

1. What were the main characteristics of the institutions of foreign policy in the Soviet Union? How have they changed in the past twenty-five years?
2. Which nongovernmental organizations deal with foreign policy in Russia? Do you personally think that the role of NGOs in foreign policy should increase, decrease, or remain the same?
3. What foreign policy issues are within the competence of the Defense Ministry of the Russian Federation? Speaking of Russia and other countries, what are the potential negative outcomes of the military influencing a country's foreign policy?
4. What is the role of the president of the Russian Federation in the country's foreign policy?
5. Compare (using help from your professor) Russia's foreign policy institutions with similar foreign policy institutions in a different country. You may select the United States as an example. Compose a list of similarities and differences. Discuss them in class. Describe your personal view: How open to the public's control should a country's foreign policy be? How significant should the role of the public be in a country's foreign policy?

Chapter 4
Players and Processes

We are ready for a dialogue with NATO ... Even if it will be only a monologue.

Vladimir Putin, 2014

Learning objectives

- Outline the ideological, political, cultural, and psychological factors affecting Russia's foreign policy.
- Describe key ideological that influence Russia's international behavior.
- Discuss the impact of the "Putin factor" on Russian foreign policy.
- Discuss the role of elites in foreign policy decisions.

Which ideas influence Russia's foreign policy? Where did these ideas and viewpoints come from and whose interests do they represent? How different are these viewpoints from those that influence foreign policy in other countries? This chapter discusses the ideological and political roots of Russia's foreign policy. It also pays attention to the carriers of these ideologies – the political elites who directly and indirectly impact Russia's foreign policy. This influence is exercised through at least two pathways. One is **political communication**: the general ways in which information related to politics, government, and foreign policy is distributed. This influence often requires **political mobilization**, or ways to preserve (or change) the existing political system and government's policies.

On Russia's political ideologies

The left and the right

Most of us have at least a general sense of the meanings of "left" and "right" in politics: as groups, for example, the left represents liberal, and the right conservative, beliefs and policies. However, as students of political science and comparative politics, we should realize how broad and imprecise these terms often are. There are huge variations in the way different countries interpret these terms.

In Russia, the left is typically associated with communist and socialist parties and groups, who promote a larger share of the government in the economy, the nationalization of key industries, and price control of most important products and services, including food and energy. The left, as a group, actively supports the welfare state, with a vast range of social benefits and services mobilized for the least protected categories of the population. The left generally wants to preserve the political and cultural legacy of the Soviet Union. The left today acknowledges the necessity of a multiparty system and it supports basic political liberties. It also supports higher taxes on the rich and big spending programs for education, housing, and health care. The left also shows a very strong support for the Russian military. In terms of international relations, the left:

- Is critical of capitalism, international corporations, and globalization in general.
- Considers the West, and especially the United States, as major adversaries of Russia.
- Criticizes Western liberal democracy, its sources, principles, and institutions.
- Believes that the relationships between Russia and the West benefits only the West. Russia, therefore, must show its strength when dealing with Western countries.
- Views the 1991 dissolution of the Soviet Union as a negative development.

For the most part, the right supports elements of the Russian welfare state but does not reject the free-market economy. The ideology of the Russian ultra-right embraces (among other views) monarchism, isolationism, populism, homophobia, and anti-Western attitude. The right, in a general sense:

- Represents a wide range of views focused primarily on regaining Russia's strength as a state and a global actor.
- Scorns Western liberal democracy.
- Supports nationalistic attitudes based on the glorification of certain developments in Russia's history associated with expansion and strengthening of Russia as a state.
- Promotes xenophobic and anti-immigrant views.

Some confusion may occur when one deals with concepts and labels containing the word "right." As in English, Russian translations of this word also mean – in addition to indicating the direction of the political spectrum (left-right) – the state of being "correct," "accurate," or "true."

Russian "centrists" generally support the Kremlin and its policies and often identify themselves as moderates by aligning neither with the right nor the left. The centrists in Russia tend to support a moderate nationalistic platform, which is less drastic than the views of the right and the left. In general, centrists also support a bigger and more assertive role for Russia in global affairs, but they reject xenophobic, anti-immigration views. Keep in mind that for some people, however, centrism is a convenient label for the lack of particular political preferences or for the lack of general knowledge about politics.

Liberals and conservatives

The use of the terms "liberal" and "conservative" in today's Russia is different from their use in the United States and the United Kingdom (and most other Western countries). In the classic textbook sense "liberal" stands for a range of views supporting basic political, economic, and personal freedoms, as well as group rights. If you are a liberal in Russia today, then you are likely to support predominantly Western models of government, a free-market economy, a free press, a transparent government, and independent courts. Russian liberals vehemently oppose authoritarianism. It is also, in most cases, inaccurate to equate Russian liberals with the left and conservatives with the right. Unlike most people on the left, Russian liberals support friendly relations with the West.

A conservative person in Russia generally stands for stability, order, and tradition (Nesterova, 2016). A conservative supports the government's protection of social welfare, the idea of Russia's greatness as a world power, a mixed economy with a large portion of it being under government control, and tolerance of authoritarianism. Russian conservatives tend to believe that the West has been undermining Russia for centuries and is continuing to do so today. In a brief summary, liberal and conservative individuals in Russia significantly differ in their lenience toward authoritarianism, acceptance of free-market principles, views of the West and the United States, and views of Russia's role in the world.

Russians who maintain conservative attitudes (unlike most Western conservatives who tend to be economically liberal) support the government's regulation of business, including the nationalization of large industries. They stand for substantial government support for the needy, higher taxes, and the restoration of Russian global military power. Most communists support these views as well, except that the communists for the most part reject capitalism and support socialism instead. Russian liberal groups, on the other hand, tend to advocate free enterprise and less government intervention in the economy and business. Prosocialist attitudes are often identified in Russia as conservative, although communists tend to reject being called "conservatives" (see Figure 4.1).

Authoritarianism

In Western analytical publications and media reports Russia's political system is often called authoritarian. **Authoritarianism** is a form of government with a highly centralized and often personalized power structure and a relatively weak civil society. Individual leaders, and not necessarily elected organs, hold much of the power, and political freedoms are often limited (Brownlee, 2007). The view in Russia remains popular that under the existing conditions authoritarian methods of government are the best option. According to this logic, without an authoritarian core the country would be significantly worse off domestically and internationally. Some Russian experts have long maintained that the Russian people tend to seek out

Political Ideologies: Russia

In summary, **liberal and conservative** individuals in Russia differ in their:

tolerance of authoritarianism

acceptance of free market principles

views of Russia's role in the world

views of the West

...and overall evaluation of the Soviet Union as a social and political system.

Figure 4.1 A brief comparison of liberal and conservative ideologies in Russia

strong leaders and be suspicious of uncertainties of free choice. The experiences of the older generations under communism contributed to these views (Gozman and Etkind, 1992; Grunt et al., 1996). Individuals who are uncertain about the economic and political future and disappointed with the present are apt to search for a strong guarantor of stability and order (Mikulski, 1995).

A predominant view among the elites (a view that seems to be encouraged by the Kremlin today) is that a strong government's power is necessary to make the country function. Although back in the 1990s and in the early 2000s "democracy" and "market economy" were very much in use in public comments, today members of the elite tend to state openly that an authoritarian version of capitalism, such as the one in Russia, is significantly more effective than capitalism's liberal forms. Moreover, they believe that Russia is ready to prevail in a global competition among these models. Positive comments about authoritarian leaders of the past are frequent. Strong military rulers are praised. For example, the former Chilean leader Augusto Pinochet (1915–2006) and the "Chilean model" of governance – that was a mixture of the free market and authoritarianism – receive positive reviews in many Russian sources (Yasin, 2017). The leaders of the White Movement during the civil war (the label to describe most of the groups that for several years fought against the Communist government after it took power in 1917), those who were scorned and belittled in Soviet communist propaganda for decades, today are viewed positively in the media, including books and online publications. This glorification of Russia's military history seems to be part of the Kremlin's policy. For example, General Anton Denikin (1872–1947), one of the most prominent leaders of the White Movement (who emigrated to the United Kingdom, then France, and died in the United States), has been reburied with honors in Russia. This powerful symbolic act could not have been implemented without the Kremlin's consent. Another person who was reburied at the same time was Ivan Ilyin (1883–1954). A philosopher and ardent nationalist, he was exiled by the Soviet government and became a principal ideologist of White émigré groups in Europe. Putin often mentioned Ivan Ilyin in his speeches. Increasingly, proponents of nationalism and authoritarianism have returned to the cultural milieu of Russia's elites in the second decade of this century.

Nationalism

Nationalism has many forms. In a general context, **nationalism** is support and glorification of one's nation, its past and present policies, and its culture. Nationalists in Russia believe that whatever political developments take place, they should be judged by how well they serve Russia's core interests, which usually include Russia's territorial integrity, safety of the borders, the absence of ethnic conflicts within its territory, and resisting the West. Nationalists argue that for the sake of Russia's interests the country needs a strong national leader. Russia still needs a multiparty system but these parties must ensure social stability and economic development. Russian ultra-nationalists, sometimes referred to as **Russophiles** (like their nineteenth-century predecessors), generally believe that Russian history has a unique nature rooted in an exceptional culture, traditions, and morals. Russophiles are not unified and politically organized. Some of them focus on cultural issues. Others promote economic and political isolationism. Yet others support the "Russian idea" formulated by émigré philosopher Nikolai Berdyaev (1874–1948). The "Russian idea" espoused Russia's moral exclusivity and even spiritual superiority over the West. Russia's mission is to save the world from self-defeating decadence. To these types of Russophiles, the communist Soviet Union was a tragic deviation from a "natural" course of Russia's historical development. It is common today to see comments portraying Russian emperors in a very positive light. Overall, Russophiles see Russia as an exceptional and even superior country compared to others.

The idea of national exclusiveness is not new in Russia. It was also fundamental to Soviet official ideology. Images of the Soviet Union as the first socialist society and the liberator of oppressed people were central to Soviet propaganda. Stalin recognized, above all during the war against Germany, that it was necessary to combine the ideas of socialist loyalty and Russian exclusiveness. The term Soviet patriotism appeared. After Stalin's death the idea of Russian exclusiveness was downgraded, but it has never completely vanished from official documents.

Today, the most conservative Russophile intellectuals scorn liberal democracy of the Western type. In their view, Russia was mortally wounded by modernization, secularization, and Westernization – the processes initiated by Gorbachev in the 1980s (Rupnik, 1989). Many Russophiles promote the values of the Orthodox religion and oppose the expansion of political freedoms as well as anything coming out of the West, including music, fashion, entertainment, or food choices. They endorse self-sacrifice and asceticism as genuine "Russian" values. Homophobic views, unfortunately, are also common.

At least two trends emerged within Russian nationalism now. The first focuses on Russian imperial ambitions and the restoration of the Soviet Union (some supporters of this view even discuss the future inclusion of Poland and Finland in the new entity). The other trend focuses on the status of ethnic Russians and their culture inside the Russian Federation and demands a special, even superior status for this group.

As you can see, authoritarian and nationalist views overlap. Opinion polls conducted in the past fifteen years show that nationalist ideas, prejudiced views against minorities, and support for a "strong hand" in the Kremlin are correlated, and the correlation becomes more significant when the economic situation worsens (Gudkov, 2008). However, polls also indicate a relatively weak public support for ultra-radical or extreme nationalist ideas (CSR Report, 2012).

Populism

Support for authoritarian ideas and nationalism frequently fuel **populism**, which consists of political strategies that pursue the goal of mass support of a person or party by appealing directly to most people's immediate needs. Populism is based on simple solutions, promises, and corresponding actions designed to give people what they want at the time. It is also associated with scare tactics and exaggerated threats, persuading people that their main values, assets, and way of life are in danger (Albertazzi and McDonnell, 2008). If people are anxious or uncertain about their present or future, they are likely to turn to politicians who offer simple solutions to the emerging – real or imaginary – problems. As the history of Russia and other countries shows, poverty and injustice frequently make ordinary people particularly susceptible to populism, and it has always been a policy of choice for both Soviet and Russian leaders. The lack of democratic principles of openness and accountability also helps some populist politicians in winning support. Because of all the uncertainties of the past thirty years, many people in Russia have often looked for simple answers and trusted politicians who could easily promise a better life and soon. Because populism was a common and convenient strategy for most political parties in Russia, it becomes difficult to distinguish between different political parties and their rather populist electoral platforms. The problem with populism, however, is that in foreign policy populism can be used to exaggerate foreign threats and external enemies. Fear, in turn, often keeps people close to authoritarian leaders who promise protection.

Ideological guidelines and concepts tend to change rapidly in Russia. This often happens not because of the evolution of the views of Russia's top public figures but solely for considerations of opportunistic expediency. The problem is that most of Russia's social groups do not have strong and long-lasting ideological affiliations. Under these conditions Russian politicians are free, depending on the situation, to use different names and labels to describe themselves, their policies, as well as foreign countries and their actions. A "culprit" may become a friend overnight and vice versa.

Foreign policy and the domestic political climate

"Foreign policy begins at home," says the title of an insightful book on the international behavior of the United States (Haas, 2014). This almost self-evident statement refers to foreign policies of other countries as well, including Russia. The foreign policy of any country – to a significant degree – depends on domestic political processes and predominant opinions about how certain policies should be conducted. A country's political climate is a general reflection of such dominant views relevant to policies. Foreign policy, in turn, influences domestic politics and the domestic political climate. How have foreign policy and the domestic political climate interacted in Russia?

The Cold War consensus

World War II has affected the Soviet society's views of foreign policy for many years. The Soviet Union suffered devastating losses in that war (see Chapter 2). The Communist Party used the memories of the devastation of the war and the country's victory against Nazi Germany as an important unifying and motivational argument about their country's liberating role in history and the Soviet Union's international mission. The Cold War was a period of a foreign policy consensus: Most people in the Soviet Union saw their country as the "savior" of Europe and the "liberator" of the entire world from Nazi oppression. Many also saw their country as a genuine global defender of the poor, the oppressed, and the disenfranchised. People generally agreed with the Kremlin's foreign policy and its anti-Western stance. By the 1980s this view of the Soviet Union's policies was greatly diminished. Instead, many Soviet citizens saw their government as a cynical player in international affairs: although the country proclaimed the highest moral standards in foreign policy, it constantly violated them. The Soviet leaders supported many brutal dictators in Africa and Asia. Moscow's unpopular war in Afghanistan (1979–1989) was one of many illustrations of why such critical attitudes emerged (Shlapentokh, Shiraev, and Carroll, 2008).

Polarization of foreign policy views

A majority of Russians supported Gorbachev's liberal domestic reforms and a new foreign policy. They wanted to see their country not as an international pariah but rather as a part of the global community. However, as you will remember from Chapter 2, these attitudes began to change in the 1990s. Several international setbacks (including the expansion of NATO and the disintegration of Yugoslavia, the country that Russia supported) and the strengthening of domestic political opposition have shifted foreign policy arguments in Russia. By the end of the 1990s a change of course to a tougher, more assertive, even confrontational line with the West had been welcomed by a few. It was later embraced by many.

Consolidation of foreign policy views

The tone of foreign policy debates was changing early in the twenty-first century. The discussions in the media about the growing external threats from the United States and NATO intensified. The conflict in Georgia in August 2008, which was seen in the West as an undisputable Russian aggression, was perceived completely differently in Moscow. Russia's military success (the official propaganda in Moscow emphasized that although the West was giving Georgia direct support, Russia had prevailed) was regarded by the bulk of society as proof of Russia's increasingly assertive role in international relations. Russia was apparently becoming an independent power capable of defending its interests outside its borders. The popularity of Prime Minister Vladimir Putin and Dmitry Medvedev (who was president in 2008) rose.

The uprisings in the Middle East and North Africa in 2010–2012, often referred to as the Arab Spring, have received serious attention in Russia. One of the common themes in the media was that Washington and its European allies had orchestrated these popular uprisings. The events in Libya in 2011 were important as well. According to Russian officials, the West had deceived Russia so that the UN Security Council adopted the resolution authorizing the use of force by the West and its Arab allies to topple Libya's leader, Muammar Gaddafi.

The Ukrainian crisis that started in 2014 has had a profound impact on foreign policy debates in Russia. The fall of President Viktor Yanukovych was greeted with great anxiety. The official sources in Moscow as well as the media portrayed the events in Ukraine as a clash between "good" and "evil" forces (in which pro-Russian forces were fighting on the "good" side and Ukrainian nationalists were on the other). In March 2014 Russia seized Crimea (which was denounced as an annexation in the West and most other countries). Opinions polls registered a surge in nationalist attitudes. More than 80 percent of Russians, in several national opinion polls, considered Crimea as a legitimate part of Russian territory (Levada, 2015). Putin's personal popularity in surveys exceeded 80 percent. A considerable part of Russia's population shared the belief that Russia was still "surrounded by enemies" and that the diminishing living standards in the country after 2014 were caused by a massive Western plot to lower oil prices and discriminate against Russia economically and financially (Levada, 2018a).

Carriers of ideology: Russian power elites

In political science, an **elite** is a small group of people who control a disproportionate amount of wealth, political power, or both. In comparative politics this group is often called the establishment. It typically has significant power to influence public opinion as well as most government policies. For decades political scientists have studied elites and their political influence. These studies, known as elite theory, propose that the establishment holds the most power in every country and that the democratic process does not necessarily impact the elite's power (Bottomore,

1993). Elite theory also argues that policy does not result from people's demands but rather from elite inner agreement (Dye, 2001).

Russia's new political elites were forming in the 1990s, after the collapse of the Soviet Union. Unlike in Poland (just to compare), where in the 1980s a formidable political opposition took shape and challenged the communist government, the Soviet Union faced a different political reality. Although by the early 1980s the country was mostly disappointed with the policies of the Communist Party, the opposition was weak and disorganized. Gorbachev began the reforms from the top while realizing that he needed grassroots support. He believed that he would be able to maintain control of many emerging political groups and movements, steer them in the right direction, and preserve his own power and the political system. He was mistaken.

The last years of the Soviet Union

In the second half of the 1980s an informal coalition developed within the reformist faction of the Communist Party, especially within its upper echelons. They never enjoyed a clear majority in the party. Yet the top rank party bureaucrats knew the real state of affairs in the Soviet economy and social life. They believed that in the competition with the West their country was already losing. They also believed that to reach Western standards of living the Soviet Union should follow the path of reforms that could end the confrontations of the Cold War. These views gained popularity among a growing number of people in the Soviet Union by the end of the 1980s. During that period tens of thousands of people turned to private entrepreneurship and profit-making (which had been illegal before perestroika). The educated class of the Soviet Union was abandoning the Marxist-Leninist doctrine. They longed for political, economic, and individual freedoms – which are the most essential Western values. The disintegration of the Soviet Union in 1991 was seen (and welcomed) as the beginning of Russia's integration into a global world. To many it was a kind of political reconciliation with the West. The nationalist camp was weak and disjointed. The orthodox communists were in disarray. Both the Russian public – particularly the intelligentsia – and the Western public praised the victory for liberal democracy in the Soviet Union (Shlapentokh, 2014).

The Yeltsin years

In the 1990s several groups of Russia's new emerging elites influenced President Yeltsin and Russia's foreign policy. At least four such groups appeared.

The first one was vast, diverse, and fragmented. It was comprised mostly of political leaders and officials loyal to Yeltsin, most of whom came from Russia's regions. Some of them had been his supporters in the past. Others began to emerge immediately after the breakup of the Soviet Union. They were mostly liberal in their views of the economy yet had very little experience in foreign policy (except for very few of them, mostly from Moscow).

The second influential group was comprised of a wide range of intellectuals, such as liberal economists, sociologists, journalists, and social scientists. Most of them had hardly any experience in governance. They joined various offices in the Russian government and influenced its policies for several years. With a few exceptions, they believed in the free market, and supported the country's new nonideological role in international affairs. To them Russia was supposed to be an equal player within the global community, but the country was willing to learn from the West (Gaidar, 2007).

Another group can be identified as new business leaders – a small but increasingly influential cluster that had gained significant wealth during the early period of Yeltsin's reforms. This group of political elites extended their power in the mid-1990s. After the rapid denationalization of property in the early 1990s, big portions of the national wealth were already in private possession, including factories, banks, and media networks. In the early 1990s considerable chunks of the country's natural resources, such as coalmines and oil fields, were also privatized. Using legal and illegal means, in a very short period, the most successful individuals (commonly called the *oligarchs* in Russia) became owners of these vast resources. In a few years a few individuals acquired enormous wealth. They all supported the political system that had allowed them to become rich. Now they needed political power for themselves (Gatman-Golutvina, 2000).

The fourth group included military, law enforcement, and security officials (known as *siloviki* in Russia, or the "muscle people"). They were gaining influence under Yeltsin's rule, especially after the 1993 violent confrontation between the forces supporting the parliament and the president's backers. In the late 1990s Yeltsin – who was physically ailing and becoming inefficient as a statesman – increasingly relied on his loyal *siloviki*. They provided a solid support for his personal power as well as the political forces backing him (Roxburgh, 2012; Gudkov, 2012). In his memoirs Yeltsin stated that he wanted to have a military man as his successor in the Kremlin; after considering several candidates he chose an almost unknown colonel, Vladimir Putin, who represented an elite group that, unlike the previous ones, maintained generally conservative and nationalist views of Russia and its foreign policy. Many military and security officials retained their old, Soviet-era views of Russia and its role in global affairs (Yeltsin, 2000).

Public opinion, which had initially supported Yeltsin's reforms in the early 1990s, was getting more polarized in the late 1990s. Economic hardship caused disappointment across the country: The liberal reforms that had been introduced in the early 1990s as the only choice for Russia did not bring improvements to most families. Inflation was rampant. Salaries of state employees were routinely delayed for months. Economic inequality skyrocketed. The financial crisis of 1998 made the economic situation even worse. Populist and nationalist politicians and harsh critics of Yeltsin's policies gained popularity. Many Russian intellectuals, looking for better opportunities in the West, were leaving Russia. Their departure considerably

its control of foreign policy. This certainly increases the role of an individual's personality in politics and the country's foreign policy. Constructivism as an approach to the study of foreign policy, and especially political psychology, directs our attention to how and why certain decisions are made in foreign policy from the position of the individual.

Before Putin: The Gorbachev factor

Before we turn to Putin, let's consider the case of Gorbachev, whose individual role in transforming his country's foreign policy was historic. Back in 1988 Mikhail Gorbachev, the last leader of the Soviet Union, fundamentally changed international relations by declaring that the United States, Canada, other NATO countries, and a reformed Soviet Union could share similar values, including worldwide peace. Gorbachev called for nuclear disarmament and the renunciation of the use of force in international relations (Brown, 1997; Rey, 2004). Although some dismissed Gorbachev's vision as unworkable, his ideas were a catalyst for the peaceful overthrow of communism in Eastern and Central Europe. Gorbachev's visionary ideas were rooted in his individual character. First, he became convinced that the West was no longer an enemy. Second, he turned to the West not only because of growing Soviet economic difficulties but also because he believed in Western economic and social models. Culturally, Gorbachev was a **Westernizer**, a person who believes that Russia's development depends upon the adoption of Western European technology, culture, and liberal governance, in sharp contrast with previous and contemporary leaders in Moscow (Rey, 2004; Zubok, 2007).

Gorbachev's values and perceptions played a huge role in Soviet foreign policy's changes. Other political leaders do not pursue radical policy transformations and remain mostly cautious, because they are dealing with domestic and international events based on practical calculations rather than value considerations. To most of them avoiding crises, consolidating their power, or winning the next election are far more important goals than becoming embroiled in uncertainty of ideological battles. Yet other leaders combine the mobilizing power of values with practical considerations. President Vladimir Putin is perhaps one of them.

Understanding Putin's worldview

Putin's worldview is certainly not one-dimensional, as it has frequently been portrayed in the media outside Russia. His worldview has evolved and is evolving with time. In practical terms, it also appears that one of the Putin's main concerns has been the preservation of his own power. This requires the protection of the political system that he has been building since his ascendance to the highest office in 1999. Unlike the communists in China, who have changed the constitution to extend the term limits for presidents, Russia is unlikely to change the constitutional rules, according to the Kremlin. Putin, who was himself chosen as an heir to Yeltsin through inner dealings in the Kremlin, is likely to stay in power as long as legally possible according to the Russian Constitution (Shlapentokh, 2014). As some experts have informally admitted, the violent revolts and revolutions in Georgia, Ukraine, Egypt, and Libya have had a profound impact on the president and spurred him to do everything possible to prevent similar violent events in Russia. This belief is associated with a very cautious and restrictive view of Russia's political opposition and, therefore, of any foreign organizations that have ties – real or alleged – with the opposition. The belief that foreign powers, especially the United States, have been behind popular revolutions was expressed back in 2007, when Putin made a speech in Munich about Russia's vision of the world (Putin, 2007). From that moment on, this view has increasingly impacted his foreign and domestic policies, and anti-Western attitudes have become an important block in the Kremlin's official ideology.

Another idea that could be helpful in understanding Putin's worldview is his belief that he had to resist the increasingly anti-Russian position and policies of the West. The United States and its allies have chosen to undermine Russia, because the Russian president has saved Russia from an economic collapse and political disintegration at the end of the 1990s. Putin intentionally linked his personal political survival to the survival of Russia as an independent country. The prominent expression circulating in the Russian media since 2012 has been about Russia being "no longer on its knees." To endorse this saying is also to believe that Russia had been on its knees at some point earlier and that the president has ended the humiliating decline of the country. Anti-Western ideas tend to dominate Putin's worldview because of the way he sees the West. According to this vision, throughout Russia's thousand-year history the West has always intended – as Putin said in November 2014 – to undermine and even destroy the Russian state, exploit the country's natural resources, and isolate Russia from the rest of the world. He specifically claimed that the United States has always intended to weaken and subordinate Russia (Putin, 2014). For many years Washington has been frequently accused of an arrogant view and ingratitude toward Russia (Shlapentokh, 2014).

Putin's ideas reach the hearts and minds of people who live within a political culture called **paternalism**, a social system where the leader plays the role of a "benevolent parent," making decisions on behalf of apparently grateful family members, in this case citizens. In a paternalist culture people accept the decisions of a central authority. This power is necessary for the people's good. Most people trust their top leaders, and the leaders in turn offer their guiding role. Russian leaders also justify their paternalistic role by the necessity to brush off the country's enemies and to keep their country a great world power (Kuchins, 2007; Treisman, 1999–2000).

In the context of paternalism, Putin as a politician can also be viewed as a **charismatic authority**. This type of authority is rooted in the masses' acceptance of, respect for, and admiration of a leader because of the leader's perceived individual features, typically associated with heroism, decisiveness, and benevolence. Numerous opinion polls conducted in Russia in recent years show Putin's very high approval ratings (Levada, 2018c). This image is maintained by Putin's advisers and willingly and uncritically promoted by the media. Photos of the president taken at different periods show him in good athletic shape, swimming, horseback riding,

Putin's publicity stunts have included:

- piloting a fighter jet;
- swimming in a Siberian river;
- scuba diving in the strait connecting the Black and Azov Seas;
- shooting a polar bear to tranquilize him;
- shooting a whale with a crossbow;
- participating in a car race;
- riding a motor bike;
- driving a heavy truck;
- riding bare-chested on a horse through the Siberian wilderness;
- copiloting forest fire planes; and
- fake piloting a hang-glider to lead cranes on a migratory route.

Figure 4.2 A short list of Putin's publicity stunts in recent years

scuba diving, performing dangerous stunts, riding trucks and bikes, or acting like an "average man" while sharing a drink with friends (see Figure 4.2).

Ruling elites and their foreign policy interests

The general attitudes of Russia's elites for the last fifteen to twenty years have appeared to be in sync with the Kremlin's foreign and domestic policies. Although the elite groups are not politically homogeneous and some differences exist within them on various aspects of foreign policy, there has been no significant challenge since 2000 to key Kremlin foreign policy strategies and decisions.

Russia's government bureaucracy in many ways resembles similar bureaucratic structures in other countries, including the United States, Canada, or the United Kingdom. A few important differences exist, however. In the current political conditions, Russia's federal bureaucracy has accumulated substantial and arbitrary powers, much greater than the powers of bureaucracies in other countries. On the other hand, Russian government officials of all levels are prohibited from making financial deals overseas or owning stock in foreign publicly traded companies. Serious limitations also exist on the ownership of foreign property.

At least two general types of attitudes of the ruling elites have emerged (Shlapentokh, Shiraev, and Carroll, 2008). One concerns Russia's treatment by Western countries. The dissatisfaction with the dismissive attitude toward Russia after the Cold War is obvious. The other is about seeking a much bigger role for Russia in global affairs and the projection of Russia's power globally. Most international events are presented and receive interpretations in Russia through the prism of these two general attitudes, illustrations of which will appear in the next chapters. At home the elites tend to see the strong authoritarian rule in the Kremlin as a safeguard of their interests domestically and globally.

Business interests and foreign policy

The ruling elites in Russia – the bureaucracy and the business elites in particular – pursue three goals. First, expectedly, they seek favorable global conditions that will protect their wealth and strengthen their power at home and internationally. Second, and this has already been mentioned, they seek an increasingly growing and assertive role for Russia in international affairs. Third, if such an integration of Russia as an important global player is impossible at the moment due to the West's resistance, Russia should create its own alliances and international organizations, in which Moscow could play a leading role.

The most important Russian industries early in the twenty-first century have been (1) the energy sector and (2) the military industries. The government controls nearly 70 percent of the energy sector. The military industries are almost entirely under the state's control. Among the biggest purchasers of Russian weapons are China, Iran, and India. Russia uses its arms sales not only to generate revenue but also to gain political weight in the countries with which they have business relations. Russia occupies top global positions as an oil, natural gas, and arms exporter. Exports of oil and gas have been, as you know, the main source of Russia's federal revenue. Due to these exports Russia considerably improved its people's living standards during the first decade of the twenty-first century. This was one of the main reasons for President Putin's popularity in opinion polls. Energy products have been used as a form of political leverage on some neighboring countries, including Ukraine. New energy agreements with foreign countries, the construction of new pipelines, and increases in exports of oil and gas have been important strategic goals. Some Russian experts even called Russia "an energy superpower" (Grigoriev, 2006). However, the plummeting oil prices in 2014–2015 drastically weakened Russia's economy and worsened its financial situation. Russian economy was picking up slightly in the following years, yet most experts labeled this period as economic stagnation. The opinion polls showed a slight decline in Putin's popularity after 2015 and also in 2018 after he endorsed an unpopular pension reform. Opinions are likely to have changed, like the oil prices, when you read these pages. Putin's popularity ratings also depend on many domestic factors. You can always check the latest dynamics in financial markets involving Russia as well as global carbohydrates prices.

Political parties and foreign policy

The Constitution of 1993 declares that the Russian Federation recognizes ideological and political diversity and a multiparty system (Article 13). As you should remember, the Soviet Union had a single-party system. After 2003 only four parties have been represented in the State Duma: United Russia, A Just Russia, the Communist Party of the Russian Federation (CPRF), and the Liberal Democratic Party of Russia (LDPR). All of them have shown a noteworthy degree of agreement on most foreign policy issues. For example, the overwhelming majority of the Duma approved the resolution on Ukraine (2014) and the "cooptation" of Crimea into Russia, the act that the United States and other Western countries called annexation.

The most powerful party in present-day Russia is United Russia. President Putin has always been *de facto* leader of the party (although officially the formal leadership role has been given to Prime Minister Medvedev). Practically all members of the Federation Council belong to this party. The majority of the State Duma members, as well as members of the regional legislative assemblies and even municipalities, nearly all the governors, most federal ministers, most of the managers of state budgeted institutions, eminent figures in science, education, culture and art, as well as top journalists, all belong to United Russia. The law forbids members of the armed forces, special services, and police to join political parties, but many of them maintain close contacts with this party. The party leaders often claim that their ideological platform is conservatism, centrism, and pragmatism. The party also emphasizes its patriotism – especially in the context of Russia's history and in relation to the military. The party supports the Kremlin's foreign policy regardless of its direction, strategies, and even small nuances.

The second most influential party is the Communist Party of the Russian Federation, which was established in 1992. The party is in effect the successor of the Communist Party of the Soviet Union. In the area of foreign policy, the CPRF maintains an anti-Western, antiglobalist, and protectionist view of international relations and Russian foreign policy. Of all the Russian parties, the communists maintain the most robust international ties with other countries' parties – mostly with communist and left-wing groups (including the communist parties in China, North Korea, Vietnam, Cuba, and Laos), as well as the communist parties in the Commonwealth of Independent States (the formal structure that appeared in place of the defunct Soviet Union; see Chapter 2). The CPRF used its ties with the Communist Party of Ukraine to support the separatists in Eastern Ukraine. In the past the communists' views on foreign policy could be different from Kremlin's position. After the events in Ukraine these views appear to have become inseparable.

A Just Russia is a left-leaning party that supports vast welfare policies and social programs. In foreign policy matters the party's main discord with the president was Russia's membership of the WTO, which this party opposes, arguing that the memberships hurts the Russian middle class and the poor. On other foreign policy issues this party, like the Communist Party, follows the course of the president.

The popularity of the Liberal Democratic Party of Russia is largely associated with the charismatic personality of its leader, Vladimir Zhirinovsky. The party's positions are a mixture of nationalism, populism, and anti-Western sentiments. The LDPR believes that, to achieve its foreign-policy goals, Russia should actively align itself with all anti-American governments, regardless of their political ideology. Zhirinovsky has a tendency to make provocative statements that become headlines. To illustrate, at a meeting in 2014 Zhirinovsky mused, in Putin's presence and without his direct objection, that Russia should have conquered France in 1812 and should have controlled all of Europe at the end of World War II in 1945. Zhirinovsky's provocative rhetoric is often shocking to the point of being irrelevant.

There are several small parties that are not represented in the Duma and that maintain a critical view of Russian policies abroad. Among such parties, to name just two, are Yabloko and the Civic Platform. These parties maintain a mostly liberal view of foreign policy and they do not proclaim a clear anti-Western or anti-American position, as other major parties do.

As you should remember from Chapter 1, the role of leading political parties in Russia's policy-making is limited. Foreign policy is "baked" in the Kremlin and the Ministry of Foreign Affairs implements it. Political parties have two general venues of influence: through the legislature and, indirectly, through the media. The executive branch, by concentrating in its hands all the leverage of influence, has no wish to have another competitive center of political power emerge in Russia and therefore opposes any party-building activities, though Russian political parties receive substantial financial support from the federal budget. In Germany and many other democratic countries political parties also receive funding from the state, yet the government's share in party revenues is small, compared to Russia's. Despite its numerous claims to the contrary, top executive leaders in Moscow view strong parties as potential rivals.

Overall, major political parties have a limited impact on foreign policy in Russia. Yet some of them often serve as mouthpieces of the government, help in shaping public opinion, and assist in implementing the government's foreign policy.

Political experts

Most developed countries, especially those with a long democratic tradition, have a network of established and authoritative institutions – including universities and research centers, both state-funded and independent – that teach and study international relations and make critical assessments of foreign policy.

Russia is only now developing such institutions. Back in the 1940s the only college that educated and trained diplomats in the Soviet Union was the Moscow State Institute of International Relations (MGIMO), which was a part of the Foreign Ministry. The Communist Party had its own group of experts who studied international affairs and delivered expert opinions to serve the party's top decision-makers in Moscow. In addition, the government began building a network of research institutions within the framework of the Academy of Sciences (such as the Institute of the World Economy and International Relations, the Institute of the United States and Canada, the Institute of Latin America, etc.) to conduct fundamental and applied studies, as well as issue policy reports on global affairs. These institutions resembled, to some degree, modern Western "think tanks." The major difference was that in the Soviet Union they were serving an ideological function: they were part of the government and justified its foreign policy under all circumstances.

After 1991 several new and independent intellectual "centers" for foreign policy studies and education emerged. During a short period educational programs in international relations and area studies were launched in nearly ninety universities across

Russia. One of the most successful programs was launched at the School of International Relations of St. Petersburg State University. The success of this new school established in 1994 as well as the Moscow State Institute of International Relations was acknowledged by their admission into the Association of Professional Schools of International Affairs (APSIA) first as an associate and then as a full member.

Many research institutes, analytical centers, and "think tanks" exist in Russia today. Most of them are partisan; a few others remain relatively independent in choosing their research and promoting their opinions. The degree of independence of such institutions is difficult to judge. Take, for example, the Institute of Contemporary Development, which (among other activities) examines foreign policy and relations between Russia and the West. Formally it is an independent think tank. Yet it has been linked to several individuals close to Prime Minister Medvedev.

The Russian Institute of Strategic Studies works directly with the Presidential Administration and other government agencies. One of its directors served as prime minister. *The New York Times* called the Institute a "semiretirement refuge for former intelligence officers" and a government mouthpiece (Nechepurenko, 2017).

Among the analytical centers set up by foreign organizations the most active is the Carnegie Moscow Center, which is a research center focusing on Russia's domestic and foreign policy, international relations, international security, and the international economy. The center is an affiliate of the Carnegie Endowment for International Peace in Washington DC, which is a nonprofit organization.

Unfortunately, Russian top businesses and political parties, as a rule, for many years did not express significant interest in research and analytical materials related to international relations, except for applied data on world markets. Only a few years ago the Russian leadership decided to create an institutional base to promote interaction between foreign policy experts and the government. The Russian Council for International Relations and the National Committee for BRICS (Brazil, Russia, India, China, and South Africa) studies have been founded. Their founders included the Ministry of Foreign Affairs and the Ministry of Education and Science. Time will show whether these institutions are effective.

In sum, the role of the expert community in the formulation of Russia's foreign policy remains very limited. The experts have little influence on decision-makers in foreign policy, in contrast to the considerable influence often seen in the United States and in the West.

Conclusion

Russia's foreign policy these days is rooted in at least three interconnected conceptual foundations. First, after Moscow dropped ideology (Marxism) as a source of foreign policy and declared a transition to a new, more pragmatic approach in global affairs, the country now seeks to secure its global positions as an energy power and a serious trade partner that is embracing free market principles. In a way, Russia has turned to the Realist view of international relations. Under these conditions Russia needs to strengthen its international status and sell its energy resources, such as oil and gas, in large quantities, for a high price, and to as many countries as possible.

Second, Russian military and security leaders in the recent past had a hard time coping with the country's ex-superpower status. Most of them wanted and continue to pursue the goal of rebuilding Russia as a global power (they also realize that Russia is unlikely to be a superpower again). Historically Russia has always pursued expansionist foreign policy strategies. Therefore, it is likely that Russia will maintain an energetic, robust foreign policy today and in the future. Because of the nature of Russian elites' values, Russia will try to dominate in some policy areas and geographical regions and seek compromises in others.

Third, the critical view of Western policies is not only a direct response to particular international developments. It is also about a growing self-assurance, which is currently strengthened by domestic nationalism and authoritarianism. It is generally believed in Russia that the country is surviving and developing in a hostile environment dominated by the United States and its most loyal Western allies. According to Realism (see Chapter 1), this leaves Russia little chance but to respond to challenges by strengthening itself militarily and by launching a comprehensive "strategic deterrence," as officials prefer to say recently. Thus Russia's mission in this international context is to resist foreign pressures and form alliances with other countries, especially in Asia, to counterbalance the policies of the West (Trenin, 2017). The opposition pushes for a more ideological (the Communists) or nationalistic (the Liberal Democrats and others) strategy in foreign policy. Some, and their number has been growing recently, support Russian isolationism. Some insist on Russia's exclusive "eastern" (Eurasian) orientation. Others emphasize the importance of cooperation with the West once their relations normalize. See if this is still the case today.

Summary

- In Russia the left is typically associated with communist and socialist parties and groups, who promote a larger share of the government in the economy, the nationalization of key industries, and price control of the most important products and services, including food and energy. For the most part, the right supports the elements of the Russian welfare state but does not reject the free-market economy.
- If you are a liberal in Russia today, then you are likely to support predominantly Western models of government, a free-market economy, a free press, a transparent government, and independent courts. Russian liberals vehemently oppose authoritarianism. A conservative person in Russia generally supports the government's protection of social welfare, the idea of Russia's greatness as a world power, a mixed economy with a large portion of it being under government control, and tolerance of authoritarianism. Russian conservatives tend to believe that the West has been undermining Russia for centuries and is continuing to do so today.

- A predominant view encouraged by the Kremlin today is that a strong state power is necessary to make the country's economy and society function.
- Russophiles believe that Russian people are exceptional and that Russian history is rooted in a unique culture, traditions, and morals. Russophiles typically reject anything foreign, especially Western.
- Public support for authoritarian practices and nationalism frequently fuel populism, meaning political strategies that pursue the goal of mass support of a person or party by appealing directly to most people's immediate needs.
- Supporters of Putin's policies maintain that a shift in Russia's foreign policy attitudes was inevitable and even desired: after the decade of economic and political instability a "strong hand" in the government has finally emerged.
- Russian foreign policy has always been personalized: it was rooted in the individual choices of its leaders. This is applicable to political leaders in every country, yet to a different degree.
- In practical terms it appears that Putin's main concern has been the preservation of his own power. This requires the protection of the political system that he has been building since his ascendance to the highest office in 1999. In the context of paternalism, Putin as a politician can also be viewed as a charismatic authority.
- Although the elite groups are not politically homogeneous and some differences exist within them on various aspects of foreign policy, there has been no significant challenge since 2000 to key Kremlin foreign policy strategies and decisions. The role of leading political parties in Russia's policy-making is limited.
- Most developed countries, especially those with a long democratic tradition, have a network of institutions – including universities and research centers, both state-funded and independent – that teach and study international relations and make foreign policy assessments. Russia is only now developing such institutions.

Glossary

Authoritarianism is a form of government with a highly centralized and often personalized power structure and a relatively weak civil society.

Charismatic authority A type of authority that is rooted in the masses' acceptance of, respect for, and admiration of a leader because of the leader's perceived individual features, typically associated with heroism, decisiveness, and benevolence.

Elite A small group of people who control a disproportionate amount of wealth, political power, or both.

Nationalism Support and glorification of one's nation, its past and present policies, and its culture. Nationalists in Russia believe that whatever political developments take place, they should be judged by how well they serve Russia's core interests.

Paternalism A social system where the leader plays the role of a "benevolent parent" making decisions on behalf of apparently grateful family members, in this case citizens. In a paternalist culture people accept the decisions of a central authority, which also believes its power is necessary for the people's good.

Political communication The general ways in which information related to politics, government, and foreign policy is distributed.

Political mobilization The ways of preserving (or changing) the existing political system and government policies.

Populism Political strategies that pursue the goal of mass support of a person or party by appealing directly to most people's immediate needs. Populism is based on promises and corresponding actions designed to give people what they want.

Russophiles People who generally believe that Russian history has a unique nature rooted in a unique culture, traditions, and morals.

Westernizer A person who generally believes that Russia's development depends upon the adoption of Western European technology, culture, and liberal government, in sharp contrast to the attitudes of previous and contemporary leaders in Moscow.

Review questions

1. Explain the "liberal" and "conservative" labels related to political views and foreign policy in Russia. Compare to the ways that these terms are used in the West.
2. What were the main stages in the formation of the Russian elites in the post-Soviet period? How did these elites influence Russian foreign policy?
3. What are the similarities and differences between the foreign policy interests of the bureaucracy and those of big business in Russia?
4. What are paternalism and charismatic authority? Do the United States or the United Kingdom (or choose any other country) have charismatic leaders these days?
5. What are the similarities and differences between major Russian political parties regarding their views of foreign policy?

Chapter 5
Principles and Strategies

We are all different ...
No one has to conform to a single development model that someone has once
and for all recognized as the only right one.

Vladimir Putin speaking at the United Nations (2015)

Learning objectives

- Describe several periods of Russian foreign policy's evolution.
- Identify the key principles that define Russia's foreign policy.
- Describe major goals of Russia's foreign policy and the strategies to achieve them.
- Critically analyze Russia's principles and strategies in its foreign policy.

In the previous chapter we looked at some basic sources of Russia's foreign policy. Now we will further detail them to better identify Russia's foreign policy principles. The term **principle** refers to a fundamental idea or belief that becomes a base for other ideas that essentially derive from that principle. The term **strategy** means a general plan of action, the particulars of which are clarified in the process of a strategy's implementation. During nearly the three decades after the disintegration of the Soviet Union an important evolution of principles and strategies of Russia's foreign policy was taking place. The most significant changes occurred in the 1990s–early 2000s. In later periods a relative stabilization and consolidation of foreign policy strategies occurred. To explain the key principles and strategies of Russia's foreign policy, we first need to ask at least three questions.

First: What is the state of international relations today from Moscow's viewpoint?
Second: What are Russia's place and role in today's world?
Third: How should Russia as an international player act?

As we have learned earlier in this book, the answers to these questions can be as diverse as they can be ambiguous, because the strategic and tactical plans of

101

Russian leaders evolve. Even within the elites, disagreements abound about a few essential details of foreign policy. The evolving international situation and domestic economic and political factors instantly influence both the principles and strategies of Russia's foreign policy. Its history provides supportive evidence for that.

Foreign policy principles: An evolution

Three Views of the 1990s

In the 1990s at least three major views of Russia's foreign policy principles and strategies appeared in the discussions of the country's foreign policy. Let's call them – using the direct translations from the Russian language – Westernism, Eurasianism, and neo-anti-imperialism. Although these labels appear self-explanatory, they need additional comments (Shlapentokh, Shiraev, and Carroll, 2008).

The **Westernists** assumed that after the collapse of communism, Russia would be able to carry out rapid democratic and market reforms and simultaneously join the community of developed democratic states, which were mostly Western. Former minister of foreign affairs, Kozyrev, called the Western democratic governments "congenial" toward Russia and referred to them as allies (Kozyrev, 1995). The main foreign policy objectives, according to the Westernists, were at least three: the creation of favorable international conditions for the implementation of domestic reforms in Russia; rapprochement with the United States, Western Europe, and Japan; and the integration of Russia into the European and Euro-Atlantic international organizations. Many politicians and foreign policy experts openly talked about possibilities for Russia to join NATO.

Those whom we refer to as **Eurasians** disagreed. They emphasized that Russia, as a Eurasian power and a unique civilization, should find its own exclusive way in the postcommunist world. Russia has its own vast resources, the intellectual power of its educated people, and a rich cultural legacy to continue and sustain its own, independent development. Russia's strategy should also oppose "Anglo-Saxon domination" and challenge the key global "culprits" such as the United States and the United Kingdom.

The **anti-imperialists**, too, called for international solidarity and resistance against the United States' imperialistic policies and Western domination. Yet they discussed this view from a different position. In a nutshell, it was a mixture of a Marxist and anticolonial rhetoric mostly borrowed from the debates of the Cold War era and then applied to today's.

Since the ascendance of Vladimir Putin to the presidency in 2000, these three approaches have essentially morphed and merged into one. The consolidating factor or process that has strengthened the role of the state in foreign policy was rooted in Putin's strategy known as the "power vertical," which we have discussed earlier. In the end, the Westernists, Eurasians, and anti-imperialists had to adjust to the realities of twenty-first-century Russian politics, which was increasingly directed from the Kremlin. A new, consolidated view of foreign policy has emerged, which we call the **pragmatic approach** (Khudoley, 2006).

The pragmatic approach

The term "pragmatic" in the context of foreign policy means acting out of practical rather than theoretical or ideological considerations. Many supporters of the Realist approach to international relations (see Chapter 1) tend to share this position. Russian leaders assumed that to become an equal and efficient partner in the international community, Russia must not act from a position of weakness. The flow of petrodollars (mostly the revenues from gas and oil exports), the stabilization of the economy, steady economic growth, and the improvement of the living standards of the population – these and other encouraging changes should have strengthened, as it was assumed, Russia's role in world affairs. The modernization of the armed forces should have indicated Russia's assertiveness and strength, while not posing a threat to other countries. Russia was likely to remain friendly with the West but not dependent on it. Russia, according to this approach, would also review its specific policies from the position of pragmatism. While remaining a partner of the United States, especially in the fields of antiterrorism and global security, Russia would most certainly bargain a new international role for itself in other areas. From the logic of these pragmatic positions, the existing international order would last for some time. Yet the balance of power could and would change in Russia's favor sometime soon.

A few cautious critics of the pragmatic approach emerged. They argued from two positions. Unsurprisingly, supporters of Eurasianism and anti-imperialism both agreed with the idea of the necessity for Russia to be strengthening its position in the world. Yet they wanted more assertive international behavior and more meaningful foreign policy moves. It was already, in their view, the time for Russia to regain a dominant status in the world. Russia should recover some of its lost territories, especially in Transnistria (in today's Moldova), Abkhazia, South Ossetia, and some other parts of the post-Soviet space. Russia should also seek broader cooperation with countries such as China, India, and Iran, and not necessarily with the West. Indeed, the West, with its decadent political and social models, should be treated with skepticism and even resisted. The political vocabulary of the old Soviet Union (such as calls for justice, collectivism, and equality) should be retained, at least in some form.

There were even more radical assessments and suggestions about Russia's foreign policy, its principles and strategies. Such ideas were coming mostly from anti-imperialists and nationalists. For example, they often saw international terrorism and jihadism as a legitimate political struggle against the United States' global domination. Others expressed sympathy toward rogue states. They admired, for example, North Korea, which was trying to become a nuclear state. The main argument of nationalists was that international conflicts involving Washington and international instability would likely weaken the United States and thus give Russia a chance to ascend politically.

Westernism was steadily losing its supporters after the 1990s. Fewer experts felt comfortable openly expressing pro-Western views. There were several reasons for the West's soft power decline in Russia. First, the perceived failures of Russia's foreign policy of the 1990s convinced many people in Russia that the West had essentially ignored their country during that time, when the help was urgently needed. Second, a chain of international developments challenged many of the Westernists' policy choices and opinions. The most difficult challenge was Washington's

"War on Terror" and the invasion of Iraq in 2003. Most commentators in Russia disagreed with the White House about the necessity to remove Saddam Hussein from power in Iraq. They vigorously criticized America's occupation of this country. Third, more people in Russia went along with the Kremlin's growing disdain for liberal ideology at home (Gudkov, 2014). Liberalism, as many believed, was a cornerstone of Western foreign policy. Finally, supporters of Westernism could not offer a coherent set of principles and strategies for Russia's foreign policy. The positions of Westernists were also weakened by serious divisions among them, including their debates about the Iraq conflict: some justified Washington's actions while others criticized them.

Putin's speech at an international security conference in Munich in February 2007 was among the first and most noteworthy affirmations of Russia's strengthening of the pragmatic approach to international relations (Putin, 2007). Not only did he criticize the United States and NATO for their global policies, he also insisted that Russia would no longer follow Western policies uncritically. From now on, he said, Russia would conduct its own, independent foreign policy. Russia would also understand the grievances of other countries dissatisfied with the global status quo and the domination of the West. The speech was an indication that Russia was shifting its foreign policy toward a significantly tougher, less cooperative (from the Western view) approach to the United States and Western Europe. Most Western experts considered the speech by the Russian president to be unexpectedly confrontational.

After 2012: A new tone

Views of foreign policy evolved again in 2012, when Putin was reelected president for a third term. One of his main international projects at that time, especially after 2014, was the formation of the Eurasian Union. This was his strategic idea, which he had already promoted during the presidential campaign. Russian political and business elites realized that this would be Moscow's top priority, which would give them a chance to create a new global center of power in an emerging multipolar (or polycentric, as Russians commonly say) world. It was expected then that the majority of post-Soviet states, as well as some other countries, would join this pan-Eurasian organization and that the Eurasian Union could succeed economically and politically. As a result of this success, Russia would regain its global leadership role. These perceived possibilities gave a moral boost to those commentators who envisioned Russia's special role in Eurasia. Russia's big business also saw a range of new possibilities in Eurasia, including new markets and, feasibly, a large and relatively cheap labor force.

One should not think that the emerging "Eurasian pivot" in Moscow's policies received total support in Russia. Many experts, among the left and the right, liberals and conservatives, have expressed their concerns and reservations (Trenin, 2017). Liberals feared the Eurasian orientation would weaken Russia's ties with the United States and the European Union. Conservatives also disliked the idea of cultural integration within the envisioned Eurasian confederation: they feared the potential erosion of Russian cultural values. The moderates and pragmatics questioned whether the new proposed union would become Russia's exclusive and thus prohibitively expensive project to carry out. It might, as they feared, drain Russia's financial and economic resources. The nationalists were also divided. Some of them, who believed in a new Russian Empire, generally supported the idea of the Eurasian Union. Others remained skeptical and continued to express their concern about growing legal and illegal immigration to Russia. Their argument was that Russia must have a far less ambitious foreign policy and that Russia's core interests should be mainly confined within its own borders. This populist and anti-immigrant view referring to their own countries, in fact, has gained strength among many politicians in the West in recent years.

So how did Russia react to its new "pragmatic" principles of foreign policy?

Specific principles

To understand the core principles of any country's foreign policy, it is often necessary to understand its view of today's world. This view (or outlook) is usually articulated by the country's top officials and often included in official documents related to foreign policy. In the case of Russia, this view is related to the world's polarity.

On polarity in international relations

According to International Relations theory, the distribution of power in the world can be of at least three types: unipolar, bipolar, or multipolar (Waltz, 2010). **Multipolarity** stands for a global situation in which the world has several centers of power. Look at the structure of international order in the nineteenth century. A few European states, including France, Britain, and Russia, dominated the world, with the exception of the Western Hemisphere, where the rising power of the United States was a decisive factor. Britain at the same time was the most powerful state financially. It had the strongest navy to protect the largest colonial empire. Yet its dominance was not a complete hegemony (the unconditional political, economic, or military predominance of one state over others). Britain had to balance its power with other strong states. Thus during the first forty years of the twentieth century the world remained largely multipolar (Shiraev and Zubok, 2016).

The defeat of Germany and Japan in World War II and the decline of Britain and France in the 1940s transformed the old multipolar order (with several global centers of power) into a new bipolar order (with only two centers), dominated by the United States and the Soviet Union. During the 1970s and 1980s the emergence of other regional centers of power (an integrated Western Europe, Japan, and the oil-producing countries of the Middle East) began to somewhat erode this bipolarity. The **Non-Aligned Movement**, which was established in 1961 and included many countries (such as India, Yugoslavia, and Egypt) not belonging to any major power bloc, gained influence by exploiting the struggle between the two superpowers.

In addition, China confronted the Soviet Union in the 1960s but did not accept the United States' hegemony (Willets, 1983).

When the Soviet Union imploded in 1991, the international order became unipolar because no single state or coalition of states could seriously challenge the military might of the United States. Thus the United States appeared to be the world's hegemonic power. In the past several years there have been signs of a possible return to a multipolar order. Among the causes of such a change is the economic ascendancy of a number of countries (Zakaria, 2008; Hiro, 2010) as well as Washington's policy choices during the Obama administration in the White House (2009–2017). India became a regional power and China became the second largest world economy. Together with Brazil and Russia, they account for nearly 30 percent of the world's land and are home to almost 45 percent of the world's population (Borah, 2011). Although these countries faced serious economic challenges after 2014, they continued pursuing their own interests and did not accept the global dominance of the United States, which has stated the importance of reclaiming its global leadership position after president Trump took office in 2017. Although the debates about today's world polarity continue (such as whether the world remains essentially unipolar), in Russia, for the most part, this debate has apparently been settled in favor of multipolarity, at least for some time (Westad, 2018).

Russia sees the world as multipolar

By the time of President Putin's return to the Kremlin in May 2012, the ruling elites were warming up to the view that a Eurasian pivot could be one of the first tangible results of Russia's new role: Russia was acting as a key player in a new multipolar world. They believed that President Putin has restored Russian authority by preserving the country's inner stability and sticking it to the West as often as possible (Westad, 2018). Several developments after 2012 provided supporting evidence for Russia's view that the world indeed was becoming multipolar and that the Russia should act more assertively in it (see Table 5.1).

Table 5.1 The arguments justifying Russia's view of the world as multipolar

The Western world is in decline.	The global financial crisis of 2008, the following economic crisis that lasted approximately until 2012, and the euro crisis of 2015 served as evidence that the West was losing its dominant position in the world economy and finances.
Non-Western countries are on the rise.	The perceived economic success of non-Western countries, especially the BRICS' development, indicated the rise of a new economic and financial "center."
The West undermines Russia's domestic stability.	It was assumed that the West actively undermined Russia's stability via various outlets of "soft power," thus pushing Russia out of the Western "orbit." Russia had no choice but to form its own power center.

In 2012 it appeared from Moscow's point of view that the Western world was in serious decline. The signs of the decline appeared obvious. The economic slowdown, the global financial crisis of 2008, and the following economic stagnation that lasted for several years served as evidence that the West was losing its dominant position in the world economy and finances. In official Russian documents references were made to the dismal state of the American and European economies (Concept of the Foreign Policy of the Russian Federation, 2016). Back in 2013 many Russian politicians and experts were making pessimistic forecasts about the anticipated decline and collapse of the US dollar and a gloomy future for the Euro. The financial difficulties in Greece, an EU member, only added to this belief. The 2016 referendum in the United Kingdom deciding in favor of Brexit was also considered as a sign of a major crisis in the West. Several Russian experts foresaw the inevitable end of NATO as a military and political organization that, as they claimed, had long lost its sense of a mission. Some commentators in the media even hazarded a guess as to the exact date of an inevitable collapse of this international organization.

Furthermore, the non-Western world appeared to be on the rise economically during the first decade of this century. Several economic indicators from China, India, Brazil, South Africa, and some other developing countries made a major impression on the Russian elites. It appeared that these countries had weathered the economic problems associated with the global financial crisis and recovered much better than the rest of the world, especially the economically advanced countries. The Chinese economy appeared the strongest and most promising. Russia has long seen the BRICS countries (in addition to Russia they include Brazil, India, South Africa, and China, as you should remember) as a future global coalition, as a new political, economic, and financial center of the world. As an international organization, the BRICS seemingly could challenge and replace G7 as a global force. When the BRICS rise and the West declines, global changes in the balance of power should follow as well. This did not happen, and the BRICS countries have been struggling financially and economically in the second decade of the century (Nwosu, 2015).

At the same time, at home, government elites' confidence in their own tenure was under serious threat for the first time since the 1990s. In 2011–2012 a series of mass protests swept Moscow and a few other cities. These protests were mostly peaceful, but on the Bolotnaya Square in Moscow in May 2012, during a public rally against the presidential inauguration of Putin, violence broke out. Western media and public opinion turned against Putin and his government because of the harsh methods they used to break this public protest. Criticisms coming from abroad strengthened an already existing opinion (shared by the elites and the state-controlled media in Russia) that Western countries were behind these protests. It was also assumed that Western intelligence, for years, had planned and then deliberately exploited Russian and international journalists, environmental activists, human rights observers, and NGOs to stage a revolt and undermine the government in Moscow.

The government's tough reaction to the protests (which was seen in the West as unjustifiably violent) also involved a series of significant legal and administrative actions that had been implemented in 2012 and later. These actions were designed to limit open displays of public disagreement, to curb the activities of Russian NGOs that used foreign funding, and to constrain the activities of international organizations, advocacy groups, and individuals promoting human rights, civil liberties, transparent elections, and environmental issues. These actions were designed, in part, to curb the influence of the West and to negatively portray its influence on Russian social and political life. In these conditions, Russian officials believed that they had had no choice but to focus on themselves. In addition, the country's new geopolitical interests were shifting to other countries, and Asia in particular (Trenin, 2017). With a new geopolitical focus Russia should have become a rising global leader.

In addition to these actions, Moscow launched a media campaign to discredit the West and to promote its own conservative values – which were seen as a necessary alternative to Western consumerism, liberalism, and feminism as well as the West's seemingly "excessive" commitment to human rights. The West was portrayed as a key source of immorality, vice, homosexuality, corruption, greed, individualism, and other signs of moral decay – all seen and critically judged, of course, from Moscow's standpoint. The Russian Orthodox Church was often used as a moral backer of true Russian cultural values of collectivism, patriotism, and traditionalism. The government sponsored local historians to promote patriotism, to create a "true" history of Russia's glorious past, and to portray Russia's moral values in a positive light (Nesterova, 2016).

Russia's imperatives in foreign policy

Based on these main arguments – about the multipolar world and the necessity to protect the established political system at home – the Kremlin formulated several key goals of its foreign policy (Concept of the Foreign Policy of the Russian Federation, 2013 and 2016).

First, Russia needs to regain its lost status as a world power and claim its position as a formidable nuclear, economic, and political force of the twenty-first century. To achieve this goal, Russia has its own reserves and potentials. Russia has vast oil and gas resources. Russia should further modernize its economy as well as its armed forces. Russia also produces good-quality competitive products to generate trade, including firearms, aircraft, and military equipment. One of the country's advantages is its educated population. Yet Russia's global ascendance needs favorable international conditions.

Second, current world conditions require a new system of international relations and a new type of decision-making. The existing structures rooted in the power of the United States and the West should no longer be accepted. They must be reformed. However, Russia does not need full-scale confrontations. To challenge and diminish the power of the United States and its allies, Russia should use various methods, including existing international organizations and international law. The United Nations, and its Security Council where Russia has veto power, is considered as one of Russia's venues to conduct foreign policy.

Next, Russia not only needs to resist the existing world order; Moscow needs to lead. It should form an alliance of countries – regardless of their political systems – that agree with Russia's foreign policy, accept its strategic goals and support their implementation. In particular, Russia seeks partnership in Asia, the Middle East, and the Pacific. China has already become a major economic and political partner of Moscow.

Fourth, Russia needs to strengthen its currency and make the ruble (Russia's currency) one of the world's key reserve currencies – comparable to the dollar or the Euro. In addition, Russia should and will support any financial arrangements that that discourage countries from using those traditional (that is, the dollar or the Euro) currencies.

Fifth, Russia must promote a new ideology, which is rooted in conservative social values and common sense. These values should gain respect and acceptance around the world. In Moscow's view, emphasizing and responding to the individual's key economic and social interests (such as employment, societal stability, etc.) is more appealing to most people than pushing for some abstract "human rights." At least three key ideas here will be important:

- Russia will support liberal political freedoms but only to a certain degree. Political freedoms, which the West promotes, should come with the citizen's responsibilities, and they can exist only within an orderly political system.
- Russia will support economic freedoms, yet the government should retain significant control over many key industries, as well as the production, consumption, and distribution of goods and services.
- Russia will also support personal freedoms; however, the basic rules of morality must be defended against the encroachment of those who promote same sex marriages, homosexuality, secularism, pedophilia, and other decadent principles or behavioral "deviances" (which are embraced and promoted, according to Moscow, by the West).

Finally, Russia as a country will need to create a new image. The country should be seen as generous and caring. Russia should pursue very high standards in business and service. Therefore, among many things, Russia has placed an emphasis on tourism and showed its eagerness to host big international events. The Russian leadership treated the Sochi Olympics (2014), the Kazan Summer Universiade (2013), and the World Soccer Cup (2018) as Moscow's top international priorities relevant to Russia's foreign policy. Expectedly, Russian state and private corporations, such as Gazprom and many others, have sponsored these and other big tournaments. Success in sport, according to Moscow's strategies, should add to Russia's prestige abroad.

Not everything went smoothly in the area of international sports, however. The doping scandal involving Russian athletes had a negative impact on Russia's international prestige. The track and field team was banned from the 2016 Olympic Games in Brazil, and the entire Russian national team was excluded from the Winter Olympics in South Korea in 2018 (some athletes were allowed to participate). Moscow maintained that these sanctions were biased and unfair. According to surveys, 71 percent of Russians did not believe the evidence presented by the World Anti-Doping Agency showing that Russian sport authorities manipulated urine samples of Russian athletes during the 2014 Sochi Olympics (Levada, 2016d).

Goals of foreign policy

Russia seeks a new role in international relations. Some changes in Russia's priorities may, of course, have occurred by the time that you are reading these pages. Others goals will remain the same for some time: they have already been determined by Russia's priorities and formulated in Russia's key documents related to foreign policy (Concept of the Foreign Policy of the Russian Federation, 2016). Russian foreign policy is conducted in coordination with defense policies (Military Doctrine, 2014). From the geopolitical standpoint, Russia's defense policies are based on constant attempts at the containment of emerging threats from different directions. West of Russia, defense strategists perceive a growing threat from NATO and the possibility that several new countries, including Ukraine, Georgia, and Moldova, might join that military and political organization, which continues to be dominated by the United States. South of Russia, one of the major concerns is the possibility of a violent attempt to spark ethnic conflicts in the Caucasus region. In the southeastern and eastern directions, one of the major concerns is the prevention of foreign countries' attempts to establish a military presence in the former republics of the Soviet Union. Russia intends to maintain its potentially superior military capabilities in this region, which has tremendous strategic importance for the Kremlin. To secure its strategic defense goals, Russia has been implementing new military strategies including so-called *strategic deterrence*. This is about using a combination of military and other methods, applying soft and hard power, meddling with national elections, and employing cyber, economic, and political tools in pursuit of various defense and foreign-policy goals (Lukassen, 2018).

Regaining a dignified position in the world

The task of restoring a country's international prestige or regaining respect is not uniquely Russian: many states pursue the same goal, including Cuba, Iran, North Korea, and a few others. The case of Russia is different because of Russia's size, historical experiences, perceptions, and its current influence on global affairs (Tsygankov, 2012). Russian elites continue using the United States as a benchmark to which they compare Russia's policies and assess their country's prestige. During the Cold War the Soviet Union was seen as a global competitor equal to America. In the 1990s this equal status was lost. This has seriously affected Russia's perception of its relations with Washington. Although a nuclear parity still exists between the two countries, Russian elites (and President Putin as well) feel that in the past Russia has not been treated with the esteem it deserved. The negative experiences of the 1990s (such as Russia's perceived humiliation in Bosnia and Kosovo and the expansion of NATO) gave President Putin moral ammunition to complain about the West's disrespect of Russia and argue for the necessity for Moscow to regain its prestige and status. Moscow cooperated with Washington on several projects, including their joint counterterrorism policies after the attacks on the United States in 2001. However, as you should remember, the invasion of Iraq in 2003 displeased Russia. The Kremlin believed that America's actions were ill advised and, most importantly, arrogant. Russia's critical warnings about the dangerous consequences of the wars in Afghanistan and Iraq were (as Moscow believes) ignored in Washington.

To regain its "deserved" and meaningful place in the global world Russia has undertaken several steps, including the promotion of new non-Western international institutions (such as the BRICS), building new alliances (such as those with Iran and Venezuela), actively advocating against the "side effects" of globalization (the problems detrimental to non-Western countries), and designing new venues for Russia's soft power.

In addition, one of the general strategies became putting pressure on Western countries and their policies. To paraphrase, for an observer, this strategy appears to be based on the principle that "what is appearing beneficial to the West, must be undermined." It is not about stirring conflict and war. Moscow believes this strategy is about rearranging the old and building a new international system.

National security goals

The main document determining the policy of the Russian state in the field of national security is the *Strategy of National Security of the Russian Federation*. It was endorsed by President Medvedev in 2009 and was left without modifications by President Putin after his return to the Kremlin in 2012. In December 2015 Russia's new National Security Strategy was published to cover the period until 2020 (National Security Strategy, 2015). The new document contains serious criticisms of the West. The United States and its allies are accused of seeking to maintain dominance in world affairs. Moscow also accuses the West of creating "levers of tension in the Eurasian region" to undermine Russian national interests. The new strategy also condemns the support given by the United States and the European Union to the 2014 revolt in Ukraine (Russia labels it as a coup), which has led to a protracted armed conflict there.

The document underlines that Russia has preserved its "sovereignty and territorial integrity," protected its national interests, become competitive, and begun the formation of a polycentric world. However, the threats to Russia's national security remain. Among them are (National Security Strategy, 2015):

• the desire of the United States and its allies to maintain a dominant position in the world and to pursue a policy of containing Russia by exerting political, economic, military, and information pressure;
• the growing global and regional contradictions between different centers of the modern world and an increasing competition between different models of social development;
• modernization and build-up of offensive weapons and a weakening system of treaties and agreements in the field of arms control;

- the expansion of NATO, the advancement of its infrastructure close to the Russian borders, and the deployment of the American ballistic missile defense system;
- counteractivities of the West against the process of integration in Eurasia and the emergence of new hotbeds of tension there;
- popular uprising, terrorism, national and religious hatred, extremism, particularly in the post-Soviet space;
- the risk of proliferation of nuclear, chemical, and other weapons of mass destruction;
- the lack of global information security systems.

The key threats are coming from the West, according to the document. The probability of a full-blown war between major powers with the use of nuclear weapons is believed to be low. Yet the threat of regional crises and conflicts is real (Foreign Policy Concept, 2016). Moscow will use military means only when nonmilitary ones fail. In particular, it is stated that nuclear weapons may be used only as a last resort. Overall, the document spends more than a third of its content discussing health, education, social policies, and the financial stability of Russia. The Kremlin clearly understands that problems related to these issues can have important security consequences.

Sovereignty

The Russian political elites have been paying particular attention to what they called Russia's **sovereignty**, a country's capacity and ability to make independent decisions. The financial crisis of 1998 (see Chapter 2) has raised in the minds of many people a critical question: should Russia follow the path of Argentina (and other countries that were in dire financial straits) and allow international organizations to essentially control the country's finances? Moscow rejected that option. It turned to strengthening its sovereignty and independence in making important decisions. Russia's views of sovereignty focus, among other things, on the following issues:

- making independent legal decisions regardless of the provisions of international law or the rulings of international organizations;
- not allowing supranational structures (such as the European Union and other institutions) to impose their decisions on Russia;
- reducing the country's dependency on foreign loans and other forms of foreign financing;
- reducing the role of foreign capital in Russia's economy and regulating foreign investments in key industries;
- reducing the role of international NGOs and other foreign organizations in Russia's social and political life;
- banning foreign investments in Russia's mass media such as television networks and social media; and
- limiting the range of financial activities of Russian federal officials in foreign countries.

The idea of protecting the country's sovereignty – in a variety of ways – has gained support among a substantial majority of the Russian population, including the young, according to opinion polls (Levada, 2015).

Territorial integrity

Safeguarding the country's borders is one of the most important goals of any government. Russia has a few unresolved border disputes, such as the one with Japan related to the Kuril Islands. This chain of more than fifty islands is under Russian jurisdiction. Japan claims four of these islands (called "Northern Territories" in Japan). Any territorial concessions have been very unlikely due to the current political environment in Russia. (Despite some hopes in Japan, this issue was not resolved during Putin's visit to Japan in December 2016; both sides agreed to continue consultations.) However, warnings that other countries could seize Russian lands, especially those rich in oil, natural gas, and other mineral resources, remain persistent in the Russian media. Analysts frequently use the case of Kosovo (and the civil war there that has lead to the creation of an independent state in the late 1990s) to warn of possible annexations of Russia's territory. For a similar reason, Russian public opinion is unsupportive of labor migration into Russia from China: there is the popular belief that Beijing is using the official emigration from this country to create settlements in Russia and then claim some parts of Russian territory in the future. Some Russians have also had concerns about the Kaliningrad Region – which is geographically separate from Russia (check the map) – especially after Poland and Lithuania joined the EU and NATO; however, these concerns have not been significant in the past few years.

The Arctic region

A new and sensitive issue in Russia's foreign policy is the Arctic region. In the Soviet Union Arctic exploration was a nation-unifying policy. This region was the Soviet Union's "frontier," almost like the North American frontier – the land that needs its explorers, heroes, and heroic myths. During the Cold War the Soviet government considered this region as a possible zone of future conflicts between the Soviet Union and the United States. During the 1990s a few complicated and contradictory processes were taking place in and around the Russian Arctic. On the one hand, there was a substantial demilitarization of the region. The attention shifted to civil and economic issues. The region was open to various international projects. On the other hand, economic difficulties and a lack of investments led to the region's decline and depopulation. In the twenty-first century Moscow has renewed its attention to the Arctic area. The new federal program, Foundations of the Russian Federation State Policy in the Arctic until 2020 and Beyond, was a clear indicator of such an interest.

What are the reasons for Russia's heightened attention to the Arctic? First, it has a lot to do with the significance of the Arctic region in the Russian economy. Though only 1.5 percent of Russians reside in the Arctic, the share of this region in the GDP is about 20 percent. The region has huge oil and gas reserves. About 17 percent of Russian oil and about 80 percent of the total volume of gas are extracted from the Arctic (Novak, 2017). Early in the 2000s, when oil prices were rapidly increasing, most experts predicted windfall profits going in Russia's direction during the next few decades. However, oil prices dropped in 2009 and then again, even more substantially, in 2015. The plans for an active economic exploration of the region to increase extraction of oil and gas have been postponed (the cost of exploration of new oil and gas fields would be prohibitive).

Second, the Arctic region was gaining in importance from the perspective of global transportation. The polar ice may thaw in certain regions (due to climate change, for example), thus allowing countries to navigate in the area, especially during summer. The Arctic Ocean route from Northern Europe to China, for instance, is approximately 40 percent shorter than the currently used ocean routes through the Suez and Panama Canals. To control this northern corridor, Russia constantly emphasizes that it maintains legal sovereignty over islands and the seabed in the area.

Third, during the period of worsening relations with the West, Russia turned to militarization of the Arctic, including revamping some of the military facilities that were shut down in the 1990s. In 2014 Russia established The Arctic Joint Strategic Command and proposed a new military district there by 2020 (TASS, 2016a).

Russia faces a legal challenge in the Arctic area because of different interpretations of international law allowing countries to claim an *exclusive economic zone*. This is an area over which a state has exclusive rights to exploration and use of marine resources. Russia respects the Maritime Boundary Agreement between Washington and Moscow (1990) and the 1920 Treaty of Spitsbergen; Russia signed an agreement with Norway (2010) on Maritime Boundary in the Barents Sea and the Arctic Ocean and joined (1987) the UN Convention on the Law of the Sea. Russia claims its rights over an expanded economic zone in the Sea of Okhotsk and other parts of the Arctic Ocean, the Mendeleev Ridge and Lomonosov Ridge, near which huge oil and gas reserves are believed to be located. One of the legal arguments that Russia uses is that these underwater ridges are in fact extensions of the Eurasian continent. To symbolically back up its claim, Russia launched several scientific expeditions, the most spectacular of which were in 2005 and 2007. During the latter a manned bathyscaphe plunged to the seabed at the geographic point of the North Pole where a titanium alloy flag of the Russian Federation was planted. This action triggered harsh criticism from the United States and Canada. The UN agreed with the Russian position on the Sea of Okhotsk, but the Commission did not rule on the claim on the Arctic Ocean and suggested additional research (UN, 2009).

Another important aspect of Russia's policy in the Arctic is Moscow's reliance on the current international organizations responsible for the area, such as the Arctic Council, which includes eight countries with sovereignty over the lands within the Arctic Circle; the Barents Regional Council; the Arctic Five (Russia, the United States, Canada, Norway, and Denmark through Greenland). Russia is not eager to engage other countries that do not have direct access to the Arctic. Russia rejects the idea that most Arctic areas are supposed to be parts of the **global commons** – zones not under any one country's sovereign control; today global commons include the open ocean, most of the seabed, the atmosphere, outer space, and Antarctica. The idea of the global commons has gained noteworthy international support (Nonini, 2007). International agreements have long protected the global commons from hostile takeovers and depletion. Russia sees its policies in the Arctic as legitimate actions of a sovereign state within the spirit and the letter of international law.

Respect for international law

In general terms, **international law** is a set of principles, rules, and agreements that regulate the behavior of states and other international actors. In theory, states and international organizations should agree on these rules and then enforce them properly. In reality, this is a daunting mission: international legal regulations are effective only as long as key international actors, such as sovereign countries, recognize and follow them rather than ignore or reject them. Countries often interpret international law differently, and we should always take this into consideration when studying comparative politics and Russian politics in particular.

The judgments of international organizations often serve as an important source of international law. Russia increasingly calls for a bigger role of the United Nations in international affairs. A permanent member of the Security Council, Russia has the right to veto any decision of the Council. Russia opposes the actions of states that do not get approval of the UN Security Council. These actions have included, for example, the NATO strikes against Yugoslavia in 1999, the campaign in Iraq in 2003, and the strikes against Syria in 2017. Russia has also criticized North Korea on several occasions, such as the ballistic missile launch and a nuclear test in 2016, all in violation of the UN Security Council's resolutions. Russia joined international sanctions against North Korea in 2017 and did not object in 2018 to US overtures to improve relations with North Korea.

However, international law has other sources, including international customary law (that derives from the past practices of sovereign states) and general principles of law, which are shared, cross-cultural principles of morality and common sense. Russia disagrees with certain actions of states based on such principles and customs, including the **responsibility to protect**. Often known as R2P, this policy states that if a sovereign country does not protect its own people from identifiable causes of death and acute suffering, then the international community must act and military force is likely to be used (Evans, 2009). Moscow believes that R2P has a weak legal foundation and is largely based on any powerful country's desire and opportunity to use force against other states.

Russia also has a constitutional obstacle that does not necessarily match Moscow's efforts to reconcile its foreign policy with international law. Article 15.4 of the Constitution of the Russian Federation states that the universally acknowledged norms of international law and the international agreements of the Russian Federation are a constituent part of its legal system; moreover, if there is a discrepancy between an international treaty and domestic legislation, the rules of the international treaty should prevail. Russian politicians and officials have called to abolish this provision (Bastrykin, 2015).

Safeguarding Russian business abroad

In the official documents (The Concept, 2016), one of the most important priorities of Russia is protecting the interests of Russian business abroad. Different suggestions have been discussed for some time about creating a federal agency to support Russian business abroad. Meanwhile, one important step has already been taken: Russia joined the World Trade Organization in 2012 (the negotiations about Russia's entering the WTO began almost twenty years earlier, in 1994). Russia has been given a sufficiently long transition period, seven years, to adjust its domestic laws to the WTO requirements. As most experts believe, Russia's WTO membership should bring better opportunities to Russian private business; better-quality products should be available in Russia; in addition, Russian entrepreneurs should enjoy more favorable conditions in foreign markets. However, the opposition within Russia claims that WTO membership and the new international rules that Russia must now follow will significantly limit Russia's options. The economic sanctions against Russia imposed after 2012 (will discuss them in Chapter 7) and later have undermined Moscow's trust in international economic cooperation. We will return to these sanctions later in the book.

The Russian government certainly cares about the country's international trade, especially in the most successful areas such as natural resources (including oil and natural gas) and arms (such as weapons, aircraft, military technologies, and equipment). For example, most foreign visits by President Putin and Prime Minister Medvedev during the past several years have been linked in some way to Russia's negotiations related to energy deals. Russia also tries to coordinate its energy policies with the Organization of the Petroleum Exporting Countries (OPEC). Some of these attempts have been successful while others have failed. Arms exports also get considerable support from the Russian leadership. Among major military clients so far have been India, China, Vietnam, Venezuela, and Iran. The list is most likely to expand in the future.

Russians abroad

Russian government frequently uses the term **compatriots**, which applies not only to Russian citizens but also to ethnic Russians (or even Russian-speaking individuals with ancestral ties to Russia) regardless of where they live. In such cases, ethnicity is determined loosely, either by kin (a person's origin) or in several other ways, including a person's active use of language or personal identification with his or her cultural heritage. In other words, "compatriots," in Moscow's view, can live within Russia's borders as well as abroad. In the United States (as well as in many other countries) there is a special agency, such as the Bureau of Consular Affairs at the State Department, which deals with United States' citizens traveling or living overseas. Russia has a similar institution at the Ministry of Foreign Affairs. In addition, there is a separate federal institution called the Federal Agency for the CIS Affairs, Compatriots Residing Abroad, and International Humanitarian Cooperation, established in 2008. This agency coordinates Moscow's policies related to Russian-speaking individuals in foreign countries.

There are at least four categories of compatriots. The first group is former Soviet citizens who, after the breakup of the USSR, identify as ethnic Russians. Many of them acquired citizenship of their new countries after 1991. The second group is identified as the "old emigrants"; most of them are the descendants of people who had fled Russia early in the twentieth century, especially after the 1917 Revolution and the Civil War. The third group is the "new emigrants," a wave of people who left the Soviet Union and Russia in the 1980s, 1990s, or later, who have permanently settled in foreign countries as legal residents or citizens. And finally, the fourth group consists of current Russian citizens who have moved overseas for various reasons, mostly recently, yet who keep their Russian citizenship.

Moscow pursues several policies toward these Russian compatriots. One offers permanent relocation of individuals back to Russia – if they wish to relocate. The government encourages ethnic Russians, especially from the former Soviet republics, to return to their homeland. There was a special federal program launched in 2006 to assist ethnic Russians and their families if they chose to relocate back to Russia. Moscow also has a policy of issuing short-term grants and fellowships to former Russian citizens, mostly scientists and other professionals, for their agreement to return and work in Russia at least for some time.

Russia accepted the role of the defender of the political rights of compatriots. One of the issues is the citizenship status of former Soviet citizens living abroad. Many of them have already obtained formal status in their new countries; some remain noncitizens for various reasons. In Latvia estimates suggest that about 60 percent of ethnic Russians have become citizens. In Estonia this number exceeds 90 percent (Amnesty International, 2018). Of course, people have different reasons for not applying for citizenship. One of them is the local language requirement: all who apply for citizenship must pass a special test. Moscow considers the language requirements to be discriminatory against ethnic Russians. It insists that they should be given citizenship without significant delays and legal obstacles. Another issue is the status of the Russian language in former Soviet Republics and the right of Russian-speaking individuals to study their own language at school. In Belarus, for example, this issue has been addressed: Russian now is the second official language.

The Russian government has discontinued an old Soviet tradition of condemnation of and discrimination against individuals who had emigrated from the country. During his visit to Paris in 2000 President Putin laid a wreath at the cemetery where many Russian immigrants were buried – including members of the White Guard who fought the Bolsheviks during the Civil War. Putin also played an important role in healing the long-standing rift within the institutions of the Russian Orthodox Church outside Russia that lasted about ninety years. In 2007 Russian Orthodox Church Outside Russia and the Church authorities in Moscow signed an act of unification.

Russia does not restrict its citizens' travel overseas (except in certain cases when the law restricts a person's travel). Russians may leave their country freely – if they obtain a visa from another country – for short trips and for longer engagements such as education and work. Approximately one hundred states have established a visa-free travel policy with Russia. These days millions of Russians work in North America, Europe, and other continents: some visit for a brief vacation, some stay there only for several months or years to study or work, and yet others leave Russia permanently.

Since 2002 Russia has regularly held the World Congresses of Compatriots, sponsored by the Kremlin. Such gatherings, among other functions, aim at promotion of a positive image of Russia. In addition, the Russian government and several NGOs (of course, some of them use government funds) continue promoting the Russian language, literature, and the arts among Russian-speaking populations abroad.

Promotion of the Russian language

Moscow considers the Russian language an important instrument of soft power. The language policy has at least two aspects or directions.

First, Moscow insists that the Russian language should receive official status or some kind of formal recognition in the post-Soviet states. Ideally, Russia would like to see Russian as a second state language there. Moscow refers to tradition, practical considerations, and the rights of ethnic Russians as the reasons to seek the special status of their language. In reality, this goal is difficult to achieve due to political and legal obstacles in most countries. Quite often Moscow's policies to promote the Russian language and obtain a special status for it are seen as expansionism. In addition, Russian is widely spoken in the former Soviet republics, and in some states official government documents are already issued both in the local language and (as a courtesy or a practical consideration) in Russian.

The second direction is the promotion of the Russian language and literature overseas. The president established a special agency, called the *Russkiy Mir Foundation* (Russian World Foundation), in 2007. The foundation is financed from the federal budget and for many years was controlled by the Foreign Ministry and the Ministry of Education and Science of the Russian Federation. The agency promotes exhibitions, festivals, tours, and Russian-studies programs. *Russkiy Mir* sees its mission as global and focuses also on cultural issues, including artistic creativity, collectivism, and spirituality. The Russian Orthodox Church is often a sponsor and an active participant in many of the Foundation's projects. Many foreigners who travel to former Soviet republics, however, admit that local elites there also prefer to learn English as a key international language.

Regional priorities

We shall turn to Russia's specific policies in various world regions in the following chapters. On these pages we shall only highlight the most important goals and priorities. The Foreign Policy Concept of the Russian Federation approved by President Vladimir Putin in 2016, gives serious attention to so-called regional directions of Russia's foreign policy. It specifies six of these directions.

- Development of bilateral and multilateral cooperation with the countries from the Commonwealth of Independent States.
- Development of relations with countries of the Euro-Atlantic region.
- Reinforcement of Russia's position in the Asia-Pacific region.
- Substantial contribution to the stabilization of the situation in the Middle East and North Africa.
- Comprehensive strengthening of relations with the countries of Latin America and the Caribbean.
- Enhancement of complex cooperation with African states on a bilateral and multilateral basis.

Of the six directions mentioned here, the first two are particularly emphasized. Within the first direction (development of cooperation with the post-Soviet states) Russia sees the importance of building mutually useful bilateral relations with all countries of the Commonwealth and favors economic, political, and military integration in the Commonwealth's space. Russia believes that not only do the CIS countries have a common historical past and cultural roots, they also should jointly confront a number of international challenges and threats. Russia focuses on the Eurasian Economic Union (EEU), which in Moscow's view, should become both a unification model open for other states to join and an effective connecting link between Europe and the Asia-Pacific region. In this context Russia is particularly devoted to the EEU's development. In the sphere of security and defense in the post-Soviet space Russia relies on the Collective Security Treaty Organization.

Russia insists that it is committed to peacefully settling all regional conflicts near its borders. Russia, for example, is promoting a peaceful settlement of the conflict in Nagorno Karabakh (involving Armenia and Azerbaijan) and finds cautious support from both sides of the conflict. However, some disagreements with other countries are serious. Russia, for example, supports the independence of Abkhazia and South Ossetia, which are not recognized as independent states by the vast majority of UN members.

The second key direction of Russia's foreign policy is in the Euro-Atlantic region (which includes European countries and North America, the United States in particular). Russia always emphasizes the important historical, geographical, and economic links between these countries and Russia. Moscow needs secure, productive, and stable relations with the West. Russia opposes NATO's further expansion. Despite the sanctions against Russia (see earlier chapters), Moscow was interested in preserving and even developing economic links with the European Union, which remained Russia's major trading partner. We will further discuss Russian relations with the West in the following chapters.

Official Russian documents have stressed for some time the increasing role of the Asia-Pacific direction in Russian foreign policy. Russian positions in this region remain relatively weak. Yet, as Moscow believes, Russia's influence in the Asia-Pacific should be increasing. Russia desires to see the region stable and peaceful and speaks against nuclear proliferation in this area. Russia believes in the special economic, security-related, and political role of the Shanghai Cooperation Organization, in which Russia is an active member. Moscow also develops economic and political ties with China, while calling mutual relations with Beijing "strategic."

In the Middle East and North Africa, Russia is increasingly active. Today Russia maintains relations with both Israel and all Arab countries. It supports a two-state solution for Israel and Palestine. Russia supports sovereign Israel and condemns violent acts against it. On the other hand, Russia has ties with Hamas and other openly anti-Israeli groups. In 2015 Russia started military operations in Syria by supporting the government in Damascus. In Central Asia, Russia's key partner remains the Islamic Republic of Iran.

During the Cold War Russia maintained close ties with Latin American and African communist parties and various liberation movements. Today Russia tends to maintain, with some exceptions, a nonideological strategy based on pragmatic goals. In Latin America, Russia particularly values its relations with two clusters of countries. One cluster represents mostly anti-American governments such as those of Cuba, Nicaragua, and Venezuela. The other cluster is a trio of Latin America's emerging economic giants: Brazil, Chile, and Argentina. Moscow wants to play the role of a reliable economic partner. Russia also shows increasing interest in the multilateral alliances of states in the region – particularly in the Community of Latin American and Caribbean States (CELAC) and Mercosur (an economic bloc of several Latin American countries).

The Soviet Union's policy in Africa was based for decades on ideological and geopolitical considerations: Moscow supported African countries of procommunist orientation and tried not to let the United States obtain strategic advantages on the continent. Today's Russian policies in Africa are largely geopolitical and economic. Russia played an active role in resolving the Sudan crisis and recognized the independence of South Sudan. Russia supports the UN Security Council's decisions related to Africa. To boost its reputation and to contribute to regional stability, in 2008 Russia sent, for example, a small peacekeeping contingent to Chad.

Again, we will discuss specific policies in several world regions in greater detail later in the book.

Conclusion

Russia is a sovereign and powerful country. It pursues its own strategic interests through foreign policy. It has its own vision of the world. It conducts an independent foreign policy. Russia sees the world as increasingly multipolar and seeks a more assertive role for itself in it. It also seeks a more respected role and wants to be seen as an equal partner in the world's affairs. Russia, according to all official documents and statements, is interested in global stability. Moscow pursues nuclear nonproliferation, supports antiterrorist policies, and hopes to expand trade and develop other forms of economic cooperation with almost every country. Yet, in the geopolitical context, Russia feels insecure about NATO and the West's economic expansion either through the European Union or by other political and economic means. For number of years Russia has criticized and confronted most policies conducted by Western countries, especially the United States and the United Kingdom.

Russia is also a major competitor for global energy resources. Having its own oil and gas resources and supplies, Russia often used them as bargaining chips in foreign policy. However, the falling oil prices in 2014 and the low prices in the following years have diminished Russia's economic strength and sent an alarm signal to Moscow about the necessity to diversify its economy to become more competitive on international markets.

Although Russia has been turning to a pragmatic foreign policy, ideology sometimes becomes a serious factor determining Russia's international strategies and moves. Thus Russia commonly sides with countries that are vocal critics of the United States and the West. Russia is extremely sensitive about its treatment by other states as a junior partner; it is determined to become an equal player in global affairs. One of the venues to achieve such equality is international law. Since the beginning of the century Russia has improved its relations with quite a few countries. Yet in recent years, especially since 2014, Russia's relations with most countries have worsened. They may have improved or become even more complicated by the time you are reading these pages.

Summary

- In the 1990s at least three major views of Russia's principles and strategies appeared in the discussions of the country's foreign policy: Westernism, Eurasianism, and neo-anti-imperialism. Later Russia adopted a predominantly pragmatic approach to its foreign policy.
- After 2012 Russia was increasingly turning to the "Eurasian project" and toward creating a new center of power in an emerging multipolar (or polycentric, as Russians commonly say) world.
- Based on these main arguments – about the multipolar world and the necessity to protect the established political system at home – the Kremlin formulated several key goals of its foreign policy.
- The main document determining the policy of the Russian state in the field of national security is the *Strategy of National Security of the Russian Federation*. It was endorsed by President Medvedev in 2009 and was left without modifications by President Putin after his return to the Kremlin in 2012. In December 2015 Russia's new *National Security Strategy* was published to cover the period until 2020.

- Russia says it pursues a "dignified" position in the world; it strengthens its national security and enhances its sovereignty.
- Russia declares that it pays attention to its territorial integrity; safeguards Russian businesses abroad; pursues an ambitious plan in the Artic region; stands for the rule of law in international relations; and promotes Russian culture and the Russian language abroad.
- Russia also pursues a host of other international goals and underlines several priorities in every world's region. These priorities are based on the strategic goals and specific regional developments.

Glossary

Anti-imperialists Individuals who call for a resistance against the United States' imperialistic policies and Western domination. It is a mixture of Marxist and anticolonial rhetoric mostly borrowed from the debates of the Cold War era and then applied to today's international relations.

Compatriots The term that applies not only to Russian citizens but also to ethnic Russians (or even Russian-speaking individuals with ancestral ties to Russia) regardless of where they live. In such cases ethnicity is determined loosely, either by kin (a person's origin) or in several other ways, including a person's active use of the Russian language or personal identification with his or her cultural heritage.

Eurasians emphasize that Russia, as a Eurasian power and a unique civilization, should find its own, exclusive way in the postcommunist world. Russia should also oppose "Anglo-Saxon domination" and challenge the key global "culprits" such as the United States and the United Kingdom.

Global commons Zones not under any one country's sovereign control; today global commons include the open ocean, most of the seabed, the atmosphere, outer space, and Antarctica.

International law A set of principles, rules, and agreements that regulate the behavior of states and other international actors.

Multipolarity stands for a global situation in which the world has several centers of power.

Non-Aligned Movement A group of states that are not formally aligned with or against any major power bloc.

Pragmatic approach With reference to foreign policy this means acting out of practical rather than theoretical or ideological considerations.

Principle A fundamental idea or belief that becomes a base for other ideas that essentially derive from that principle.

Responsibility to protect Often known as R2P, this policy states that if a sovereign country does not protect its own people from identifiable causes of death and acute suffering, then the international community must act and military force is likely to be used.

Sovereignty A country's capacity and ability to make independent decisions.

Strategy A general plan of action, the particulars of which are clarified in the process of a strategy's implementation.

Westernists Individuals who assumed that after the collapse of communism Russia would be able to carry out rapid democratic and market reforms and simultaneously join the community of developed democratic states, which were mostly Western.

Review questions

1. Explain the meaning of the concepts "principles" and "strategies" in the context of foreign policy. Compare Russian and any other country's foreign policy in the context of their principles and strategies (ask your professor for assistance). What are the similarities and differences?
2. What are the new features of Russia's foreign policy after Vladimir Putin's return to the Kremlin in 2012? Describe the essence of the pragmatic approach to Russia's foreign policy.
3. Explain unipolarity, bipolarity, and multipolarity in international relations. What is the Russian view of unipolarity?
4. Explain the goal of obtaining a "dignified position" in the world. What does it mean for Russia? Why do the Russian elites attach such great significance to the issue of safeguarding the country's sovereignty?
5. Why does Russia emphasize the importance of international law? Why is Russia critical of so-called R2P principles?

Chapter 6
Russian Policies toward Post-Soviet States

Only by standing together will all our countries be able to take their
places as leaders of global growth and drivers of progress, only
together will they succeed and prosper.

Vladimir Putin, 2011

Learning objectives

*   Describe the main historical, ideological, and political roots of Russian policies toward the post-Soviet space.
*   Describe several key stages in the relationships between Russia and the former Soviet republics.
*   Critically explain Russia's contemporary strategies and specific policies toward the post-Soviet space.
*   Apply the facts and their critical analysis to predicting the future of Russian foreign policy in the post-Soviet space.

After the breakup of the Soviet Union the Russian Federation shared borders with eight of its former republics, including Estonia, Latvia, Lithuania (via the Kaliningrad region), Belarus, Ukraine, Georgia, Azerbaijan, and Kazakhstan. Together with the six other former republics that did not share borders with Russia, such as Moldova, Armenia, Turkmenistan, Uzbekistan, Tajikistan, and Kyrgyzstan, these countries are often called in Russia, "the post-Soviet space" or "the post-Soviet states". Geographical proximity and a shared history have always been important factors influencing international relations. We will now briefly review Russia's strategic interest in the region and then look at the relationships between Russia and the "near abroad" (how the post-Soviet space was often called in the past) from a historical perspective, which is closely connected to contemporary developments. The relations of Russia with Baltic states (Estonia, Latvia and Lithuania) will be discussed in Chapter 8.

Key motivations of Russia's foreign policy in the post-Soviet space

The term **post-Soviet space** refers to Russia as well as several countries that used to be republics of the former Soviet Union. Russian politicians, in documents and official statements, usually underline the utmost importance of productive and successful relations between Moscow and these countries. It will be natural to expect that any country would pursue normal relations with its neighbors. Russia is not an exception. It certainly needs stable and reliable neighbors and partners. Yet at least two reasons explain the particular importance of the "near abroad" to Moscow. The first reason is that Russia has been a dominant power in the region for the past three or four centuries. Some of Russia's neighbors see it as an important protector of their security and their core economic interests. Others look at Russia with ambivalence: they appreciate its help yet often question the selfish motives behind Russia's foreign policy decisions. The second reason is closely connected with the worsening of Russia's relations with the West during the past decade or so. To "compensate" for poor relations with Western Europe and the United States, Moscow seeks reliable partners elsewhere.

What else motivates Russia and its foreign policies in the post-Soviet space? Consider at least four points:

- **Geopolitics.** Moscow sees the post-Soviet space as special, exclusively connected to Russia politically and economically. The term "near abroad" has emerged to indicate the perceived dual status of the countries that are assigned to this category: they all are independent and yet they are closely attached to Russia. Russia naturally seeks a leading political role among these states because of Russia's geographic proximity to them.
- **Historical and cultural ties.** Moscow believes that Russia and the former republics of the Soviet Union are closely interlinked due to a shared historical and cultural past within the Soviet Union and the Russian Empire. The Russian language remains common in government and business communications in most countries (although the English language is gaining popularity). Millions of people in the region have mixed ethnic identities including Russian.
- **Security factors.** Russia underlines the importance of friendly relations with its neighbors for national security reasons. A stable "near abroad" is a factor positively contributing to Russia's domestic security and social stability. From the standpoint of the realist approach to international relations, Russia is interested in maintaining a stable security regime within the region. Moscow also hopes and tries to be playing a key role in such a security regime.
- **Economic factors.** Russian businesses need new markets; thus the "near abroad" becomes a natural area for economic expansion, trade, and investments. Similarly, businesses in the former republics of the Soviet Union need Russia's energy supplies and professional expertise, as well as Russian investors and consumers. On the other hand, Russia needs cheap labor; immigrants from the former Soviet republics constantly seek jobs in Russia.

Is Russia seeking mostly partnership or domination in the post-Soviet space? From the strategic standpoint, how does Russia see the post-Soviet space? What are Russia's strategic interests in the region? To answer these and other questions, we need to look first at the historical context of Russia's relations with its close neighbors.

Historical background

The Imperial period

In the nineteenth century Russia expanded and absorbed large parts of Poland, Finland, the Caucasus, and Central Asia (see Chapter 2). In this process some ethnic and religious groups were subjected to open discrimination, such as the imposition of the Pale of Settlement on the Jews, in which permanent residency to them was allowed only in certain areas, beyond which Jewish permanent residency was generally prohibited. In some other cases local national aspirations were taken into consideration. Finland had a status of Great Duchy, where the Russian tsar was a constitutional monarch. The citizens of Finland had a range of political rights, including the right of women to vote, granted in 1905. In Central Asia Russia established a protectorate over the two states (Khanates) of Bukhara and Khiva. Russia seldom interfered in their internal affairs but controlled their foreign policy and trade. A special system of administration by a governor general operated in the Caucasus. Russia attempted to keep ethnic tensions at a low level and suppressed any forms of nationalism in the regions under St. Petersburg's control.

The Soviet period

The Russian revolution of 1917 gave a boost to many national sovereignty movements across the country. Finland, Estonia, Latvia, Lithuania, Poland, Ukraine, Georgia, Armenia, and Azerbaijan declared independence. The new Soviet government almost immediately recognized them. Some of these states retained their independence later, while others were incorporated back into a newly formed Soviet state. By 1922 the Bolsheviks exercised control over nearly the entire territory of the former Russian Empire, except the territories in the West. Poland, Lithuania, Latvia, Estonia, and Finland successfully defended their independence, and Bessarabia was annexed by Romania.

Lenin favored the creation of a union of several republics as equal members. Stalin, at that time Lenin's associate, proposed that all ethnic republics should be incorporated into Russia as autonomies. Lenin's approach prevailed, and in December 1922 the four Soviet Republics, Russia, Ukraine, Belarus, and the Trans-Caucasus Federation – including Georgia, Armenia, and Azerbaijan – signed a treaty on the formation of the Union of Soviet Socialist Republics (USSR).

Table 6.1 The evolution of the Soviet Union

Republics	Year/Comments
Russia, Ukraine, Belarus, and the Trans-Caucasus Federation	1922; the four initial members of the Soviet Union
Turkmenistan and Uzbekistan	1924; created as separate republics
Tajikistan	1929; created as separate republic
Kirghizia and Kazakhstan	1936; created as separate republics
Georgia, Armenia, and Azerbaijan	1936; after the dissolution of the Trans-Caucasus Federation
Estonia, Latvia, and Lithuania	1940; forcibly incorporated
Moldavia	1940; after Bessarabia was handed over from Romania

Communist leaders in Moscow believed that this new state would soon become a political base to coordinate a global communist revolution. Even the initially proposed name of the new federation was The Union of Soviet Socialist Republics of Europe and Asia. Yet in the final version the title "Europe and Asia" were omitted to show the global ambition of the new state. The Communist International openly pushed for a new global state called the World Soviet Union. It has never emerged, as you already know (See Table 6.1).

Over the following years the Soviet Union underwent important changes. Five new republics were created: Turkmenistan (1924), Uzbekistan (1924), Tajikistan (1929), Kirghizia (1936), and Kazakhstan (1936). In 1936 the Trans-Caucasus Federation was dissolved. Georgia, Armenia, and Azerbaijan joined the USSR as three republics. In 1940 Estonia, Latvia, and Lithuania were forcibly incorporated in the Soviet Union. After Bessarabia was handed over from Romania to the Soviet Union, the Moldova Republic was created in 1940. Borders between the republics within the USSR were often changed at will to mix several ethnic groups together or to increase the number of ethnic Russians in the republics. Thus, Azerbaijan and Georgia ended up with areas populated by Armenians; Kirghizia had many ethnic Uzbeks and Tajiks; and Kazakhstan, Ukraine, and Belarus had to accept a significant number of ethnic Russians. In Moscow's view, this was a way to control underground nationalist and separatist movements in the regions.

All three Constitutions of the Soviet Union (1924, 1936, and 1977) granted the republics substantial powers, even the right to secession from the USSR. Yet in practice this was hardly possible (in fact, the formal rules of succession were adopted only in 1991). The Communist Party of the Soviet Union controlled the communist parties in the republics as well as all the particulars of their economic and social life. All forms of disagreement or protest in the republics were suppressed. The Communist Party of the Soviet Union had a long-term, careful policy of appointing ethnic Russians for the most important party and government positions in the ethnic republics' bureaucracy.

After Gorbachev's ascendance to power in 1985, and after he granted political freedoms and relaxed political censorship, nationalism and separatism began rapidly gaining influence in the ethnic republics. Newly formed nationalist political groups grew in number and strength. Ethnic tensions emerged in Uzbekistan, Tajikistan, Azerbaijan, Georgia, Moldavia, Estonia, Latvia, Lithuania, and in many other places. The 1989–1990 elections to the USSR's Congress of People's Deputies and the Supreme Soviets of the republics resulted in the ascendance of many nationalist-minded politicians, which has strengthened the position of local nationalist and separatist forces.

The Soviet leadership attempted to reverse the disintegration of the Soviet Union by holding an all-state referendum. Yet the new leaders of Armenia, Georgia, Moldavia, Latvia, Estonia, and Lithuania declined to participate in it. Gorbachev was preparing a new union treaty assuming the anticipated exit of at least six former Soviet republics. The failed August 1991 coup further weakened the federal institutions of the Soviet Union. Most of the executive power that Moscow still possessed shifted to the republics. In September 1991 the USSR officially recognized the independence of Estonia, Latvia, and Lithuania. In December 1991 the leaders of Russia, Ukraine, and Belarus (without Gorbachev) signed the Accords on the Creation of the Commonwealth of Independent States (CIS) accompanied by a number of other documents. On December 21, 1991, the leaders of eleven republics met in Alma-Ata and signed the Protocol establishing the CIS. On December 25, 1991, Mikhail Gorbachev, having lost almost all of his powers as the Soviet leader, announced that he had "discontinued his activities" as president of the Soviet Union. The red flag flying over the Grand Kremlin Palace was lowered and the tri-color Russian banner was raised. The Soviet Union ceased to exist. Yet its legacy will continue to affect international relations in the post-Soviet space for many years to come.

The evolution and the current status of Russia's foreign policy toward the post-Soviet states can be understood as a process unfolding in several stages. Each of them should also be understood not as a discrete period but rather a transitional and evolving phase (see Figure 6.1).

Period	Brief Description
A Civilized Breakup: 1991–1994	Relations are insignificant. Countries are preoccupied with their own domestic issues. Estonia, Latvia, and Lithuania are on their way to join NATO and the European Union.
Approaching the Post-Soviet Space: 1994–2000	Early attempts to cooperate and manage mutual trade and commerce are made.
Attempting a Consolidation: 2000–2008	Early attempts to create a more interconnected system are underway; many countries need more integration yet are reluctant to accept Russia's domination. Some international institutions are formed. Political problems emerge.
Advancing the Consolidation Process: 2008–2012	New agreements are reached; institutions of cooperation are formed.
Advancing the Consolidation Process: 2012–today	New institutions of cooperation are formed; new forms of economic, military, and political cooperation are discussed.

Figure 6.1 Evolution of Russia's policies toward the post-Soviet states

A civilized breakup (1991–1994)

After the disintegration of the USSR, Russia declared itself its legal successor. As a result, it retained its seat as a permanent member of the UN Security Council and in other international organizations. This did not cause any objections from other countries. Almost simultaneously all the post-Soviet states became new members of the UN and other international organizations.

During the early period of Russia as a sovereign state Moscow was certainly trying to establish and build relations with the former Soviet republics. Yet this was not the most precious foreign policy task for several reasons. First, Russia faced many urgent problems at home. In the early 1990s the economic and political situation across the post-Soviet space was critical. Only the Baltic countries had specific plans related to their speedy integration into the European and Euro-Atlantic structures. Other countries, including Russia, were at a crossroads and had to determine which direction their foreign policy should take. Second, Moscow's main concern was the establishment of good relations with the West. Russia needed economic assistance and international acceptance. Yeltsin and his associates believed that Russia would be able to rapidly and successfully introduce market reforms and establish new democratic institutions: such transformations should have allowed Moscow to regain stability, built its reputation, and thus remain an indisputable leader in the post-Soviet space.

The "civilized breakup" that took place in 1991 and after suited both Russia and the other post-Soviet states. Immediately upon the dissolution of the USSR, Russia established diplomatic relations at ambassadorial level with the former Soviet republics. Presidential visits were held between Russia and a number of the newly formed independent states. Several bilateral economic treaties were signed. In the early 1990s Russia, Kazakhstan, Armenia, Kirghizia, Tajikistan, Uzbekistan, Azerbaijan, Belarus, and Georgia signed the Collective Security Treaty. Things were looking good on paper.

Weapons of mass destruction

The Soviet Union possessed significant arsenals of weapons of mass destruction (WMD) including nuclear weapons. They were located in various parts of the country, primarily in Russia, Ukraine, Belarus, and Kazakhstan. Both Belarus and Kazakhstan immediately agreed to hand over those arsenals to Russia. Some politicians in Kazakhstan believed that their new country should retain at least some nuclear weapons as a bargaining chip against possible territorial claims by Russia. However, many others thought that Russia would never make such claims and that Kazakhstan would be much better off as a non-nuclear state. Washington, in fact, supported this position as well. In Ukraine similar concerns emerged. Some politicians believed that without nuclear weapons Ukraine would not be able to resist

Russia's efforts to reclaim the Crimean Peninsula (these arguments were recalled again in 2014 after Russia annexed Crimea). Ukraine decided that it needed international guarantees about its territorial integrity, and Kiev (Ukraine's capital) received them. On December 5, 1994, the leaders of Ukraine, Russia, the United Kingdom, and the United States signed a memorandum to provide Ukraine with security assurances in connection with its decision to become a non-nuclear state (Budapest Memorandum, 1994). Ukraine then handed over to Russia its nuclear and chemical weapons. According to this agreement, the Russian Federation, the United Kingdom, and the United States promised to refrain from the threat or use of force against the territorial integrity or political independence of Ukraine and pledged that none of their weapons would ever be used against Ukraine except in self-defense.

Having proclaimed itself a legal successor to the USSR, Russia established control over Soviet property abroad and simultaneously assumed all the Soviet foreign loan obligations. The process was not as smooth as it may seem today. Several newly formed independent states expressed displeasure about Russia taking over the buildings and property of all Soviet embassies, while very little or even nothing in some cases was left for other countries.

Dividing the Soviet Union's territory and property

The borders between the republics of the Soviet Union, as you should remember from previous chapters, were set arbitrarily. Regions with predominantly Russian populations were often included in other ethnic republics. In 1991 many ethnic Russians who grew up in the Soviet Union suddenly found themselves living in other sovereign states. From the standpoint of international law, and according to the agreements signed at the Conference on Security and Cooperation in Europe (1975), European borders should have remained unchanged. Yet there were many politicians in Russia, especially among communists and populists, who openly discussed the necessity of expanding the borders of Russia to accommodate the Russian-speaking population living there. Such claims certainly could not strengthen trust toward Moscow. For a few years the countries of the former Soviet Union maintained a visa-free policy for travelers. This policy was gradually discontinued later in the 1990s.

Although the newly formed sovereign states have retained factories, communication networks, and other assets of the former Soviet Union, Russia was able to establish control over the most important production facilities in the energy sector. Russia has also retained most major deposits of oil and natural gas (they were mostly in Siberia and the Far North).

The newly established countries' transition to a market economy was difficult. Every one of them suffered a substantial economic decline and staggering financial difficulties. Seeking financial stability, in 1992–1993 many post-Soviet states negotiated the possibility of creating a key single currency zone with the ruble as its only currency. Russia favored this idea. However, later on, all the post-Soviet states backed off and decided to create their own national currencies instead. One of the most important reasons for refusing a single currency was their concern about becoming too dependent on Moscow in both fiscal and monetary areas.

In the military sphere Russia tried to preserve as much of the united infrastructure as possible. The CIS member states signed an agreement about preserving a united system of air defense and joint border guarding. It was clear, however, from the beginning that this and many other similar agreements would not last. Although Russian troops remained on the territory of nearly all post-Soviet states, their governments expected that the Russian soldiers would be soon redeployed back home. Disagreements emerged about the Black Sea navy. It was decided to put it under joint Russian-Ukrainian control until 1997. Kazakhstan also signed an agreement to allow Russia to lease the former Soviet and world's largest operational space launch facility in Baykonur.

Settling conflicts

Addressing the violent conflicts in the post-Soviet states was an especially challenging task. The majority of these conflicts were ethnic and surfaced in the middle and late 1980s. The problems of the Trans-Dniestr region (in Moldova), Nagorno Karabakh (in Azerbaijan), and Abkhazia and South Ossetia (in Georgia) were among the most difficult ones. During the last months of the Soviet Union the Russian-speaking population of the Trans-Dniestr region violently protested against Moldova's secession from the USSR. A new Trans-Dniestr sovereign state was later declared, but it did not receive the necessary formal international recognition. Several international agreements, which included Russia, the United States, and the European Union, settled the tensions in this republic for some time. However, this area remained a source of instability for many years.

The Nagorno Karabakh ethnic conflict involving the Armenian and the Azeri groups had grown into a bloody military confrontation in the late 1980s. Russia took the side of Armenia, which occupied Nagorno Karabakh, an Azerbaijan territory with the majority of its population being Armenian. Armenia also took over seven adjacent Azeri districts. In 1994 a ceasefire was reached, thanks to international mediation and Russia's active role. Yet Russia did not recognize Nagorno Karabakh's independence in order not to antagonize its relations with Azerbaijan.

The situation around Abkhazia and South Ossetia was also very difficult. In the late 1980s the Abkhaz Autonomous Republic and the South Ossetia Autonomous Region opposed Georgia's desire to secede from the USSR. In the 1990s Russia's sympathies were with Abkhazia and South Ossetia, which *de facto* broke away from Georgia. Russian troops were deployed in these regions as the CIS peacekeeping force. Yet tensions in these regions continued. New hostilities would erupt in 2008, resulting in a military conflict between Russia and Georgia (see again Chapter 2).

1994–2000: Approaching the post-Soviet space

The next period of Russian policies in the post-Soviet space (approximately from 1994 to 2000) was marked by Moscow's increasing motivation to develop good relations with post-Soviet states. During that period bilateral relations were underway; several states informally recognized Russia's special role in the region and accepted Moscow's role in the security and economic development of the post-Soviet space.

The Commonwealth of Independent States was steadily emerging as a two-tier structure, with most of the Central Asian states and Russia on the one end and the European countries on the other. In 1999 Azerbaijan, Georgia and Uzbekistan did not renew the Treaty on Collective Security. The treaty's remaining members were Russia, Armenia, Belarus, Kyrgyzstan, and Tajikistan – the latter interested mostly in receiving Russian military aid. Relations between Russia and Belarus remained solid yet were compromised by the lack of mutual trust: Moscow wanted assurances of loyalty from its neighbor; Belarus, on the other hand, did not want to be too dependent on Moscow. Some progress was made in Russo-Ukrainian relations. In 1997 a new treaty was signed on sharing the Black Sea navy. Russia was granted the right to lease the seaport of Sevastopol until 2017 and to keep its naval base there. The economic ties between these two countries remained fairly strong, but in 1993–1994 a trade conflict emerged between them related to the natural gas that Russia was delivering to Ukraine. Moscow was also displeased with Ukraine's apparent pivot toward Europe and Kiev's increasingly independent foreign policy.

In the Caucasus Russia supported Abkhazia and South Ossetia (which had already declared independence from Georgia, an independent state) and Adjara, which had demanded and received a greater autonomy within Georgia. Russia also regarded Armenia as its chief ally in the region and viewed its relations with Azerbaijan through the prism of its alliance with Armenia. Russia's relations with the newly emerged Central Asian states were steady. Some of them acted with confidence, such as Turkmenistan, which had vast gas reserves and anticipated substantial revenues from their sales. Others needed Russia's political, economic, and military assistance.

All in all, from 1994 to 2000 Russia made certain efforts toward the consolidation of its influence in the post-Soviet space. Yet it failed to slow down the processes of disintegration of the traditional economic and political ties. Several attempts were made to create, separate from Russia, new economic and political structures. For example, in 1997 the GUAM alliance emerged, which comprised Georgia, Ukraine, Azerbaijan, and Moldova. Moscow reacted to this organization negatively, believing that it had been created mostly to push Russia to the sidelines. Moscow realized, however, that formal treaties could become almost irrelevant. Indeed, despite many agreements between Russia and the neighboring states, most of them remained only formalities. One of the examples of such meaningless treaties was the 1995 custom union agreement among Russia, Belarus, and Kazakhstan.

There are several reasons why Russia failed to consolidate its influence in the post-Soviet space. First, the majority of business and political leaders in the former Soviet states did not want to become too dependent on Russia. They did not want the restoration of the Soviet Union, or whichever new political institution it would become. Most local leaders preferred the uncertainty of their sovereignty to the certainty of a new integration dominated by Moscow.

Second, Russia as a country was struggling with its own economic and social problems so that it could not lead by example. Moscow did not accumulate enough soft power (see Chapter 1) – the power to inspire and lead – to encourage and inspire other states without pressure or threats.

Third, it was evident that former Soviet states were different from one another in terms of their political and economic systems. Therefore, any substantial integration of all ten or even twelve sovereign states (i.e., former Soviet republics, except the Baltic states, which have never considered any form of integration with Russia) would have required changes in their political institutions, as well as foreign and domestic policies, which the majority of the local elites did not want to attempt after several years of independence and self-governance. Meanwhile, new Russian leaders had a new plan in the works.

Attempting a consolidation: 2000–2008

The new Russian president in 2000 already sought a new international role for his country. Putin wanted more effective and assertive Russian policies in the post-Soviet space. It was a difficult task. At the end of the last millennium Russia as a country had few economic and political resources to support Putin's strategic plans. However, the economic situation in Russia was improving, thanks in part to the rising oil prices that began bringing Russia windfall profits. In fact, this money has encouraged Russia's assertiveness and improved its confidence in international affairs.

Russia in part relied on the CIS, an international organization that for a decade was mostly formal and rather ineffective, yet legitimate in the eyes of the international community. In 2000 the CIS had become a kind of a "discussion club" rather than an efficient intergovernmental organization capable of making binding decisions. Moscow was eager to turn to new and presumably more efficient mechanisms of foreign policy within the existing CIS structure. Such mechanisms, in Putin's view, should have included new international institutions.

New institutions

In 2000, with Russia's energetic support, the ineffective Customs Union was formally transformed into the Eurasian Economic Community, which included Russia, Belarus, Kirghizia, Kazakhstan, and Tajikistan. The new organization aimed at easing and even eliminating many customs restrictions; it was also planning a common currency, as well as common labor and market policies. These policies were expected to take effect within ten years or so. One of the models for this union was the European Community and its institutions. However, the Eurasian Economic Community, almost two decades after its inception, remained far from being what it was expected to be.

After 2000 a few important changes took place in Russia's security policies. Russia initiated the creation of the Collective Security Treaty Organization, which was formally established in 2002. Some states, under the provisions of this treaty, have purchased Russian arms. To other states, this treaty provided some security assurances. However, it was also clear to observers that most states did not want to see Moscow's military presence and influence grow in the post-Soviet space.

Meanwhile, Russia was becoming more assertive in its international behavior. It continued viewing GUAM (see earlier in this chapter) negatively. Although this organization was generally inefficient, its members were increasingly looking for closer relations with the European Union. To disrupt this process and to become a more attractive economic and political partner, Russia began offering other states new economic incentives, such as low fuel and natural gas prices as well as new trade benefits.

Bilateral relations

During his first two presidential terms from 2000 to 2008 Putin pursued a robust policy of developing bilateral ties with most post-Soviet states. A treaty was signed establishing a new international organization – the Union State of Russia and Belarus. Russia's greatest interest in this Union State was a cooperation of the two countries in defense and security. Belarus was mostly seeking trade benefits and Russia's economic aid. Moscow also used this precedent to signal to other states that they were welcome to follow suit and develop closer ties with Russia. Yet the proposed integration with Belarus stalled due to many problems. Some of them were bureaucratic, but most were political.

In addition to Belarus, Russia sought friendlier ties with Moldova. A key issue was an ethnic conflict in this country involving several hundreds of thousands of ethnic Russians living in Transnistria. After some initial welcoming signals, however, the government of Moldova rejected a Moscow-sponsored plan to settle the ethnic conflict in the Transnistria region. Moscow's plan provided for a federalization of Moldova (thus giving ethnic Russians a special legal status) and for Russian troops to stay there indefinitely. The reason for Moldova's rejection of the plan was its fear of dependency on Russia and the strengthening of Russia's geopolitical position in the region. The failure to settle the conflict caused a further deterioration of relations between the two countries for a long period (Treschenkov, 2013).

Relations with Ukraine took many dramatic turns. Before the presidential election of 2004 Moscow supported Prime Minister Viktor Yanukovych, who had on his side considerable bureaucratic and economic resources and the support of the majority of the Russian-speaking population. His opponent, Viktor Yushchenko, had substantial support in Ukraine's western and central regions from the majority of ethnic Ukrainians. He also favored closer ties between Ukraine and NATO and the European Union. An acute political crisis occurred in Ukraine during the elections. Mass protests erupted in several cities including the capital; the protests were sparked by accusations of massive electoral fraud in favor of Yanukovych. These protests became known later as **the Orange Revolution** (named after the orange color of flags and ribbons that the protesters were wearing to identify themselves). As a result of a new and transparent recount of the ballots, Yushchenko won the presidency. Russia was displeased and accused Western governments and other organizations of meddling with Ukraine's domestic affairs (Gretskiy, 2010). In the following months and years relations between Russia and Ukraine cooled. In 2006 both countries clashed again over the payments for natural gas that Russia supplied to Ukraine. Russia threatened to cut off the shipment of gas to Ukraine and shut off the gas pipes coming through the country, which could have affected several countries in Europe heavily dependent on Russia's gas supplies. These and several other similar trade disputes between Ukraine and Russia received the name **the gas wars**. These conflicts were settled, at least for the time being.

Russia's relations with Georgia also deteriorated. Georgian President Eduard Shevardnadze (1928–2014) refused Putin's request to allow Russian troops to pass through Georgian territory during Russia's military operations against Chechnya in 1999. This position certainly displeased Moscow, which – quite predictably – did not support Shevardnadze when he was pressured to resign in 2003 in the midst of public protests. Russia helped the new political leaders of Georgia to restore their authority in Adjara (a province in Georgia). However, Moscow soon became annoyed with the new Georgian President Mikheil Saakashvili and his policy of pursuing closer relations with NATO and the European Union. George W. Bush's visit to Tbilisi in 2005 added more negativity to the relations between Georgia and Russia. They now were clashing about the status of Abkhazia and South Ossetia, which had declared their independence from Georgia earlier. Georgia insisted that its territorial sovereignty must be respected. Moscow supported the separatists and continued its diplomatic and political pressure on Georgia. As a politically provocative gesture, Russia offered citizenship to the residents of Abkhazia and South Ossetia. Many of them accepted the offer. One of the reasons was the welfare benefits (including pensions and other subsidies) that Russia offered to its new citizens.

Although no major changes in Russia's relations with Armenia and Azerbaijan were taking place early in the 2000s, several cardinal changes took place in Central Asia, where Russian influence grew considerably. Russia developed closer economic ties with neighboring Kazakhstan. In September 2001, after the terrorist attacks against the United States, Russia joined the antiterrorist coalition and advised the Central Asian states to support the United States' military operation in Afghanistan. Kirghizia and Uzbekistan let the United States use their airbases. However, after the 2003 invasion of Iraq, Russia was increasingly critical of Washington's policies in the Middle East and Afghanistan. At the same time, Washington and the West criticized the authoritarian and often brutal methods used by the leaders of Central Asian states against their domestic political opposition, and many

Central Asian leaders were displeased by such criticisms. Probably not without Moscow's encouragement, the government of Uzbekistan decided to discontinue the American military presence there (Gleason, 2006).

During the first eight years of Putin's presidency Russia was becoming more self-assured in its relations with the states that used to be the republics of the former Soviet Union. Moscow did not achieve its geopolitical goals of a closer integration due to its limited political power and insufficient economic resources. The countries that Russia courted also sought economic and political cooperation with the European Union, the United States, and the People's Republic of China. The challenge was that Russia was their closest and jealous neighbor. And its influence was growing.

Advancing the consolidation process: 2008–2012

During the presidency of Dmitry Medvedev (2008–2012) politicians in Moscow took to frequently using the term a **multipolar world**. This term, also known as *multipolarity*, stands for a distribution of power in which more than two countries project equal measures of military, economic, and political influence. Its use reflected the view that Russia was becoming strong enough to play a considerably bigger role in international affairs as one of the "centers" of power in today's global world.

Russia's aspirations

Russia has already joined several international forums, including the most prestigious such as G8 and G20. (These forums include the most developed countries that hold annual meetings to foster agreement on several global issues such as economic challenges, crisis management, security, energy, and international terrorism.) Despite the devastating impact of the global financial crisis of 2008 and the subsequent economic slowdown, which certainly affected Russia, the ruling classes in Russia still believed that the balance of power in the world and in the post-Soviet space was changing in favor of Russia. They also believed that the time was ripe for their country to take even more assertive steps in foreign policy. Moscow assumed that during the financial and economic crisis most of the post-Soviet states would be interested in Russian aid (primarily in the form of oil and gas deliveries and other kinds of economic assistance). Russia was actively pursuing an efficient international organization in Eurasia to boost economic cooperation and trade among the countries of the region. As a result of these efforts, in 2010 a "renewed" Customs Union consisting of Russia, Belarus, and Kazakhstan was formally created. Unlike the Customs Union of 1995, which essentially failed, the new union was designed to conduct a set of specific policies. Kyrgyzstan and several other countries expressed interest in joining the union in the future.

However, the Collective Security Treaty Organization (see earlier in this chapter) experienced difficulties. Most member states showed only lukewarm support for the CSTO's decisions. Although it had been planned to create a joint rapid deployment military force to deal with the threats to regional security including terrorism, the implementation of this plan was very slow. Uzbekistan quit the organization in 2012. The CSTO and NATO did not establish formal relations.

The 2008 Georgia conflict

The armed conflict in Georgia in August 2008, known as the **Russo-Georgian War**, became one of the most critical world developments of that period. It was the first large-scale European war of the 21st century. For several years prior to this conflict the official declaration of the independence of Kosovo and its quick recognition by the United States and the majority of European countries had led to an animated discussion in Russian political circles about the future of Abkhazia and South Ossetia. Some urged Moscow to push for these regions' total independence. Moscow hesitated. However, when hostilities erupted between the Georgian forces and the Russian troops located in South Ossetia and Abkhazia, Russia chose action and moved into Georgia. The West condemned this action as an aggression. Although Moscow was displeased with Georgia's turn to the West, Russia had not invaded a neighboring country since it occupied Afghanistan in 1979 (Saakashvili, 2018). Moscow defended its right of self-defense. A ceasefire was achieved through the relentless mediation of French President Nicolas Sarkozy. Meanwhile Russia formally endorsed the independence of Abkhazia and North Ossetia. In protest, Georgia immediately exited the Commonwealth of Independent States. Relations between Georgia and Russia deteriorated and were further worsened by Russia's sanctions against some Georgian products (mostly food and beverages) sold on Russia's markets. Only in 2011, when a new president of Georgia was elected, did the relations between the two countries turn toward normalization (see Map 6.1). The process of normalization, however, was slow.

Relations with Ukraine

Ukraine openly supported Georgia in the 2008 war. Making steady moves toward NATO membership, Ukrainian leaders have further irritated Moscow and caused a serious deterioration of the Russo-Ukrainian relations. A new gas war erupted (see earlier in this chapter). The disagreement about the prices for natural gas resulted in a serious interruption of the natural gas supplies going through the pipelines in Ukraine to Central Europe. Later in 2009 Ukraine and Russia signed a new agreement, which many in Ukraine considered unfair because they were expecting to pay significantly lower gas prices than the agreement suggested. Russia was undaunted. Although Moscow referred to its legal obligation to stick to high market prices,

Map 6.1 Georgia, Abkhazia, and South Ossetia

Kiev saw the Russian position as an attempt to economically pressure Ukraine or even punish it for an apparent pro-Western course.

Yanukovych was elected president of Ukraine in 2010, which pleased Moscow. Immediately both sides signed a new gas accord, more affordable for Ukraine. The Russian navy received the legal right to use the seaport of Sevastopol until 2042. Although Yanukovych no longer formally pursued NATO membership, the main direction in Ukraine's foreign policy was a closer cooperation with the European Union. Moreover, the Ukrainian leadership hoped for a more radical revision of the gas contract of 2009 to lower the cost of gas. Russia, however, did not want to give Ukraine much lower rates. There were at least two reasons why. Russia had already made a commitment to the WTO to use only market prices in trading at home and abroad. Second, Russia needed new revenues. Gazprom, the state-owned company that was involved in gas deals with Ukraine, had been already experiencing financial difficulties (it has to compete with other global gas producers, including those in the United States). A long-term gas contract with Ukraine was a source of significant and steady revenues to Gazprom and thus to the government of Russia.

Other countries

Relations with Belarus were improving in the military and economic domains. Both countries carried out a large-scale military exercise. Belarus stepped up its participation in the CSTO and joined the Customs Union. Russia's relations with Moldova remained uneasy and at times tense. Both Armenia and Azerbaijan acted prudently and were avoiding serious complications in their relations with Russia. Meanwhile in Central Asia Kazakhstan has effectively become Russia's chief partner in the post-Soviet space.

The Georgian War of 2008 and the reaction of other countries to Russia's behavior demonstrated at least two tendencies. On the one hand, it was obvious that Russia could act independently, regardless of other countries' criticisms and objections. Moscow realized it could use many tools, including economic and even military, to "reward" or "punish" other countries. On the other hand, Russia realized the limitations of its own power. None of the post-Soviet states openly supported Russia's actions in Georgia or recognized the independence of Abkhazia and South Ossetia.

Despite these setbacks, Russia was attempting to build new foundations for a tighter cooperation with most post-Soviet countries.

Advancing the consolidation process: 2012–today

The next stage of Russia's foreign policy evolution in the post-Soviet space covers the period from the return of Putin to the presidency in 2012, his reelection in 2018, to the most recent days. During this period Russia was energetically moving toward rebuilding the post-Soviet space, which was, as seen from the Kremlin, a new center of world power. As president, Putin suggested the idea of a new geopolitical organization, the Eurasian Union (Putin, 2012a). In the fields of economic policies, a new CIS Free Trade Zone Treaty was projected to replace about one hundred bilateral and multilateral agreements on trade and commerce. This new treaty now included Armenia, Belarus, Kirghizia, Kazakhstan, Moldova, Tajikistan, Ukraine, and Russia.

The Eurasian Union

The initial plans for the Eurasian Union were very ambitious. This international organization was supposed to be a confederation of states that would resemble, in some ways, the European Union. It was also projected that the new intergovernmental organization would have structures such as the Council of Heads of States and Governments, the Eurasian Parliament, and the Council of Foreign Ministers. Several intergovernmental financial and economic institutions were proposed, including the International Investment Bank, the Economic Commission, and the Commission for Mineral Reserves. It was also proposed that the states establish a common currency (like the Euro, the currency of the European Union).

However, such an impressive plan was very difficult to implement from the start (Sadri, 2014). Neither government bureaucracies nor political or business elites of the proposed union wanted to surrender their power to Moscow. The task of building a joint parliament was especially daunting. A vital question was about the composition of the proposed legislature. Which country should have most deputies in there? Should it be the one with the largest population? Then how powerful will Russia become in this institution? While Moscow saw this parliament as a source of political integration, most other countries pursued mostly economic coopera-tion, not necessarily close political ties. Moscow was using various arguments to persuade several countries to join the Customs Union as a pretext for their future membership in the Eurasian Union. At the same time Russia faced competition from the European Union. The Eastern Partnership program of the European Union was a very attractive opportunity for Ukraine, Moldova, Azerbaijan, Armenia, Georgia, and Belarus to develop closer ties with Europe. The dilemma that many countries of the former Soviet Union were now facing was difficult (Treschenkov, 2014). On the one hand, developing partnership with the wealthy European Union was very appealing from economic and political standpoints. On the other hand, an obvious "pivot" toward the West could have jeopardized these countries' apparently good relationships with Moscow. Open conflicts were about to occur.

The Ukraine crisis

Russia's relationships with Ukraine during almost three decades after the disso-lution of the Soviet Union, and particularly after 2012, should illustrate the dra-matic ambiguity of Moscow's policies toward the former Soviet republics. From the beginning, the course of political and economic reforms in Ukraine was extremely rough. Several governments came and went, but the overall economic situation in the country was difficult, at times dismal. President Victor Yanukovych, who was elected in 2010, curbed civil liberties and harassed political opposition. For instance, his key political adversary and former prime minister, Yulia Timoshenko, a charismatic politician, was imprisoned, and her sentencing was viewed in the West as political retaliation against her. Corruption in Ukraine was rampant. With eco-nomic opportunities for the middle class diminishing, the gap between the wealthy and the rest of the population was huge and growing. These and many other factors caused a growing discontent in society and a conflict among Ukraine's political and business elites. Russia's strategy to dominate in Ukraine was often overshadowed by Moscow's frustrations over the political battles in Kiev as well as the two coun-tries' mutual disagreements.

The foreign policy strategies of the Ukrainian president were highly inconsistent. He was explicitly advocating the necessity of closer ties with the European Union, which could bring substantial financial relief for Ukraine. He was also pushing for closer ties with China, even for a possibility of getting financial aid from Beijing. At the same time, he was openly pursuing a cozy relationship with Moscow: he was aware of the importance of getting natural gas from Ukraine's big neighbor and of having Russia's economic and political backing.

Putin and his advisers tolerated Yanukovych's discussions with the European Union and assumed that Ukraine would continue leaning toward Russia. It was gen-erally believed that Ukraine would be playing a very important role in a possible alli-ance involving Russia, Belarus, and Kazakhstan. This political alliance, if created, would have been the biggest in Eurasia. Some in Russia even considered this new intergovernmental organization as a viable alternative to the European Union and the United States. The political and economic consequences of such an alliance would have influenced global affairs for years to come. Moscow's commentators, especially the nationalists, claimed that the cultural and religious ties between the people in Ukraine and Russia should make a new political union between the two nations inevitable (Wilson, 2014).

Meanwhile, Ukraine's leaders continued their indecisive policies of trying to simultaneously please both Russia and the West. In the fall of 2013 Kiev announced its intention to sign an agreement with the European Union on a closer economic association and free trade. However, a few months later President Yanukovych backed off, announcing a course toward closer ties with Russia instead. The motives behind this switch in proposed policies seemed to be reasonable. The European Union was about to deliver about $800 million in loans. This was about thirty times less than Ukraine had initially asked for. Russia was offering a considerably larger aid package: $15 billion and discounted gas prices on top of it (CNBC, 2013a). Furthermore, the European Union demanded major legal changes in Ukraine's business regulations. Russia's aid, by contrast, was supposed to be delivered with no specific conditions attached to it.

The decision to back away from the deal with the European Union and to realign with Russia sparked mass protests in Ukraine's major cities including Kiev. Violence erupted and, after the police's pushback, escalated. Dozens of civilians were killed in clashes with the police. Some members of the government called for decisive measures against the protesters; others refused to use force against civilians. On February 21, 2014, President Yanukovych and several oppositional leaders from the parliament moved to resolve the escalating conflict. They signed an agreement on a political settlement in the country; they even agreed on moving the presidential elections forward to May. However, violence continued in Kiev. The protesters captured several key government buildings. Losing the support of his own law enforcement units, Yanukovych left the capital. An interim government was formed without him. These 2014 events are called in Ukraine the **Revolution of Dignity**.

These sudden and stunning developments caused a great deal of anxiety in Moscow. In fact, it was obvious that a democratically elected government in Kiev was forced to resign under pressure of the violent protests. In the West such protests are commonly called a revolution. Moscow saw this differently, calling the protesters, "extremists" and "fascists." The events in the capital also sent emotional shock waves across the Ukrainian regions with predominantly Russian-speaking populations. In Crimea, which was a part of Ukraine, Russian nationalists supported by the majority of the population seized power. They were encouraged by the presence of Russian troops, which had been quickly and surreptitiously deployed there under the Kremlin's directives. In fact, a sizable Russian contingent, about twenty-five thousand troops, has already been stationed in Crimea after the collapse of the USSR according to an agreement with Ukraine. Russian forces quickly took over most important strategic locations on the Peninsula. Given the presence of a foreign country's armed forces, a referendum was hastily organized to consider Crimea's independence. A quickly formed new government petitioned Moscow about the incorporation of Crimea into the Russian Federation. This military and political operation, planned in Moscow, resulted in an obvious outcome: Russia accepted the "offer."

The United States, the European Union, and many other countries immediately condemned Russia's actions. They called it an **annexation**, which is the forceful transition of land from the control of one state to another. The annexation was viewed as a flagrant violation of international law. Ukraine protested, and a majority of countries supported the Ukrainian position. Russia rejected the criticisms, arguing that the decision to secede was made by the residents of Crimea (Rosenfielde, 2016). The West ruled out military actions to defend Ukraine's sovereignty and chose a series of economic sanctions against Russia instead. In 2014 Ukraine signed an agreement on its association with the European Union, which was ratified in 2017. At the same time, Ukraine and the European Union agreed on a visa-free travel regime.

Despite the global condemnation of Russia's actions in Crimea, the government in Moscow received the support of the majority of its people according to polls (Levada, 2014, 2018d). One of the major arguments in favor of the annexation (in Russia it is called reunification or "historic justice") was that according to the results of the popular referendum in Crimea, the vast majority of voters wanted Crimea be a part of Russia. Russian nationalists rejoiced. The United Nations did not recognize the referendum.

In the spring of 2014 Russia offered military and political support to ethnic separatists in the eastern part of Ukraine (mostly in the Donbass region) where large numbers of Russian-speaking population lived. After a series of deadly clashes between the separatists and the Ukrainian military, the conflict turned to a lingering warfare. Russia vehemently denied any direct participation in the conflict. However, Western powers disagreed and condemned Russia's involvement. Ultimately, to punish Russia's actions in Crimea and in Eastern Ukraine, the United States and its allies continued with a wide range of economic and political sanctions against Russia. Moscow responded with its own sanctions against the West by drastically limiting the sales of Western products in Russian markets.

In February 2015 Russia, Germany, France, and Ukraine met in Minsk – the capital of Belarus – and agreed on a solution to the conflict in the eastern Ukraine. It became known as the Minsk Protocol. The Protocol called for an immediate bilateral ceasefire and withdrawal of all illegal armed groups, military equipment, and mercenaries from the territory of Ukraine. In 2017 the United States undertook a consultation with Russia. Both sides agreed that UN should play a more active role in the conflict. Meanwhile, Moscow was leaning toward an option that would allow peacekeeping troops and international observers to be deployed between the separatists and Ukrainian troops. The West favored a special UN administration for the Donbas region. Despite the 2015 Minsk Protocol, deadly violence in the region continued.

During the four years of conflict more than ten thousand people lost their lives, including three thousand civilians (UN, 2018). One of the deadliest single tragedies caused by the conflict was downing of the Malaysia Airlines Flight 17 headed from

Amsterdam to Kuala Lumpur. The plane that was shot down on July 17, 2014. Dutch investigators concluded that a rocket that hit the plane was launched from pro-Russian separatist-controlled territory in Ukraine. All 283 passengers and 15 crew on board died. In 2018, after three years of investigation by national and international teams, the governments of the Netherlands and Australia issued a joint statement in which they laid responsibility on Russia "for its part" in the crash. The statement calls on Russia to accept its responsibility and help establish the truth and achieve justice for the victims (MH17 Statement, 2018). Russia continues to officially deny any involvement in this tragedy (Reuters, 2018). In 2015 more than 40 percent of Russians blamed Ukraine for the downing of the plane, 17 percent accused the United States, and only 5 percent mentioned either Russia or the Ukranian separatist forces (Levada, 2015). A willing public in any country is an easy target of conspiracy theorists, sensation-seeking journalists, and professional government fabricators – the Russian public is no exception.

Other countries

The Ukrainian events sent alarm signals to the residents of Transnistria. Almost 500,000 people living there are predominantly Russian speaking. For years they have been protected by the Russian military deployed in the region, and the government of Moldova has become increasingly displeased with the Russian military's presence on its territory.

Georgia, despite certain positive changes in its relations with Russia, still sought closer ties with the European Union and, possibly, NATO. Moldova and Georgia also signed the association agreements with the European Union and received visa-free status with the countries of the Schengen zone. Armenia was initially willing to sign an agreement with the European Union but later backed off, mostly because of Russian pressure. Yet again, in 2017 Armenia signed a cooperation agreement with the European Union. A new government that took office in 2018 continued to seek greater ties with the European Union, including visa-free travel. At the same time, Armenia maintains friendly relations with Moscow.

Azerbaijan has notably improved its relations with Russia since 2012 but relies mostly on bilateral agreements instead of joining any intergovernmental organizations controlled by Moscow. Both Armenia and Azerbaijan are maintaining good relations with Moscow. They both needed Russia's mediating role in settling the conflict in Nagorno-Karabakh, which has been lingering on for more than thirty years. Nagorno-Karabakh, based on a referendum, declared itself a sovereign republic and assumed a new name, The Republic of Artsakh. Most countries consider Artsakh a part of Azerbajjan.

The **Eurasian Economic Union (EEU)** was finally launched in 2015. This is an economic union that initially consisted of Russia, Belarus, and Kazakhstan. Armenia and Kyrgyzstan also joined. Moscow hopes that the EEU will consolidate Russia's political and economic influence in the post-Soviet space. The main weakness of the EEU as well as the Kremlin's entire "Eurasian project" is that it remains largely a bureaucratic venture mostly designed by elites. Without serious economic incentives available to all its members, the EEU, at least for some time, is unlikely to produce any significant and positive changes in Russia or Eurasia.

Conclusion

The breakup of the Soviet Union was a major historic event affecting the lives of tens of millions of people in Europe and Asia. The newly formed states had to establish their mutual relationships based on a brand new foundation requiring mutual respect and useful cooperation. History shows – for example, consider the implosion of Ottoman Empire earlier in the twentieth century or the breakup of Yugoslavia in the 1990s – that such processes of disintegration are seldom smooth. Open conflicts between newly formed countries are common.

Since the early 1990s Russia has pursued stable and productive relations with all the former republics of the Soviet Union. After 2000 Russia's position became even more assertive. The adjective "common" became a key word to accompany most talks of Russia's strategic goals in the "post-Soviet" space – a *common economic space, common energy policies, common civilizational goals*, and so on. Russia certainly hoped for a more robust and efficient integration of states within the post-Soviet space. Other countries, however, had different expectations, concerns, and strategies. They wanted closer economic ties yet hoped not to become too politically dependent on Moscow.

Estonia, Latvia, and Lithuania, from the early days of their independence, did not have any desire for a closer collaboration with Russia. On the contrary, they expected to be quickly integrated into the European Union and NATO. Russia was certainly displeased with these developments (seeing them as a threat to Russia's interests) but could not influence the integration of these countries into the European institutional structures. Central Asian states for years maintained relatively stable relations with Russia. The ruling elites in these countries understood the importance of Moscow's support. Russia has demonstrated that its major concern is stability in Central Asia, regardless of the type of government or political leaders these countries have. As a result, Russia has been continuously backing several authoritarian regimes in that region.

In the Caucasus region Russia has maintained steady relations with both Armenia and Azerbaijan. However, the relationship with Georgia has been poor for more than two decades. An armed conflict between both sides broke out in 2008. Relations worsened after the war. Russia continues to defend its actions as self-defense. Most countries, including the United States, have maintained a very critical view of Russia's aggression against Georgia.

Russia's relations with Belarus remain mostly productive and friendly. Although European countries and the United States for many years criticized Belarus's authoritarian government, Russia took a different position. The relationship between Ukraine and Russia has been turbulent and drastically worsened after 2014. Russia's actions in Crimea and in Eastern Ukraine sparked substantial global criticism and tough economic sanctions against Russia.

Despite a few setbacks, in the future Russia is likely to continue its efforts at consolidation of countries that used to be the republics of the former Soviet Union. Moscow will consider pursuing an ambitious project to reestablish itself, along with aligned countries, as a new center of power and a new center within the global economic and trade system (Putin, 2011). Moscow believes that this consolidated organization or an efficient structure of states will play a great role in decision-making, setting the rules, and shaping the future of the world. This is, of course, a very ambitious plan, and every ambitious plan needs constant reality checks.

Summary

- The term post-Soviet space indicates Russia as well as several sovereign countries that used to be the republics of the former Soviet Union. Security concerns, geopolitics, economic interests, and historical ties – these and other factors generally motivate Russia and its foreign policies in the post-Soviet space.
- After Gorbachev's ascendance to power in 1985, and after he granted political freedoms and relaxed political censorship, nationalism and separatism began gaining influence in the ethnic republics.
- The evolution and the current status of Russia's foreign policy toward the post-Soviet states can be understood as a process unfolding in several stages. Each of them should also be understood as a transitional and evolving phase.
- The Soviet Union possessed significant arsenals of weapons of mass destruction (WMD) including nuclear weapons. They were located primarily in Russia, Ukraine, Belarus, and Kazakhstan. Both Belarus and Kazakhstan immediately agreed to hand over those arsenals to Russia. Ukraine received international guarantees for its territorial integrity in exchange for the country's nuclear weapons.
- From 1994 to 2000 Russia made certain efforts to consolidate its influence in the post-Soviet space. President Putin after 2000 sought a new international role for his country. Putin wanted to see Russia's policies in the post-Soviet space becoming more effective and assertive.
- During the first eight years of Putin's presidency Russia was becoming increasingly confident in its relations with the states that used to be the republics of the former Soviet Union. Moscow, however, did not achieve its geopolitical goals due to its limited political power and insufficient economic resources.
- The armed conflict in Georgia in August 2008 became one of the most critical international developments. Russia's actions were condemned by a number of countries.
- Ukraine openly supported Georgia in the 2008 war. Making steady moves toward NATO membership, Ukrainian leaders further irritated Moscow and caused a serious deterioration of Russo-Ukrainian relations. Disagreement about the prices for natural gas resulted in an interruption of the gas supplies going through the pipelines in Ukraine to Central Europe.

- After 2012 Russia has been energetically moving toward rebuilding the post-Soviet space, which the Kremlin sees as a new center of world power. As president, Putin suggested the idea of a new geopolitical organization, the Eurasian Union.
- Russia's relationships with Ukraine during almost three decades after the dissolution of the Soviet Union, and particularly after 2012, illustrate the dramatic complexity and ambiguity of Moscow's policies toward the former Soviet republics, policies often employing "carrot-and-stick" strategies.
- The United States, the European Union, and many other countries condemned Russia's actions in Ukraine in 2014 and after. The annexation of Crimea was viewed as a flagrant violation of international law. The majority of the international community supported the Ukrainian position. Russia rejected the criticisms.

Glossary

Annexation The forceful transition of land from the control of one state to another.
Eurasian Economic Union An economic union launched in 2015 that initially consisted of Russia, Belarus, and Kazakhstan. Armenia and Kyrgyzstan have also joined.
Gas wars Trade disputes between Ukraine and Russia about the natural gas sold by Russia.
Multipolar world or multipolarity stands for a distribution of power in which more than two countries project equal measures of military, economic, and political influence.
Orange Revolution A series of protests in Ukraine in 2004 named after the orange color of flags and ribbons that the protesters were wearing to identify themselves.
Post-Soviet space The term refers to Russia as well as to the current CIS countries that used to be the republics of the former Soviet Union.
Revolution of Dignity A series of violent events in Kiev, Ukraine, in February 2014, resulted in the ousting of the Ukrainian President, Viktor Yanukovych, and the overthrow of the executive branch of the government.
Russo-Georgian War A large-scale military conflict in 2008 between Georgia, Russia, and the Russian-backed self-proclaimed republics of South Ossetia and Abkhazia.

Review questions

1. Explain the post-Soviet space. What does it include from Russia's standpoint? Do other countries, such as the United States and the United Kingdom, have similar assumptions about their own "spaces"?

2. What factors and developments motivate Russia and its foreign policies in the post-Soviet space?
3. What are the causes of the ethnic and political conflicts in the Trans-Dniestr region (in Moldova), Nagorno Karabakh (in Azerbaijan), and Abkhazia and South Ossetia (in Georgia)?
4. What was the "Orange Revolution" (or "revolutions") and why is it relevant to Russia and its foreign policy?
5. Why is Russia's takeover of Crimea called "annexation" in most Western sources? Why does Russia reject this definition?

Chapter 7
Russia's Policies toward the United States

*Russia expects that US actions in the international arena will be strictly
guided by international legal norms, primarily the UN Charter, including
the principle of non-interference in domestic affairs of other states.*

Concept of the Foreign Policy of the Russian Federation (2016)

Learning objectives

*   Describe and critically review the historical milestones in the relationship between the Soviet Union and the United States.
*   Describe and critically analyze the periods of Russian-American relations after 1991.
*   Critically discuss the multiple international and domestic factors affecting the relationships between Moscow and Washington.
*   Describe major problems as well as key perspectives in the relations between the two countries.

Historical background

Over the past two centuries bilateral relations between Russia and the United States have always played a major, even decisive role in international affairs. At certain historical periods these countries were allies fighting a common enemy. During other periods they were partners. They were also, and quite often, adversaries. Great success stories of these countries' cooperation were followed by no less significant setbacks. These days, while Moscow and Washington continue cooperating in some areas, they are competing in far more others.

Early periods

During the American Revolutionary War (1775–1783), Russia did not support Great Britain and declared neutrality in the conflict between London and its North American colonies, which certainly was seen as a goodwill gesture toward the United States (Korshunov, 1995). In the nineteenth century Russia accepted – without formally announcing this – the **Monroe doctrine**, the US strategic approach and policy toward the Western Hemisphere that stated that any efforts by European nations to interfere with sovereign countries in North or South America would not be accepted (Ivanyan, 2001a). The United States was one of only a few countries that were on the side of Russia in the Crimean War of 1853–1856. Russia fought against the Ottoman Empire, which was supported by Britain, Sardinia, and France. Washington criticized as unfair the articles of the 1856 Paris Treaty that officially adjudicated the results of the Crimean War: Russia surrendered territories and was banned from having a navy in the Black Sea as well as military fortresses nearby (Kurilla, 2005). During the Civil War in the United States Russia's sympathies were with President Lincoln and the North (Ivanyan, 2001a). At the same time Russia was gradually pulling its settlements out of North America and sold Alaska in 1867 for $7.2 million, which would be roughly $125 million today (Bolkhovitinov, 1991). Russia also repeatedly declined requests from the Kingdom of Hawaii to assume authority over this Pacific territory.

Although Russia no longer had permanent settlements in America, emigration from Russia to the New World was growing, especially at the end of the nineteenth century and later. Caused mostly by economic factors, this massive migration also had political and religious causes, including the authoritarian, antidemocratic policies of Emperor Alexander III, which drew criticism from the United States (Zhuravleva, 2012).

During the Russo-Japanese War of 1904–1905 the United States took a neutral position and helped to settle the conflict between Japan and Russia by mediating the Portsmouth Treaty of 1905. About a decade later Russia and the United States fought in the anti-German alliance in World War I (Russia from 1914, the United States from 1917). In the spring of 1918, however, the Soviet government abrogated all the international obligations of the Russian Empire and separately signed a bilateral peace treaty with rival Germany. Washington did not fight against the new communist government in Russia. Although the United States sent several thousand troops to Northern Russia, this was done in hopes of resurrecting the Eastern Front in the war against Germany. And the United States' military presence in the Russian Far East was aimed against Japan, which had already occupied parts of the Russian Far East and Siberia. As one of the Bolshevik leaders, Mikhail Kalinin, said in Vladivostok in 1923: "If we look seriously at the past now, then pretty often when one talks to simple peasants and workers and asks them which of the interventionist armies was softer, more cultured, treated the population better, did less harm, one gets an indication to America, that its troops behaved more correctly, did less moral and material harm in a given territory, and this is no accident."

The United States was among the last of the major powers in Europe to recognize the Soviet state and establish diplomatic relations with the USSR in 1933. Even prior to the formal establishment of bilateral relations, though, the two countries interacted. In the early 1920s the American government and several charitable organizations provided considerable aid to the famine-stricken regions of Soviet Russia and, after 1922, the newly formed Soviet Union (Makarov and Khristoforov, 2006). The Soviet Union began to purchase American heavy machinery for various construction and manufacturing projects as early as the late 1920s (Shpotov, 2015). In the 1930s economic relations between the two countries were robust. In the geopolitical arena the governments of both countries were concerned about Japan's expansionist policies in Asia. At the same time, Washington expressed displeasure with Moscow's suppression of religious freedoms in its own country as well as with the policies of the Communist International, which the Soviet Union, as you may remember, sponsored. For example, the American Communist Party was a member of the Communist International and called during various meetings in Moscow for a socialist revolution in the United States and a violent removal of the American government.

World War II

World War II began in September 1939. During its early stages relations between Moscow and Washington were lukewarm. Stalin initially was skeptical about President Roosevelt's efforts to prevent German aggression in Europe. The United States, on the other hand, was very critical of the 1939 Molotov-Ribbentrop Pact, the agreement between Germany and the Soviet Union on the division of both countries' spheres of influence in Europe. Washington also condemned Moscow's invasion of Finland in 1939 and refused to recognize the forcible incorporation of Lithuania, Latvia, and Estonia into the USSR in 1940. Yet after Germany invaded the USSR in June 1941 and after Japan attacked the United States in December of that year, both countries began actively cooperating politically and militarily. Great Britain too joined this emerging anti-German alliance. This historic cooperation among the three countries became the backbone of the global anti-Hitler coalition. The summits in Tehran (November–December, 1943), Yalta (February, 1945), and Potsdam (July–August, 1945) helped in coordinating these countries' efforts to end the war, establish a new international order, and draw the new postwar political map of the world. This wartime cooperation was one of the most recognized and celebrated periods in Russian-American relations.

The Cold War begins

After 1945 the world entered a period of dramatic global confrontation. It went down in history as the Cold War (see earlier chapters). It was a state of political and military tension between the powers aligned with the Soviet Union, on the one hand, and the countries aligned with the United States and the West, on the other. The confrontation was global. It touched practically all areas of life, military, economic, political, ideological, and social. The two countries were the leading forces of two seemingly irreconcilably antagonistic social-political systems.

The Cold War for more than forty years had a substantial and continuous impact on the entire international order. The two opposing military and political blocs – NATO headed by the United States and the Warsaw Pact headed by the Soviet Union – emerged as two major global forces. They were called the **superpowers** because of their global military and economic strength that at that time could not be matched by other states. Several times during this period the world was on the brink of a global war. Fortunately, every time the Soviet Union and the United States were able to find a way to avoid it. The Cold War was also a period of massive nuclear arms buildup. In the 1950s the United States maintained a policy of massive nuclear retaliation against the Soviet Union should it attack America or its allies in Europe. From the 1960s and later both the Soviet Union and the United States realized that they had reached strategic parity in terms of the quality and quantity of their nuclear weapons. Yet the massive nuclear arms race continued (Zubok, 2007).

One of the most dramatic events of recent history, which brought the world to the brink of a nuclear confrontation, took place in October 1962. The **Caribbean Crisis**, as Russians tend to call it (in British and American sources it is called the Cuban Missile Crisis), unfolded after Moscow secretly deployed nuclear missiles in Cuba. In response Washington imposed a naval blockade of the island, preventing all vessels going to Cuba from landing there. Soon the leaders from both sides realized how easily a rapid escalation of a regional conflict could turn into a nuclear war. The Soviet and American leaders chose negotiations instead. This conflict was resolved, but both sides realized that negotiations bring better results if they are held from a position of strength. The nuclear arms race continued along with negotiations.

During the 1960s and 1970s the United States and the Soviet Union (along with a few other countries) signed several pacts, including the 1963 Treaty on Partial Banning of Nuclear Tests; the 1968 Treaty on the Nonproliferation of Nuclear Weapons; and the 1972 Convention on Banning the Development, Production, and Accumulation of Stocks of Biological Weapons and on Their Destruction. Several steps were made to curb the strategic arms race. In 1972 the USSR and the United States signed the Anti-Ballistic Missile Treaty (supplemented by the 1974 Protocol) and the Interim Agreement on Offensive Arms, which was developed into the 1979 Treaty on the Limitation of Strategic Arms (also known as SALT).

Both countries' leaders recognized the importance of a continuous dialogue. Summits between the Soviet and American heads of states – and there were about twenty of those during the Cold War – became regular. Among the most productive were the meetings that took place between 1972 and 1975 and between 1987 and 1991. After the 1962 Cuban Missile Crisis the White House and the Kremlin established a direct telephone line. It has been regularly used in difficult and critical international situations.

Spheres of influence

On the basis of the agreements in Yalta and Potsdam (1945), the Soviet Union and the United States gradually established their **zones of influence** (often called spheres of influence). These are specific geographical regions and countries over which a state claims (formally or informally) political, military, economic, and cultural exclusivity. In practical terms, if a state establishes such zones of influence, other states usually do not interfere in the affairs of countries in the designated spheres. The Soviet zone of influence included Central and Eastern Europe as well as some Asian states such as Mongolia and North Korea. The United States traditionally considered both North and South America and Western Europe as its spheres of influence. However, throughout the Cold War fierce competition continued between the United States and the Soviet Union for influence in Africa and Asia. Moscow at different times actively supported the governments in Laos, Angola, Mozambique, Syria, Libya, Ethiopia, South Yemen, and several other countries. Moscow was actively pursuing friendly relations with any country that declared nonalliance during the Cold War. One of them was India. Washington during the same period pursued strategic relations with Pakistan – India's major rival. Establishing good relations with India and thus challenging America's strategies in Asia was a major foreign policy strategy of the Soviet Union.

Despite formal agreements and robust diplomatic interactions, Washington and Moscow continued their global competition and used almost every noticeable development, every international conflict as an opportunity to put pressure on each other. The United States provided military and financial aid to the countries and political groups that resisted Moscow's policies. The Soviet Union tried to check the United States' advances as well and supported almost any government that refused to support American policies or expressed lukewarm attitudes toward Washington. The principle "an enemy of my enemy is my friend" was used by both countries throughout the Cold War. For example, the 1979–1989 Soviet invasion of Afghanistan (during the civil war) served as an apparent and legitimate cause for Washington to support the local and regional armed resistance against the Soviets (Brzezinski, 1980). Washington launched a proxy war against Moscow and started sending electronic equipment, guns, ammunition, and anti-aircraft rockets to the Afghani resistance – *the mujahidin.* Years later many of them turned their arms against the United States and the international coalition deployed in Afghanistan after 2001.

The election of president Reagan, a devout anticommunist, in 1980 resulted in Washington's increasing military pressure on the Soviet Union. The deployment of American medium-range missiles in Western Europe (in response to a similar deployment by the Soviets on their territory) signaled the beginning of a new phase of a dangerous nuclear buildup. Reagan's plans to create an effective, space-based, antimissile defense system (known as the Strategic Defense Initiative or SDI) forced the Soviet Union to make its own plans for a similar, computer-based defensive system to counter America's SDI. However, in the 1980s the Soviet Union was already lacking the necessary financial, economic, technological, and scientific resources to implement these plans.

Ideological battles

A major area of the Cold War's battles was ideology. Both countries, the elites and ordinary people alike, saw each other as principal rivals in the sphere of ideas. America believed that it was defending the free world from the "evil empire" (the term coined by Reagan and attached to the Soviet Union). This evil empire, according to America's books and printed and broadcast media, was spreading dangerous communist ideology targeting capitalism and civil liberties on a global scale. The Soviets, through the lenses of their education and media, generally saw America as a belligerent, imperialist, inhumane, and expansionist state. As a matter of policy Soviet leaders historically supported communist, socialist, left-wing, and anticolonial parties around the world. On the other hand, any political party's anticommunist position almost guaranteed support from Washington.

While stressing (after the death of Stalin in 1953) the importance of a peaceful coexistence with the West, Moscow has never has given up the belief that global ideological battles must continue. As you should remember from earlier chapters, Soviet ideology was rooted in the basic ideas of Marxism-Leninism, which denounced private property and rejected capitalism, profit, and the market. Marxism emphasized the importance of state control over the economy and social life and attacked the basic political liberties of Western countries because they were seen as serving only the rich and powerful. All official documents of the Communist Party emphasized the belief that capitalism shouldn't have a future and that communism would eventually prevail in every region of the world. The old ideological belief in violent communist takeover has subsided. Communism, as a new set of principles proposed, could and should peacefully win over the hearts and minds of the world's population.

After the 1940s the Soviet leaders embraced the **Iron Curtain** policy – the term fashioned in the West to portray the Soviet Union's efforts to block its people (as well as the people from the satellite socialist states) from interacting with and getting information from capitalist countries. In fact, people's contacts with foreigners were not completely banned during the Cold War. Soviet citizens could travel overseas. However, tourist delegations to the West – the tours either organized or permitted by the Communist Party – were few and far between. The United States was a country that was especially difficult to visit for an ordinary Soviet citizen. As you should remember from earlier chapters, Soviet radio, television, and newspapers were under complete control of the government. The media maintained an anti-Western and anti-American agenda, which the Communist Party directed. Washington did not idle either. In 1947 the **Voice of America (VOA)** – the official external broadcast institution of the United States – began its shortwave radio broadcasts to the Soviet Union. Soviet security authorities responded to the VOA's regular programs by starting electronic jamming of the radio signals coming from the West. This was a difficult and a very expensive task, as it turned out. Moscow contributed significant funds and human resources to block foreign "voices" and strengthen domestic censorship. The main fortified line of ideological defense was built to resist the United States and its Western allies. However, with the rapid proliferation of technologies later in the twentieth century, the task of blocking information was becoming increasingly difficult to implement (Shiraev and Zubok, 2000).

Relations in other areas

After Stalin's death Khrushchev's strategic goal was the Soviet Union's economic success achieved in direct competition with the United States. He wanted to catch up and then surpass America in economic production and labor efficiency. He believed that the Soviet Union would soon produce consumer products of the highest quality and design. However, these goals were practically unachievable. The country had neither the financial nor organizational potential necessary for massive technological innovations and sustainable economic growth. The Soviet Union was steadily falling behind the United States and the West in the development of major modern technologies, including computers. The quality of most Soviet-made consumer goods was dismal.

Could the Soviets ask for economic help from the West? Could the West offer assistance? Perhaps. Yet it was practically impossible, as it seems from today's perspective. Moscow and Washington did not eagerly facilitate their trade relations generally for political reasons. The leaders of the Soviet Union did not want to become dependent on Western technologies and products. Washington did not want to support and advance the Soviet economy and political system either. Moscow believed it could overcome its economic difficulties. After all, the Soviet Union had massive natural resources, including oil and gas on whose sale the Soviet Union relied for many years. Yet after 1981 global oil prices began to decline, which drastically reduced Moscow's financial resources. Besides, the management of the economy was grossly inefficient.

The Cold War between the Soviet Union and the United States continued in the field of science and education. The Soviets had very limited access to American research publications. Bilateral contacts between teachers, students, and researchers were infrequent. In the 1970s the father of one of this book's authors (he was a Soviet researcher and geologist) published a book in the United States without any direct contact with his coauthor (they met many years later, in the 1980s). Perhaps a notable exception to the realities of the Cold War was the **Fulbright Program**, a competitive, merit-based system of grants for international educational and research exchange between the United States and other countries. Such exchange programs use the Fulbright's grants given to students, scientists, artists, and other professionals. Every year dozens of American scholars and students visited the Soviet Union and remained there for weeks and even months doing research, lecturing, and studying. A few Soviets visited the United States as Fulbright scholars as well.

Another highlight of Soviet-American cooperation was the joint space program, highly publicized in the Soviet Union, called The Apollo-Soyuz Test Project (ASTP), which culminated after months of training in the first joint US-Soviet space flight in 1975. Some American consumer products did reach the homes of ordinary Soviet citizens. For example, Pepsi-Cola built large production facilities in the Soviet Union, and the first Pepsi bottling factory was opened in Novorossi-ysk in 1974. In the 1980, months before the summer Olympic Games in Moscow (which most Western countries ultimately boycotted, to protest the Soviet invasion of Afghanistan), American cigarettes appeared in Soviets stores. But these examples were exceptions. The government in Moscow exercised a bureaucratic monopoly on purchasing foreign goods, and ideology was the key reason (besides the lack of funds) why American and Western products were unavailable in the Soviet Union. Yet even if we imagine for a second that they were available, most Soviet people could not have afforded them.

The Gorbachev factor

In previous chapters we have already discussed the importance of individuals, their visions and specific actions, in domestic and foreign policy. After Gorbachev came to power in 1985 and proposed his new strategies for the country (see Chapter 2), Moscow and Washington signed several agreements including the Intermediate-Range Nuclear Forces Treaty (INF, 1987), which proposed total elimination of these forces by both sides, and later the Strategic Arms Reduction Treaty (START, 1991) pro-viding for the first time a process of reduction of strategic arsenals. This period of easing tensions and the development of mutual understanding between the USSR and the United States played an important role in the success of the 1986 Stockholm Conference on Confidence and Security Building Measures and Disarmament in Europe. The 1990 Treaty on Conventional Forces in Europe drastically reduced both countries' military presence in Europe and established a mechanism of con-sultations and dialogue. (In 2015, however, Russia halted its participation in this treaty, referring to the fact that most European countries did not ratify it and that the mechanism of mutual consultation was no longer useful.)

Soviet troops, as you should remember, left Afghanistan in 1989. Moscow stopped supporting leftist insurgencies around the world. The Kremlin played an important role in the reunification of Germany in 1990 and did not interfere in the internal affairs of allied socialist countries undergoing significant political changes in the late 1980s. Communist parties eventually lost their grip on power in Central Europe. The White House welcomed these foreign policy outcomes as well as the democratic changes in the Soviet Union, all of which reinforced mutual trust between the two countries.

Important changes also took place in ideology. Gorbachev abandoned Marxism as an official ideology of the Soviet Union; the country was now turning to liberal polit-ical values and capitalism. The tone of the American leaders' comments changed as well: the "evil empire" label was no longer in use. In the spheres of business, science, and education both countries experienced a short yet remarkable period of curiosity, shared interest, respect, and cooperation. Mutual visits of scholars, teach-ers, and engineers were frequent. In 1989, when Mikhail Gorbachev and President

George H. W. Bush had a summit in Malta, the countries no longer regarded each other as rivals. In effect, that was the end of the Cold War (Zubok, 2007). The late 1980s was perhaps the best period in US-Russia relations in all areas.

Russian-American relations before 1991: The stages

During the Cold War Soviet-American relations played the most essential role in international politics. Since the disintegration of the Soviet Union, though, these relations lost their global significance, and America emerged as the sole global superpower. Russia, on the other hand, had to adjust to a new role and a new position in international relations. This adjustment process was uneasy and full of twists and contradictions. It continues today.

Several periods in Russian-US relations emerged (see Table 7.1, which briefly describes them).

During the first period, from 1991 to approximately 1993, Russia and the United States

- declared their willingness to build their bilateral relations in a spirit of partnership and friendship;
- supported a policy of demilitarization of their relations;
- reaffirmed earlier agreements to reduce nuclear arms;
- pledged cooperation in settling international conflicts;
- attempted to move their economic relations into the domain of the free market;
- stopped sponsoring media propaganda campaigns against each other;
- promoted a wide range of interpersonal contacts between individuals and organizations (both government and NGOs).

During the next stage, lasting from 1993 to the end of 1999 and early 2000, a few conflicting patterns in these countries' mutual relations have emerged. Among them were

- institutionalization of the bilateral dialogue through the intergovernmental Gore-Chernomyrdin Commission (Al Gore was US vice president; Victor - Chernomyrdin was Russia's prime minister);

Table 7.1 The five periods of Russian-US relations after 1991

Period	Description
1991–1993	Friendly mutual relations and cooperation based on trust
1993–2000	Friendly yet lukewarm mutual relations
2000–2008	Fluctuation: Cooperation in some and competition in other areas
2008–2012	Fluctuation: Competition in some and cooperation in other areas
2012–	Competition and tensions; cooperation in few areas

- expansion of cooperation in business, education, culture, and other areas;
- growing disagreements about NATO's expansion and the armed conflict in the countries of the former Yugoslavia;
- growing criticism in Washington of Russia's domestic policies that were seen as antidemocratic and influenced by corruption;
- considerable deterioration of US-Russian relations coinciding with the 1998 financial crisis in Russia and the Kosovo crisis of 1999.

The third stage was from 2000 to approximately 2008. During this period President Putin spent his first two terms in office. This period was characterized by fluctuations in US-Russian bilateral relations the key features of which were

- Russia's joining the antiterrorism coalition and supporting the United States' operations in Afghanistan in 2001;
- continuing business and economic relations;
- the United States' formal withdrawal from the 1972 Anti-Ballistic Missile Treaty (Washington intended the development of a new antimissile defense system, which was seen as being incompatible with the 1972 treaty);
- Moscow's opposition to this decision by Washington;
- the emergence of a powerful nationalist trend among the ruling elites and in Russia's public opinion (caused in part by (1) the perceived actions of Washington around the world, such as the 2003 Iraq invasion, and (2) the increased assertiveness of the Russian government in both domestic and foreign affairs);
- Russia's marked displeasure with the alleged role of the United States in popular revolts (called "color revolutions" in Russian sources) in Georgia, Ukraine, and Kyrgyzstan.

The fourth stage, lasting from 2008 to 2012 (the presidency of Dmitry Medvedev), was also marked by considerable fluctuations, although several positive trends in both countries' relations reemerged. The main features of this period were

- a growing strategic belief among the ruling circles in Russia that the 2008 global financial and economic crisis would inevitably end America's global economic and political domination;
- Russia's growing anticipation that one of the outcomes of this crisis would be Russia's strengthening as well as its accession to global power status;
- a sharp deterioration in bilateral relations caused by Russia's role in the war in Georgia in 2008 and the United States' condemnation of Moscow's actions in and around Georgia;
- an attempt to "reset" US-Russian relations under US Secretary of State Hillary Clinton in 2009;
- further development of business and trade relations;
- Russia's growing concerns with, as Moscow saw them, the United States' and NATO's attempts to "encircle" Russia and sponsor "regime changes" in many countries.

The fifth stage, which began in 2012 and continues to this day, is characterized by a worsening of Russian-American relations. This was evident from

- the weakening of institutional and diplomatic links between the two countries;
- persistent anti-Russian and anti-American rhetoric in statements of public officials and leading commentators in both countries;
- explicit disagreements about Crimea and the conflict in Ukraine;
- deterioration in business and economic relations as well a major decline in educational and cultural contacts;
- the suspension of arms control negotiations (since the Cuban Missile Crisis of 1962 up to 2010 such negotiations had been suspended only once, during the tense period in mutual relations between 1982 and 1984);
- the political and diplomatic drama based on Washington's belief that Russia interfered in the 2016 US presidential elections and arguments about a "collusion" between Trump and Putin back in 2016, which has been denied by both sides;
- sharp disagreements about the conflict in Syria and each country's role in the conflict.

Now we will critically discuss these stages as well as the specific features of Russian-US relations in some detail. This discussion is important: to understand the events of today, one needs a better understanding of the past.

Russian-American relations after 1991: Key features

The 1990s: A honeymoon

Washington supported the birth of a new Russian state and cheered the creation of fourteen other new independent states that emerged after the collapse of the Soviet Union. Russia and the United States started a new phase in their relations. It was difficult to imagine a better start. Many specialists in Russia considered the United States as the most successful model of political, social, and economic development, the one that Russia could and should follow. They also expected that the United States would offer significant assistance – something similar to the Marshall Plan of the 1940s. Russian people now could freely travel overseas (they still had to apply for visas to visit Europe or the United States, but the Soviet system of exit permits to leave the country was gone). Russians could possess foreign currency. Some federal ministries and institutions in Russia turned to foreign advisers in the hope of learning from them about the market economy and democratic governance. According to opinion polls, Russia in the early 1990s was one of the world's most pro-American countries (Shiraev and Zubok, 2000).

In 1992 President Boris Yeltsin visited the United States. It was a historic visit. Both sides confirmed that they no longer regarded themselves adversaries. They were prepared to establish a new type of relations rooted in partnership. In 1992 Moscow and Washington signed the Charter of Russian-American Partnership and Friendship. The document formalized the readiness of Russia and the United States to cooperate, strengthen peace and security globally, and promote exchanges in the fields of economy, science, technology, culture, and education. The United States reiterated its support for the Russian reforms and promised assistance in restructuring Russia's military industry. Both countries wanted to overcome the negative consequences of the Cold War. Although in November 1992 many in the Russian leadership were surprised by the victory of the young candidate Bill Clinton over the incumbent President George Bush (with whom Russians had established a very productive relationship), the overall atmosphere in Moscow in regard to strengthening Russian-American ties remained very positive.

Russia was the USSR's legal successor. Russia assumed all the Soviet obligations arising from previously concluded international agreements. The Strategic Arms Reduction Treaty signed in July 1991 (when the Soviet Union still existed) mentioned the strategic arms located in four republics: Russia, Ukraine, Belarus, and Kazakhstan. The United States acted as an intermediary during the transfer of the nuclear weapons under Russia's control. A new agreement, START II (Strategic Arms Reduction Treaty), was signed in January 1993. It offered new reductions in strategic arms, including intercontinental ballistic missiles with multiple independently targetable warheads.

At the end of 1991 the US Congress approved the Cooperative Threat Reduction Program, better known as the Nunn-Lugar Program (after the names of the two US Senators who sponsored the bill). According to this program, the United States provided CIS countries (including Russia) with funds to eliminate weapons of mass destruction, to facilitate the conversion of defense industries, and to develop contacts with the United States in military areas. In June 1992 a seven-year agreement was signed between the United States and Russia to provide security for transportation of nuclear weapons for their storage and destruction. Washington was to provide the equipment, services, and expertise for this project (Nunn-Lugar Program, 1991). The newly elected Senator Barack Obama went to Russia as a participant in this program. About 20 years later Russia discontinued it.

Because of the joint efforts of Russia and the United States, the UN General Assembly approved the Convention on the Prohibition of the Development, Production, Stockpiling and Use of Chemical Weapons and on Their Destruction. The Soviet Union over the years had stockpiled massive arsenals of chemical weapons. Their liquidation was a measure of the utmost importance. The United States agreed to finance the destruction of some of the Russian chemical stockpiles within the framework of the Nunn-Lugar Program (1991). Overall, within a relatively short period Russia and the United States were able to halt the arms race and move toward disarmament.

Furthermore, the positions of Russia and the United States on many international issues became noticeably close. In the UN Security Council and other international organizations both countries voted the same way. Russia folded its relations with North Korea, a country that maintained an anti-American foreign policy. The massive propaganda campaigns supported by both governments and orchestrated by the media during the Cold War were over. New agreements were planned for cooperation in business, science, culture, and education. The US Freedom Support Act of 1992 played a very positive role in bilateral contacts. The program sponsored several hundred Russian schoolchildren to attend American schools for expended periods. American charity organizations started delivering different forms of humanitarian aid, including food supplies and medications, to the most impoverished Russian cities.

In April 1993 the first summit between Yeltsin and Clinton took place in Vancouver. Both presidents signed several important agreements. The positive relations between the two leaders received institutional support: a bilateral commission was formed under the chairmanship of Vice President Al Gore and the Russian Prime Minister Victor Chernomyrdin. Clinton supported Yeltsin during the October 1993 political crisis in Moscow. America considered the results of the 1993 Constitutional Referendum in Russia as legitimate (Chapter 2).

The Vancouver agreements gave a new impulse to Russian-American relations. Washington helped Russia in obtaining loans through the International Monetary Fund. President Clinton also lobbied for the inclusion of Russia in the G7 Group, which was an informal bloc of developed democracies and economic powers comprising the United States, Canada, France, Germany, Italy, Japan, and the United Kingdom. They met annually to discuss international security and coordinate their economic and other policies. Yeltsin took part in the Denver meeting in 1997 for discussion of political, though not economic, problems. President Clinton pushed for the expansion of the G7 Group (to make it the G8, despite some other countries' objections) to help Russia in building its international prestige, bring it closer to the West, and boost Yeltsin's domestic image (Group of Seven, 2015).

Problems emerge

The White House was pleased with Yeltsin's victory in the 1996 presidential elections in Russia despite a few warning signs indicating that many liberal reformers and supporters of pro-Western policies were losing their positions in the top echelons of power in Moscow. In the second half of the 1990s the balance of power within the ruling elites in Russia began to change. Massive American aid – which was eagerly anticipated in Moscow – did not materialize. The transition to a market economy, which was initially hailed with great enthusiasm, did not bring noticeable economic and social improvements. The gap between the rich and the rest of the country was widening.

NATO's decision to enlarge and include in 1999 three countries of the former Soviet block triggered a negative response in Russia. Many saw this expansion as orchestrated by the United States, despite its assurances about seeing and treating Russia as a friend, not a foe. Communists and nationalists now blamed the West for Russia's difficulties. Problems in mutual relations emerged. For example, the United States' Senate ratified the START II agreement in 1996. It took about four years for Russia to do so. Moscow then withdrew from the treaty in 2002 in response to the US departure from the ABM treaty. Russia and the United States disagreed about Iran's nuclear program: Moscow, unlike Washington, did not see Iran as having nuclear ambitions. Russia began openly improving its relations with the government of North Korea. Many in Moscow were now questioning the United

States' global dominance and calling for a new multipolar world structure (Shiraev and Zubok, 2000). The worsening of bilateral relations and the perceived problems with the Russian democratic process did not particularly encourage American lawmakers to revisit an old artifact of the Cold War: Russia had not yet received the status of most-favored nation in trade relations with America.

The Kosovo crisis of 1999 further aggravated Russian-American relations. Four years earlier, in 1995, the Dayton Agreement to end the war in Bosnia and Herzegovina had been signed. The United States and Russia became the international guarantors of the agreement. Russia had troops in Bosnia as a part of the international peacekeeping force. In Kosovo, however (the region was engulfed by a deadly ethnic conflict between Serbian and Albanian populations), NATO acted militarily to stop Serbian forces from launching a massive violent campaign against ethnic Albanians. Russia complained that the UN Security Council, where Russia had veto power, was not consulted. US and British planes bombed several targets in Serbia and the Serbian positions in Kosovo, thus providing support to Albanian separatist groups. The United States later supported the future independence of Kosovo. Russia did not. This disagreement would remain a serious source of tension between Moscow and Washington for years to come. The events in Kosovo gave additional ammunition to Russian nationalists who argued that Yeltsin and his government were too weak to conduct an independent foreign policy and to defend Russian allies such as Serbia (which at that time was ruled by a communist autocrat). Yeltsin's political position and public support inside Russia weakened. So did Russian-American cooperation. The 1999 incident at the Pristina airport in Kosovo was just a reflection of growing tensions between Russia and the West. For several days Russian troops occupied the airport ahead of a scheduled deployment of NATO troops there. Although this standoff between Russia and NATO ended peacefully, Moscow had demonstrated that it could act at will without consulting Washington or other Western powers. In a theatrical gesture the Kremlin handsomely awarded the military commander for his actions in Pristina.

New "Ups" and "Downs"

During the first two terms of the presidency of Vladimir Putin relations between the two countries went through major "ups" and "downs." A wide range of international and domestic developments contributed to these fluctuations. As you should remember from earlier chapters, in the late 1990s and early 2000s the Kremlin and the Russian media argued that the United States and the West treated Russia unfairly after the collapse of the Soviet Union. After a difficult period of consolidation, it was argued, Russia had reached a new stage of development that required the country's fresh and more assertive role in global affairs. Moscow persistently underlined that a sovereign state such as Russia had the right to conduct its independent foreign policy. It was an implicit criticism of America's dominant position in international affairs (Glad and Shiraev, 1999).

Both countries still wanted to build effective mutual relationships. Putin succeeded in persuading the Federal Assembly of Russia to ratify the START II treaty, which Boris Yeltsin had failed to do. President Bush met Putin for their first summit in Slovenia in 2001, and they established good personal relations. Yet Bush discontinued America's participation in the Gore-Chernomyrdin Commission. Bush, according to his plan, was cutting unnecessary layers of bureaucracy. Russia saw this development differently, as a sign of Washington's fading interest in Russia.

The reaction of the top Russian officials to the terrorist acts against the United States in 2001 was quick and supportive. On September 11 Putin made a brief televised statement in which called the acts "barbaric." He sent a message to George W. Bush to express sympathy to the American people and to say that the attacks must not go unpunished. Putin ordered flags to be lowered and a moment of silence to be observed throughout Russia at noon Moscow time on September 13. On that day Putin held a telephone conversation with Bush to discuss joint actions. Russia joined the antiterrorism coalition and made a statement pledging support of the NATO operation in Afghanistan and readiness to help – just short of sending troops there. Russia also supported the creation of American temporary air bases in Uzbekistan and Kyrgyzstan to help America with a supply line to Afghanistan. In the fall of 2001 the Russian public, according to polls, was very supportive of the American people (Shlapentokh, Woods, and Shiraev, 2005).

Relations between Russia and NATO were improving as well, as evidenced by the 2002 Rome agreement. The NATO-Russia Council was created as an official diplomatic institution for coordinating joint security, personnel training, fighting international terrorism, and other projects between NATO and Russia. Russia also toned down for a while its criticism of the ongoing NATO enlargement. Russia became a full-fledged member of the G7 Group, now G8. Moscow closed its military surveillance facility at Lourdes (Cuba) and a naval base in Kamran (Vietnam). In 2002 the United States officially revoked the Anti-Ballistic Missile Treaty (again, Washington believed the treaty limited its ability to develop new defensive anti-missile systems.) Yet in 2002 both countries signed the Strategic Offensive Reductions Treaty (SORT), which was in place until 2011. Moscow and Washington also agreed to limit operationally deployed nuclear warheads.

The 2003 war in Iraq, unlike the 2001 invasion of Afghanistan, provoked fierce criticism in Russia. Moscow criticized Washington for acting unilaterally, without UN Security Council approval. Russia also objected to the decision in the United States to build a new ballistic missile defense system in Europe. American officials explained this as a necessary measure to protect the West from any surprise missile attack coming from Iran. Russia disagreed. It believed that this proposed defense system was designed to weaken Moscow's capability to respond to an attack should it come from NATO. Such a disagreement is an illustration of the constructivist approach to international relations: two international actors viewing a fact or a development from different positions – reflecting their strategic views of international politics.

Russian government elites did not like what they believed was America's intrusion into the internal affairs of former Soviet republics. The revolutionary events in Georgia (2003), Ukraine (2004), and Kyrgyzstan (2005) appeared to Moscow to be sponsored by Western governments and nongovernmental organizations acting (allegedly) on behalf of the West. President Bush in 2005 visited Georgia – a country from the post-Soviet era that was seemingly moving into the Western orbit. The Bush administration also increased its criticisms of Russia's foreign policy. In a speech in Lithuania in 2006 Vice President Dick Cheney criticized Russia's energy policy, portraying it as antagonistic and unfair toward Russia's neighbors. Russia was criticized for behaving like a bully toward some countries (such as Ukraine) and maintaining cozy relations with countries conducting anti-American policies (such as Iran and Venezuela).

The United States stepped up its criticisms of Russia's domestic policies, including increased Russian government control over the mass media and NGOs. The case of the billionaire Mikhail Khodorkovsky is salient, because he was perhaps the most prominent Russian businessman to be given a lengthy prison sentence based on multiple charges of tax fraud and other financial violations. Khodorkovsky's key asset – the company named Yukos, one of the largest energy companies in the world at that time – was forced into bankruptcy and then was taken over by companies controlled by the government. No compensation was paid to American and international shareholders, including pension funds, which suffered around $8 billion in losses (Cohen, 2012). Most Western watch groups considered the Khodorkovsky case as politically motivated (he had been increasingly involved in politics and sponsored several groups and parties opposed to Putin). In 2013, before the Winter Olympics in Sochi, Putin pardoned Khodorkovsky, who immediately left Russia and remained a vocal critic of Putin's policies.

Despite worsening relations in the political field, useful contacts between Russia and the United States still developed in the business area. Exports of Russian oil into the United States increased. Three Russian industrial giants, the oil concern Lukoil, the steel company Severstal, and the nickel company Norilsky Nikel, continued their business cooperation with American companies and strengthened their positions on US markets. Some American companies were increasing their investments in Russia. In 2005 the United States was Russia's sixth biggest foreign investor. During Putin's first term in office Russia, due to the profits from oil revenues, started purchasing United States' Treasury bonds as well as investing in America's currency (Russia was also buying Euros and British pounds). In 2006 Russia and the United States agreed on almost all conditions allowing Russia to enter the World Trade Organization. Special agreements were signed about the protection of intellectual property, agricultural technologies, and trade in farming products. Russian-American contacts were also developing in the fields of science, culture, and education. Joint space projects, such as the **International Space Station (ISS)**, received global publicity. ISS is a space research laboratory (the largest human-made body in low Earth orbit), a joint project that began in 1998. It involves a multibillion-dollar budget as well as several space agencies in the United States and Russia. Both countries agreed to sponsor this program until 2024 (Foust, 2015).

Yet a few warning signs already suggested even deeper tensions looming in US-Russia bilateral relations. In February 2007, as you should remember, Putin delivered a historic speech at an international conference in Munich on security policy, which most Western experts considered the symbolic beginning of a long-term confrontation between Moscow and the West (Putin, 2007). He sharply criticized the unipolar model of the world and the role of Washington in it. Putin called the continuing NATO expansion "a serious provocation" that diminished mutual trust between Russia and the West. He accused the West of building new dividing lines and walls. He also called for a new "reasonable balance" among the interests of all countries in the international dialogue, thus critically referring to US dominance in global affairs. Putin also promised that Russia would carry out an "independent foreign policy" to ensure security and prosperity "not only for a select few, but for all." In this critical context, he blasted international organizations for working on behalf of a few dominant countries. He certainly meant that one of these dominant countries was the United States (Putin, 2007).

The "Reset"

President Dmitry Medvedev entered office in May 2008. The acute global financial crisis of that year and the following global economic crisis coincided with a short period of improvements in Russian-American relations. Yet significant difficulties persisted. Despite the poor economic forecast for Russia, in 2009 the ruling elite in Moscow still blithely believed that Russia would come out of the global crisis strengthened, while the United States and the European Union would be weakened. Some even believed that a new economic world order was in the making, the order in which Russia and other BRICS countries (China, Brazil, etc.) would very soon play a central role in global affairs. This did not happen.

Relations between Russia and NATO suddenly deteriorated again in 2008 as a consequence of Russia's war against Georgia. Russia, as you should remember, accused Georgia of being an aggressor and intervened in a conflict between Georgia and South Ossetia. The United States and its allies saw this conflict differently and sided with Georgia. The United States criticized Russia for recognizing the breakaway Georgian regions of South Ossetia and Abkhazia. For the first time after the end of the Cold War Washington was openly supporting a country involved in a military conflict with Russia.

Yet soon after Barack Obama was elected president in 2008 he spoke in favor of improving relations with Russia. Washington viewed Medvedev as a new-generation politician, more a pragmatic technocrat than an ideologue. In the summer of 2009 Barack Obama and Dmitry Medvedev agreed to chair a new government commission on bilateral relations (modeled on the Gore-Chernomyrdin commission). The commission had sixteen working groups in charge of a range of issues from economic cooperation to the advancement of a civil society. One of Medvedev's signature domestic strategies was "modernization" (especially technological), and now it appeared that a robust partnership with America should facilitate Russia's technological developments. In 2010 the **New Start Treaty** was signed.

It was an agreement on measures for the further reduction and limitation of strategic offensive arms. Moscow and Washington agreed to limit their strategic nuclear weapons to 1,550 nuclear warheads by 2017. The treaty also cut the number of strategic nuclear missile launchers by half. That was an important step in bilateral relations and a promising development related to global nuclear security. No progress, however, was achieved in the matter of antiballistic missile defense. Although President Obama announced that he would scale back the development of the new ballistic missile defense system in Europe proposed by President Bush, Russia did not see that policy change as meaningful enough.

Russia and the United States continued supporting nuclear nonproliferation. Both countries condemned the announced nuclear tests in North Korea in 2006 and 2009, and neither Moscow nor Washington wanted to see Iran developing nuclear weapons. At the same time, Russia continued helping Iran in constructing a nuclear power plant in Bushehr, claiming it was meant only to fulfill Iran's energy needs. Russia also opposed what Moscow saw as harsh sanctions that the United States and its allies were imposing on North Korea and Iran. Moscow believed that the potential for negotiations had not been exhausted yet. (Moscow later agreed and voted at the UN Security Council for imposing sanctions against Iran and North Korea.)

Washington and Moscow continued their cooperation in counterterrorist policies and regarded Al-Qaeda and other terrorist groups as major threats to international security. Russia welcomed the killing of Osama Bin Laden in 2011 but insisted that only joint international efforts in the future could produce tangible results in fighting terrorism (CNN, 2011). The two countries, however, differed in their views of the events of the **Arab Spring** – a series of uprisings that spread across the Arab world in 2010–2011 and involved Tunisia, Egypt, Libya, Syria, Yemen, Jordan, and Bahrain. The position of Moscow was that America and the West were somehow behind (directly or through financial support and political maneuvering) these uprisings. Initially Russia did not oppose the 2011 international military campaign involving the Arab League and NATO against Libya. The violent death of its leader, Muammar Gaddafi, had a significant impact on Russia's political elites. Putin – who served as Prime Minister at that time – was very critical of a discussion in Western media that Russia's elites might some day follow the same path as Libya's leader (CNN, 2011a). Russia gave support to the government of Bashar al-Assad in Syria, which had been Russia's long-time ally, to keep him in power. In 2015 Russia entered the conflict militarily on the side of Al-Assad whose forces were fighting multiple opposition groups within his country, including ISIS militants.

Human rights and civil liberties still remained a key problem in relations between Washington and Moscow. The United States paid attention to the Moscow public protests after Duma elections in 2011 and accused the Russian police of suppressing the demonstrations in May of 2012. The West was also critical about what was perceived as the increased attacks on civil rights in Russia and the empowerment of security institutions vis-à-vis corruption, censorship of the independent press, and the widespread harassment of political opposition. The Russian government rejected these accusations. From the official point of view, the protests were limited and largely inspired (even provoked) by the American Embassy and several pro-Western NGOs. However, in 2017, when the opposition organized a series of anticorruption demonstrations in Moscow and other cities, the Kremlin did not find any signs of foreign influence (Peskov, 2017). Yet in January 2018 Russian officials again accused the American Embassy of supporting the opposition.

Opinion polls that measure Russian people's views of the United States (professional polling began in the early 1990s when independent survey companies emerged) show at least two general trends. One is a decline in favorable opinions about America over almost three decades – from mostly supportive in the early 1990s to mostly critical in the twenty-first century. The other trend is the ambivalence of Russians toward the United States; polls show several periods of rapid worsening of opinions toward America. For example, trends in opinion polls since 1990 show at least four major declines: in 1999, 2003, 2008, and 2014. All these changes have been linked to four major international developments about which Moscow and Washington (and the West) had profoundly opposite opinions, such as NATO's airstrikes against Serbia, the US invasion of Iraq, Russia's war with Georgia, and Moscow's annexation of Crimea (Smeltz et al., 2016).

Russian-American relations after 2012

The period after 2012 when Putin returned to power as president was characterized by a serious deterioration in Russian-American relations. Disagreements and tensions between the governments of these two nations intensified on a wide range of issues.

In recent years most Russians have held negative views toward the United States, a shift from 2014 (before the events in and around Crimea), when more than four out of ten Russia had positive feelings toward the United States. (See Table 7.2 for opinions about the United States in Russia from 2014 to 2018.) In the past several years opinion polls have shown that Russians generally disapprove of Washington's handling of international affairs. In 2016 more than two-thirds of Russians believed that their country should focus on limiting US power and influence (68 percent), and only 32 percent trusted in cooperation with the United States. More than half of Russians thought that Washington's ambitions to exert control over other countries was a critical threat to Russia (Smeltz et al., 2016). Opinions began to change in 2017 and later: more Russians saw America positively: in 2016, for instance, only 23 percent of Russians maintained a good image of the United States; in 2018 this number rose to 41 percent (Levada, 2018e). At the same time, about 40 percent of Russians maintained a negative view of the United States, down from 65 percent in 2016.

The polling data from the 2016 and 2017 Chicago Council Survey and the Levada Analytical Center in Russia – both these organizations are nonpartisan and independently funded – show that mutual perceptions between Russians and Americans were at their lowest levels since the Cold War ended in the early 1990s. In 2017 only a quarter of Russians expressed a favorable opinion of the USA

Table 7.2 How do you, in general, feel about the United States?

	2014	2016	2017	2018
Very Good	2	2	2	3
Mostly Good	41	21	35	39
Mostly Bad	36	39	40	28
Very Bad	8	26	16	12
Don't Know	13	13	16	18

Source: Created using Levada, 2017, 2018e

(24 percent) and 60 percent unfavorable, similar to opinions in 2016. Among those Russians who thought their country had enemies (66 percent), about half mentioned the United States as an enemy. While there were shared concerns about global threats, the surveys also revealed mutual distrust. Russians expressed their insecurity about US strength and power and wanted their country to limit Washington's international influence. Although most Americans believed that Russia was acting to keep US power in check, the US public still favored collaboration and engagement rather than a confrontation with Russia. Only 31 percent of Russians thought that their own country tried to influence the domestic affairs in the United States. Overall, at least seven in ten Americans thought that Russia tried to influence the domestic affairs of the United States and that Russia is actively working to undermine US international status and influence (74 percent) (Smeltz, Wojtowicz, and Goncharov, 2018). Surveys also showed that experts in both countries maintained that both sides – and both presidents – were responsible for the strained relationship (Smeltz et al., 2018).

Russians tend to believe that Washington's policies over the years were an important cause of many of Russia's economic and social problems, ranging from the collapse of the Soviet Union in 1991 to the financial crisis of the late 1990s, or from the large popular anti-Putin protests in Moscow in 2011 and 2012 to the major economic slowdown in 2015–2018. The common narrative was that the United States was behind the "color revolutions" across the post-Soviet world (the name for popular uprisings against corrupt governments in post-Soviet states; people during these chose specific colors for their ribbons and flags for self-identification) and in Georgia and Ukraine to change governments there, create friendly regimes, and (most importantly) to undermine Putin's hold on power in Moscow (Yaffa, 2016).

Several issues remained very important for US-Russian relations. The 2012 **Magnitsky Act** had a special significance; this was a bipartisan bill passed by the US Congress and signed by President Obama to penalize Russian officials believed to be responsible for the death of Russian lawyer Sergei Magnitsky in a Moscow prison back in 2009. The case was singled out to make a statement of Washington's disapproval of the ongoing harassment and discrimination of political opposition and the individuals who dared to go public and revealed examples of massive government corruption in Russia. The Russian government rejected the accusations and considered this Act as an interference in Russia's domestic affairs. Almost immediately, at the end of 2012, as an act of retaliation, the State Duma banned the international adoption of Russian children in the United States and imposed a travel ban to Russia on a number of US officials. Later another important bill was passed forcing nongovernmental organizations with foreign (including US) funding to register in Russia as "foreign agents" and thus make themselves vulnerable to additional and substantial financial scrutiny.

The **Snowden case** has also played a very negative role in Russian-US relations. Edward Snowden is an American computer professional, formerly employed by the CIA, who in 2013 illegally copied and leaked classified information from the National Security Agency. By doing this, he revealed massive domestic surveillance programs managed by the US government. These programs were in place as part of counter terrorism policies. Snowden, who fled the United States, was charged with espionage and theft of government property. He received temporary asylum status in Russia (it may have changed by the time you read these pages). Although Snowden's actions sparked a major international debate about national security and individual privacy, the United States was very critical of Russia's cozy relations with Snowden and Moscow's approval of his status as an asylum seeker.

The Russian government and the media have stepped up the anti-American campaign, reaching at times Cold-War levels in terms of the methods and the scope of the information and arguments used (Shiraev and Zubok, 2000). For example, the Russian Foreign Ministry issued several reports criticizing the United States for violating the rights of American citizens. The Russian Central Electoral Committee published a paper about the American electoral system being essentially undemocratic (mainly, as it was argued, due to the United States' use of the electoral college to elect presidents). Russia's television networks continued their relentless attacks of America's policies. President Putin published a critical article in the *New York Times* (Putin, 2013; Murray, 2013). American commentators on major television networks turned to criticism of Russia as well. Social networks became a new domain for confrontation.

At that time, Russia stepped up its attempts (you should remember from Chapter 6) to build the Eurasian Union – an apparently new center in the emerging – in Russia's view – polycentric world. The United States saw these efforts differently. It perceived them as an opportunity to recreate the Soviet Union but in a new format (Clover, 2012). Both countries increasingly saw each other as competitors, both accused each other in aggressive intentions. The clearest sign of a crisis in Russian-American relations was the cancellation by Washington of the official presidential visit to Moscow in September 2013.

The most difficult problems between Russia and the United States emerged over the conflict in Ukraine and the incorporation of Crimea into the Russian Federation. Washington as well as European capitals supported the new government in Kiev, which had been put in place of the defunct administration headed by the fugitive president Yanukovich. The United States, as you know, condemned Russia's actions in Crimea, labeling them as an "annexation," which is the forceful transition of land from the control of one state to another. In March 2014 the United States imposed sanctions against several Russian senior officials and took steps to weaken Russia's positions in international organizations. As a symbolic yet powerful gesture, G7 resumed its meeting but without Russia. Moscow replied with defiance and introduced its own counter-sanctions against Western countries, including the United States. These sanctions included a ban on a range of agricultural and food products from Western countries. For years scores of products from Western countries disappeared from Russian supermarkets' aisles. Substantial problems remained in the area of nuclear arms control. Although both countries were implementing the agreements based on the 2010 treaty, any new initiatives related to disarmament suggestions have been shelved.

In 2016 Russia adopted Law FZ-318 (31 October), which underlined a few conditions for a potentially new stage of cooperation with the United States. Moscow wanted the suspension of the Magnitsky act (see earlier in this chapter). Russia also hoped for the suspension of the US Ukraine Freedom Support Act of 2014, which was designed, from Washington's view, to assist the government of Ukraine in restoring its sovereignty and territorial integrity. Washington also aimed at deterring the government of the Russian Federation from further destabilizing and invading Ukraine and other independent countries in Eastern Europe and Central Asia (Ukraine Freedom Support, 2014). Moscow also wanted the reduction of the United States' military presence in Europe as well as financial compensation from the West for the losses associated with the anti-Russian sanctions. Moscow also signaled that many arms control issues have no longer been its priority, at least for some time.

Russia's impact on the 2016 US elections

Russia played an unexpectedly noticeable role in the 2016 US presidential elections. American security experts and politicians alleged Moscow's deliberate cyber intrusion into the 2016 electoral process. The outgoing administration of President Barack Obama clearly stated that the Russian government had attempted to interfere in the elections. Several government sources including US intelligence suggested the reason for the intrusion: President Putin was supportive of Donald Trump and wanted Hillary Clinton to lose (Blake, 2017). The US government also stated that Russia orchestrated the hacking of emails of several political organizations of the Democratic Party. (The hackers allegedly could not or did not break into the Republican Party's online communications.) Those hack attacks resulted in the public release of thousands of stolen emails, many of which included damaging revelations about the Democratic Party and former Secretary of State Hillary Clinton, the party's nominee, who eventually lost the election to Donald Trump (Diamond, 2016).

According to the published comments of several government officials, hackers also broke into the email accounts of Clinton's campaign chair, John Podesta. The content of the emails was then passed to *WikiLeaks*, an international nonprofit organization that had gained notoriety in the past for publishing secret government information, usually stolen or obtained by other means. The content of the Podesta emails was made public during the summer and fall of 2016. US officials also insisted that the hackers were Russians. Moreover, multiple sources revealed that the Russian government has directly and indirectly trained numerous trolls to generate fake accounts in social networks with the purpose of confusing, antagonizing, discouraging, or agitating American public opinion (Bump, 2018). It is quite possible that this was just a tryout, an experiment to see how significantly such interferences could affect the political process and public opinion in the United States.

However, disagreements abounded about who directed or ordered these hack and troll attacks. Politics often motivated these disagreements. Clinton's supporters as well as several government sources in the Obama administration claimed that any form of discrediting Clinton during the electoral campaign was the key focus of the alleged Russian operation (Yaffa, 2016). Trump supporters either rejected the allegations about Russia's involvement or insisted that if the hacking did take place it had nothing to do with Clinton's election loss. Yet these attacks could have had a bigger, more strategic impact. A new kind of informational warfare that Russia was rehearsing in case of the 2016 US elections was focusing on deliberate disinformation, exaggeration, misinterpretation of facts, creating confusion – all to achieve a range of political or diplomatic objectives. Such cyberattacks can create a "new reality" or multiple realities with the ultimate aim of affecting the opinions and ultimately, the decisions of hundreds of millions of people in foreign countries. Sometimes, as research into the electoral process in the United States shows, it only takes a few thousand votes to sway elections in many constituencies (Dudley and Shiraev, 2008).

The real extent and political impact of the Kremlin's involvement in hacking Democratic servers and the *WikiLeaks* disclosures will probably never be accurately measured and assessed (Walker, 2016). The Russian government continues to deny any involvement. Most Republicans downplayed the impact, while Democrats tended to claim that the hacking was a key factor leading to Donald Trump's electoral victory in 2016. It seems likely that the actual or alleged "hand of Moscow" in the US presidential campaign will be studied and debated for years to come.

Conclusion

For the past thirty years Russian-American relations have been experiencing periods of optimism, followed by years of disappointment and frustration. In the early 1990s Russia's top elites regarded the United States as a model for successful economic and political development, a standard that Russia could emulate. Since the middle of the 1990s both international and domestic developments changed the direction of the US-Russian relations. The continuing economic difficulties in the late 1990s have convinced most Russian leaders as well as most ordinary Russians that Western – and American in particular – models of economic recovery did not work out well in Russia. The expansion of NATO and the 1999 Kosovo crisis have also convinced most Russian officials and the media that the United States was ignoring Russia in international affairs (Tsygankov, 2016). Many American investors would be reluctant to invest in Russia's economy siting bureaucracy, corruption, and lack of transparency there.

Common international threats often give states new incentives to cooperate. Both countries found a new ground for cooperation after the terrorist attacks against the United States in 2001. Washington and Moscow agreed about the significant global threat coming from several radical groups (those sharing the values of radical Islamism) and began political and military cooperation in the fields of counterterrorism. This collaboration continues.

Meanwhile, nationalist and hawkish tendencies grew among the key decision-makers in Russia after 2000. More individuals in a position of power considered a tougher approach toward the United States as the only effective direction of Russia's foreign policy. President Putin gradually accepted a tougher – compared to the 1990s – policy strategy toward Washington. This hawkish (Russians prefer to call it "assertive") position gained popular support in the country. At the same time, in the United States both Democrat and Republican politicians grew increasingly critical of Russia's domestic and foreign policies. Washington was very critical of Moscow's involvement in the Georgia conflict in 2008.

Relations between the United States and Russia remained lukewarm for years. The bilateral contacts in the fields of science, education, and culture continued, yet remained limited. Attempt at a "reset" of relations initiated by the Obama administration did not bring noteworthy changes. The United States played an instrumental role in initiating and imposing a wide range of sanctions against Russia for taking over Crimea and Russia's involvement in the crisis in Ukraine after 2014. Moscow rejected all accusations and imposed its own sanctions in retaliation.

The election of Donald Trump in 2016, despite expectations in some political circles in Moscow, did not generate immediate changes in Russian-American relations. In August 2017 the US Congress passed the Law Countering America's Adversaries through Sanctions Act (H.R. 3364). According to this law, Russia was an "adversary" of the United States together with Iran and North Korea. The Russian reaction was, of course, very critical, which gave the supporters of a tough approach in foreign policy with the West new political ammunition. It hardly needs repeating that any serious change of a policy course in Russia is largely based on the decision of one person, the president. In July 2018 presidents Putin and Trump met in Helsinki. Almost all experts in the United States and Russia expressed little hope for any rapid improvements the US-Russian relationship (Smeltz et al., 2018). Yet there is always a path toward positive developments.

US-Russian relations may have changed by the time you read these pages. If they have it will be most likely in response to new regional and global challenges. Hopefully, the challenges will not be overwhelming and relations will change for the better.

Summary

- Over the past two centuries bilateral relations between Russia and the United States have always played a major, even decisive role in international affairs.
- The United States was among the last of the major powers to recognize the Soviet state and establish diplomatic relations with the USSR in 1933.

- After 1945 the world entered a period of dramatic global confrontation. It went down in history as the Cold War, which lasted until the late 1980s. The Cold War for more than forty years had a substantial impact on the entire international order.
- The Soviet Union and the United States have gradually established their zones of influence.
- A major feature of the Cold War's battles was ideology. Both countries saw each other as principal rivals in the sphere of ideas and values.
- After Gorbachev came to power in Moscow in 1985 both countries experienced a remarkable period of mutual interest, respect, and cooperation in the fields of international security, disarmament, business, education, and science.
- Between 1993 and early 2000s a few conflicting patterns in these countries' mutual relations emerged. Between 2000 and 2008 the relations were characterized by fluctuations, growing problems, as well as accomplishments.
- In 2009 there was an attempt to "reset" relations under US Secretary of State Hillary Clinton. Russia was concerned with the United States' and NATO's attempts to "encircle" Russia and sponsor "regime changes" in many countries.
- The attempt at a "reset" did not bring noteworthy changes. The political and diplomatic drama intensified on the basis of accusations that Russia interfered in the US presidential elections and that there was a deliberate "collusion" between Trump and Putin back in 2016.
- The most difficult problems between Russia and the United States emerged over the conflict in Ukraine and the incorporation of Crimea into the Russian Federation.

Glossary

Arab Spring A series of uprisings that spread across the Arab world in 2010–2011 and involved Tunisia, Egypt, Libya, Syria, Yemen, Jordan, and Bahrain.

Caribbean Crisis The Russian term for the 1962 Cuban Missile Crisis, which unfolded after Moscow secretly deployed nuclear missiles in Cuba. In response Washington imposed a naval blockade of the island, preventing all vessels going to Cuba from landing there. Soon the leaders from both sides realized how easily a rapid escalation of a regional conflict could turn in to a nuclear war.

Fulbright Program The competitive, merit-based system of grants for international educational and research exchange between the United States and other countries.

International Space Station A space research laboratory (the largest human-made body in low Earth) and a joint project started in 1998. It involves a multibillion-dollar budget as well as several space agencies in the United States and Russia. Both countries agreed to sponsor this program until 2024.

Iron Curtain The term fashioned in the West to portray the Soviet Union's efforts to block its people (as well as the people from the satellite socialist states) from interacting with and getting information from capitalist countries.

Magnitsky Act The 2012 bipartisan bill passed by the US Congress and signed by President Obama to penalize Russian officials believed to be responsible for the death of Russian lawyer Sergei Magnitsky in a Moscow prison back in 2009.

Monroe doctrine The US policy toward the Western Hemisphere that stated that any efforts by European nations to interfere with sovereign countries in North or South America would be regarded as unacceptable.

New Start Treaty The 2010 agreement on measures for the further reduction and limitation of strategic offensive arms. Moscow and Washington agreed to limit their strategic nuclear weapons to 1,550 nuclear warheads by 2017.

Snowden case An episode that played a very negative role in Russian-US relations. Edward Snowden is an American computer professional, formerly employed by the CIA, who in 2013 illegally copied and leaked classified information from the National Security Agency. By doing this, he revealed massive surveillance programs managed by the US government.

Superpowers The label used to describe the United States and the USSR because their global military and economic strength that at that time could not be matched by other states.

Voice of America (VOA) The official external broadcast institution of the United States.

Zones of influence Specific geographical regions and countries over which a state claims political, military, economic, and cultural exclusivity. In practical terms, if such zones of influence are established, other governments usually do not interfere in the affairs of countries from the designated spheres.

Review questions

1. Which geographical areas did the Soviet and the US zones of influence include? What are Russia's zones of influence today, in your view?
2. What was the Gorbachev factor in Soviet-US relations? In your view, is there a "Putin factor" in today's relations between Moscow and Washington?
3. What was the "reset" policy and what were the consequences of this policy?
4. What was Moscow's view of the Arab Spring and the Orange Revolutions? How was it different from Washington's view?
5. Russia played an unexpectedly noticeable and controversial role in the 2016 US presidential elections. Explain.

Chapter 8
Russia's Policies toward Europe and the European Union

If for many European countries, sovereignty and national pride are forgotten concepts and a luxury, then for Russia, true sovereignty is an absolutely necessary condition of our existence.

Vladimir Putin

Learning objectives

- Describe and critically review the historical milestones in the relationships between the Soviet Union and Europe.
- Describe and critically analyze the periods of Russian-European relations after 1991.
- Critically discuss the multiple international and domestic factors affecting the relationships between Moscow and European countries.
- Describe major problems and key perspectives in the relations between Russia and the European Union.

About one quarter of Russian territory is located in Europe and more than two-thirds of the country's population lives there. Russia has had traditionally robust trade and multiple political links to European states. Yet – in the context of economic integration, government institutions, and ideology – is Russia today a part of Europe or not? How close is Russia to Europe politically and culturally? There are no simple answers to these questions. On the one hand, Russian leaders and ordinary people believe that they belong in Europe geographically and culturally. On the other hand, Moscow often distances itself from the continent and emphasizes deep disagreements between Russia and the West. Which process, toward Europe or away from it, will prevail in the near future? Or maybe Russia will idle for years before it chooses its path? You should make your own call after reading this chapter.

Historical background

Earlier periods

The Dukes in Kiev had close relations with the Byzantine Empire as well as with many early states in Central and Eastern Europe. Between the twelfth and fifteenth centuries the Novgorod Republic had trade relations with Germany, Sweden, Denmark, and some other countries and was a member of the Hanseatic League of North European cities. With the ascendance of Moscow as a center of Russian lands between the fifteenth and seventeenth centuries the aristocracy conducted mostly an ambivalent policy toward Europe. On the one hand, they sought access to many European manufactured products and technologies. On the other hand, they feared falling under Europe's control. As a result of this cautious approach, Russia at that time projected little influence on European politics and was part of none of the European coalitions.

The beginning of Russia's effective participation in European politics is associated with Peter the Great. As emperor he reformed Russia in many ways (see Chapter 2). One of his strategies was modeling Russia after Europe. In comparative politics this is often called **Europeanization** – the process in which an apparently non-European subject (such as a state, a city, or a social group) embraces particular European features such as government institutions, policies, or cultural trends including learning European languages. Since the early 1700s Russia's governing institutions, the military, and the aristocracy's daily customs, including their fashion, had been changing – often as a result of forceful imposition by the Emperor – to resemble some European mores and patterns, influenced at different times by the Netherlands, Prussia, Italy, Great Britain, and France, among the most influential countries. Along with many cultural changes, Russia was building a formidable army and navy. It was gradually becoming a major player in European affairs. From the eighteenth century on Russia was an active participant in key European coalitions and treaties. It was also engaged in many European wars (Bieleń, Khudoley, and Romanova, 2012). We have overviewed some of these developments in previous chapters.

After the end of the Russian Civil War in the early 1920s the newly formed Soviet state chose an isolationist and often confrontational policy toward Europe. As you should remember, Soviet leaders followed a Marxist-Leninist ideological doctrine and pursued a strategy based on the dogma of the "world socialist revolution." They later embraced the concept of the "world revolutionary process," which was a less confrontational strategy of supporting communist, left-wing, and other friendly regimes globally. Up until the 1930s the influence of the Soviet Union on European affairs was insignificant. Although most European states had *de jure* recognized the Soviet Union, they refused to have friendly relations with Moscow. There were no official visits of European heads of state. Most international congresses and conferences (except for international communist gatherings) saw no participants from Moscow.

However, from 1934 to 1939 the Soviet Union joined the League of Nations. A more robust foreign policy toward Europe emerged. Two general strategies stood out. First, Moscow leaders were against any type of a pan-European integration. Moscow saw a strong and united Western Europe as an adversary and tried to exploit any disagreement among European countries and thus use them to Soviet advantage. This has been an essential strategy of Soviet diplomacy and then Russian diplomacy in the twentieth and twenty-first centuries.

Second, Moscow pursued its own integration with European countries – based on ideology. The victory in World War II turned the Soviet Union into a global power and a major actor in European affairs. Communist regimes were established in several European countries. In 1955 Soviet leaders created the **Warsaw Pact**, formally the Treaty of Friendship, Cooperation, and Mutual Assistance, which was a military and political alliance as well as a collective defense treaty of the European communist governments. It included East Germany, Poland, Czechoslovakia, Hungary, Romania, Bulgaria, and Albania (which withdrew in 1968 on account of an ideological conflict with Soviet communists: Albanians accused Soviet leadership of acting too cozy with capitalist states).

During the Cold War most Western European countries joined NATO as a security measure to counter the perceived threat from the Soviet Union. For decades the division of Germany in 1949 and the building of the Berlin Wall in 1961 had been the symbols of this ideological, political, and military confrontation in Europe and globally. After World War II the Soviet Union turned down the assistance plan by the United States (known as the Marshall Plan) and forced the other countries in Central Europe that were under Moscow's control to reject this plan as well. Moreover, to counter the influence coming from Washington, the Soviet Union created its own economic alliance with the socialist countries in Europe called the Council for Mutual Economic Assistance (Comecon) (Lipkin, 2016).

After Stalin's death in 1953 the Soviet Union's policies toward Europe gradually changed. On the one hand, Moscow continued its attempts at weakening the United States' influence on Europe and strengthening its own dominance in Central and Eastern Europe, including East Germany. On the other hand, Moscow took several practical steps to reduce tensions in Europe. In fact, these steps had for a couple of decades cemented – both legally and politically – the fundamental division in Europe. In 1970 the Soviet Union and West Germany signed the Treaty on normalization of relations. An agreement about the status of West Berlin was signed in 1971. Both West and East Germany formally joined the United Nations in 1973. The Soviet Union also pursued economic cooperation with Europe and called for productive relations between the European Economic Community (EEC) and Comecon.

Why did this policy change occur? In the West this process received the name **détente**, that is the easing of strained relations between countries. The key reason for such a major shift in Soviet policy was the need to earn hard currency by selling oil, gas, and some other natural resources to Europe in return for new technologies from the West. The Soviet economy displayed signs of weakness at that time, so the money and technologies, as Moscow expected, should have given the economy a substantial boost. To some degree the desire to ease tensions in Europe and to develop economic ties with European partners was also driven by poor relations – which deteriorated after the late 1950s – with communist China. Facing a hostile China in the east, the Soviet leaders believed that any improvement of relations with Europe should bring them at least some economic and even political benefits. Another reason was that the Soviet leaders acknowledged the tremendous economic and technological progress achieved by the West and wanted to use modern technologies to advance the development of socialism at home (Glad and Shiraev, 2001).

One of the most significant events of the late twentieth century took place on August 1, 1975, when the heads of thirty-three European states, as well as the United States and Canada, signed the **Helsinki Final Act** of the Conference on Security and Cooperation in Europe. This document contained the principles of mutual relations among European states. According to the Final Act, the Soviet Union formally agreed to respect human rights and guarantee liberties to its citizens (an obligation that remained mostly on paper). The Final Act also gave a boost to negotiations and talks on specific measures to reduce tensions, strengthen security and trust, economic ties, cooperation in the fields of science, education, and culture, and direct contacts among ordinary people. Relations in many areas were improving. In the 1980s, when the Cold War entered a period of turbulence due to the Soviet invasion of Afghanistan and the deployments of American and Soviet missiles in Europe (see earlier chapters), relations between Western European countries and the Soviet Union were almost at their peak in many years.

Perestroika and European policies

During perestroika (see Chapter 2), in the second half of the 1980s, the Soviet Union introduced a policy of new thinking in international affairs and pursued improvements in its relations with European countries.

In 1985 Soviet leader Gorbachev declared that the EEC was not merely an economic entity but also a political reality, thus acknowledging its importance for Soviet foreign policy. In 1989 the USSR and the EEC agreed to reciprocate their diplomatic missions and signed the Agreement on Trade and Economic Cooperation. This Agreement contained references to the Helsinki Final Act, thereby underlying the latter's lasting influence on politics. In 1989 Gorbachev visited Strasbourg and spoke before the Parliamentary Assembly of the Council of Europe (PACE). There the Soviet leader outlined his vision of a "common European home," a popular metaphor in the Russian language to indicate geographical proximity and the pursuit of common goals for all European countries (Gorbachev, 2006). The Soviet Union was granted a special provisional status in PACE. It was a symbolic achievement, yet an important step for the new Soviet diplomacy. By the 1990s the Soviet Union and its institutions seemingly were on the path of unprecedented political and economic cooperation with Europe.

In 1990 the Soviet Union and other European leaders as well as leaders from the United States and Canada signed the *Charter of Paris for a New Europe* proclaiming that democracy had to be the only system of government in Europe. In the military arena NATO and Warsaw Pact countries signed the 1990 *Treaty on Conventional Armed Forces in Europe* providing for a mutual and substantial troop and arms reduction. Both sides agreed on several practical measures to reinforce mutual trust. Together with the earlier signed agreements between Moscow and Washington on nuclear missiles, these agreements signaled an apparent end to a decades-long confrontation in Europe between the two military blocs and their supporting political systems. The Cold War was heading to its end. The collapse of communism in 1991 and the creation of a new Russian state apparently lifted most of the remaining ideological and political barriers between Russia and Europe. A new era for Russia as a part of Europe was about to begin.

The European focus of Russia's foreign policy

About half of Russia's foreign trade over the past twenty years has been with the countries of the European Union. For many years Russia has been the largest supplier of oil and natural gas to Europe. On average, more than one-third of all European oil and gas imports were from Russia (European Commission, 2009). From the late 1990s millions of Russians in increasing numbers were buying European agricultural products, clothes, and cars. Hundreds of thousands of Russian tourists every year visited European resorts, discovered European art in Paris and Madrid, and shopped at malls and supermarkets in London and Budapest. However, while mutual business interests encouraged more productive and robust relations between Russia and Europe, many opportunities to move forward have been missed. Unfortunately, new political developments have been constantly creating obstacles in diplomatic, corporate, trade, and cultural affairs.

There have been at least five distinct stages in the development of Russian-European relations during the last three decades. The first stage was approximately between 1991 and 1994. It was marked by mutual enthusiasm, good will, and a measure of wishful thinking typical for both sides. Russian and European countries, their governments, elites, and the majority of their people no longer considered each other foes. Moreover, the idea that Russia was a part of a new Europe and should participate in the process of European integration was popular in Russia as well as in the European Union. The discussions turned to several possible forms of this integration. Russia was using the 1975 Helsinki agreements as a liberal framework to build its new relations with Europe. In 1991 the European Commission launched a program called the Technical Assistance to the Commonwealth of Independent States. It was to help Russia and the other members of the Commonwealth of Independent States in their transition to democratic governance and market-oriented economies. The program made some early impact on the emerging market economies but later was largely ineffective.

Russia's decision to comply with the Treaty on Conventional Armed Forces in Europe (1990) was noteworthy. Although the military and political situation had considerably changed in the early 1990s – neither the Warsaw Pact nor the Soviet Union existed any longer – the Russian leadership decided to continue observing the treaty. Russian troops returned home from Central European states. The reduction of troops and conventional weapons of the 1990s had led to a significant improvement of the political climate in Europe. To many people the military tensions as well as the anxieties of the Cold War were history. Having acknowledged the importance of its relations with Europe, Moscow was also focusing on its interactions with the United States. Russia was simultaneously developing its ties with NATO. There were talks – although mostly informal – about the ascendance of Russia into this organization in the future. The agreement on partnership and cooperation between Russia and the European Union was signed in 1994. These and other developments provided a solid foundation for taking relations across Europe to a new level.

The second stage was associated with a general cooling of mutual relations. It lasted from 1994 to approximately 2000. A previously positive and optimistic attitude toward Russia was changing in most European capitals. A key reason was that the Russian democratic and market reforms were failing and Russia was not transforming into a liberal democracy of a Western type – at least not as fast as most political leaders and experts in the West had anticipated. Russia was also heavily criticized for its use of force in the breakaway province of Chechnya. Moscow didn't take these criticisms calmly. It had its own grievances. The decision to enlarge NATO, which had been made early in the 1990s, caused a very negative reaction in Moscow (Goldgeier, 1999). Most commentators in Russia argued that by expanding NATO the West took Russia for granted and did not acknowledge Russia's geopolitical interests. Anti-Western sentiments in Russian society grew, as you should remember, during the war in Bosnia in the early 1990s and especially during the Kosovo crisis of 1999. Unlike the vast majority of European governments, Russia was on the Serbian side during that conflict (Sobel and Shiraev, 2003). Although Russia joined the Council of Europe, the practical effect of this formal membership was limited.

Relations with Central European countries, as well as with the Baltic states, were lukewarm at best –mostly due to the NATO enlargement. Russia, on the one hand, and Estonia, Latvia, and Lithuania, on the other, were suspicious of each other's motives. Moscow did not want to see the expanding NATO too close to its borders. The Baltic states did not want to be dominated again by their eastern neighbor.

The third stage lasted from 2000 until the outbreak of the global financial and economic crisis in 2008. This period was marked by a growing departure from the strategic goals pursued by Russia and Europe. We have learned earlier in this book that Russian leaders were gradually turning toward the Eurasian "project." Several important differences between Russia and Europe emerged:

- Russia turned to building an economic model based on state capitalism, while Europe continued to follow a liberal economic model.
- Russia essentially maintained an economy with two main sources of export: hydrocarbons (such as oil and gas) and arms. Europe was turning to service and information technology.

- Russia's policies were increasingly paying attention to and strengthening its sovereignty, while most European countries were turning away from sovereignty and delegating power to supranational institutions. The major institution was the European Union.
- Europe was strengthening liberal political values and the institutions protecting them. In Russia liberal values were increasingly questioned and even criticized.

Several political developments did not help Russia score political points in the eyes of most European observers and the public. The government in Moscow was seen as strengthening its control over big business. The case of billionaire Mikhail Khodorkovsky stood out. His arrest and a lengthy prison term seemed unfair and orchestrated by the government. His case showed to most Western observers that the government in Moscow could use any excuse to suppress domestic political opposition. Moscow disagreed with the critics, arguing that no type of political pressure from the West would be tolerated. The 2008 war with Georgia put Russia again under heavy criticism. Although Russia continued to prioritize its relations with Germany and France (and they were satisfactory at that time), its relations with the United Kingdom significantly worsened due to a series of political scandals, to which we will return to later this chapter. Russia continued having only lukewarm relations with the Baltic countries and most countries in central Europe (with the exception of Hungary and Slovakia). Russia and Europe were drifting further apart in many areas.

The fourth stage was from 2008 – marked by the beginning of the global financial and economic crisis – to 2012 the year when Vladimir Putin was elected president for the third time. During this period the European Union was very critical of most of Russia's domestic and foreign policies. Moscow attempted to engage Europe in Russia's policies of "modernization" – the catch word associated with a new initiative by president Medvedev to rapidly renovate his country's economy and social life by means of new technologies. However, Russian politicians and experts were increasingly convinced that the ongoing economic crisis would severely weaken European states and the European Union in general. Putin and his close circles (although Putin was serving as Prime Minister, his influence on Moscow's decision-making in domestic and foreign affairs was significant) believed that a new center of global economy and politics would soon shift to East Asia and the Pacific Region. During this period Moscow was strengthening its economic and political ties with China.

The fifth period, which started in 2012, has been the time of the most serious difficulties and even tensions between Russia and European states and transnational institutions since the end of the Cold War. Russia's increased focus on Eurasian integration (see Chapter 6 on policies toward post-Soviet States) was also pushing Russia away from Europe – both politically and economically. In terms of cultural identity, most discussions in the media about Russia being a part of European "civilization" subsided. The European "model," based on a market economy, democracy, and respect for human rights, often seen elsewhere as an attractive standard of socio-economic and political development, especially in many post-Soviet countries, was gradually abandoned in Moscow. Russia showed decreasing interest in cooperation with the European Union, NATO, and other pan-European institutions. The 2013–2014 crisis in Ukraine and Russia's violent actions during this crisis (see earlier chapters), including the events in eastern Ukraine and the annexation of Crimea, caused a storm of criticisms in Europe. Together with the United States, European governments imposed a range of economic and financial sanctions against Russia (Romanova, 2016). Moscow, in turn, responded with its own sanctions against the West. The level of mutual trust dropped lower that it had been for years.

Russia and the European Union

According to opinion polls, many Russians after 2014 maintained a negative view of the European Union. This attitude was caused by – among several other factors – the worsening of official relations between Russia and the European Union especially after Russia's annexation of Crimea and its actions in Ukraine (TASS, 2016b). These attitudes, from a historical perspective, appeared as an anomaly. For more than twenty-five years after the creation of the sovereign Russian state in the early 1990s, most Russians had had a favorable view of Europe and the European Union and considered Russia a part of Europe (see Figure 8.1).

The past two decades since the 1990s (Britain's referendum on the exit from the European Union in 2016 was an exception) have been marked by European integration. Russia witnessed the signing of the Maastricht Treaty to create the European Union; the issuing of the single European currency – the Euro; the signing of the Schengen Agreement allowing easy border crossings among EU countries; more coordinated actions in foreign and security policies; the enlargement of the European Union to include most European countries except a few from the former Soviet Union and the former Yugoslavia. The European Union has turned into a powerful actor exerting considerable influence on the world stage and regularly striving to resolve conflicts peacefully and provide assistance to lesser developed countries and regions. Even the serious financial crises involving Greece in 2012–2015 and the promised departure of the United Kingdom after the referendum in 2016

	2015	2016	2017	2018
Very Good	2	1	2	3
Mostly Good	18	26	37	29
Mostly Bad	43	39	38	33
Very Bad	28	19	9	13
Don't Know	9	14	14	22

Figure 8.1 Russian people's views of the European Union
Source: Created using Levada, 2018f

apparently showed the ability of the European Union to adjust to new challenges. Russia found itself in an ambiguous position. On the one hand, Moscow formally maintained a positive view of closer ties with Europe including institutional cooperation and economic partnership. On the other hand, a weaker European Union suffering from policy rifts (especially those related to the relationships with Russia) seemed a desirable development. The more countries disagree with and defy the EU policies toward Russia, the better they seem to be for Moscow.

The legal basis for relations between Russia and the European Union was the *Partnership and Cooperation Agreement* (PCA). It was signed in 1994 and came into force in 1997. After 2007 it was renewed annually due to a procedural agreement. The PCA contained several important statements including future policies: Russia and the European Union share common values and they would strive to create a free trade area within a decade and develop cooperation and partnership in various fields such as the arts, education, and science. The PCA defined a mechanism of political interactions between Russia and the European Union, such as regular summit meetings. The main part of the agreement dealt with economic cooperation and trade. The European Union recognized Russia as a country with a transitional economy. Russia agreed to adjust its legal system to the requirements of the European Union. Both sides promised to respect democratic values and human rights as well as to sustain a mutual commitment to international peace and security.

This agreement was a clear success of Russian and European diplomacy. However, it failed to bring most of the expected results. Notwithstanding multiple declarations of intent and extensive negotiations, Russia and the European Union did not manage to sign a new agreement replacing the Partnership and Cooperation Agreement that expired in December 2007. The participants on both sides failed to even agree on the basic principles of a new document. The sides, by default, went along with formal, automatic extensions of the agreement. The European Union gave an additional stimulus to relations between Russia and the West. In 1999, during the European Council meeting in Cologne, the European leaders adopted the Common Strategy of the European Union on Russia (Chronology, 2015). It appeared that a new political ground was being built to stimulate relations between Moscow and other European capitals. It wasn't the case.

Why did such a failure take place? Several reasons should be mentioned including differences in business culture, protectionism, bureaucratic delays, and, most importantly, the lack of political will. For example, Russia already had its own reservations about the envisioned partnership between Moscow and the European Union. Specifically, the Kremlin's *Medium-Term Strategy for Development of Relations between the Russian Federation and the European Union* (2000–2010), an official guideline, stated that Russia would not seek either full or associate membership in the European Union. It mentioned Russia's obligation to its CIS partners and criticized the European Union's enlargement eastwards to include Estonia, Latvia, and Lithuania as well as some Central European countries. Russia also openly announced a possibility of protectionist measures regarding some domestic industries. The EU-Russian integration was a formality. Take trade as an illustration. Russia joined the World Trade Organization only in 2012 rather than in 1997 as had been anticipated in the PCA. Therefore, Russia for many years was not formally ready for the implementation of the free trade policies with Europe. To simplify the process, Russia and the European Union signed several separate agreements on steel, textiles, and energy. Other agreements were signed in the fields of science and technology. Yet these contracts did not make a significant impact on trade.

Nonetheless, Russia was also trying to explore possibilities with the European Union. In 2003 the European Union and Russia agreed to give their cooperation a boost by launching a program based on the four Common Spaces: Economic; Freedom, Security, and Justice; External Security; and Research, Education, and Culture. In 2005 special roadmaps (or plans) to develop such spaces were designed. At the 2010 Russian-EU summit the two sides agreed on a program called the *Partnership for Modernization*. The goal of this program was to stimulate greater opportunity for investment in the key sectors that boost economic growth and innovation. The program was also aiming at helping Russia to comply with European technical standards and regulations related to business, manufacturing, and trade. Yet again, these and other agreements did not produce the projected results, and the roadmaps were impressive only on paper. Moreover, in Russia many political groups and experts – the communists and nationalists in particular – insisted that the Common Spaces agreements had benefited mostly the European Union, not Russia.

The EU enlargement brought new challenges to the relations between Russia and Europe. Many of Russia's former neighbors now were members of the European Union. With travel and tourism developing, Moscow wanted to establish visa-free travels for Russians. Yet the negotiations had been dragging on for years and stalled in 2014. (Some Russians joke that instead of the "Iron Curtain" of years ago they now have to face the "Visa Curtain.") Or consider the case of Kaliningrad – the city and the adjacent region that shares no border with Russia (surrounded by Poland and Lithuania, see Map 8.1). Russia wanted to discuss the right of its citizens to visa-free passage to and from Kaliningrad through Lithuania. It could have been

Map 8.1 The Kaliningrad Region

a turning point in moving forward and working out a broader deal to allow Russians to travel to EU countries visa-free. However this proposal was turned down, although residents in some Russian areas received the right to travel visa-free in limited parts of Poland, Latvia, and Lithuania. Furthermore, in 2016, as part of a broader package of sanctions against Russia, Poland toughened the rules for Russians to travel visa-free there. Moscow's proposal to make Kaliningrad a kind of a pilot project for fine-tuning the relations between Russia and the European Union was initially welcomed in European capitals. However, on the practical side of things (such as unlimited travel of residents or free trade within a designated zone) there have been only limited results.

Despite these setbacks, Russia and the European Union remain very much interdependent. Europe's dependency on energy, Russia's dependency on modern European technologies, and meaningful interactions in the fields of culture, education, tourism, and science explain their interconnectedness. There are large Russian-speaking communities in Germany, the United Kingdom, Spain, and other countries. Nevertheless, in the second half of the 1990s most political leaders and experts in Western Europe shared an opinion that Russia was not ready for a broader integration in Europe. Almost nobody discusses a full integration. This opinion remained and strengthened later.

Politicians and experts in Russia are divided about how to deal with the European Union. Two broad categories have emerged by the end of the second decade of the century. **Euro-optimists**, in general terms, tend to believe that increasing European integration and the emerging common border should bring Russia benefits. Some hope for serious economic benefits. Others believe that political changes will follow: the integration eventually should encourage Moscow to reform and accept European political values and business practices. **Euro-pessimists**, on the other hand, tend to believe that Russia's integration into Europe did not and does not serve the country's core interests. Euro-pessimists tend to feel that the European Union is using Russia to its own advantage and that Russia's economic and social success should take place outside the European Union's structure. Some pessimists criticize liberal values as decadent. Others reject European models of free-market capitalism and endorse authoritarian forms of state capitalism. Some of them go further and speak about a "post-European Russia" (Lukyanov, and Miller, 2016).

Euro-pessimists are not a uniform group of nationalists or retrogrades, as one might think. Russian business elites, at least some of them, were not rushing into the European Union either. To them, open competition with European businesses would end up in a loss for the Russian side: it is less technologically advanced, less skilled, and less experienced compared to its European counterparts. Next, during the global economic crisis that started in 2008 Russia and the European Union acted together using international institutions, above all the G-20, and stood against unilateral protectionist measures. At the same time, many Russian entrepreneurs maintained a belief, mentioned earlier, that the troubles with the European Union's economy and finances would continue over a long period and that the European Union's share of the global market and its political clout would shrink. Why then invest in EU-Russia ties? Significant disagreements and even tensions exist regarding energy policies.

The gas conflicts between Russia and Ukraine (2005–2006 and 2008–2009) and Belarus (2006–2007), and threats from Russia to cut off the delivery of natural gas – although this would have had little effect on most people of the EU countries – compelled the influential political and business circles in Europe to seek alternative sources of gas supply. The European Commission made urgent calls to diversify energy imports, especially of natural gas. Russia was seen as a bully in these and other conflicts related to gas products, their delivery, and pricing. Populist and nationalist sentiments in Russia (which were strengthened during the economic crises of 1998 and 2008) also played a role in Euro-pessimists' logic: Russia seemed to be able to weather economic storms without Europe.

Ideology also played a role in the growing problems between Moscow and Brussels. Russia's domestic human rights policies remained under constant criticism from the European Union. Over recent years the European Parliament passed several resolutions criticizing the Russian authorities for restricting the activities of NGOs, limiting public rallies and peaceful demonstrations, and restraining political freedoms such as freedom of speech and assembly. Moscow usually dismissed such statements as inaccurate. In recent years Moscow has treated the criticisms as foreign meddling in Russia's domestic affairs. Many Russians agreed with this official point of view. Some political scientists and journalists turned to discussing a fundamental value gap between the citizens of Russia and the European Union. Europe and the West were increasingly associated with liberal values and criticized. Russia was increasingly associated with conservatism and its righteousness. The logic was that while Europeans have become unreasonably focused on specific liberal rights related to race, religion, and gender, Russia was the country that preserved the "traditional" values very much related to morality, decency, economic stability and security for all. President Putin himself outlined the importance of Russian conservative values without mentioning liberal ideas (Putin, 2014; Popova, 2004).

A difficult test of EU-Russian relations was the August 2008 conflict in the Caucasus. We have already discussed it earlier. Unlike NATO, the European Union did not suspend its relations with Moscow. The European Union, having voiced its support for Georgia, opted to act as a mediator (the mission was entrusted to French President Sarkozy, since France presided in the European Union at that time). Sarkozy helped secure a ceasefire. Yet Russia's use of military force and its swift recognition of the breakaway regions of Abkhazia and South Ossetia provoked serious criticisms from the European Union. After the 2008 crisis the competition between Russia and the European Union for influence on the post-Soviet space became tougher (Gretskiy, Treshchenkov, and Golubev, 2014).

The Ukrainian crisis brought relations between Moscow and Brussels to their lowest point. The European Union condemned Russia's actions in the Crimea and in eastern Ukraine. Like most other countries in the world, the European Union considers the peninsula an integral and legitimate part of Ukraine. Despite Russia's predictable objections, the European Union signed the association and free trade-zone agreements with Ukraine, Georgia, and Moldova. Ukraine received substantial financial aid in 2014–2018 and was saved from financial collapse. A series of sanctions followed to curb imports and other forms of interaction between both sides. The scope and frequency of political contacts was drastically curtailed. Regular

Russian-EU summits, which used to be held twice a year, were cancelled. The nego-tiations on a new visa-free travel between Russia and the European countries of the Schengen Area were suspended. For the first time in the history of Russian-EU rela-tions severe sanctions were imposed against a number of Russian political figures, entrepreneurs, and companies. As a counter-measure Moscow approved its own list of European politicians who were forbidden to visit Russia. It was a serious down-turn in relations between Russia and the European Union.

As you can see, despite many declarations and efforts on both sides over many years, a strategic partnership between Russia and the European Union has not taken place so far. The socioeconomic and political models of the European Union and Russia remain very different. Most importantly, and perhaps sadly, at the end of the second decade of this century the level of trust between both sides remains at its lowest since the Cold War.

The European Union and Russia still shared several common views on some international problems. Both Moscow and Brussels supported the Obama nuclear deal with Iran and criticized the US withdrawal from it in 2018. The European Union and Russia spoke against the imposition of the new trade tariffs on a range of goods by the United States, considering it a violation of WTO rules. This, however, did not lead to an improvement in relations between Russia and the European Union. There are few chances that Russian-EU relations will seriously improve in the second decade of the century or even perhaps in the early 2020s (Khudoley, 2016). On the whole, one might state that the United States, Russia, and the European Union are drifting along the opposite vectors, and the existing gap between them not only is not shrinking but, in fact, widening.

Russia and NATO

Until its disintegration at the end of 1991 the Soviet Union had had no official relations with NATO except a few contacts occurring during the negotiations on arms limitation. However, already in the fall of 1991 the new Russian leaders were discussing the possibility of joining NATO. They signaled their willingness through public statements and interviews and by means of diplomatic channels.

In December 1991 the newly created North Atlantic Cooperation Council had brought NATO members together with the former members of the Warsaw Pact and some other participants. Yet no major breakthrough related to the Russia-NATO integration took place. From the beginning the Western partners were not rushing to admit Russia. The reasons for such reluctance were somewhat obvious. In the early 1990s, when discussing NATO's enlargement with the members of his administra-tion, US President Bill Clinton remarked that Russia's joining NATO was "blue-sky stuff" which would require a different Russia, different NATO, different Europe (Talbott, 2003: 132). Obviously, Clinton was referring to the necessity to have the right conditions that were important for the integration process. NATO's reluctance to discuss Russia's membership disappointed Russian leaders and triggered frustra-tion among many who hoped for a new role for their country. They knew that NATO was about to enlarge, but without Russia. This was happening vis-à-vis NATO's active engagement with countries of the former Soviet Union. Yeltsin did not object to the NATO expansion initially, but later on, influenced by domestic political circumstances (including the mounting opposition to his "soft" foreign policy), he changed his view. During the 1996 presidential race he criticized the NATO enlargement, and his criticism was one of the centerpieces of his election campaign.

Certain positive developments, of course, emerged in the 1990s. Russian and NATO soldiers now participated in an international peacekeeping force in Bosnia. In 1997 Russia and NATO signed the Founding Act, proclaiming that the two organizations no longer considered each other adversaries, and proposed the creation of several formal institutions of cooperation. The main role was assigned to the Permanent Joint Council (PJC) with all the NATO countries and Russia participating in it. Regular security-related consultations between the Ministers for Foreign Affairs, Defense Ministers, and top military officials began.

However, a serious crisis in relations between Russia and NATO broke out in the spring of 1999. It was triggered during the events in Kosovo described earlier in this book. The international community in general blamed the Serbian government for the violence against ethnic Albanians (mostly Sunni Muslims) in Kosovo. Russia disagreed and supported Serbia. After the failed attempts by international mediators to manage the conflict, NATO bombed Serbia and forced it to withdraw its troops from Kosovo, which eventually declared independence in 2008. Russia objected the NATO's actions and condemned the forceful partition (as Moscow called it) of Serbia, but to no avail.

A new chance to improve relations came with the election of Russia's new president. During the March 2000 campaign not only did Putin avoid using anti-Western rhetoric, but, on the contrary, he cautiously reexamined the possibility of Russia's future partnership with NATO. In the aftermath of the 9/11 tragedy in New York and Washington, DC, Russia joined the antiterrorist coalition, urged countries in Central Asia to provide assistance to the United States including the opening of US military bases there, and aided the NATO military operation in Afghanistan. Russia and its Western partners again discussed the possibility of Russia joining NATO. In 2002 in Rome the top leaders of Russia and NATO agreed to create the NATO-Russia Council. They wanted to boost their military cooperation in areas such as counterterrorism, nonproliferation of nuclear weapons, and coordination of search and rescue operations at sea and during natural disasters. In the following years the Russia-NATO collaboration developed mostly around the counterterrorist operation in Afghanistan. In addition, Russia closed its military installations in Vietnam and Cuba. And in 2003 Russian troops left the Balkans. There was also softening of criticism of the 2004 NATO enlargement, despite the fact that it had involved the Baltic countries now bordering Russia.

Relations, however, were worsening again after the 2003 US invasion of Iraq. Moscow had already opposed the war preparations in 2002. In the following years Putin was changing his tone and rhetoric of his speeches. One of his toughest statements was the 2007 speech in Munich (discussed earlier in this book). It contained sharp criticisms of the West and particularly NATO. Yet the most serious crisis between Russia and NATO occurred in August 2008 when the war in the Caucasus broke out involving Russia, Georgia, and the self-proclaimed states of Abkhazia and South

Ossetia. As a result NATO suspended its relations with Russia, including the activities of the Russia-NATO Council. Russia too suspended its activity in the Partnership for Peace and a few other joint programs. The council resumed its work some time later.

Throughout the twenty-first century Russia and NATO continued their cooperation in the field of counterterrorism. For this reason Russia agreed in the past to allow certain supplies for the NATO troops in Afghanistan to be transited through Russia. However, Russia opposed any further NATO enlargement, especially of countries such as Ukraine and Georgia. Missile defense too has become one of the most critical issues in Russia-NATO relations. Over the past decade or so Russia has been getting more assertive in the Arctic, where it is anxiously watching NATO's activities. Russia also gives special attention to cybersecurity and views the Internet as a possible venue for future conflicts. Russian leaders (as well as their counterparts in China) often use the terms "information security" and "information sovereignty" to justify tighter control over the Internet in their countries.

After the 2014 crisis in Ukraine NATO has essentially frozen its relations with Russia, except conveying meetings of the Russia-NATO Council. Although Russia expressed disappointment about the diminished contacts, it started increasing its military presence in areas close to NATO countries' borders, including the Baltic Sea and the Black Sea. After 2015 Russian and then NATO officials started to publicly call the other side an "adversary" or a "threat" (thus challenging the Founding Act of 1997 when both sides declared that they were no longer enemies).

Russian political elites have always recognized the real military potential of NATO. It is the most powerful military and political bloc of the modern world, and Moscow maintains that it does not want return to the Cold War hostilities. Yet NATO is under constant criticism from Russia's government and the media. The reasons are ideological, political, and pragmatic (many refer to the legacy of the Cold War), and we have discussed them in various chapters earlier in this book. A very negative attitude toward NATO reflects Russia's general perception of the West and Russia's view of its own position in the world. NATO is a convenient target for Russian nationalists regardless of their political affiliation (some of them are conservative, others are communists). The Communist Party and the Liberal Democratic Party, since the 1990s, have also been harsh critics of NATO and especially of its eastward enlargement. Attacks on NATO also allow the Kremlin to consolidate the country's public opinion and rally people behind the government, especially during difficult economic periods. The Russian military elites also need to have "a foe" to justify large spending on defense and national security.

Russia and the Council of Europe

The Council of Europe (CoE) is an international organization founded in 1949 to promote democracy, human rights, the rule of law, and economic development in Europe. The CoE cannot make binding laws, yet it has certain executive powers and prestige. One of its enforcement bodies is the European Court of Human Rights (ECHR), which enforces the European Convention on Human Rights.

Since the inception of Russia as a sovereign state Moscow has sought admission to the CoE. Democratic circles in Russia had long considered their country's cooperation with the Council of Europe as a critical lever for domestic reforms and a mechanism to ensure the strengthening of civil rights in Russia. In the 1990s Russia was shedding its authoritarian past. The 1993 Constitution includes an entry about the necessity to respect human rights. Russia had formally committed itself to restructuring the old institutions and creating a civil society in accordance with the standards of the Council of Europe. However, a slow pace of political reforms, the weakness of many civil institutions, and the first Chechen military campaign (as you should remember, Russia was accused of serious human rights violations there), and other developments have slowed down Russia's admittance to the CoE. Only in 1996 did the Russian Federation officially join the Council of Europe and sign the European Convention on Human Rights. Now Russia had to adjust its laws.

One of the greatest challenges has been the abolition of the death penalty, which was prescribed to Russia by the agreement. Russians are split on the issue of capital punishment: 44 percent supported it and 41 percent opposed (BBC, 2017). Under these circumstances the Council of Europe agreed to accept a deal. There has been a written commitment signed by top Russian officials to legally "suspend" the death penalty without going through a series of legislative procedures. As a result, Russia has not executed any convicted criminal since 1996. This suspension should be in place today (please check if this is the case). The constitutional court in Russia in 2016 affirmed the moratorium on the death penalty. As a member of the CoE Russia has to reform its prison system to make it more transparent and committed to due process. Moreover, Russian citizens can appeal to the European Court of Human Rights if they believe that their rights have been violated in Russia.

Most Russian commentators viewed the Council of Europe from a pragmatic position. On the one hand, they wanted Russia's membership in it, hoping that it would give Moscow an equal role in Europe and bring more influence in international politics. On the other hand, they were not inclined to rush too fast with domestic reforms related to human rights. The reasons for the delays were bureaucratic as well as ideological. For example, what is considered an individual's "right" is highly contested in Russia – a type of debate that is common even in developed democracies, such as the United States (Etzioni, 2014). However, Russian populists and nationalists have gained support for criticizing the concept of human rights as decadent, too liberal, and therefore inappropriate for Russia. Such arguments appeal to some parts of the Russian electorate. In addition, the West is often accused of using the concept of human rights to interfere in Russia's domestic affairs (Shtepa, 2018). Such accusations were common in the 1970s during the Soviet times. All in all, Russia's place and its role in the Council of Europe remains a disputed political issue.

Russia fell under heavy criticism yet again during the second Chechen campaign. From 2000 to 2001 the Parliamentary Assembly of the Council of Europe suspended the Russian delegation's voting rights. Several times PACE adopted resolutions criticizing the Russian authorities for serious human rights violations in many areas of social and political life. These criticisms referred to the government's actions against NGOs and the independent media. Others referred to unlawful arrests and detentions of citizens. The Ukraine crisis has complicated the situation even further. PACE refused to recognize the inclusion of Crimea in the Russian Federation and condemned Russian policy in Ukraine. The Russian parliamentary delegation's voting right at PACE has been suspended again. As a countermeasure the Russian delegation withheld its activities at PACE – an action short of quitting the organization altogether.

Russia's dissatisfaction with the Council of Europe has been growing during the second decade of the twenty-first century. Moscow was accused of meddling with Russian domestic affairs, undermining Russia's security on behalf of human rights, and "scapegoating" Russia for its independent policies. After Putin's comeback as president in 2012 and during Russia's obvious pivoting toward a Eurasian integration, Russia significantly decreased its activities as a member of the CoE. The Russian ruling class increasingly saw the CoE as an instrument of the European Union, intent on limiting and even undermining Russian influence across the post-Soviet space. To add to this negative perception, Russia's government officials were losing case after case in the European Court of Human Rights. As a result some political forces in Russia were calling on Moscow to quit the CoE altogether. The Kremlin disagreed. Russia did not want to demonstratively cut ties and self-isolate. It responded legally. The Constitutional Court of the Russian Federation was given the right to block the ECHR's decisions if they contradicted the Russian Constitution. Russia could depart from its requirement to enforce any ECHR rulings if this was the only way to avoid a violation of the Russian Constitution (Library of Congress, 2016). Thus, Russia underlined the supremacy of its laws above the country's international agreements.

Russia in the Organization for Security and Cooperation in Europe

In the late 1980s and the early 1990s the disintegration of the Soviet Union, the changes in Central and Eastern Europe, and the end of the Cold War were undoubtedly positive developments in the context of the Helsinki agreements (see earlier in this chapter). It appeared that many political and humanitarian problems had been addressed. The Russian government initially paid serious attention to the Helsinki process. Moscow took part in the subsequent summits held in Helsinki (1992), Budapest (1994), Lisbon (1996), and Istanbul (1999). The adapted Treaty on Conventional Armed Forces in Europe was signed at the Istanbul Summit after the dissolution of the Soviet Union and the Warsaw Pact. Russia did attach great significance to the implementation of all provisions of the Final Act of 1975, including those on issues of humanitarian cooperation and human rights. During the first Russian military campaign in Chechnya, in the 1990s, the Organization for Security and Cooperation in Europe observers were invited to the war zone. Russia supported the initiative for the establishment of new institutions, including those to ensure the observance of democratic principles during elections.

However, differences emerged between Russian and Western approaches to the future of the Helsinki process. Russia insisted on transforming the Helsinki process into a new and functional international organization with considerable powers. The West agreed to the formal establishment of the OSCE (1995) but wanted this organization to focus on elections and humanitarian cooperation. Security issues were increasingly assigned to NATO, thus causing unease in Moscow. Speaking at the 1994 Budapest summit Boris Yeltsin cautioned that an emerging new "Cold Peace" could replace the Cold War. At the subsequent summits Russia also criticized NATO's enlargement plans.

Since 2000 Moscow has expressed its dissatisfaction with the OSCE's critical reports about the undemocratic electoral practices in the post-Soviet states. The OSCE, like the Council of Europe, was seen as interfering in Russia's domestic affairs. Nevertheless, Russia backed the idea of holding a new summit (2010), and actively participated in its preparation. The Russian government also agreed to the OSCE monitoring the 2008 conflict with Georgia and in the Donbass region as part of the Minsk agreements related to Ukraine in 2014 and 2015. There are voices in Russian political circles demanding Russia's withdrawal from the OSCE. Yet the leadership's opinion has been different. Russia is likely to continue pushing for a greater role of the OSCE in European politics.

Here we will summarize several important points in relations between Russia and several key European players. We have already covered many aspects of these relations earlier in this book, so now we focus on several highlights.

Russia's relations with major EU players

Germany

By 1994 Russia had finally withdrawn all its troops from Germany. They had been stationed there (in East Germany) since the end of World War II. Despite the logistical difficulties associated with the withdrawal of a large military contingent (there were up to six hundred thousand service men and women including their families), Russia carried it out within a quite short time. The early 1990s was a remarkable period for peace and cooperation. Germany had already become one of Russia's most valuable trade partners. Germany had assisted Russia in the financing of the troops redeployment. Germany welcomed ethnic Germans living in Russia and in the territories of the former Soviet Union. In the eyes of German public opinion Russia acted fairly: it helped with the German reunification in the 1990s and then withdrew its military for good.

Berlin played a central role in EU and NATO policies. Despite the normalization of relations after the Cold War, Berlin and Moscow in the 1990s held different views on the conflict in the former Yugoslavia. Germany was the first to recognize the independence of Croatia and Slovenia, a diplomatic move, that Moscow opposed

(Shiraev and Terrio, 2003). Germany was also very critical of Russia's actions in the Chechen conflict. Russia, as you remember, treated this conflict as a domestic issue and as a counterterrorism operation, as a forceful response against violence. Germany emphasized the brutality of the Russian forces against the civilian population. There was a negative impact on relations when the State Duma refused to ratify the agreement that provided for a possibility for Berlin to reclaim German cultural property, which the Soviet Union had confiscated after Germany's defeat in 1945. Yet Germany and Russia were on the same side in criticizing Washington for the 2003 US invasion of Iraq.

Putin, when he became president, pursued a special relationship with Germany. His knowledge of Germany and the German language and personal relations with Chancellor Schroeder facilitated diplomacy. In September 2001 Putin made a speech at the Bundestag in German (Putin, as a KGB officer, lived for many years in Germany in the late 1980s). Both countries in the early 2000s established a range of intergovernmental institutions responsible for a dialogue in the areas of economy, science, and education. German investments in the Russian economy were also growing. Some legal groundwork was drafted in the European Commission for the construction of the "Nord Stream" – a gas pipeline from Russia to Germany across the Baltic Sea. Nevertheless, relations began to worsen.

The first reason was Russia's domestic policies that were becoming more authoritarian under President Putin. German political parties, NGOs, and the media were increasingly critical of the direction that Russian politics was taking. Angela Merkel, the new Chancellor, was much more critical of Russia than her predecessor Schroeder. The second reason for a worsening trend in relations was Russia's changing view of its role in the world and its foreign policy. Although on the surface both Russia and Germany called for broader international cooperation, respect of other countries' interests, and the necessity to act cautiously in international conflicts (such as the bombing of Libya by an international coalition in 2011), many significant points of disagreement were emerging. Russian actions in Georgia in 2008 and in Ukraine in 2014 (and later) were the signs – in the eyes of German observers – of Russia's boorishness and disregard for international law. Germany voted in the UN General Assembly as well as in other international organizations for the resolution condemning Russia's actions in Ukraine. At the same time, Germany participated in the Normandy contact group, including Germany, Russia, Ukraine, and France to resolve the situation in the eastern regions of Ukraine. Both governments had a different view (although they recognized the Islamic State as an enemy) of the conflict in Syria and the need to support the embattled President Assad, whose government Russia defended militarily.

The financial crisis of 2008 and the following economic crisis negatively impacted Russian-German trade, but all in all Germany remained Russia's top trade partner. Germany remained in the top-five ranks for both exports and imports (Global Edge, 2018). Both countries wanted to implement the Nord Stream 2 project – a pipeline across the Baltic Sea to deliver gas directly from Russia to Germany (two pipelines were laid between 2001 and 2012). At the same time, although Germany still relies on oil and gas exports from Russia, German political leaders see the necessity to decrease their country's energy dependency on Russia. High-level contacts between Russia and Germany continued. Yet the disagreements between them remained serious.

France

Russia and France have fought a few wars against each other. The most noteworthy conflict took place in 1812 when France invaded Russia and occupied Moscow. Russia pushed back. Russian Emperor Alexander I and the six-countries coalition army entered Paris in 1814. Russia and France had not been at war with each other ever since until the Crimean War (1853–1856). They were later allies during both world wars. During the Cold War France often played a reconciling role, trying to mediate and sooth various conflicts and confrontations between the United States and the Soviet Union. After the collapse of the Soviet Union France immediately recognized Russia as the successor state.

In February 1992 President Yeltsin visited France. It was one of his first official visits abroad. He signed a new treaty of mutual cooperation. France backed Russia's application to the Council of Europe and a few other international organizations. France played a noteworthy role in the 1994 Agreement on Partnership and Cooperation between the European Union and Russia. France also played a positive role in accepting Russia to the Council of Europe (1996) and the signing of the Founding Act between Russia and NATO (1997). However, France as well as other European countries was critical of certain Russian domestic practices and foreign actions (see the part on Germany) and attached Russia's integration into European institutions to changes in Moscow's domestic policies and its international behavior.

A major deterioration of Russian-French relations happened during the 1999 Kosovo crisis and the second (1999) Chechen campaign. The active participation of France in the bombing of Yugoslavia (the second largest participating air force after the United States) caused frustration in Russia (Sobel and Shiraev, 2003). Moscow was displeased when the French Foreign Ministry held a meeting with a representative of Chechen separatists and the French parliament (the National Assembly), which organized his press conference (JF, 1999). It was a French initiative for the EU Council to adopt a resolution condemning Russia for its actions in Chechnya. Probably, this had only a symbolic meaning, but Putin visited Paris in 2000 after he had already met with US, German, and UK leaders.

Meanwhile, the volume of trade between France and Russia tripled from 2001 to 2008. Both countries began their cooperation on antiterrorist policies. In 2002 Russia and France agreed to establish the Council for Security Cooperation with the Ministers for Foreign Affairs and Defense holding annual meetings. For a brief moment Russia was on the side of France and Germany in their harsh criticism of the US invasion of Iraq in 2003. France welcomed Russia's decision to send its navy vessels to combat piracy off the coast of Somalia and its helicopters in 2008 for the

European Union's force in Chad and the Central African Republic. Both countries supported nonproliferation of nuclear weapons and other weapons of mass destruction. Yet France criticized Russia's decision to suspend its participation in the Treaty on Conventional Armed Forces in Europe.

France stressed that security on the continent not only required a balance of power but also demanded strengthening democracy and human rights, as well as maintaining the priority of the existing institutions, especially the European Union and NATO. During the 2008 conflict in Georgia the French President acted as a mediator between Russia and Georgia. He was able to implement a cease-fire agreement. However, France did not approve of Russia's recognition of independence of Abkhazia and South Ossetia: Paris supported Georgia's position in this conflict. France for years, together with the United States and other European nations, supported sanctions against Iran to curb its nuclear ambitions, a policy that Russia continuously criticized as unfair to Iran and unjust (Russia insisted that such measures must be approved only by the UN Security Council). Russia and France supported the nuclear deal with Iran and opposed President's Trump's decision to leave the agreement.

Russia and France also had different views on the necessity and scope of the military action against Libya in 2011. The two countries had different views on the war in Syria. Although Moscow and Paris acknowledged the need to weaken and eventually destroy the self-proclaimed Islamic State, they disagreed on the status of Syrian President Assad and his government. Russian policies have for many years received the support of some French political groups, especially the National Front, which is a socially conservative, nationalist political party. Its leaders were very critical of the sanctions against Russia during the conflict in Ukraine. The National Front's anti-NATO, anti-American, and anti-immigrant positions all find sympathy and positive reactions in Moscow (National Front, 2018).

In the second decade of the twenty-first century France became the fourth largest foreign investor in the Russian economy. France occupied the fifth place in imports to Russia, behind China, Germany, the United States, and Belarus (Global Edge, 2018). However, Russian investments in France remain relatively small. As in Germany (and other countries), French media, both liberal and conservative, tend to be very critical of Russia's domestic and foreign policy, which are perceived as anti-Western and boorish. France also backed the EU sanctions against Russia for its actions in Ukraine. One illustration of the scope of these sanctions stands out. Earlier in 2009 France had agreed to sell Russia two amphibious assault ships of the *Mistral* class. These helicopter carriers were supposed to be delivered to the Russian navy sometime in 2015. However, in 2014 the French president decided to cancel the deal because of Russia's actions in Ukraine. Principled politics tramped a massive business deal. France agreed to return almost $1.5 billion to Russia for the failed contract (AFP, 2015).

During the 2017 French presidential elections some French officials accused Russian media of interference on the side of the French right-wing parties. Russia denied the accusations. Yet high-level contacts between the two countries continued.

The United Kingdom

Throughout history, relations between Russia and the United Kingdom have been constantly swaying from tense to friendly, from openness to mutual isolation – depending on particular events, leaders, and policies. During the Napoleonic Wars early in the nineteenth century both countries were allies. Then Russia and Britain clashed in the Crimean War (1853–1856). They were allies again during World War I and World War II. Stalin for some time in the 1930–1940s viewed Britain, not the United States, as the major opponent of the Soviet Union (Zubok and Pleshakov, 1997). The attitude of Khrushchev was different: his first official visit to the West was to the United Kingdom. In the early 1960s London was the main political and trade partner of the USSR in Western Europe. Yet as a nuclear power and a member of NATO the United Kingdom was also a key strategic foe of the Soviet Union during the Cold War. Relations began changing for the better during perestroika in the late 1980s. Personal contacts between Mikhail Gorbachev and Margaret Thatcher played a very important role in both countries' improving relations.

In January 1992 President Boris Yeltsin visited London – this one of his first trips abroad after the collapse of the Soviet Union. During the visit he signed an agreement on the principles of relations between Russia and the United Kingdom. Both sides formally agreed to cooperate in many areas, including disarmament, science, technology, energy, agriculture, banking, environmental protections. Queen Elizabeth II visited Russia in 1994. Not surprisingly London, like Berlin and Paris, was critical of Russia's slow transition to democratic institutions and democratic governance during the 1990s, the lack of civil liberties, and Moscow's military actions in Chechnya. Moscow was increasingly frustrated by what it saw as a deliberate effort by the West to keep Russia "out" and direct its domestic and foreign policy.

After 2000 President Putin took steps to improve relations with London. Alas, several events contributed to the worsening of these countries' bilateral affairs. In 2003 Moscow requested the **extradition** – the official transfer of a suspected or convicted criminal to another country – of several influential Russian citizens who had already been under criminal investigation in Russia. One was Boris Berezovsky, a prominent billionaire and a close ally of former president Boris Yeltsin. Berezovsky had sought and received political asylum in the United Kingdom. In Russia he faced multiple charges including embezzlement and fraud. London refused the extradition request believing that the Berezovsky case was politically motivated and thus that he would not receive fair treatment in Russia.

This decision displeased Moscow. In 2007 it was London's turn to ask for an extradition. This time the request was related to the poisoning with a radioactive substance of a former Russian security officer and spy, Alexander Litvinenko, who died in London under suspicious circumstances. What became known as the **Litvinenko case** involved the evidence of the use of radioactive polonium-210 against the former Russian spy. Suspicion for the assassination fell on the Kremlin.

The British government wanted to extradite a key suspect in the case from Russia. The Kremlin refused, citing a law prohibiting the extradition of Russian citizens to foreign countries. The Russian government and the media were very energetic in promoting the Kremlin's position. Probably as a result of this progovernment media campaign, a substantial proportion of Russians, about 36 percent, believed that the Litvinenko murder was an anti-Russian provocation (WCIOM, 2009h). The fallout of the Litvinenko case was the mutual expulsion of diplomats in 2007 and the cutting of British ties with Russian security agencies. Other disagreements included the judgments of the infamous **poisoning scandal** of 2018. The scandal was about the poisoning in the United Kingdom of Sergei Skripal, a former Russian security agent, and Yulia, his daughter. According to the British investigation, the Skripals were poisoned by an exremely potent chemical agent traceable to Russia. These and other serous issues have unfortunately seriously disrupted contacts in business, diplomatic, and cultural areas between Britain and Russia. The poisoning scandal also caused Washington's additional economic sanctions against Russia in 2018.

The 2003 invasion of Iraq further worsened relations between Russia and the United Kingdom (as well as with other European countries, as we have learned). Unlike the leaders of Germany, France, and Russia, the British Prime Minister Tony Blair supported (reluctantly, as he has insisted) the US military operation against the Iraqi regime of Saddam Hussein (Blair, 2016). A further complication in relations between London and Moscow was brought about by the diametrically opposed positions of Russia and Great Britain in regard to the August 2008 conflict in Georgia.

There were some signs of improving relations, nevertheless. In September 2011, for the first time in a number of years, the British Prime Minister visited Russia, and in the summer of 2012, during the Olympic Games, both Putin and Medvedev visited London. It appeared that the formal mechanism of high-level talks was about to get restored. There were a few points of mutual agreement. Russia and the United Kingdom both stood and continue to stand for a strict adherence to nonproliferation of nuclear weapons. Both countries participated in the *Group of Six* in negotiations with Iran on its nuclear program. Several significant business disputes involving both countries were also settled.

Russia and Britain had a similar view on the importance of the 2015 nuclear deal with Iran. Yet Russia did not support the unilateral sanctions against Iran reimposed by the United States in 2018. Significant differences also appeared about Syria, where Russia and Britain supported the opposite sides in the armed conflict. Obviously, the Ukraine crisis triggered a drastic worsening of already poor relations. From the floor of the UN General Assembly and in many other international organizations Britain voted for resolutions criticizing Russia's actions. London supported the initiative to have the 2014 G-7 Summit without Russia. Britain declared that it continued to recognize Crimea as Ukrainian territory, condemning the actions of separatists in Eastern Ukraine. All military cooperation between the two countries was put on hold. When Putin was elected to his next term in 2018 there were no signs of a quick improvement of the countries' bilateral relations. Moscow and London continue to have very different perceptions of history and the present international relations.

Russia and the countries of Central Europe

After the break-up of the communist bloc and the Soviet Union, most former communist countries of Central Europe (including the Czech Republic, Hungary, Slovakia, Slovenia, and Croatia) were no longer sharing borders with Russia, except
Poland. For convenience, we will include Romania and Bulgaria (both countries
were members of the communist bloc) in Central Europe, although some scholars
consider them geographically and geopolitically a part of Eastern Europe.

The 1990s represented a period of decreased mutual significance as well as only
lukewarm relations between Russia and the Central European countries. Early in
the 1990s several major obstacles in their interactions remained. Among them were

- the logistical problems associated with the withdrawal of Russian troops from
  some of these countries' territories;
- the challenges of establishing a new type of diplomatic relations based on the
  principle of equality;
- restructuring economic ties based on the free market principles; and
- addressing the negative legacy of the Soviet Union's past: Central European
  countries were now turning toward the West.

The first obstacle was resolved relatively fast. Russia withdrew its forces from Europe
by 1994. Next, Moscow signed new bilateral treaties with the states in Central Europe
including agreements recognizing each other's sovereignty and ruling out interferences in domestic affairs. Russia was acting very cautiously in the armed conflict in
the former Yugoslavia and always called for an end to the violence and a peaceful resolution of the conflict. By 1994 Russia began to form its own view of the conflict
which was increasingly critical of all Western involvement, especially in Bosnia (Sobel
and Shiraev, 2003). In the end, multinational peacekeeping forces (including Russian
troops) were introduced there to stop the deadly violence. Addressing the second obstacle, Moscow tried to establish a new type of diplomatic relations. Russian leaders
were hoping to build trust by denouncing the crimes of communism. For example, the
Soviet intervention in the popular uprising in Hungary in 1956 and the Soviet occupation of Czechoslovakia in 1968 were now officially condemned. Russia tried to show
its former satellites that the negative legacy of communism should be put aside and
a new type of equal relations created. The third obstacle was especially challenging.
Although most remaining trade disputes as a legacy of the 1980s were settled by 1994,
the economic ties established with the Soviet Union that existed for decades have been
crumbling since the late 1980s. New relations based on market principles were only
emerging slowly. Russian businesses initially sought but soon abandoned their attempts
to seek big financial, commercial, and other opportunities in Central Europe. Emerging Russian businesses could not successfully compete with most Western investors in
Central Europe. Similarly, both businesses and governments in the Czech Republic,
Hungary, and Poland preferred a closer European integration to developing business
contacts with Russia, which could offer them very little at that time.

While Russia hoped for a new type of relationship based on equality and goodwill, for the former socialist countries the priority of the time was to prepare for an

early accession to NATO and the European Union. The legacy of communism and Moscow's dominance in the past were among the reasons why Central European countries wanted to distance themselves from Moscow. Another reason was the speed and direction of Russia's own political reforms after 1991. Initially, Russia did not object to the NATO enlargement. President Yeltsin stated this opinion to Polish President Lech Wałęsa (b. 1943) in 1993. Later, Russia's position on the expansion changed. The development of relations with any particular country in Central Europe and the Baltic States was being increasingly often linked directly to whether they were going to join the North Atlantic Alliance or not. Moscow objected particularly intensely to the NATO inclusion of the Baltic countries, arguing that the boundaries of the former Soviet Union were the "red line" that NATO should not cross. Russia cited its own security concerns as a reason for resisting NATO. For some time in the 1990s the only active bilateral relations, including military cooperation, remained between Russia and Slovakia – a country that, unlike the Czech Republic, was temporarily outside the focus of NATO and the European Union. You remember that the Kremlin saw very negatively the inclusion of Poland, the Czech Republic, and Hungary in NATO.

Russia, as we know, condemned the NATO bombings of Serbia in the 1990s, but its support of Belgrade was mostly moral. For example, the Russian government turned down Serbia's request for advanced air defense systems. This action would have been violating international sanctions against Serbia, and Moscow did not want to see an escalation of the conflict. In some other instances Russia acted decisively and quickly. The deployment of Russian paratroopers from Bosnia to Kosovo in 1999 in advance of the NATO troops triggered a short-lived feeling of hope and excitement among the Serbs and a positive reaction in Russia. The public and the media commented that this event was a sign that Russia was restoring its international influence and power (Shiraev and Zubok, 2000). By the end of the Kosovo crisis in 1999 Russia's relations with the West, as we have studied, had worsened. Although Russia withdrew its support for the Serbian leader Milošević in 2000, the views on the conflict in Moscow and other European capitals differed: unlike the Central European countries, Russia refused to recognize Kosovo's independence. The tensions began to subside only in 2001 when the antiterrorist coalition involving Russia and the United States emerged.

The legacies of the Cold War continued to influence Russia's policies. Russia has repeatedly accused Estonia and Latvia of violating the rights of their Russian-speaking residents. Moscow disagreed with the Baltic countries' policies regarding the Russian language as well as their policies toward reassessing some events that took place during World War II (Lanko, 2009, 2013). For example, how one should judge the local resistance in Latvia, Estonia, and Lithuania that fought against the Soviet occupation? As you remember, Russia rejects the very idea that an "occupation" took place. Next, how should one judge the role of the Soviet Army during the war? The official view of Moscow has always been that the Soviet Union played a crucial role in liberating Europe from the Nazi occupation. On the other hand, there is a common view in the Baltic states as well as in the countries of Central Europe that the Soviets used the war against Germany to their own advantage and that it led to establishing communist regimes across Europe.

Moscow was taking important steps in improving its relations with Poland. Unfortunately, the tragic events in 2010 have worsened them. A plane crash near the Russian city of Smolensk would likely to remain a source of disagreements for years to come. President Kaczynski, together with his wife and other politicians and senior military officers, headed for the ceremonies at the site of the 1940 Katyn massacre were killed in the crash. The **Katyn massacre** refers to the events in April 1940 when Soviet authorities ordered the execution of more than 22,000 Polish officers after the Soviet Army had occupied a portion of Polish territory. The Nazis discovered the mass graves in 1943. They used them as a propaganda tool in hopes of weakening the anti-Nazi coalition of the Soviet Union, Great Britain, and the United States. Stalin's government resorted to denial, accusing the Nazis themselves of committing the murders. The Western allies of the Soviet Union, accepted the Soviet government's version and downplayed reports of an international medical commission suggesting that the murders were committed by the Soviet secret police (Zaslavsky, 2004). During the Nuremberg trials in 1945 and 1946 the Katyn massacre was, with connivance of Western powers, ascribed to the Nazi regime. Only in 2010 did the Russian government openly acknowledge the murders, calling the tragedy a "military crime."

The two countries view the events in 1940 differently: Poland considers them as an act of genocide; Russia disagrees. In the aftermath of the crash many conspiracy theories emerged. Russia took measures to calm public opinion in Poland and dismiss many unfounded allegations. Later that year the Duma passed a resolution to acknowledge that Stalin and other Soviet officials secretly directed the Katyn massacre. Following the tragedy political contacts between Russia and Poland continued. Poland, however, continued its commitment to NATO, which was articulated during President Obama's 2014 visit to Warsaw.

During the events in Ukraine virtually all the Central and Eastern European countries had demonstrated their support for ousting the government of the pro-Russian president Yanukovych, who fled the country in 2014 as a result of revolutionary turmoil. Under those circumstances Central and Eastern European countries condemned Russia's actions by voting for the relevant resolutions in the UN General Assembly as well as in some other international organizations. Moreover, most Central European countries spoke for the toughest sanctions against Russia. Poland and the Baltic countries aligned themselves more strongly with the United States than with France and Germany on that issue. The Baltic Sea region remains a potentially volatile region due to the presence of Russian and NATO armed forces there essentially a few miles away from each other (Khudoley, 2016). On the other hand, Hungary, Slovakia, and Slovenia continued a dialogue with Russia. Time will tell whether these dynamics remain or change.

Conclusion

During the 1990s the Russian elites were looking forward to the possibility of the quick "inclusion" or integration of Russia into Europe. They sought good, neighborly relations with all European countries, including former socialist, so-called satellite states. These hopes have not materialized thirty years later. According to one view, it was mostly the fault of European countries that were reluctant to see Russia as an equal partner and were even prejudiced against Russia. Europe was too complacent and self-absorbed in the last thirty years, so that it overlooked the importance of building stable and efficient relations with their powerful neighbor in the East. If Europe had not made that historic blunder, the relationship would have been much better today.

The discussions about Russia's "integration" in Europe – quite common in the 1990s – have been postponed at least for the meantime. In part the reason lies in Moscow's gradual reversal of its foreign policy course. Russian experts and politicians these days increasingly see their country as a powerful and independent player in international affairs, on a par with Europe, America, and China.

Moreover, Russia remains critical of Western liberal political values and often presents itself as a guarantor of conservatism and traditionalism in social life and politics. The sanctions imposed on Russia after 2014 have strengthened a critical sentiment against the European Union and the Western world in general.

At the same time, despite a significant downturn in relations, many Russians continue to travel across Europe, spend vacations and buy property there, buy European products that are not sold in Russia due to the sanctions, imitate European interior designs, follow European fashion, sports, and music, and send (those who can afford this, of course) their children to study at European universities.

However, whether Russia is a part of Europe (or the West) – culturally and politically – has been a challenging question for many Russian politicians, intellectuals, and ordinary people. According to opinion polls, nearly 30 percent of Russians are oriented toward Western values, but about 20 percent want the return of the Soviet society, and about 40 percent insist on Russia's "special way" in the world. What the Russian choice will be depends on two factors: the leader in Moscow and the way the international situation is interpreted there. A lot depends on the West too.

Summary

- From the eighteenth century on Russia was an active participant in major European affairs, including joining coalitions and treaties. It was also engaged in many European wars.
- The Soviet Union conducted a robust foreign policy toward Europe from the 1930s. The Moscow leaders were against any type of pan-European integration. Yet Moscow pursued its own integration with those European countries under the rule of communist parties.
- In 1955 the Soviet Union created the Warsaw Pact – formally the Treaty of Friendship, Cooperation, and Mutual Assistance, which was a military and political alliance as well as a collective defense treaty of the European Communist governments.
- During the Cold War most Western European countries joined NATO as a security measure to counter the perceived threat from the Soviet Union. For decades the division of Germany in 1949 and the building of the Berlin Wall in 1961

had been the symbols of this ideological, political, and military confrontation in Europe and globally.

- During the perestroika period, in the second half of the 1980s, the Soviet Union introduced a policy of new thinking in international affairs and pursued significant improvements in its relations with European nations.
- The collapse of communism in 1991 and the creation of a new Russian state apparently lifted most of the remaining barriers between Russia and Europe. A new era in their relations was about to begin.
- There have been at least five distinct stages in Russian-European relations during the last two-and-a-half decades.
- Many Russians after 2014 maintained mostly a negative view of the European Union. This attitude was caused by – among several other factors – the worsening of official relations between Russia and the European Union, especially after Russia's annexation of Crimea and its policies in Ukraine.
- The legal basis for the relations between Russia and the European Union was the *Partnership and Cooperation Agreement* (PCA). It was signed in 1994 and came into force in 1997. However, the agreement failed to bring the expected results.
- A serious crisis in relations between Russia and NATO broke out in the spring of 1999. It was triggered by the events in Kosovo.
- Since the inception of Russia as a sovereign state, Moscow sought admission to the Council of Europe.
- Differences emerged between Russian and Western approaches to the future of the Helsinki process.
- Politicians and experts in Russia today are divided about how to see and treat a strong European Union. Two broad categories of opinions have emerged: Euro-optimists and Euro-pessimists.
- A difficult test of EU-Russian relations was the August 2008 conflict in the Caucasus (Georgia). The Ukrainian crisis brought relations between Russia and the European Union to their lowest point.
- Russia's relations with key European players, such as the United Kingdom, France, and Germany, have remained uneasy and even tense since 2014. These countries disagree with Russia's foreign policy and criticize Moscow's domestic record, especially in the fields of civil liberties and transparency.
- Russia's relations with Central European countries remain steady but mostly lukewarm;
- Despite the setbacks, Russia and the European Union remain very much interdependent. Europe's dependency on energy, Russia's dependency on modern European technologies, and significant interactions in the fields of culture, education, and tourism can explain their interconnectedness and offer a promise for the future.

Glossary

The Council of Europe (CoE) An international organization founded in 1949 to promote democracy, human rights, rule of law, and economic development in Europe.

Détente The easing of strained relations between countries.

Euro-optimists Tend to believe that increasing European integration and the emerging common border should bring Russia significant benefits. The integration should encourage Moscow to reform and accept European political values and business practices.

Europeanization The process in which an apparently non-European subject (such as a state, a city, or a social group) embraces particular European features such as government institutions, policies, or cultural trends.

Euro-pessimists Tend to believe that Russia's integration into Europe does not serve the country's core interests.

Extradition The official transfer of a suspected or convicted criminal to another country.

Helsinki Final Act A 1975 agreement on the principles of mutual relations among European states in an attempt to reduce tensions between the communist countries and the West.

Katyn massacre The tragic events in April 1940, when Soviet authorities ordered the execution of more than 22,000 Polish officers after the Soviet Army had occupied a portion of Polish territory.

Litvinenko case The 2007 poisoning of Alexander Litvinenko, a former Russian spy, by radioactive polonium-210 while he was living in London. Suspicion for the assassination fell on the Kremlin.

Poisoning Scandal The 2018 poisoning of Sergei Skripal, a former Russian security agent, and Yulia, his daughter, in the United Kingdom. According to official US and UK sources, this poisoning was secretly organized by the Russian government.

Warsaw Pact The Treaty of Friendship, Cooperation, and Mutual Assistance, which was a military and political alliance as well as a collective defense treaty of the European Communist governments.

Review questions

1. There have been at least five distinct stages in Russian-European relations during the last two-and-a-half decades. Name and describe them. How can you describe the major direction of these changes?
2. Many Russians after 2014 maintained a negative view of the European Union. Why? Give several reasons for the changes in Russian people's attitudes.
3. Why did the 2003 invasion of Iraq further worsen relations between Russia and the United Kingdom? Which events, in your view, could rapidly improve relations between Russia and the United Kingdom (or the United States)?
4. There is a view that one of Moscow's foreign policy goals is to stir disagreements among European countries. If this is the case, why would Moscow pursue such policy goals?
5. Which European countries could be the most interested in developing close and effective relations with Russia today?

Chapter 9
Russia's Policies toward China

With regard to Russia, strategic comprehensive interaction between Russia and China remains our foreign policy priority.

Vladimir Putin, November 10, 2017

We have a truly trust-based strategic partnership, and our practical cooperation brings new records.

China's President Xi Jinping, November 10, 2017

Learning objectives

- Describe and critically review the historical milestones in the relationship between the Soviet Union and China.
- Describe and critically analyze the periods of China-Russia relations after 1991.
- Critically discuss the multiple international and domestic factors affecting the relationship between Moscow and Beijing.
- Describe major perspectives in the relations between the two countries.

In the twenty-first century, when Moscow's relations with Washington and Western European countries have been worsening, the relatively robust relations between China and Russia have drawn substantial attention from politicians, scholars, and journalists. How long will these good relations last? Will China and Russia form a new strategic alliance, or is this just a convenient partnership in trade, as some suggest (Ying, 2016)? Opinions have differed. Some believed in a long-term strategic political and military partnership. Others maintained that this is just a temporary business of convenience: both countries have less in common in terms of their fundamental interests than people might think. Yet others saw in this relationship a new trend of the twenty-first century when the political elites in a growing number of countries have decided to trade the promise of economic and social stability to its citizens for a share of these citizens' fundamental political and personal freedoms.

As in previous chapters, we will provide a brief historical background of Russia-China relations and then critically analyze them from different angles.

Historical background

Before the Chinese revolution

At the end of the seventeenth century advancing Russian troops clashed with the Chinese military. Negotiations followed. In 1689 in the town of Nerchinsk the first border treaty was signed. The Aigun (1858) and the Beijing (1860) treaties further detailed the demarcation line between the two countries. These accords receive different assessments these days in Moscow and Beijing. China, for example, considers these nineteenth-century agreements unfair. Russia disagrees and sees these treaties as valid legal documents. In the late nineteenth and early twentieth centuries Russia was actively engaged in the struggle with other great powers over the spheres of influence in China. Russia was able to seize new areas in the east, thus connecting its territorial possessions in Siberia and East Asia with the Pacific Ocean. Russia then used the economic and political weakness of China to its own advantage. Yet, following Russia's defeat in the war with Japan (1904–1905), its influence continued only in northern parts of Manchuria. In the twentieth century the newly established Soviet state was expanding its power in the Far East by making deals with multiple Chinese warlords (who maintained control over Chinese territories in the North) and increasing Moscow's political influence in the aftermath of several armed conflicts there.

After the 1917 revolution the new Soviet government in Moscow facilitated the creation of the Communist Party of China (1921) and simultaneously sought good relations with the nationalists led by Chiang Kai-shek (1887–1975). A problem in their relations occurred over the question of Mongolia, which the nationalists considered an inseparable part of China but the Soviets did not. The Soviets helped Mongolian communists establish an independent state in 1921. The Mongolian People's Republic was established in 1924 and remained a close ally of the Soviet Union for many decades. Moscow also hoped to see the end of the civil war in China and facilitated a united front against the Japanese aggression.

In August 1945, three months after World War II was over in Europe, the Soviet Union (acting under agreement with Washington and London) attacked and defeated the Japanese troops occupying the northeastern Chinese province of Manchuria. The Soviet invasion of Manchuria, the Soviet military presence in that region, together with the United States' relentless bombing of Japan in August 1945, all contributed to Tokyo's imminent surrender and defeat in World War II. Soviet support (the Soviets provided weapons and helped in the Northeast region of China) was also an important factor in helping Chinese communists take power in the country in 1949.

People's Republic of China (PRC)

After the creation of the People's Republic of China in 1949 the Soviet Union became China's strongest ally. The reasons for building the alliance were ideological and practical. Both governments were under control of communist parties. Their ideologies were rooted in Marxism-Leninism. The Chinese and Soviet leaders shared a similar ideological, anti-imperialist view of international relations. Exhausted by the long war, China's leader Mao Zedong (1893–1976) needed external help for China's reconstruction. China urgently needed economic assistance. One of Mao's first acts was to visit Moscow, where he was seeking military protection and economic aid. He met with Stalin. The Soviets welcomed a potentially reliable partner in the East. The Sino-Soviet Treaty of Friendship, Alliance, and Mutual Assistance was signed in 1950. It was a mutual defense treaty, which also guaranteed economic aid to China. Moscow sent hundreds of economic advisers, engineers, military officers, nurses, and doctors to assist its emerging strategic partner. Thousands of Chinese students arrived at Soviet universities, medical, and technical schools.

In 1950 North Korea – with Soviet and Chinese support – attacked South Korea and then fought the UN-backed American forces there (Torkunov, 2000). Tens of thousands Chinese were killed in the **Korean War** (1950–1953) – one of the earliest and perhaps the bloodiest battle of the Cold War (some Western sources suggest more than four hundred thousand Chinese soldiers dead; Chinese sources believe the casualties were just over one hundred thousand).

The Soviet Union provided assistance in the early Chinese nuclear program by sending advisers and blueprints to help in building and testing the facilities for nuclear material production. China – also with Soviet assistance – was on the path to developing its own nuclear weapons (the first successful nuclear bomb test was conducted in 1964). The emerging Soviet-Chinese political alliance caused serious concern in the West in the 1950s. To contain communism in Asia Washington developed new strategic programs and assisted with a military buildup in Taiwan.

The split

Stalin's death in 1953 had a profound impact on Mao Zedong and the Chinese communist leaders. Although Mao conducted an independent foreign policy, he had long respected Stalin as an authoritative and strong leader. Khrushchev, who emerged as a new head of the Soviet government, hoped for a strong Beijing-Moscow alliance with Moscow playing a "big brother" role. Yet Mao did not want to be a puppet in the hands of the Kremlin. Serious problems between these two countries emerged, which led to a conflict and split in the early 1960s. Several reasons for the conflict can be identified. Mao was displeased with Khrushchev's criticism of Stalin and Stalin's **personality cult**, as it was labeled in the Soviet Union. The decision in Moscow to stop the support of the Chinese nuclear program (the Soviets at that time began consultations with the United States on nuclear arms control) was another crucial point that had worsened Soviet-Chinese relations. Khrushchev also changed the view of the United States and the West: the Soviets began seeing them mostly as competitors, not as deadly enemies. This position further alienated Mao Zedong (Zubok, 2007).

Chinese leaders criticized Moscow's new policy of peaceful coexistence between socialist and capitalist countries. Moscow, in turn, was displeased with Mao's radical domestic policies. A grandiose plan ("The Great Leap Forward") to quickly transform China into a rich world power seemed to the Soviets naïve and dangerous: Moscow believed that Chinese leaders had abandoned scientific knowledge and ignored common sense. Mao increasingly saw himself as a new leader in the global communist movement – the position that Moscow's leaders did not want to give up. The conflict between Mao and Khrushchev grew increasingly personal. Mutual insults ensued. Mao also suspected that the Soviet leadership wanted to remove him from power.

In 1963 all contacts between the communist parties of the two countries were cut off. Moscow and Beijing were accusing each other of revisionism and betrayal of the principles of Marxism-Leninism: the Soviets labeled the Chinese as dogmatic and as retrogrades; the Chinese labeled the Soviets as sellouts and revisionists. Moscow removed all Chinese sympathizers from many communist parties' leadership positions around the world. **The Great Proletarian Cultural Revolution in China**, an ideological and political "cleansing" campaign that took place between 1966 and 1969, also targeted Soviet sympathizers in China. The tensions between China and the Soviet Union soon escalated. Several military clashes took place along the Chinese-Soviet border. Both countries intensified propaganda against each other in the media, in books, and in official speeches.

From the 1960s until the 1980s the USSR and the PRC were taking opposite positions regarding almost all international issues (a rare exception was the support of North Vietnam in the war against the United States). Moscow sought any possibility to limit China's influence in international politics. Therefore, the normalization of relations between China and the United States (in 1972 President Richard Nixon visited Beijing; in 1978 the two countries established official diplomatic relations) caused serious concerns in Moscow. In part as a result of these developments, the Soviet leaders made the decision to improve relations with the United States in the early 1970s.

Only in the late 1980s, as a result of Gorbachev's reforms in domestic and foreign policy and the changes in China's foreign policy (Beijing too was turning away from ideology toward a pragmatic approach to international politics), the two countries indicated that they were ready to restore their relations on the basis of mutual respect, shared benefits, and peaceful coexistence (Ying, 2016).

The Chinese vector of Russia's foreign policy

Diplomatic relations between the People's Republic of China and the Russian Federation were gradually improving after the dissolution of the Soviet Union in 1991. These improvements were modest at first, since some difficulties in relations between Moscow and Beijing persisted. Although Marxist ideology was no longer an issue, Moscow was critical of China's domestic human rights policies. Beijing for its part was displeased with Russia's friendly relations with Taiwan and the opening of the Representative Office for the Taipei-Moscow Economic and Cultural Coordination Commission (today it issues visas to Russian citizens traveling to Taiwan). After Boris Yeltsin made his first official visit to China in 1992, a new and dynamic period of political reconciliation between the former rivals began.

During the early 1990s both governments remained careful in their assessments of their mutual relations. They referred to their contacts only as "mutually useful" and "productive." China and Russia announced that they would regard each other as a "friendly country" (Ying, 2016). In 1996 both sides reached an agreement on their strategic interaction in the twenty-first century. The term "strategic" when referring to China-Russian relations later became common in speeches and transcripts of diplomatic talks. When a certain term or phrase becomes frequent in official documents, this is likely to mean that the term has become a part of a political strategy.

China and Russia now were regularly reaching common opinions on most strategic and specific international issues. To illustrate, both countries criticized NATO's enlargement and both denounced the bombing of Yugoslavia by NATO forces in the 1990s. China did not criticize Russia for its violent actions in Chechnya, considering the situation in that breakaway region as Moscow's domestic problem. Moscow supported the one-China policy (in regard to Taiwan). Moscow and Beijing emphasized the importance of ending America's global domination and the importance of a multipolar world structure; they called for the respect for sovereignty in international affairs and criticized the Western concept of humanitarian intervention, which is interference in the affairs of other states in case of a humanitarian crisis. After the major financial crisis of 1998 Russian business and financial elites were paying increasing attention to China's economic models, which seemed at that time to be crisis-immune.

In 2001 the close relations between the two countries were formalized in the **Treaty of Good-Neighborliness and Friendly Cooperation**, which is a twenty-year strategic, economic, and defense international accord. The agreement signaled the development of solid ties between the two countries in many economic and social spheres. The treaty also indicated the closeness of their positions on the international stage. Russia and China were now cooperating closely in the United Nations, Shanghai Cooperation Organization, BRICS (an association of five major emerging national economies: Brazil, Russia, India, China, and South Africa), Asia-Pacific Economic Cooperation (APEC) and other international associations and organizations. They often expressed similar views about international events. In cases where their views differed the disagreements were often downplayed. China, for example, cooperates with Ukraine but at the same time does not criticize Russia's policies toward Ukraine and opposed the sanctions against Russia. China stands by Russia in the Syrian conflict. Russia supported China's position about the importance of bilateral negotiations with other countries regarding the territorial conflict in the South China Sea. After 2013 President Putin used the term "special" when referring to the relationship between the two nations. How can we explain these relations and predict their further development in the context of international politics? Let's consider three explanatory models.

First, Russian-Chinese relations can be seen as a time-sensitive "marriage of convenience". This is a temporary alliance of two countries during times of uncertainty in today's world. Russia needs cash and new investments – especially after facing an economic slowdown that began in 2012 and continued thereafter. So far, Russia's two major reliable sources of revenue have been hydrocarbons (oil and gas) and arms. China, in turn, can be a reliable buyer of these products, if the price is right. Moreover, Russia needs relatively inexpensive, affordable consumer goods. China manufactures them. Therefore, so long as both countries are happy with their trade arrangements, their economic and political alliance is likely to last. The mutual economic benefits could stimulate "good" politics between the two countries, including scientific, educational, and cultural exchanges. China, especially in this favorable political climate, may also find some new investment opportunities in Russia.

Second, China can consider Russia as a kind of "backyard". The relations between the two countries may appear as an opportunity for China to expand its influence in Eurasia and utilize Russian vast natural resources and territories. China is overpopulated and needs new territories and new energy reserves to sustain its economic growth. China also needs new markets for its products and services. Therefore, Russia has already become a convenient target (or even a potential victim) of China's geopolitical aspirations in Asia. Moreover, China does not have to depend on Russia's oil and gas: it can purchase them elsewhere. China is not particularly concerned about Russia's ability to transport China's goods to Europe by land, thus benefiting China (Gubuev, 2017), because it is building its own infrastructure, including roads and pipelines, deep into Central Asia. It is likely to invest tens of billions of dollars in a transportation path stretching from western China across Pakistan to the Indian Ocean (Kaplan, 2016). Thus Beijing wants Russia to be dependent on China, not vice versa. This also means that Russia is likely to reluctantly accept China's economic expansionism, masking it under the slogans – all for domestic consumption – of mutual cooperation and goodwill.

Third, Russia and China are likely to pursue ambitious geopolitical goals. They would cooperate mostly for domestic political as well as global purposes so long as their strategic interests do not clash. Both countries have adopted somewhat similar authoritarian domestic models. In both countries governments and the elites use democracy as a convenient "smokescreen" vis-à-vis the world's public opinion for suppressing civil freedoms, silencing the opposition, creating a culture of dependency on government – all to extend their grip on power. Both governments cultivate

Table 9.1 Three paths of China-Russia relations

Views of China-Russian Relations	Descriptions
"An alliance of convenience"	Russia and China will last as partners so long as they see this partnership as mutually useful.
"Russia is China's backyard"	China is exploiting Russia's vulnerabilities and uses its ties with Moscow to gain unilateral advantages.
"A new center of power"	Russia and China need each other to successfully compete with the West and dominate geopolitically.

nationalism to mobilize the masses. Both countries share a few strategic goals related to the West. They both see the United States and the West as their key competitors, even opponents, in the global world. Moscow and Beijing thus need each other to successfully compete with the West (Xi Jinping, 2016). See Table 9.1.

Russia-China relations: Key features

Borders

The border between Russia and China is about 4,200 km or 2,600 miles. It is the world's sixth-longest international border (could you name the other five that are longer?). After years of disputes both countries agreed to settle their territorial disagreements. Several small Amur River islands had been under Russia's control since the signing of the treaties of 1858 and 1860, but for many years these islands had still been claimed by China. The Soviet Union and China signed an agreement on the mutual border in 1991, which was amended in 2004. Russia transferred these small islands along with several small adjacent territories to China. Thus, seemingly a small a border dispute, which was a source of tensions for years, was resolved. The agreement also had an important symbolic meaning, because it reflected the process of reconciliation and growing understanding and goodwill between the two countries. After the parliaments in both countries ratified this territorial agreement (there were, of course, criticisms from the nationalist groups in Russia), the official transfer ceremony took place in 2008. For the Russian public the surrendered islands were too small to be emotionally significant. On the other hand, despite the resolution of the border issue, some Chinese commentators were making critical references to the nearly 600,000 remaining square miles of Chinese territory that Imperial Russia annexed in the late nineteenth century (Ying, 2016). But these claims did not become a serious political issue for the governments to discuss.

Economy

By 2011 China had become Russia's largest trading partner (China's GDP is about nine times larger than that of Russia). China's fast-growing economy needed to secure and diversify energy imports, while Russia's economy was largely driven by the demand from other countries for natural resources. China became a petroleum importer (due to its rapidly growing economy) for the first time in 1993. It had also become the world's second-largest oil consuming country around 2011 and the world's largest overall energy consumer around 2010 (IEA, 2017). In 2016 Russia surpassed Saudi Arabia as China's main oil supplier, with Rosneft, a state company, playing a major role in Russia's oil exports (Hess, 2018). Given its geographical proximity to China, Russia has been a clear candidate for meeting China's energy demands. In addition to the availability of natural resources, both sides benefited from the mutual trust that has been growing between the two countries. Yet certain challenges appeared.

Russia obviously needed a stable partner and purchaser of gas and oil for reasonably high prices. China, too, needed stability in partnership with Russia but, certainly, hoped to pay less for the products it purchased. In addition, China – like Europe – did not intend to be too dependent on Russia as its only energy supplier. Reasonably, China also wanted to diversify its sources of energy by getting oil and gas elsewhere. Russia, also understandably, wanted a degree of exclusivity as a trade partner. To further complicate the issue, Russian leaders did not want to see their country as merely a natural resources "warehouse" for China. Moscow needed investments to create employment, boost wages, bring new technology, and improve its country's infrastructure. China, however, has not been too eager to commit huge resources to invest in Russia's economy. One of the reasons is that China did not see a potentially promising return for its investments (Yuejin and Na, 2008).

Therefore, despite frequent declarations about the importance of their economic cooperation, Chinese-Russian relations have been limited by mutual doubts, delays, and pricing worries. Russia could offer to China a convenient route to transport products to Europe. Yet so far the price of land shipments has been considerably more expensive than shipments by sea (Gubuev, 2017). A new strategic concern affecting the relationship between China and Russia has also emerged: it is growing economic competition from other countries in Eurasia (Weitz, 2011). China's increasing oil and gas partnerships with former Soviet Central Asian republics such as Kazakhstan, Turkmenistan, and Tajikistan concerned Moscow. As you should remember, Central Asia has been Moscow's traditional region of influence.

Russia and China cooperate regarding nuclear energy. The **Tianwan Nuclear Power Station** is the largest nuclear plant in mainland China. It was built mostly by Russian companies and launched in several steps between 2006 and 2007. Still, Russian officials have been reluctant to transfer advanced nuclear energy technologies and other strategic knowhow to their Chinese partners. It seems understandable: Russia's possession of technology should protect Russian exports. Yet this position was likely to reinforce China's doubts about Russia's reliability as a long-term energy and economic partner (Weitz, 2011).

The Russian company Lukoil has been China's largest Russian oil supplier since 2006. The same year Gazprom – which is one of the biggest gas companies in the world – took over all exports of natural gas from Russia's eastern Siberian fields. In 2014 China and Russia reached a thirty-year gas deal, according to which Russia would send – beginning in 2018 – about 38 billion cubic meters of natural gas each year to China (Perlez, 2014). Russia, on the other hand, allows China to invest in Russia's energy sector and infrastructure. According to estimates, China's investments in Russia were around $1.4 billion in 2007 and were expected to reach $12 billion by 2020 (Yuejin and Na, 2008). However, many of these plans and estimates have to pass the reality test. For example, the planned substantial investment ($9.1 billion) proposed by the CEFC China Energy (a private Chinese conglomerate) in the Russian state-run oil company Rosneft fell apart in 2018. It seems that many companies in China consider the Russian government-run companies as too risky for investments (Hess, 2018).

Relatively low or even moderate oil prices, as well as other economic and political complications, could, of course, affect economic and trade relations between Russia and China. Take, for example, the delay until 2020 of the construction of two gas pipelines – the *Power of Siberia* and *Altai* – intended to bring gas to China from Siberia. Significant doubts emerged over these projects' economic viability and profitability. Russian energy companies, constrained for some time by Western sanctions (including Russia's actions in Ukraine), had difficulties developing oil and gas fields in eastern Siberia. Gazprom and Rosneft owned billions of dollars to Chinese banks (Eder and Huotari, 2016). China's and the world's shift to renewable sources of energy (such as wind and solar) is likely to further diminish Russia's chances of becoming a global energy superpower. Russia was also hoping to boost its agriculture by selling its products to China. However, by 2015 Russia accounted for only about 1 percent of China's chief imports – soybeans and corn.

Overall, trade between China and Russia had been growing steadily for more than a decade early in the twenty-first century. It took a hit after 2013. Troubled by Western sanctions, falling oil prices, and the unstable ruble, Russia's economy contracted. The difficulties are likely to continue for years to come. China, too, has acknowledged that the period of rapid growth of its economy, which was taking place early in the century, was seemingly over. See Figure 9.1.

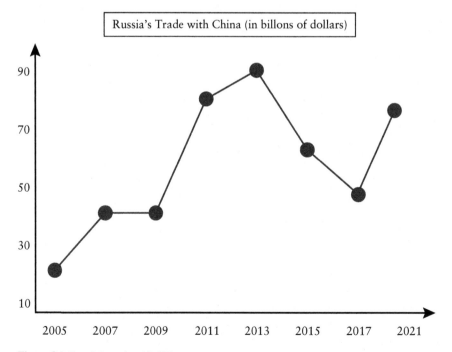

Figure 9.1 Russia's trade with China
Sources: Created using UN Comtrade Database; Russia's Federal Trade Statistics Service

Financial relations

For years China and Russia maintained policies of making their currencies – the ruble and the yuan – competitive on a global scale. They both see the global domination of the US dollar – the most potent reserve currency – as an obstacle to their ambitious economic and financial policies. On many occasions they have stated their desire to see global trade gradually abandoning the dollar. In 2010 Russian and Chinese leaders decided to use their own national currencies for bilateral trade, instead of the US currency. The move was meant to improve relations between Beijing and Moscow and to protect their domestic currencies and economies from the consequences of the world financial crisis, which began in 2008 and affected the global economy. The trading of the Chinese yuan against the Russian ruble began in the Chinese interbank market and the yuan's trading against the ruble started on the Russian foreign exchange market in December of 2010. In 2014 Beijing and Moscow signed an agreement on cash exchanges to get around American sanctions imposed on Russia and indirectly affecting China (Smolchenko, 2014). China also pledged its financial backing of Russia to support its currency, in case the ruble depreciates too low against the dollar and the euro. China and Russia are cooperating on new multinational financial institutions, such as the Asian Infrastructure Investment Bank, the New Development Bank, the BRICS and the BRICS foreign exchange reserve pool. In many ways such policies have been a calculated measure in hopes to gain advantage in case the dollar suddenly weakens or collapses.

The Shanghai Cooperation Organization

Back in 1996 China, Kazakhstan, Kyrgyzstan, Russia, and Tajikistan signed the *Treaty on Deepening Military Trust in Border Regions* in Shanghai and later agreed to reduce their military forces in those areas. This security organization in 2001 came to be called the **Shanghai Cooperation Organization**, or Shanghai Six after Uzbekistan joined the treaty. India and Pakistan also joined in 2017. Turkey has also expressed its interest in joining the "six." The initial purpose of the group was to reduce and then eliminate border disputes, reduce the presence of the countries' military forces near state borders, and coordinate efforts related to the countries' mutual security. One joint concern was and remains ethnic separatism and terrorism in Asia. Therefore, the members of this organization conduct joint military counterterrorism training and pursue wider cooperation in antidrug policies. The countries also coordinate their efforts in economic, investment, and trade areas. Russian and Chinese leaders regularly call for greater cooperation and coordination in the Shanghai Cooperation Organization as a form of multilateral diplomacy. Western experts tend to view this organization as an attempt to counterbalance the activities of the United States and NATO in Central Asia (Rozoff, 2009). There are differences in Russia's and China's positions toward this organization. China is mostly interested in economic cooperation. Russia, however, gives top priority to international security.

Military affairs

After the Western countries imposed an arms embargo on China – a consequence of the 1989 Tiananmen Square protests and violence – this country became a reliable client for Russian military exports, for many years accounting for from one-third to a half of all Russia's foreign military sales, depending on the year (Weitz, 2016). The volume of Russian sales of weapons and defense technology to China since around 2000 has reached $2 to $3 billion per year. Extensive Chinese-Russian defense cooperation these days involves consultations between high-level military personnel and joint military education and training. Military exercises have included more than a dozen joint maneuvers during the past decade or so. Since the early 2000s thousands of Chinese military personnel have studied in Russia, and hundreds of Russian military experts and officials have received short-term training at the National Defense University of China (Ying, 2016).

However, since the early 2000s China has been continually reducing its dependency on Russia's arms supplies. Beijing has already designed, developed, and mass-produced its own advanced weaponry and military equipment. China has been building a high-tech military, including cutting-edge submarines, ballistic missiles, fighter jets, and cyberwarfare units (Kaplan, 2016). Although Russia remains China's most important supplier, Moscow is gradually losing its market share because Beijing increasingly favors locally built weapons. Although the Chinese People's Liberation Army still buys key military parts from Russia – such as jet engines, radars, naval guns, and missile components – imports from Russia have dropped to less than 5 percent of China's military procurement, down by at least one-fifth from what they were in the early 2000s (Eder and Huotari, 2016).

Russia's Far East

In Russia's vocabulary **Far East** refers geographically to the parts of Russia between Lake Baikal and the Pacific Ocean. The Far Eastern Federal District of Russia had slightly more than six million residents, living mostly in the southern parts of the district and in its few large cities (Census, 2010). This is among the least populated regions in Russia and the world. The population is steadily declining due to the lack of economic and social opportunities in the region and to other opportunities emerging for the young elsewhere.

A stable Far East is vital for Russia's security. The country's fundamental goal in this region is to create a favorable geopolitical environment to provide stability and economic growth. Russian leaders and policy analysts for many years had been expressing their concerns about this region's depopulation, since mostly Chinese but also Japanese and Korean immigrants have been settling there (Trenin, 2002). The migration (although insignificant) of Chinese peasants and workers into the vast areas of Russian Siberia and Far East continued over the past fifteen or so years, and the local economy has become increasingly reliant on Chinese goods, services, and labor.

Table 9.2 Russian people's views of China

	2015	2016	2017	2018
Very Good	15	11	9	9
Mostly Good	65	61	67	61
Mostly Bad	6	10	10	9
Very Bad	2	3	3	4
Don't Know	11	16	11	18

Source: Levada, 2018f

Many regions of the world experience an influx of migrants. Russians too live now in the communities that host migrants from many countries and regions. In recent years many Chinese citizens have moved into Russia to pursue various business and trade opportunities. Their actual number is being disputed, for many of them live in Russia illegally. There is not, of course, an organized and hostile takeover of Russia's Far East by any country or ethnic group. The decline in the Russian-speaking population has taken place due to many reasons, including economic and social challenges. However,, as is happening in many other countries, immigration is becoming a sensitive political issue that can be easily exploited by any political group with a nationalist agenda. Russian tabloids often run headlines making allusions to a Chinese "invasion", and "conquest" of Russian territories (Clover, 2018). However, public opinion polls in Russia show a generally positive attitude toward China (See Table 9.2).

International relations

China and Russia, as has been stated earlier, tend to share many similar views on international affairs. Moscow supported Beijing's antiseparatist policies in Tibet and the Xinjiang province and received support from Chinese leaders for its own actions in Chechnya years ago. Russia also supports the "one China" policy and agrees that Taiwan is an inseparable part of China. Both countries have also been concerned with North Korea's dangerous behavior and have endorsed US policies aiming at reducing tensions at and around the Korean Peninsula.

Moscow and Beijing for many years did not publicly clash on a single international issue. There are differences in their positions, however. China, for example, emphasized that Russia must act with caution in Ukraine. Yet, China has not openly censured Russia's actions and did not join the West to impose sanctions on Russia (Ying, 2016). In terms of international alliances, Russia has always maintained a positive attitude toward creating a strategic alliance among India, China, and Russia. China, however, prefers a more cautious approach, understanding that such an international alliance might cause an alarmed reaction from the Arab countries, Pakistan, the United States, and possibly many other states. Therefore, China tends to be guarded and even restrained about creating and joining new alliances and has little interest in a formal military alliance with Russia. Beijing certainly cares about its relations with Washington and does not envision building any anti-US or anti-Western blocs including Russia or any other country.

According to leadership in Moscow and Beijing, Sino-Russian relations are a "priority" for both sides. These relations are not linked to fluctuations in the international situation. Chinese President Xi in 2018 called Putin a "good and old friend of the Chinese people" and "the leader of a great country who is influential around the world" (Withnall, 2018). By the beginning of the third decade of the twenty-first century, China and Russia were seemingly sharing a strategic interest in being parallel strategic competitors to the West and the United States in particular.

Russia and 'One Belt and One Road.'

In the past decade one of the most important pieces of China's foreign and economic policies has been the design and implementation of a high-capacity transport infrastructure, linking East Asia to Europe, as well as a range of economic projects adjacent to this infrastructure. These massive plans for a development strategy have received the name the **Belt and Road Initiative (BRI)**. China is working on inviting and including many Asian and European countries (the number is around 60) as well as regional organizations to implement this project. The project proposes several land corridors and a maritime transport route.

These plans of China in general correspond with Russian strategic projects for tighter cooperation in Eurasia. However, Russia's initial reaction to the BRI was tepid, for it was unclear whether the new transport routes would bypass Russia or how these initiatives would compliment the Eurasian Economic Union. Following the talks between Putin and Chinese President Xi Jinping in 2015 many of those concerns were addressed. Russia is aware that the BRI draws funding primarily from government sources. The plans include building high-speed railways in Russia, which would require cooperation with the Chinese government and many Chinese companies.

The future of Russian-Chinese relations will certainly depend, among many other factors, on how deep and effective Russia's involvement in the BRI will be and how successful and attractive this project become in the eyes of other countries and alliances.

Conclusion

Observers studying the relations between Beijing and Moscow see the evolution of their affairs – from animosity in the 1960s and 1970s, through cautiousness in the 1990s, to partnership and cooperation in the 2000s – as a model for other countries to follow. Both Russia and China have managed their differences and learned to work together on many economic, cultural, and political issues.

Russia's concern about China's economic expansion and its growing political power is coupled with both countries' desire to expand their cooperation. From the economic standpoint their collaboration should be mutually beneficial. Both countries are interested in maintaining stability in Asia and both oppose ethnic separatism, including Islamic radicalism. A common unifying goal for Moscow and Beijing could be a new "strategic partnership" as a counterweight to both the United States and Western Europe. However, this is a very delicate issue: Russia does not want to see a very powerful China at its borders. China does not need a confrontation with the West simply because it supports Russian policies.. China's Belt and Road Initiative, which in theory, should promote cooperation among Eurasian countries, could be seen in Moscow as China's drive for a larger role in global affairs. Russian nationalist groups insist that the ultimate goal of China is to capture Russian resources, mostly by financial and economic means and not necessarily through the use of force. Russia and China also increasingly often see each other as competitors for the markets in Central Asia (Eder and Huotari, 2016).

Good relations between China and Russia are likely to steadily develop. Since the beginning of this century the two countries have held regular annual meetings between their heads of state, prime ministers, top legislators, and foreign ministers. Since 2013, when Xi Jinping became president of China, until 2018, he has visited Russia five times. Putin has traveled five times to China in the same time period. Yet the frequency of visits is not always the best indicator of the effectiveness of relations. Both countries had hoped to boost their bilateral trade and reach $100 billion by 2015. In 2015, however, the volume of trade between Russia and China reached only $64 billion (Eder and Huotari, 2016). How large is this number? In comparison, US-Chinese trade reached nearly $600 billion that year; Europe's annual overall trade volume with China was around $500 billion. You can make your own critical judgment of these numbers.

To reiterate, most of the time Russia and China agree on most international issues. Sometimes they do not. But they are able to acknowledge and manage their disagreements while continuing to expand their cooperation. Both sides call it strategic. Only history knows how long strategic alliances last.

Summary

- In the late nineteenth and early twentieth centuries Russia was actively engaged in the struggle with other great powers over the spheres of influence in China. Russia was able to seize new areas in the east, thus connecting its territorial possessions in Siberia and East Asia with the Pacific Ocean.
- After the 1917 revolution the new Soviet government in Moscow facilitated the creation of the Communist Party of China and simultaneously sought good relations with the nationalists led by Chiang Kai-shek.
- After the creation of the People's Republic of China in 1949 the Soviet Union became China's strongest ally. The reasons for the alliance were ideological and practical.

- Stalin's death in 1953 had a profound impact on Mao Zedong and the Chinese communist leaders. Serious problems between these two countries appeared, which led to a conflict and split in the early 1960s.
- Diplomatic relations between the People's Republic of China and the Russian Federation were improving after the dissolution of the Soviet Union. China and Russia now were regularly sharing common views on both general and specific international issues.
- In the twenty-first century, while Moscow's relations with Washington and other Western European countries have been worsening, Russia and China have been developing relatively robust and friendly relations.
- After 2013 President Putin used the term "special" in reference to the relationship between the two nations.
- China and Russia claim that they have settled the remaining order disputes with each other.
- By 2011 China became Russia's largest trading partner. The Russian company Lukoil became China's largest Russian oil supplier from 2006 onwards. Russia and China cooperate regarding nuclear energy.
- China and Russia for years maintained policies of making their currencies – the yuan and the ruble – competitive on a global scale. They both see the global domination of the US dollar – as the most potent reserve currency – as an obstacle to their ambitious economic and financial policies.
- Differences in Russia's and China's positions toward the Shanghai Cooperation Organization exist. China pushes for mostly economic cooperation. Russia, however, gives top priority to the field of international security.
- Although Russia remains China's most important supplier, Moscow is gradually losing its market share because Beijing is increasingly favoring locally built weapons.
- Moscow and Beijing for many years did not publicly clash on a single international issue. There are some differences in their positions, however.
- Beijing and Moscow see the evolution of their relations – from animosity in the 1960s and 1970s, through cautiousness in the 1990s, to partnership and cooperation in the 2000s – as a model for other countries to follow.

Glossary

Belt and Road Initiative A development strategy proposed by the Chinese government to include a high-capacity transport infrastructure linking East Asia to Europe as well as a range of economic projects adjacent to this transcontinental infrastructure.

Far East In Russia's vocabulary this refers geographically to the parts of Russia between Lake Baikal and the Pacific Ocean.

The Great Proletarian Cultural Revolution in China An ideological and political "cleansing" campaign that took place between 1966 and 1969, which also targeted Soviet sympathizers.

Korean War One of the earliest and perhaps the bloodiest battle of the Cold War, involving the United Nations, the United States, China, North and South Korea. China came to the aid of North Korea, and the Soviet Union gave some assistance.

Personality Cult A complex worshiping and idealization of a leader (political, business, religious, etc.), often through unquestioned endorsement, flattery, and praise.

Shanghai Cooperation Organization Known also as the Shanghai Eight, an international political, economic, and military organization of eight (their number can change) countries, including China and Russia, aiming to reduce and eliminate border disputes, reduce the presence of the countries' military forces near state borders, and coordinate efforts related to the countries' mutual security.

Tianwan Nuclear Power Station The largest nuclear plant in mainland China. It was built mostly by Russian companies and launched in several stages between 2006 and 2007.

Treaty of Good-Neighborliness and Friendly Cooperation The 2001 twenty-year strategic, economic, and defense accord between China and Russia. The agreement signaled the development of ties between the two countries in many economic and social spheres and also indicated the closeness of their positions on the international stage.

Review questions

1. Since the 1990s China and Russia have been sharing common views on most general and specific international issues. Discuss the reasons why such a sharing is taking place. Use the three explanatory models of relations between China and Russia.
2. In your view, could the world's pivot to renewable sources of energy (such as wind and solar) seriously diminish Russia's hopes of becoming the global energy superpower? Discuss your opinion.
3. Since 2012 Russia's foreign policy has deliberately turned "east." Do you think this was a strategic success or a mistake, and why?
4. How should the West (including the United States and the United Kingdom) approach the developing Russia-China ties?
5. In your view, should Russia support the "one China" policy? Discuss options.

Chapter 10

The Southern Direction of Russian Foreign Policy (Russia's Policies toward the Middle East, North Africa, and Central Asia)

Today, traditional military and political alliances cannot protect against all the existing transborder challenges and threats.

The Foreign Policy Concept of the Russian Federation

Russia's "southern" direction of its foreign policy is about pursuing relationships with predominantly Muslim states, except for India, Israel, and Nepal. Some of these countries have been Russia's historical neighbors. Others were very much distant acquaintances. They all have played and continue to perform different roles in Russia's foreign policy. Some of them were constant competitors and foes. Others maintained relatively smooth relations with Russia for many decades. Yet others were constantly balanced between cooperation and competition. Ideology, politics, and economic interests all played their roles in different times. They continue to play such roles in the twenty-first century.

Historical background

The Russian Empire conducted a robust policy in the southern direction in the nineteenth and the beginning of the twentieth centuries. Russia sought and acquired new territories and was enlarging its spheres of influence. The long-term aspiration of Russian rulers to gain control over Constantinople (Istanbul), the Straits of Bosporus, and the Dardanelles was one of many factors that contributed to World War I.

The Soviet government did not take part in the division of the Ottoman Empire at the **1919 Paris Peace Conference**. It was the meeting of the Allied victors, including the United States, Great Britain, and France, following the end of World War I that set the peace terms for the defeated Central Powers, such as Germany and the Ottoman Empire, and determined new borders in Europe, the Middle East, and other regions. The Bolsheviks supported the nationalists in Turkey led by Mustafa Kemal (1881–1953) (MacMillan, 2003). They also attempted to strengthen Russia's positions in neighboring Iran and Afghanistan. The latter was considered as a possible channel for revolutionary propaganda and political influence in India and other British colonies. Yet, contrary to Moscow's anticipations, no influential communist parties emerged in any of these countries. The hope of using the local nationalist forces to the Soviet Union's advantage also fell through. On the contrary, at the beginning of the Cold War Turkey, Iran, and Pakistan joined the Western blocs. This strategic move negatively affected Moscow's policies toward these countries for many years. After Stalin's death in 1953 the USSR still pursued an active policy in the southern direction, paying particular attention to India, Afghanistan, and several Arab states. After the end of the Cold War, and especially after the 1990s, Russia was becoming more pragmatic and assertive as a player in this diverse region. Several reasons contributed to this renewed effort.

First, Russia's own apparent economic success in the early 2000s and its internal stability gave Moscow some seemingly compelling arguments to justify its increasing importance and strength as a country and as an economy. Second, the United States' frequent inability or unwillingness to address both lingering and acute problems in the region (such as the situation in Syria) created a political vacuum in the region. This environment gave various outside powers an opportunity to intervene. One such power was Russia. And finally, a chain of rapidly developing events changed the political landscape of many countries in the region (Rabinovich, 2016). From an emotional standpoint, the high hopes of many people about the opportunities sparked by the Arab Spring (2010–2011) were followed by an overwhelming and bitter sense of failure. On the one hand, several dictators had to resign or were removed by force. Yet anarchy and instability (rather than democracy and stability) have emerged. These challenges have overwhelmed the regimes in Syria, Iraq, Libya, and Yemen. These four states, alongside Lebanon and Sudan, have often been referred to as **failed states** for their inability to maintain physical safety of their people, economic opportunities, and political stability.

In the first two decades of the twenty-first century the ongoing Saudi-Iranian rivalry reflected serious differences in these two countries' policies as well as the historical Sunni-Shia conflict (Rabinovich, 2016). Iran and Saudi Arabia have clashed, as proxy powers, in several conflicts including the wars in Syria and Yemen. This time Russia was not standing on the sidelines.

Russia-Iran relations

Russia and Iran have had a long history of interaction marked at different times by turns and alterations in a course among cooperation, competition, and rivalry. Robust trade relations between the two states continued for centuries. During most of the Cold War, after the 1950s, the government of Iran, under the rule of Shah Pahlavi (1919–1980), was relying politically on the West. Iran was one of the major allies of the United States in Asia. At the same time, Iran for years maintained diplomatic and trade ties with the Soviet Union. Although relations between the two countries were satisfactory, they were not particularly cordial (Milani, 2011).

After the **1979 Iranian Revolution** and the demotion of Shah Pahlavi, the Soviet Union was among the first foreign states to recognize the newly formed Islamic Republic of Iran. The Kremlin realized that the rapid worsening of the relations between Iran and the United States could give Moscow new strategic opportunities in dealing with its southern neighbor. However, Iran's new government did not rush to treat the Soviet Union, a communist country at that time, as a new friend simply because Moscow opposed Washington's foreign policy. On the contrary, the new regime in Iran often called the Soviet Union the "lesser Satan" (Iran's authorities used the demagoguery term the "great Satan" to label and scorn Washington). Relations between Moscow and Teheran worsened after the Soviet military occupation of Afghanistan in 1979. As a result of the occupation and the lingering civil war that followed, tens of thousands of Afghan refugees fled to Iran in the early 1980s. During the Iran-Iraq war (1980–1988) Moscow proclaimed its neutrality in the conflict and attempted to increase its influence on both countries. This did not happen. Despite disagreements and political tensions between Teheran and Moscow, Iran and the Soviet Union still maintained diplomatic and trade relations.

Since the 1990s Russia has maintained notably closer and more robust trade, economic, and political relations with Iran, compared to many previous decades. As you should remember from previous chapters, according to the new Foreign Policy Concept, Moscow insists that it no longer uses ideology in dealing with other countries. It pursues, in theory, mostly pragmatic relations based on mutual interests, economic benefits, and other long-term goals. However, in reality, ideological calculations seldom disappear from Russia's foreign-policy motivations. For example, Russia and Iran share a common strategic interest of limiting the political and ideological influence of the United States in the Middle East and Central Asia. In practical terms, Russia increasingly often uses America's foreign policy missteps and inactions (and there are plenty of them) to Moscow's advantage. Russia has been taking benefit of the poor relations between Washington and Teheran and has often played a key role as an important intermediary between Western governments and the government of the Islamic Republic of Iran.

Russia constantly engages Iran and emphasizes its role as an equal player and partner in international institutions. Iran, for example, was offered full membership in the SCO. Moscow for years played a key role in the development of Iran's nuclear program. In particular, Russia assisted in constructing a nuclear power plant in Bushehr, finished in 2011. Teheran for years purchased military equipment and weapons from Russia vis-à-vis the Western sanctions against the Islamic Republic. One of the most noteworthy deals was Russia's delivery of S-300 missiles to Iran. (These missiles can be used as a defensive weapon against aircraft and cruise missiles if they are launched against Iran.) Initially, back in 2010 Russia, under pressure from the West, had suspended the delivery of these missiles. One of the reasons was that Iran had been under international economic sanctions for its noncompliance with nuclear nonproliferation policies. These sanctions affected Iran's foreign trade, financial and insurance services, energy sectors, and technologies. Later, however, in 2015 President Putin lifted the self-imposed Russian sales ban after an interim nuclear deal had been reached between Iran and the six negotiating countries, including the United States. Independent analysts have always criticized Iran's purchase of the Russian-made S-300 missiles. On the one hand, Iran asserts the defensive nature of this purchase and insists on the right to "shield" itself from foreign threats. Critics, on the other hand, claim that such a defense system gives Iran a major strategic boost: because Iran feels strategically safe, it may now develop offensive strategies and threaten its neighbors, including Turkey, the Gulf States, Saudi Arabia, and Israel (Reuters, 2016).

In addition to their military deals, Iran and Russia have also been expanding trade ties in several sectors of their economies, including telecommunications, agriculture, and technology for the oil industry. Russia continued extending financial credits to Iran to help develop its infrastructure, transport, and communications (RIA, 2015).

Iran consistently pursues new opportunities to improve and strengthen its geopolitical position in the region. Observers claim that Iran seeks regional hegemony, a policy that faces resistance from most other states (Rabinovich, 2016) such as Israel, Turkey, and Saudi Arabia. Moscow, in light of these negative reactions, tries to maneuver diplomatically in an attempt to persuade others not to see its pro-Iranian position as a manifestation of the negative intentions against Sunni Arab states such as Saudi Arabia.

Moscow's friendly and pragmatic policies toward Iran find popular support in Russia. According to a 2013 survey, 86 percent of Russians viewed Iran's role in international affairs positively, with only 10 percent expressing a negative view (BBC, 2013). Moreover, unlike the public in the United States, most Russians did not see Iran as a serious political or military threat to their country or the world. At the same time, Russians did not perceive Iran as a major ally either (Levada, 2016b).

It appears that in the future – in the context of new political developments – we should expect a continuing development of bilateral economic and military relations between Teheran and Moscow. They both supported the Assad regime in Syria. Yet very few expect that these relations will dramatically improve to become a strategic partnership (Partnership between Russia and Iran, 2017). Many of the economic deals and projects that both countries have agreed on have not been implemented. Moscow and Teheran disagreed on the use of the Caspian Sea (they have to share it with three other countries), and negotiations continue. In 2018, Iran, Russia, and four ex-Soviet states, agreed how to divide up the Caspian Sea in terms of energy exploration and pipeline projects. However, the delimitation of the seabed – a huge problem- will require additional agreements. (As you read this, check whether a better compromise has been found.) They both remain direct competitors on the global oil market. Russia also is not eager to antagonize its relations with the Arab countries or take sides in Sunni-Shia rivalry. Do not forget that most Russian Muslims are Sunni. Russia also does not want to be viewed (by unconditionally siding with Iran) as a threat to the region's stability. Moscow, for example, was silent on Washington's new administration's harsh criticism of Iran in 2018 and later, but it was strongly against Washington's rejection of the 2015 nuclear agreement with Iran.

Russia's relations with Arab countries

In the 1950s, especially after the 1956 Suez crisis, Moscow was giving increased attention to Arab countries. Soviet policies toward them were very selective. Many Arab countries in the second half of the twentieth century were choosing their own independent economic and political models as well as foreign policies. Many of these countries were turning away from the West; Moscow didn't want to miss a chance and tried to take advantage of these, apparently favorable for the Soviet Union, developments. The Soviet leaders were particularly eager to court those Arab countries that toyed with various political and economic models that were rejecting capitalism and embracing socialism. This was a typical Cold War strategy not limited exclusively to the Arab world (see Chapter 2). This was Moscow's global ideological strategy.

During the Cold War Moscow supported emerging prosocialist regimes in Iraq, Syria, Algeria, and South Yemen and pursued robust economic and political relations with them. The Soviets between the 1950s and the 1980s maintained stable and even friendly relations (which were worsening in other periods) with Egypt, Libya, the Sudan, and Somalia. Over the years thousands of students from these countries studied in Soviet universities, medical schools, and military academies. Russian engineers, builders, teachers, nurses, and military instructors worked under long-term deals in several Arab countries. (An uncle of one of the authors of this book, for example, spent three years in Algeria in the 1970s as a science instructor for a local college.) Moscow did not consider these countries as "legitimately" socialist (unlike the socialist countries in East and Central Europe or Vietnam and Mongolia, for example), but it actively engaged them in political and trade relations.

Cold War considerations played a main role in the Kremlin's decision to support the **Palestinian Liberation Organization (PLO)**, which was formed in 1964 to fight for the independence of Palestine. At that time Moscow was increasingly critical of Israel's policies, especially the policies toward Palestinians. In the 1960s Israel was moving closer to the West, which certainly irritated Moscow. After the 1967 War between Israel and its Arab neighbors, Moscow accused the Israeli government of aggression against the Arab states and broke off diplomatic relations with Tel Aviv. For almost twenty years after that war Moscow used its anti-Israel position (the struggle against Zionism, as it was officially labeled in the Soviet Union) to its own advantage in dealing with the PLO and most Arab states. The relationships with Saudi Arabia and Kuwait, as well as with several other Arab monarchies that sustained good relations with the West, were rather chilly. One of the reasons (in addition to ideology) was the fierce competition on the oil market. The possibility of losing oil revenues was an important reason why Moscow didn't join the Arab countries' oil embargo against the West in the 1970s.

Since the 1990s Russia's strategic goals in the Middle East have been focusing on gaining or regaining influence over most Arab countries. Several tasks and priorities associated with this effort have emerged in the 2000s and evolved over the years.

First, Russia needs political and social stability in the region. The revolutionary turmoil after 2011 in Tunisia and Egypt, the civil war in Syria and the rise and fall of the ISIS, the ongoing conflict in Iraq, and other conflicts have emerged as substantial challenges to both regional and broader international stability. Moscow saw the events of the Arab Spring (and similar popular revolts in other countries, as we have discussed elsewhere) as mostly harmful to regional stability and potentially dangerous for Russia.

Second, Russia actively pursues a bigger, more effective role for itself in this region's politics. This often involves the task of dropping ideological considerations and developing bilateral and multilateral ties with the countries of the region and taking advantage of the West's inaction or mistakes there. Moscow's good relations with Teheran should help Russian leaders, or so they believe, to play a mediating role between Iran and several Arab countries, especially Saudi Arabia, in the future.

Third, Russia seeks every opportunity to reduce the political domination of the United States, especially after the 2003 invasion of Iraq. Not only does Moscow support its traditional allies, such as Syria, contrary to Washington's and most other countries' wishes; Russia also actively engages Egypt, Sudan, and several Gulf states in political dialogues and consultations. By maintaining a nonideological and pragmatic policy, as Moscow claims, Russia hopes to become an important and influential force capable of solutions that neither the United States nor other Western countries could implement. For example, Russia maintains relations with both Israel and the Palestinian organizations (including Hamas, which is officially deemed a terrorist organization by the United States). Moscow abandoned its open anti-Israeli policies in the 1990s and now pursues dynamic relations with Tel Aviv. Large numbers of Soviet and Russian Jews have moved to Israel permanently over the past thirty years, and the size of the Russian-speaking population in Israel is around one million people. Moscow supports a two-state solution for Israel and Palestine and condemns violence between the two sides, regardless of which side is seen as responsible for it.

Russia and Syria

Russia's relations with Syria have been for decades robust and at times very friendly. During the Cold War Syria received millions of dollars from the Soviet Union in military and economic assistance. Moscow actively supported Syrian leader Hafez Assad (1930–2000) after he took power in 1971 in a military coup. Partly because of Assad's anti-Western and anti-Israeli attitudes, Moscow reached out to the Syrian government in hopes of gaining political influence in the Middle East. Syria reciprocated partly because it needed a reliable economic and military partner, which the Soviet Union appeared to be. In addition, Moscow offered educational opportunities for Syrians in Soviet colleges. Thousands of Syrian students studied in the Soviet Union during almost a twenty-year period until the end of the 1980s.

In 1971 both countries agreed about the Soviet naval facility in Tartus, on the coast of the Mediterranean Sea. It had been the only Soviet naval facility in that region and remains an official base for Russian ships in the Mediterranean in the twenty-first century. Although its strategic importance is frequently questioned (some experts suggest that it is an insignificant naval facility), Russia and Syria have agreed to further develop and enlarge this base. Back in 1980 Syria and the Soviet Union signed the Treaty of Friendship and Cooperation, which remains in force to this day. In 1987 the Syrian officer Mohammed Ahmed Faris became the first Arab astronaut (he travelled in space on the Soviet rocket). Russia has also played an essential role in helping the Syrian economy, specifically by writing off about 70 percent of Syria's $13.4 billion debt in 2005. Estimates suggest that Russia's contracts with Syria for arms have surpassed a billion dollars (BBC, 2013; CNBC, 2013a).

One of the most noteworthy developments of the past decade has been Russia's active support of the government of Syria, right from the onset of the political conflict and the civil war there in 2011. Russia immediately offered diplomatic support to Syria's government. The prospect of Syria falling into Washington's sphere of influence was clearly objectionable to Moscow. In the summer of 2013 it seemed that Russia helped defuse the chemical weapons crisis in Syria by offering the elimination of all Syria's chemical weapons as an alternative to a threatened American air raid against the Syrian ruler. Until October 2015 this support manifested itself primarily through the prevention (with Chinese help) of any UN Security Council resolution that would have sanctioned international military intervention into Syria. Moscow used all possible means to keep Assad in power. When the government in Damascus used chemical weapons against civilians in 2017, as most Western experts and leaders believe, Russia blocked the UN Resolution that condemned this attack; Russia also opposed sanctions against Syria. Moscow's argument was that the UN had no evidence that the Syrian government was responsible for such a barbaric act (Reuters, 2017).

Russia's policy was driven by a logical calculation: the overthrow of a legitimate government, no matter how it is perceived by others, would become a dangerous international precedent. In addition, Assad's regime was the last remaining Russian "asset" in the Middle East; thus, to remain there, Russia should support Assad by all means. As a permanent member of the UN Security Council, Moscow repeatedly vetoed Western-sponsored draft resolutions demanding the resignation of the Syrian president. To advance its military presence, Russia reclaimed the naval base in Tartus and the airfield on the Syrian coast near Latakia (Rabinovich, 2016). Moscow also started its direct military involvement in the war in the fall of 2015. These Russian policies challenged the Arab League's policy recognizing (in 2013) the anti-Assad groups – the National Coalition for Syrian Revolutionary and Opposition Forces – as the legitimate representatives of the Syrian people. The **Arab League** – which is the most influential international organization of Arab countries – also gave its members the green light to arm the Syrian rebels.

Although Russia began military operations against the Islamic State (ISIS or ISIL) in 2015, it also fought other militants fighting against the government of Assad on Syrian territory. Russia reached an agreement with Iran, Iraq, and Syria on collecting and sharing information related to ISIS. Moscow's involvement in the conflict in Syria has been its first significant military engagement outside the borders of the former Soviet Union. Russia sent squadrons of fighter jets to Syria as well as auxiliary units and started a ferocious, sometimes indiscriminate, bombing campaign against several rebel strongholds (*New York Times*, 2016). While claiming that it focused its attacks on the self-proclaimed Islamic State and other jihadi targets, the Russian air force also bombed moderate Islamist groups and groups supported by the United States and its Middle Eastern allies (*Guardian*, 2016). Moscow, however, frequently denies that such air attacks take place (Al Jazeera, 2018). Russia's actions in Syria, and especially its bombing campaign against the civilian population, caused a very negative international reaction. Moscow repeatedly argued about the necessity of using force and restoring order and stability in the region. Moscow has shown that it was not particularly concerned with one of many "byproducts" of its bombing campaign, namely a big wave of Syrian refugees trying to get into Europe or flee elsewhere. The Russian Supreme Court refused to consider the claim of Syrian citizens for asylum in Russia, because Moscow refused to consider the events in Syria as civil war but rather an antiterrorist operation (Lobanov and Kasrprzyk, 2018). Russia instead accused the West for many years, because of its actions and inaction, of creating the refugee crisis (Rabinovich, 2016). In 2018 Russia and France discussed their future efforts to ease the consequences of the humanitarian crisis in Syria including the deliveries of medicine and other crucial supplies (TASS, 2018).

Shortly after its eruption in March 2011, the Syrian crisis became the focal point of Russia's Middle Eastern politics. Yet, unlike during the Cold War years, Russia does not push for a particular ideology in Syria and does not want to impose a particular social or economic model there (Trofimov, 2018). The crisis has unfolded on four levels:

a local civil war between the regime of President Bashar al-Assad and its diverse domestic opposition, which has often been supported by foreign groups and powers;

a regional military and geopolitical conflict between Iran, on the one hand, and its rivals (Jordan, Qatar, Saudi Arabia, Israel, and Turkey) on the other;

a conflict between two branches of Islam, and two types of Islamic governance, Sunni and Shia, in which Russia was apparently on the side of Shia Iran; and

an international conflict between Russia, on the one hand, and the United States supported by its Western allies, on the other (see Table 10.1).

Table 10.1 The war in Syria and Russia's strategic outcomes

Type of conflict	The essence of conflict	Russia's strategic outcomes
Local	A civil war between the regime of President Bashar al-Assad and its diverse opposition (including ISIS and other jihadist groups) within the country.	Russia's support of Assad could improve Russia's relations with some Arab states but may worsen others; meanwhile, the defeat of ISIS will bring Russia international benefits.
Regional	A regional military conflict between Iran (which supports Syria), on the one hand, and its rivals (Jordan, Qatar, Saudi Arabia, and Turkey), on the other.	Russia may gain greater support in Iran yet may worsen its relations with most Arab states.
Religious conflict	An open conflict between the two main branches of Islam.	Russia is likely to pursue the role of a key mediator in this conflict.
Global	A global conflict between Russia, on the one hand, and the United States, supported by its Western allies, on the other.	Russia may earn prestige for its toughness, establish its permanent base in the Middle East, and challenge Western powers there for years to come.

Russia and Iraq

For decades in the past the Cold War considerations influenced the Soviet Union's relations with Iraq. They involved ideology and power politics. Formally, until 1959 Iraq was a member of the Baghdad Pact – officially known as The Central Treaty Organization (CENTO) involving Iran, Pakistan, Turkey, and the United Kingdom. One of the key goals of this treaty – encouraged and supported by the United States – was to contain the Soviet Union and its close allies. After the 1968 coup Saddam Hussein consolidated his political power in Iraq and moved closer to the Soviet Union. The Treaty on Friendship and Cooperation between the two countries was signed in 1972. Like several other states that were moving into the political orbit of the Soviet Union during that time, Iraq wanted to conduct an independent foreign policy and, at the same time, it needed a powerful ally, which the Soviet Union offered to become. Moscow supplied weapons to Iraq cheaply and often on credit. Relations worsened after the Soviet invasion of Afghanistan (Iraq did not support the war) and after Hussein launched a campaign against communists in Iraq.

However, the end of the Cold War changed Russia's global priorities as well as policies toward Iraq. An important indicator of the change was the Soviet Union's opposition to the 1990 Iraq invasion of Kuwait. Moscow formally supported an international coalition to resist Iraq and endorsed the United Nations' resolution authorizing the use of military force there. Yet gradually, during the 1990s, Russia became more protective of Iraq and its policies. Not only did Moscow maintain trade relations with Baghdad, it also was sending military advisers there. Russia agreed to the UN sanctions imposed on Iraq in the 1990s, although with some reservations. Moscow criticized and opposed, as you remember, the US invasion of Iraq in 2003 and the occupation that followed.

Russia's involvement in Iraq these days is about pursuing at least three goals: protecting Russia's energy interests, securing Moscow's regional influence, and weakening the influence of the West, especially the United States. In the 2000s Russia invested millions of dollars in Iraq's energy sector. Russian energy companies continue to work on Iraq's largest oil deposits. Moscow hopes to strengthen its commercial and security ties with Iraq, potentially eroding US influence in one of the world's most critical regions (Borshchevskaya, 2014). Moscow believe Iraq is interested in purchasing Russian arms, developing new oil fields with Russia's help, and implementing reconstruction and other projects (Mamedov, 2018). In 2015 it opened an intelligence-sharing center to coordinate actions with Iran and Syria aimed at fighting ISIS. Trade between Russia and Iraq, mostly made up of Russian exports, has risen to $2 billion, according to Russian news media (Hameed, 2016).

Russia and Egypt

In the 1950s Egyptian president Gamal Nasser (1918–1970) launched an independent anti-imperialist policy that earned him enthusiastic support in the USSR. Nasser turned to the Soviet Union for economic aid and weapons. The response of the Soviet Union to the Suez Crisis in 1956, and Moscow's enthusiastic support of Egypt, somewhat improved the Soviet image in the Middle East. Since 1967, however, after the armies of Egypt, Syria, and Jordan were defeated in the Six-Day War against Israel, Soviet influence in the region has diminished. It appeared to many Arab leaders that Moscow was unable to stop Israel. In addition, it appeared that for the Soviets better ties with America were more important than Moscow's commitments to Egypt and the Arabs. After the 1973 war against Israel Egypt was increasingly turning to the United States for political and economic assistance. Washington appeared to have been winning the Cold War battles in the Middle East. Moscow had to cope with the fact that Soviet influence was diminishing not only in Egypt but also across the Middle East.

Relations between Russia and Egypt remained steady after the end of the Cold War. In the 2000s President Putin visited Egypt, and then Egyptian President Hosni Mubarak visited Russia. Relations between the two countries were further improving following the July 2013 military coup that ousted Egypt's president Mohamed Morsi. Both countries have been working to strengthen their military and trade ties and other forms of bilateral cooperation. The official visit of Egyptian President Abdel Fattah al-Sisi to Russia in 2016 – his first overseas trip outside the Arab world since his election – and the outcome of his talks with President Vladimir Putin have clearly demonstrated that relations between Egypt and Russia were improving (Egypt did not ignore the United States; Al-Sisi visited Washington in 2017). It has been revealed that Egypt was ready to increase its supply of agricultural products to Russia, which in 2017 accounted for 90 percent of Russian imports from Egypt. Russia remains the largest supplier of grain to Egypt, providing about 40 percent of its grain consumption. Both countries have been in talks about establishing a free trade zone between them (RIA, 2014). Egypt's exports to Russia increased by 35 percent in 2017, reaching $500 million, compared to $374 million in 2016 (Egypt Today, 2018). Since the 1990s Egypt has become one of the most attractive foreign destinations for Russian tourists, which positively impacted the economy there. Unfortunately, the 2015 downing of a Russian plane over Egypt (it was a terrorist attack) has forced Russia to impose restrictions on travel to Egypt. The situation will have changed by the time you read these pages.

There have been rather serious differences in the Egyptian and Russian positions regarding the Gaza Sector (or Gaza Strip, which is a self-governing Palestinian territory on the Eastern Coast of the Mediterranean Sea). First of all Moscow still does not consider **Hamas** a terrorist organization. (Hamas is a Palestinian Sunni-Islamic fundamentalist group, which is regarded as a terrorist organization in the United States, Egypt, Israel, and the European Union.) It appears that the Kremlin does not intend to burn bridges with Hamas, and this apparent political neutrality may help Russia, as it believes, in its future role as a mediator between Israel and Palestinians. Moscow also believes that as long as Hamas retains control of Gaza, Israel will have to engage in negotiations with the movement, directly or indirectly. Moscow has always opposed the blockade of Gaza, which both Egypt and Israel support. At the same time, both Russia and Egypt are similarly interested in the defeat of the jihadists across the region. Hamas also believes that the Russians can play a bigger role in the future developments in and around Palestine (Khoury, 2018; Naumkin, 2014).

Russia's relations with Israel

After 1944 Joseph Stalin adopted a pro-Zionist foreign policy, apparently believing that the new country (Israel) would become socialist and this development would speed up the decline of British influence in the Middle East. On May 17, 1948, three days after Israel declared its independence, the Soviet Union officially granted *de jure* recognition of Israel, thus becoming the second country to recognize the Jewish state (preceded only by the United States' *de facto* recognition). During the following years, however, relations have deteriorated. Moscow maintained an anti-Israeli position in the Arab-Israel conflict. From 1967 to 1991 there were no official diplomatic relations between the Soviet Union and Israel. These mutual tensions began to ease only after 1992.

The Russian language is now the third most widely spoken language in Israel (after Hebrew and Arabic). Israel also has the third largest number of Russian speakers outside of the former Soviet republics; Russian-born people constitute the biggest group of the total immigrant population in Israel. Moscow wants to see Israel as a strategic partner in the Middle East. Both countries see Islamic extremism as a major threat. In the trade area relations are robust. Israel sells agricultural products to Russia, which one can easily find on almost every store's shelf in Russian cities. Yet Russia also wants to play a mediating role in the Middle East. Therefore, in violent confrontations between Israel and its opponents Moscow avoids condemning any of the parties for their actions; Moscow also denounces violence erupting occasionally between Israel and its opponents (Khoury, 2018; Naumkin, 2014).

The Arab-Israeli conflict remains an important issue on the region's political agenda, but its significance as a defining issue in Russia's strategies has declined in the second decade. Most Arab states are primarily concerned with the Iranian and jihadi challenges, and several Sunni states have been collaborating with Israel against these challenges (Rabinovich, 2016). Russia, for example, did not criticize Israel for its air strikes against Iranian and Hezbollah military targets in Syria. Russia understands these strategic changes and conducts a regular dialogue with Israel and other Arab states.

Russia's relations with Afghanistan

During the Cold War Afghanistan became the center of a major conflict between the superpowers. In 1978 the Soviet Union sent hundreds of advisers to Kabul in support of a new procommunist government there. Fearing the collapse of this regime, foreseeing instability in the region, and grossly miscalculating Washington's plans in the area, the Soviet Union invaded Afghanistan in 1979. In the past Moscow had used its military to intervene in Hungary and Czechoslovakia, yet it never sent tens of thousands of combat troops beyond the borders of the Warsaw Pact. The war cost Russia more than 15,000 dead and tens of thousands wounded. The United Nations General Assembly condemned the Soviet invasion. US President Carter blocked grain deliveries to the Soviet Union, launched a boycott of the 1980 Olympic Games in Moscow, and stepped up US arms spending. For the Soviets, Afghanistan had become their Vietnam, a comparison used by many observers in Russia to compare the invasion of Afghanistan with the Vietnam War (Borovik, 1990). Although the Soviet troop withdrawal was completed by February 1989, fighting among rival groups of Islamic fundamentalists, who were using US and Soviet weapons, has continued for many years.

After the terrorist attacks against the United States in 2001 Russia provided political, logistical, and intelligence support to Washington to overthrow the Taliban regime (Mankoff, 2012). Moscow has long accused the Taliban regime in Kabul of supporting violent jihadists in the Russian province of Chechnya in the late 1990s. The United States and Moscow signed an agreement about coordinating their counterterrorist efforts in Afghanistan and globally (Declaration, 2002). Later Russia, like the United States, supported a united Afghanistan and stood against the attempts to divide the country along ethnic lines. Russia also wrote off Kabul's outstanding debt to Moscow (Mendkovich, 2011).

Russia pursues at least three major goals in Afghanistan. First, Russia needs a secure and stable Afghanistan, which should contribute to the stability of Russia's southern neighbors such as Tajikistan and Uzbekistan. Russia is particularly attentive to the influence of militant Islamists in Central Asia, especially in the former Soviet republics. Russia is also concerned with the illegal trade in narcotics, such as opiates, which originate in Afghanistan and enter Russian and then global markets through Russia's southern border. Second, Russia wants to see a strengthening of its ties with Afghanistan. Moscow engages Kabul internationally, such as granting it a role of observer status in the SCO. In addition, Russia wants to see a decreasing role of the United States and its Western allies in Afghanistan as well as in the entire region. This, not surprisingly, has been part of Russia's global strategy.

Russia's relations with Turkey

From the late sixteenth century relations between the Ottoman Empire and Russia were often tense, as the two powers engaged in a number of conflicts known as the Russo-Turkish wars. The Soviet Union did not participate in the partitions of the Ottoman Empire (MacMillan, 2003) and had robust and even friendly relations with the new Turkish government of Mustafa Kemal. Relations have worsened since the late 1920s. After Turkey joined NATO in 1952 (and thus joined the Western alliance against the Warsaw Pact during the Cold War), the relations between the two countries were tense. They changed for the better in the 1990s.

Russia has rapidly become Turkey's largest provider of energy, while many Turkish companies (such as construction firms, for instance) began operating in Russia. Since the 1990s Turkey (like Egypt) became a top foreign destination for Russian tourists attracted by the country's affordable and friendly seaside resorts. Turkey was selling a wide range of agricultural products to Russia. However, the successful bilateral relations of the past two decades were severely strained after the **November 2015 jet incident**, when a Turkish F-16 combat aircraft shot down a Russian Su-24 jet close to the Turkish-Syrian border (the Russians at that time were conducting military operations in Syria). In response, Russia immediately imposed severe economic sanctions on Turkey. These included the suspension of visa-free travel to Russia for Turkish citizens, limits on Turkish residents and companies doing business in Russia, and restrictions on imports of Turkish products including vegetables. In 2016 the Russian government reopened a line of communication with its counterparts in Ankara. Moscow then lifted the travel restrictions on Russian citizens visiting Turkey and partly restored mutual trade. Turkey and Russia have turned to a more pragmatic policy toward each other (Kogan, 2016). In 2017 and later the two countries further normalized their ties through a series of meetings and negotiations. It remains to be seen if this policy of normalization is sustainable.

The Turkish president in 2016 expressed a willingness to join the Shanghai Six, as a sign of his disappointment with the European Union's policies toward Turkey, including the reluctance to admit Turkey into the union. Russia also courts Turkey as a NATO country in an attempt to take advantage of a "weak link" in the NATO alliance. The instability and uncertainty of the situation in the nearby Middle East, such as in Syria, should affect Russia-Turkey relations for a considerable period. Washington's actions in Syria (the United States supports Kurdish groups there; Turkey fights against their advances) and criticism of Turkish policies and the 2018 economic sanctions against Turkey for detaining several US citizens (Turkey claimed that they all were connected to anti-government plots) have further pushed Ankara closer to Moscow (Dettmer, 2018).

Russia's relations with India and Pakistan

Russia for decades has been one of India's closest allies. The two countries have maintained political, military, and commercial ties since the mid-1950s. The turning point was the Soviet decision to support India in its territorial dispute with Pakistan regarding the territory of Jammu and Kashmir. During the Cold War India and the Soviet Union enjoyed strong strategic, military, economic, and diplomatic relationships. In 1966 the Soviet Union served successfully as a peace broker between India and Pakistan to end an Indian-Pakistani war (Jamal, 2016). India was distancing itself from Western countries, and its leaders were interested in developing close relations with Moscow. In 1971 India and the Soviet Union signed a treaty of friendship and cooperation. India-Soviet relations have been perhaps the most successful example of Moscow's close relations with countries from the Non-Aligned Movement (see Chapter 5). Besides mutual trade, both countries have cooperated in the fields of energy and education and in the space exploration project. Rakesh Sharma, an air force pilot aboard the Soviet rocket, was the first Indian to travel in space in 1984. After the collapse of the USSR Russia continued its friendly relations with India.

In the twenty-first century Russia remains a key partner of India in the fields of energy security, nuclear energy, and hydrocarbons (Mukherjee, 2015). Another key area of trade is weapons. In the twenty-first century arms exports from Russia to India have exceeded $20 billion (Pulipaka, 2016). Russia accounts for almost 70 percent of India's arms purchases from foreign countries. Among big purchases are Russian jet fighters and helicopters. In 2012 both states signed a new arms deal worth $2.9 billion (BBC News, 2016). Both countries have reduced some trade regulations and tariffs. Russia has also agreed to build more than twenty nuclear reactors in India over the next two decades. Russia's biggest gas company, Gazprom, has continued its natural gas shipments to India of approximately 2.5 million tons a year for twenty years. India and Russia agreed to cooperate in the field of computer-related technology (Sharma, 2012).

Meanwhile, several problems in Russian-Indian relations have emerged. Some Russian companies, for example, did not fulfil their contractual obligations (such as a delay in repairing an Indian aircraft carrier). India worries about the strengthening of Russia-China relations. On the other hand, Russia is concerned about the improvement of India's relations with Washington. In comparison, in 2017 US-Russia trade was worth about $8 billion, when US-Indian trade has reached $114 billion (More, 2018).

For many years relations between the Soviet Union and Pakistan – India's neighbor and chief rival for seven decades – were robust yet not necessarily friendly. Cold War contentions and regional politics played an important role in Moscow's policies toward Islamabad. In 1954–1955 Pakistan became a member of the Southeast Asia Treaty Organization (SEATO) and the Central Treaty Organization (CENTO), political and military blocs that the Soviet Union opposed. During the Indo-Pakistani war of 1972 Moscow supported India. Pakistan helped the Afghan fighters during the Soviet occupation of Afghanistan in the 1980s and became a major venue for American equipment and weapons delivered to the Afghani mujahidin (soldiers of God, as the resistance often called themselves). During that period relations between the Soviet Union and Pakistan were at their lowest point.

The real improvements in Russia's relations with Pakistan came in the wake of the 2001 terrorist attacks against the United States. Pakistan quickly denounced the government of the Taliban and joined the NATO coalition to hunt down the al-Qaeda leaders. The decision of Pakistani leaders to join the international action against terrorism has led to an improvement in Russia-Pakistan relations in economic, trade, and political fields. Pakistan is searching for stable partners, and Russia is one of the potentials candidates.

Russia endorsed Pakistan's full membership in the Shanghai Cooperation Organization (Pakistan and India joined in 2017). Moscow has offered its assistance in developing Pakistan's power plants. Russia also sells military jets and combat helicopters to Pakistan. The Pakistan Army, together with those of other countries, have participated in Russian military exercises (Jamal, 2016). Russia, of course, is aware of India's attention to the ways in which relations between Moscow and Islamabad are developing. Moscow sends its assurances that it treats both India and Pakistan evenhandedly and that India-Russia ties should remain strong.

Conclusion

From a geopolitical standpoint, after 2008 the United States' influence in the region has weakened. Washington cut the bulk of the US military presence in Afghanistan and Iraq. President Obama refused a substantial military involvement in the Syrian civil war. America under Obama strained its relations with several conservative Arab states, such as Saudi Arabia. America did not show support for the protest movement in Iran in 2011–2012 and essentially stood on the sidelines during the Muslim Brotherhood's reign in Egypt in 2012–2013. Russia turned to playing a more assertive role in the region. It used its traditional allies as well as seeking new engagements. By taking action in Syria in 2015 Russia has made clear its intention to restore its status as a major international player (Lukyanov, 2016).

However, Washington has reversed many of its policies since 2017 when president Trump entered the White House. Washington reengaged many Arab and Muslim states and took a tough position against Iran's domestic and foreign policies by reinstating sanctions against Teheran in 2018. These and other international developments should impact Russia's actions in North Africa and South Asia in the future. Russia may choose to retain and strengthen its ties with Iran, which could leave Moscow in relative isolation in the region and globally. Russia also could reach out to the United States and its allies, thus adding to the legitimacy of its presence and policies in the region.

How the situation in and around Syria develops is likely to be a major indicator of the direction of Russia's foreign policy. You can judge – when you are reading these pages – if a coalition of predominantly Sunni states (including Turkey and Saudi Arabia) prevails in Syria or if Russia and Iran will be sponsoring a regime friendly to them in Damascus as well as gaining a geopolitical advantage in the region. Russia may also strengthen its positions in the Middle East by cooperating with the regional powers in securing a new coalition government and assisting in Syria's rebuilding after the war (assuming that the conflict is over). On the other hand, Washington's assertive political steps (which could include engagements of several leading Arab states) may shift the balance of power. It will be up to Iran if this country continues the same regional policy in the region.

Russia cannot push the United States out of the Middle East – it could not do so even after Washington somewhat disengaged in the region between 2008 and 2016. America's influence remains strong and lasting. Russia, on the other hand, has no real allies in the region, just business partners. Russia, despite its military abilities and its sophisticated diplomatic efforts, doesn't really have the means to project power across the region. Egypt, Turkey, and a few other countries can use Russia to make business deals, yet they do not really want to irritate Washington: their strategic relationship with America is vital (Trofimov, 2018).

In the twenty-first century Russia has chosen a bigger role in the Middle East. Moscow seeks to play a mediating role between the conflicting sides. Examples are Russia's relations with India and Pakistan or with Israel and its rival, Hamas. In the coming years the Saudi-Iranian and Sunni-Shia challenges are likely to remain key sources of international tensions in the region. If the United States does not mobilize the Arab states to check Iran's regional ambitions, Russia will likely attempt to exploit the difficulties in relations between Washington and the Arab capitals. Moscow has plenty of options in this regard. One key problem persists though: Russia's resources remain limited.

Summary

- Russian foreign policy's southern direction involves predominantly Muslim states, as well as India, Israel, and Nepal. Some of these countries have been Russia's historical neighbors. Others were very much distant acquaintances.

- The Russian Empire conducted a robust policy in the southern direction in the nineteenth and the beginning of the twentieth centuries. Russia sought and acquired new territories and was enlarging its spheres of influence.
- During the Cold War the USSR pursued an active policy in the southern direction, paying particular attention to India, Afghanistan, and several Arab states. After the 1990s Russia was becoming more pragmatic and assertive as a player in this diverse region.
- Russia and neighboring Iran have had a long history of interaction marked at different times by cooperation, competition, and even rivalry. Today Russia and Iran share a common strategic interest of limiting the political and ideological influence of the United States in the Middle East and Central Asia. Russia constantly engages with Iran and emphasizes its role as an equal player and partner in international institutions.
- After the mid-1950s, especially after the 1956 Suez crisis, Moscow was giving increased attention to Arab countries. Russia's policies toward them were very selective. During the Cold War Moscow supported prosocialist regimes in Iraq, Syria, Algeria, and South Yemen and pursued robust economic and political relations with them.
- Russia needs political and social stability in the Middle East and North Africa. Russia actively pursues a bigger, more effective role for itself in this region's politics. Russia seeks every opportunity to reduce the political domination of the United States, especially after the 2003 invasion of Iraq.
- Russia's relations with Syria have been for decades robust and at times very friendly. During the Cold War Syria received millions of dollars from the Soviet Union in military and economic assistance. Russia immediately offered diplomatic support to the Syrian government from the onset of the political conflict and the civil war in Syria in 2011.
- Moscow started its direct military involvement in the war in the fall of 2015. When the government in Damascus, according to most experts, used chemical weapons against civilians in 2017 (which Syria and Russia both deny), Russia blocked the UN Resolution that condemned this attack and imposed sanctions against Syria.
- During the Cold War the Soviet Union's relations with Iraq were influenced by Cold War considerations involving ideology and power politics. Russia's involvement in Iraq these days has at least two goals: protecting Russia's energy interests and securing Moscow's regional influence at the expense of the West.
- Russia's relations with Egypt remain stable. Egypt has been an attractive destination for tens of thousands of Russian tourists every year. There have been rather serious differences in the Egyptian and Russian positions regarding the Gaza Sector. At the same time, both Russia and Egypt are similarly interested in the defeat of jihadists.
- Moscow wants to see Israel as a strategic partner in the Middle East. Both countries see Islamic extremism as a major threat. In the trade area relations are very robust.
- During the Cold War Afghanistan became a center of a major conflict between the superpowers. The Soviet Union fought a protracted war there until 1989.

Russia today needs a secure and stable Afghanistan, which should contribute to the stability of Russia's southern neighbors such as Tajikistan and Uzbekistan. Moscow engages Kabul internationally, for instance, granting it a role of observer status in the SCO.

- From the late sixteenth century on relations between the Ottoman Empire and Russia were often tense, and relations with Turkey remained tense during the Cold War. Relations changed in the 1990s. Russia has rapidly become Turkey's largest provider of energy, while many Turkish companies have begun operating in Russia. Turkey became a top foreign destination for Russian tourists.

- Russia also courts Turkey as a NATO country in an attempt to take advantage of a "weak link" in the NATO alliance. The instability and uncertainty of the situation in the nearby Middle East could affect Russia-Turkey relations for a considerable period.

- Russia has been one of India's oldest and closest allies. The two countries have maintained political, military, and commercial ties since the mid-1950s. In the twenty-first century Russia remains a key partner of India in the fields of energy security, nuclear energy, and hydrocarbons. One of the key areas of trade is weapons.

- For many years, relations between the Soviet Union and Pakistan – India's neighbor and chief rival – were robust yet not necessarily friendly. Russia endorses Pakistan's full membership in the SCO. Moscow has offered its assistance in developing Pakistan's power plants. Russia also sells military jets and combat helicopters to Pakistan. Moscow sends its assurances that it treats both India and Pakistan evenhandedly and that India-Russia ties should remain strong.

Glossary

Arab League The most influential international organization of Arab countries.

Failed states Countries labeled in this way for their inability to maintain physical safety, economic opportunities, and political stability.

Hamas Palestinian Sunni-Islamic fundamentalist organization, which is regarded as a terrorist organization in the United States and the European Union but not in Russia.

Iranian Revolution (1979) The overthrow of the Persian monarchy and its eventual replacement with an Islamic Republic.

November 2015 jet incident Tragic episode when a Turkish F-16 combat aircraft shot down a Russian Su-24 jet close to the Turkish-Syrian border (the Russians at that time were conducting military operations in Syria).

Palestinian Liberation Organization (PLO) Formed in 1964 to struggle for the liberation of Palestine.

Paris Peace Conference (1919) The meeting of the Allied victors, including the United States, Great Britain, and France, following the end of World War I to set the peace terms for the defeated Central Powers such as Germany and the Ottoman Empire.

Review questions

1. After the end of the Cold War Moscow became more pragmatic and assertive as a player in the Middle East, North Africa, and Central Asia. Discuss the reasons that contributed to this renewed effort.
2. What was the policy of the Soviet Union toward Israel? Did Russia change this policy after the end of the Cold War and why?
3. Discuss the key motivations of Russia's nonideological foreign policy toward the Arab states.
4. Why did Russia take the side of President Assad in the Syrian civil war? Why did Moscow repeatedly veto Western-sponsored draft resolutions demanding the resignation of the Syrian president?
5. What were Moscow's relations with India and Pakistan like during the Cold War and how have they changed in the past twenty years?

Chapter 11
Russian Policy in Various Parts of the World: The Asia-Pacific Region, Latin America, and Africa

Russia will continue to comprehensively strengthen relations with the Latin American and Caribbean countries, given the region's growing role in world affairs .... Russia will enhance multifaceted interaction with African states on a bilateral and multilateral basis ...

The Foreign Policy Concept of the Russian Federation

Learning objectives

- Describe and critically review the historical milestones in the relationships between the Soviet Union and the countries in the Asia-Pacific region, Latin America, and Africa.
- Describe and critically analyze the periods in Russia's relations with the countries in the Asia-Pacific region, Latin America, and Africa.
- Critically discuss the multiple international and domestic factors affecting the relationships between Moscow and the countries of the studied regions.
- Describe major problems as well as key perspectives in the relations between Russia and the states in the Asia-Pacific region, Latin America, and Africa.

Russia claims the role of a global power. Russia's foreign policy has different areas of interest, not limited to the post-Soviet space, the United States, the European Union, or China. Russia considers its participation in Asia-Pacific integration as very important. Moscow explores new political and economic possibilities with countries in Latin America and Africa. Certainly, Moscow's foreign policy in these regions has to be understood in different, often unique contexts. One of them is historical.

Russia and the Asia-Pacific region: Historical background

The double-headed eagle, the Russian national symbol, looks east and west as if it is symbolizing the meaning of Russia's Eurasian destiny. However, for almost the entire history of Russia the importance of the eastern, Asian, direction of its foreign policy was only secondary to the preeminence of the Western one. Only occasionally did Russia switch its European orientation and turn east, to Asia. These were usually the years following Russia's painful military and diplomatic failures. There was, for example, a revival of Russia's interests toward Asia in the aftermath of the Crimean War in the middle of the nineteenth century (see Chapter 2); there was also the Soviet Union's pivot to the east in the 1920s, after the Soviet leaders' expectations of a communist revolution in Europe had failed. At the turn of the twenty-first century, again, Russia's foreign policy was increasingly focusing on the Asia-Pacific region. This pivot can be attributed to at least two reasons. One of them was the remarkable economic success of several countries in that region, which led to their growing share in the global economy and their developing role in world politics. Russia's worsening relations with the West, especially in the second decade of this century, was the other reason.

Early years

The first Russian explorers set foot on the Pacific shore of Eurasia in the 1600s. However, it took another two centuries for Russia as a state to become a significant Pacific power. Early, there were mostly military considerations that stimulated Russia's government drive to the East. The government also played a key role in the economic development of the region. Take, for example, **the Trans-Siberian Railroad**, a massive project that early in the twentieth century allowed people to conveniently move by train across the whole of Eurasia. However, the railroad did not become the "land Suez Canal" as some Russian entrepreneurs hoped (they referred to the economic and strategic importance of the Suez Canal connecting Mediterranean Sea and the Indian Ocean).

By the middle of the nineteenth century Russia had relinquished its overseas territories on the American continent (see Chapters 2 and 7), yet it was spreading its influence in Mongolia, China, and Korea. That robust policy triggered a confrontation with Japan that ended up in a major war (1904–1905), which Russia lost and gave up vast and important territories as well as its political influence in southern Manchuria and elsewhere in the region.

After seizing power in 1917 the Bolsheviks, even though they did not have substantial resources, were conducting dynamic policies in Asia. In 1921 local procommunist forces with the help of Soviet troops seized power in Mongolia. Moscow provided assistance to the Chinese communists fighting in the civil war against the government of Chiang Kai-shek. The Comintern (see Chapter 2) was responsible for a series of violent uprisings in several Asian countries. However, apart from Mongolia, Moscow had very little, if any, success in building communist regimes in Asia.

In the mid-1930s Moscow – fearing a new large-scale military conflict with Japan – deployed thousands of troops and heavy military equipment to Mongolia. The Soviet Union together with the Mongolian military fought Japan in a brief yet deadly military conflict in 1939. In 1941 the USSR signed a non-aggression treaty with Tokyo and only in August 1945 did the Soviet Union, after defeating Germany, declare war on Japan. After Japan's capitulation the USSR acquired southern Sakhalin, the Kuril Islands, and Port Arthur (the latter was transferred to China a few years later).

The Cold War and after

During the Cold War the US-Soviet geopolitical rivalry was greatly influencing international relations in the Asia-Pacific region. Yet other ideological and geopolitical factors were important in Soviet foreign policy. First, the China-Soviet conflict that had emerged in the late 1950s was a major and in many ways unique international development: two ideological allies could not get along and turned to a bitter rivalry instead of cooperation. Second, a number of countries (India, Indonesia, and a few others) openly declared nonalignment from the American (NATO and others) and Soviet (the Warsaw Pact) military blocs. In the 1960s–1980s the Non-Aligned Movement remained an influential force in international relations. Third, following the unpopular Vietnam War, several countries feared the possibility of deteriorating American support in the future and thus pursued friendlier relations with the Soviet Union and China.

In the twentieth century Moscow provided economic and military assistance to communist parties in Asia, including those of China, Mongolia, North Korea, and North Vietnam. Moscow supported China and North Korea, who were fighting American troops (deployed under the UN mandate) during the Korean War. The Soviets also helped Vietnamese communists in their struggle against France (the war between 1946 and 1954), the United States (the Vietnam War), and during the Vietnamese–Chinese war of 1979.

The Soviet Union certainly sought efficient economic and political ties with the nonaligned countries. Some bilateral relations were rather ambiguous, such as with Indonesia. Others were quite generous and cordial, as with India. The Soviet Union supported India in almost every conflict against Pakistan, and in the 1960s–1980s Moscow sided with Delhi in its territorial disputes with China. India, as you should remember, became one of the closest allies of the USSR and other countries of the communist bloc.

Soviet relations with the United States' allies were tense. In 1951, when the Korean War was in full swing and relations with the West were at their lowest, the Soviet Union turned down a peace treaty with Japan. Tokyo claimed four of the Kuril Islands (in Japan they are called the **Northern Territories**) seized by the Soviet Union after World War II. Hoping to improve its relations with Tokyo, Moscow was planning to return two of the four islands to Japan. However, because Japan signed the 1960 security treaty with the United States (and for a few other political reasons), this offer was withdrawn. No peace treaty between Moscow and Japan has ever been reached.

Moscow had very poor relations with South Korea, an ally of the United States. Only in the early 1980s did signs of improvement in both countries' bilateral ties emerge, and trade activities between these two countries began. However, the 1983 downing of a South Korean civilian jetliner carrying several hundred passengers flying to Seoul from the United States worsened relations for many years. Although this commercial plane flew into Soviet airspace while on its way to Seoul by mistake, and although Soviet military commanders had other options available to them to avoid the deadly outcome, they chose to shoot it down. This tragedy angered Korea and the rest of the world.

Soviet relations with Australia, New Zealand, and Singapore were also poor. The ability of the Soviet Union to influence the region economically or politically was limited. Their trade relations were insignificant. An early attempt at improving ties with China took place in 1982. However, the real change in Moscow's relations with Asian countries occurred after Gorbachev came to power in Moscow. In 1988 the USSR took part in the Seoul Olympic Games, and it established full diplomatic relations with South Korea in 1990. In 1989 Gorbachev visited China and met with one of China's top leaders, Den Xiaoping. Gorbachev went to Japan in 1991, making it the first summit in the history of these two countries. In an atmosphere of improving relations between the Soviet Union and the United States, a new and clearer border in the Bering Sea separating both countries was established. These days this agreement is generally accepted in Russia, though some groups express criticisms and some nationalistic opponents claim that Russia gave up too much and gained very little.

From the late 1980s, during the final years of the Soviet Union, for the first time in history the Pacific East of Russia was no longer seen as largely a military outpost but rather an economic region that could engage and be engaged with in a productive international cooperation.

Main features of Russia's policy

Russia's policy in the Asia-Pacific region, to a certain degree, is a continuation of the Soviet policy in the second half of the 1980s and early 1990s. At the same time it has several unique features.

First, Russia's vast Asian regions – Siberia and the far east – have opened up to the outside world. Cross-border travel is simplified, which stimulates trade and tourism with the adjacent regions. Yet Siberia and the far east are lagging behind the rest of Russia economically. Not surprisingly, Moscow uses its foreign policy to bring more economic and social benefits to the population of these regions.

Second, Russia is striving for different, deeper, and more efficient forms of integration in the Asia-Pacific region, emphasizing economic and military ties based on bilateral and multilateral agreements.

Third, the Kremlin maintains the position that the balance of power in the global world is changing from the West to other areas such as the Asia-Pacific region. Moscow was recently busy creating and formalizing various form of cooperation, including an attempt at building a Moscow-Deli-Beijing "triangle" as well as the more successful BRICS and the Shanghai Cooperation Organization (see earlier chapters). The latter has become the first large post–Cold War international organization without the presence of the United States.

Fourth, Russia declares that it is building nonideological, pragmatic relations with all countries in the Asia Pacific region. Officially, Russia does not divide the countries into those more or less important in its policies. Yet China occupies the most prominent place among Russia's partners, as we have mentioned in earlier chapters.

Main periods of Russia's policy in the Asia-Pacific region

Russia's foreign policy and relations with the countries of the region have gone through several overlapping stages. Each stage was connected to Russia's domestic situation and Russia's growing interest in regional cooperation as well as in political and economic integration in Eurasia.

Exploring

The first period of the development of Russia's foreign policy in the Asia-Pacific region demonstrated Russia's attempts at integration into the world of industrially developed and democratic nations, mostly in Europe and North America. It lasted from 1991 to approximately 1994. Russia was rapidly pivoting toward the West; yet it was also cautiously building its new relations with the East. There were many "ups and downs" in this process. Although trade with China was increasing, Beijing was unhappy about Russia's contacts with Taiwan and the Dalai Lama. (The Dalai Lama is the Buddhist leader of Tibet, who left China in 1959 and lives in exile in India.) Yeltsin's visit to China in 1992 somewhat smoothed Russia's relations with China.

Russian leaders' desire to join the G7 provided an opportunity for them to settle the territorial dispute with Japan, mentioned earlier in the book. It did not happen, because neither side could find a compromise. Meanwhile, bilateral contacts rapidly developed in nonpolitical areas including trade, educational exchanges, and tourism. In terms of policies with North and South Korea, Russia supported the unification of the Korean Peninsula. Moscow signed the

Russian–South Korean Basic Treaty in 1992, which formalized the ongoing normalization of relations. Russia has also cut its economic assistance to North Korea and did not extend the Soviet–North Korean Treaty on Friendship, Cooperation, and Mutual Assistance. Moscow remained very critical of the ongoing North Korean nuclear program. Russia's relations with Vietnam and Mongolia were weakening. Moscow stopped the Soviet-era military and economic assistance to both countries, which, as well as North Korea, have accumulated a substantial debt: the three countries acquired this debt during the Soviet era and the interest on it has been growing. Some countries, such as India in 1993, agreed on a restructuring of their debts to Moscow.

Thus, over a short period before 1994, Russia had overcome the main negative effects of the Cold War in the Asia Pacific region and began restructuring its relations with other countries in the region.

Trying out

During the second phase (1994–2000) Russia's interest in the Asia-Pacific region grew. This was the period when the idea of a multipolar world was gaining prominence in Russia. One of the most active proponents of the idea was the former Minister of Foreign Affairs (1996–1998) and then Prime Minister (1998–1999) Yevgeny Primakov. He believed in new centers of power in the East including Russia, India, and China. He even talked about a **"power triangle"** as a metaphor to describe these countries' perceived political and economic relations. This was not an older version of Gorbachev's vision of such a triangle, which back in the 1980s was symbolizing international cooperation. In Primakov's version this triangle would have had a strategic, anti-Western stance. Lenin suggested a similar idea in one of his last works in the 1920s (Khudoley, 2016).

A symbolic marker of the growing political consensus among Russia, India, and China was their condemnation of the 1999 NATO military campaign in Kosovo. All three countries rejected the concept of humanitarian intervention, which was discussed in the West by that time (Sobel and Shiraev, 2003). Although relations with India developed gradually, Russia's relations with China picked up. Moscow now referred to these relations as a "strategic partnership." Russia also began reviving its relations with Pyongyang. In 1998, initiated by Primakov, Russia and North Korea started negotiations on a new friendship and cooperation treaty, signed in 2000. Unlike in the Soviet days, the new treaty did not contain provisions about mutual military assistance.

In 1996 Russia set up dialogue with ACEAN, an intergovernmental organization that was increasingly emphasizing economic (not political) relations. In 1998 Russia became a member of the APEC forum (Asia-Pacific Economic Cooperation which includes twenty-one Pacific Rim member economies). Moscow considered the APEC membership as yet another step on the path toward joining the World Trade Organization.

In brief, during this period Russia was actively involved in the process of economic and political integration in the region, hoping to benefit from the region's rapid economic development. Yet even its modestly optimistic expectations were not fulfilled. The financial crisis of 1997–1998 that started in Asia hit Russia very hard (sending the national currency into a tailspin in August 1998). Now Moscow began to show less interest in the economic practices of Japan and South Korea and increasingly turned to China, whose economy was still booming at that time.

Dynamically engaging

The third phase of Russia's policy development in the Asia-Pacific region covers the first two presidential terms of Putin (2000–2008). During that period the country experienced the strengthening of the role of the state in every aspect of life and a more robust role in international affairs. Initially, the Russian leadership was prepared to cooperate with the United States and the West (by joining the antiterrorist coalition in 2001 and joining G8, for example), but new priorities were emerging in the Asia-Pacific region. The goal of accelerating the integration processes in the eastern direction had never been as high on Russia's foreign policy agenda.

The Moscow-Deli-Beijing power triangle, contemplated by Primakov, looked more promising. Russia tried to underline its own role in the triangle by all available means. For example, the 2006 G8 meeting and the summit of the leaders of the triangle took place back-to-back in St. Petersburg, Putin's birthplace. Russia wanted to show that by holding membership in both international groups it could mediate between them as well as connect them closer to each other. This "triangle," however, did not gain any political clout. India and China had serious disagreements between themselves (including territorial disputes). Russia, however, remained loyal to the idea of the triangle and continued efforts to build new such "triangles" with other countries.

In 2001 Russia, China, and a few other states formed the Shanghai Cooperation Organization (SCO). It did not include the United States. The emergence of the SCO was a sign that Russia and China were drifting toward each other, though some disagreements between them remained. At the time Moscow was hoping that the SCO would evolve into a military-political bloc. Some Russian experts and journalists termed the SCO an "eastern NATO." However, China rejected such labels and emphasized mostly economic ties.

During this period Russia was actively engaging with several countries as members of APEC. It was using the summits for some multilateral and bilateral negotiations. Yet, Russia's integration into the region stayed limited – there was little, if any, economic growth in the Pacific regions of Russia. Most entrepreneurs from China, South Korea, and elsewhere preferred the European parts of Russia for business and investments.

Although Russia became a full-fledged member of the G-8 group of which Japan is also a member, no major shifts occurred in its relations with Japan. The

Russian-Japanese summits, held regularly, facilitated the development of economic and humanitarian relations but not a bilateral rapprochement on the key political issue of the South Kuril Islands. Russia and India, however, improved their relations (see earlier chapters).

Russia agreed to write off 98 percent of the debt owed by Mongolia to the Soviet Union. This gesture gave a boost to trade and economic relations and, to some extent, political contacts between Russia and Mongolia. Other countries received attention too. Putin was the first Russian top official ever to pay a formal visit to Vietnam (2001). Both sides agreed to raise the level of relations and call it a strategic partnership. The same year Russia shut down its military base in Cam Ranh, but the military cooperation, including arms sales to Vietnam, continued. Russia's consent to write off almost the entire debt from the Soviet period gave an additional impetus to trade and economic relations between these two countries, including their oil exploration and extraction in the South China Sea.

More complicated and, to an extent, contradictory was Russia's policy vis-à-vis the Korean Peninsula. Russian officials no longer spoke publicly about Korean unification. In 2000 Putin paid a formal visit to Pyongyang. It was the first ever visit of any top Soviet or Russian official to North Korea. Moscow was critical about Pyongyang's nuclear ambitions. As a permanent member of the UN Security Council, Russia voted to impose sanctions on North Korea. Russia was part of the Six-Party Talks (the United States, North Korea, South Korea, China, Japan, and Russia) on the North Korean nuclear weapons program. Yet Moscow subscribed to the opinion that Pyongyang's nuclear program carried no direct threat to Russia.

As you can see, during this period Russia actively tried to improve relations with the countries in the Asia-Pacific region on both a bilateral and multilateral basis. Russia was also making efforts at regional integration, looking for any new opportunity to engage as many countries as it could.

Looking for new opportunities

The fourth phase of the Russian policy development in the Asia-Pacific region (2008–2012) took place in the midst of the global economic crisis. As you should remember, Russia's ruling elites held the belief that the West would come out of the crisis weakened, if not declining. Therefore, for the first time Russia began to shape its eastern policy not only with the hope of developing bilateral and multilateral relations but also with a vision of a changing world order. The Kremlin hoped and continues to hope to achieve this through changing the international system rooted in liberal values and the law and installing a "post-Western world order" based on power and driven by the interests within different spheres of influence (Kirchick, 2017).

The pursuit of the Moscow-Deli-Beijing power triangle continued, but the foundation for a much bigger alliance called the BRICS, bringing in Brazil and South Africa, was already emerging. Russia tried to use its presidency in the BRICS in

2010 to position the organization as an alternative to the dominant Western institutions. However, the other BRICS members were not that eager to form a political alliance. They chose to intensify coordination on economic issues rather than to go down the path of confrontation with the West.

The fact the APEC summit that took place in the Russian city of Vladivostok (2012) was declared a huge success for Russia. Moreover, Russia stood not only as the country hosting the event but also as representing the Customs Union of Belarus, Kazakhstan, and Russia. Nevertheless, Russian diplomacy has failed to convince the other APEC members to reorient their trade toward Eurasia.

New elements were emerging in Russia's relations with Japan, South Korea, and North Korea. When President Medvedev visited the South Kuril Islands, he explicitly emphasized Russia's sovereignty over that territory. Previously, neither Soviet nor Russian top executives had ever stated their positions so openly. It caused protests in Tokyo and the inevitable cooling down of Japan's relations with Moscow. On the Korean Peninsula, by contrast, Russia's policy evolved in a different direction. Some Russian politicians once again began discussing the possibility of unification. Moscow and Seoul affirmed through their statements an emerging strategic partnership between them. South Korea was the first Asian country to create a "partnership for modernization," a bilateral program that Moscow considered strategic at that time. Russia condemned the resumption of nuclear tests by North Korea and Pyongyang's withdrawal from the Six-Party Talks. Still, Russia wrote off most of the debt that North Korea had owed to the Soviet Union and went on to restore a regular railway service between the two countries.

Trying new designs

The fifth phase of Russia's policy development in Asia Pacific, which started approximately in 2012, is marked by Russia's aspiration to become an effective center of the modern world, as well as by the drastic deterioration of Moscow's relations with the West. Russian policy in the Asia-Pacific region should be seen in these contexts. Russia emphasized the importance of stability and order in countries' domestic and international affairs, which is not necessarily a goal that countries would reject. In Russian designs, however, "order and stability" stood for the status quo and the preservation of the power of the ruling elites. Russia especially supported policies of the countries in the region that would curb Washington's political and military domination. Next, Russia – facing economic pressures due to the Western sanctions – pursued the strategy of growing trade with the countries in the Asia-Pacific region. These strategies were difficult to implement though. They required time and substantial funding, which Russia did not have. Several large-scale state-sponsored programs for the development of Siberia and the Far East were idling due to the inevitable funding cuts.

Facing a period of confrontation with the West, Moscow turned to international organizations such as the BRICS and SCO. Although both these organizations voiced their criticism of the sanctions against Russia, their statements were somewhat measured as they did not want to complicate their relations with the United States and the European Union. Russia did not support the **Trans-Pacific Partnership** – a trade agreement among twelve nations to lower trade barriers and establish new rules of economic interaction among the countries. Moscow argued that this agreement would benefit only Washington and not other countries, but the United States used a completely different argument for withdrawing from the treaty in 2017 (*AAP*, 2017). The White House believed that the treaty was harmful to key American economic interests.

The importance of developing relations with Vietnam is regularly underlined in Moscow. Vietnam needs American support in the conflict over the territories in the South China Sea. Russia and South Korea had introduced visa-free travel between the two countries. On the one hand, Seoul did not support Moscow's actions in Ukraine and in Syria; on the other, South Korea did not join Western sanctions against Russia. Russia condemned the missile launches and the nuclear tests by North Korea in 2013, 2016, and 2017. At the same time, the deployment of a missile defense system in South Korea (aimed to protect South Korea from an attack from the North) aroused concern in Moscow. Like China, Russia believed that such a system could be used to give the United States an advantage in a future conflict, should it occur. As the argument goes, more missile "shields" on one side inevitably force the other side to build even more missiles that can penetrate this shield. This causes an unnecessary and costly arms race (Mullaney and Buckley, 2017). Tokyo, a major ally of the United States in the region, is constantly trying to reopen talks about a peace treaty with Russia, hoping that Moscow will be willing to compromise on this lingering territorial issue. In 2018 a number of agreements were signed between Japan and Russia, in the areas of investments, medical supplies, chemical industries, humanitarian exchanges, and culture.

Latin America: Historical background

Russia acted somewhat cautiously toward the Latin American states during their historic wars for independence in the nineteenth century. This behavior had at least three underlying reasons. First, Russia did not have any major strategic interests in the region. Second, Russia had obligations under the treaties related to the Holy Alliance, which included the recognition of the sovereign power of the Spanish King. Finally, Russia did not want to challenge the United States' foreign policy strategy (which became known as the Monroe Doctrine, as you should remember from previous chapters), which warranted Washington's opposition to any European state's intrusion into the internal affairs of the countries in North, South, and Central America. In today's terms, if we judge from the Realist perspective, the Monroe Doctrine asserted that the Americas were a distinct sphere of Washington's interests. Russia was too far away to challenge Washington and it assumed that Washington would respect Russia's strategic interests and security concerns in Europe, Asia, and elsewhere.

Early contacts

Russia first established diplomatic relations with Brazil in 1828 and then Uruguay in 1857. Brazil then was a monarchy and Uruguay was a republic. Many monarchies at that time did not seek diplomatic ties with newly formed republics. Russia did. However, the continuing exchange of ambassadors with Latin American countries did not result in any noteworthy economic projects or political breakthroughs. As an exception, indicating slowly developing ties, a number of Russian natural scientists traveled to South America in the 1800s and made substantial contributions to the study of the continent's geography and ecosystem.

During the 1920s–1930s the newly formed Soviet Union attempted to establish and give financial support to communist parties in countries across the Latin America. The results were mixed. Only Cuba and Mexico developed relatively powerful communist parties at that time (and not necessarily because of Moscow's sponsorship). On the other hand, Moscow also pursued good relations with most Latin American governments, even if they were not particularly sympathetic toward communists or openly anticommunist. According to the communist dogma, Soviet leaders believed that governments of small countries (including local property and business owners) could be potential allies within the anti-imperialist front. Although Mexico and Uruguay were among the first to recognize the Soviet government, they later severed their diplomatic relations and accused Moscow of interfering in their internal affairs. For example, Leo Trotsky, one of the most prominent figures of the Russian revolution, emigrated to Mexico after parting ways with Stalin; one of Stalin's agents assassinated Trotsky in 1940 in Mexico. In 1939 Latin American countries voted for the exclusion of the Soviet Union from the League of Nations because of Moscow's invasion of Finland that year. However, Latin American countries supported the anti-Hitler coalition, thus siding with the Soviet Union. By the end of World War II the Soviet Union had official diplomatic relations with almost all Latin American countries, although ties remained mostly formal and superficial.

The Cold War

During the early stages of the Cold War the governments of Latin American countries were on the side of the United States. A dramatic change took place after the 1959 Cuban Revolution when the country's new leader, Fidel Castro, embraced socialism as a political and economic system. Moscow provided military and economic assistance to its new ally in the Western Hemisphere, near the United States' border. Hundreds of Cuban college students studied in the Soviet Union every year. The cost of traveling to Cuba was, of course, prohibitive to most Soviet people, yet government-sponsored delegations, tours, and youth exchange programs were available. The assistance to Cuba was gradually discontinued in the mid-1980s.

In general terms, Cuba for decades coordinated its foreign policy with the Soviet Union. Yet it would be a mistake to think that Havana was a "puppet" in the hands of its big "master." Cuba exercised substantial influence over the Kremlin's foreign policy. One of the reasons for this was that for the Soviet leaders the loss of Cuba as an ally in the Western Hemisphere would have been a painful setback to their global reputation and influence. Fidel Castro could even goad the Soviets into supporting Cuba's military engagement in the wars in Angola in 1975 and the Horn of Africa in 1977 (Shiraev and Zubok, 2016; Gleijeses, 2003). In some other areas Havana also acted quite independently, at times neglecting to consult with Moscow.

The Soviet Union maintained diplomatic relations with all countries of Latin America. The only exception was Chile, and only after the 1973 coup d'état orchestrated by Augusto Pinochet (1915–2006), which overthrew the leftist government of president Salvador Allende (1908–1973). The attempts by the Soviet Union to "cozy up" its relations with several nationalist leaders, such as the Argentinian dictator J. D. Perón (1895–1974), yielded little in return. Moscow also maintained robust relations with Latin American communist parties. Ties with other leftist groups were not always cordial, due to Moscow's disapproval of the radical policies adopted by several such parties. In return, these parties criticized Moscow for its apparently reconciliatory attitudes to the West and for the Soviet revisionist domestic policies (emphasizing the importance of material consumption) that increasingly deviated from Marxist dogmas. In the late 1970s Moscow's policies in Latin America were somewhat pragmatic. Yet the Soviet leaders were always eager to support left-wing governments, such as the one that emerged in Nicaragua in 1979 after the Sandinistas seized power in this country and established a revolutionary government.

Gorbachev's policies of perestroika did not receive official encouragement from Havana. Despite the signing of the 1989 Soviet-Cuban Friendship and Cooperation Treaty – the first such document in the history of the two countries – Moscow could not convince the Cuban leadership to accept market reforms and a democratic transformation. At the same time, relations between the USSR and a majority of Latin American countries remained steady. Moscow restored its ties with Chile and gradually moved away from ideology in international affairs. The financial aid to Cuba, Nicaragua, and various leftist parties and movements was first reduced and then cut.

Key Periods in Russian–Latin American relations

Reconstructing

The first stage we shall examine lasted from the time of disintegration of the USSR in 1991 to the mid-1990s. Both sides were overcoming the legacy of the Cold War. The positive trend in relations was possible in part because of a "honeymoon" in Russia's relations with the United States and other Western countries. Many Latin American states were, like Russia, choosing democracy and developing market economies.

Russia's relations with all Latin American countries were stripped of an old ideological bias. Russia stopped delivering aid to the communist parties in the region. Russia scaled back its military presence in Cuba and stopped the aid to

Cuban military operations in a number of countries in Asia and Africa, as well as its economic assistance. The issues related to several Latin American countries' debts were quickly settled. The only problem was the massive Cuban debt (exceeding $30 billion); it was not finally settled until 2015. Russia's relations with Nicaragua took a downturn in the early 1990s when almost all the Soviet-sponsored bilateral programs were gone. Only some academic, educational, and cultural contacts continued. In 1992 Russia received an observer status in the Organization of American States. Still, Russia could not become an efficient partner overnight given the economic hardships of the transition period, the geographic distance between the sides, and their poor knowledge of each other.

Developing

Latin America was not a top priority of Russian diplomacy in the middle of the 1990s. President Yeltsin's visit to Latin America was planned but did not happen. Foreign minister Kozyrev's visit was postponed a few times and then canceled as well. His successor, Primakov, on the other hand, visited Latin America and had meetings with a few diplomats during various international forums. There were deliberate but rather sporadic attempts on the part of Russia to engage Latin America. For example, Russia was aware of the fact that not all Latin American countries backed the US–NATO bombing of Serbia in 1999, the strikes that Moscow opposed. This "common ground" allowed Moscow seek other areas of political and diplomatic engagement. Moscow signed friendship and cooperation treaties with Venezuela (in 1996) and Uruguay (in 1997). There were new agreements with Argentina and a few other countries. Russia proclaimed a course of Strategic Partnership for the twenty-first century with Brazil. Those formal treaties had little ideological motivation behind them and were not directed against any other country. They were rather declarative statements of mutual intent to develop bilateral diplomatic and economic relations. Domestic factors played a role too. Even though Russia declared a nonideological approach to diplomacy, it actively engaged Venezuela, where in 1998 a leftist leader, Hugo Chávez (1954–2013), took power.

Strengthening

The next stage in developing relations has been associated with Putin's presidency. Early during this period the political landscape in Latin America was shifting. Center-left and leftist governments gained strength and political power in several countries. Disappointed with the poor results of market reforms, some governments turned to a greater government control of the economy. At the same time, these parties and governments expressed criticism of the United States and the world's economic and financial system. Most Latin American countries strongly condemned the 9/11 attacks against the United States but did not support the US invasion of Iraq in 2003.

Some, such as Venezuela, attempted to create an alliance that would openly oppose Washington. Russia began selling arms to Venezuela and a few other governments. Other countries, such as Brazil, sought a greater role in world affairs without jeopardizing their relations with major global powers. Russia appeared a suitable partner to these as well as other Latin American countries. In 2000 Putin paid an official visit to Cuba. In 2001 Russia shut down its military base in Lourdes (in Cuba). This was done in the context of cooperation between Russia and the United States as partners in the antiterrorist coalition. This closure did not affect Cuban-Russian relations. Several Latin American leaders and officials frequented Russia and worked out the legal details of visa-free travel for tourists between Russia and their countries. Russia had signed by 2018 such agreements with nearly all Latin American states.

One of Russia's strategic goals was the strengthening of its role in multilateral relations. Key importance was given to international organizations. Russia began contemplating the formation of an economic alliance that would become known as the BRICS. By developing relations with Latin America, Russia, in addition to achieving its economic goals, had been trying to demonstrate that it was a global actor. Russia was also seeking tactical achievements in the areas where the United States had been traditionally dominant. A surge in Russian activities in Latin America, sometimes demonstrative, took place in the aftermath of the Russia-Georgia conflict in August 2008. The West criticized Russia's role in that conflict. While most Latin American countries remained undecided, Nicaragua and Venezuela openly supported Russia. They have been among few countries, including Russia itself, that officially recognized the independence of Abkhazia and South Ossetia. In 2008 Russia and Venezuela conducted their first joint naval exercises. Military cooperation between the two countries was rapidly developing. Russia continued to pay attention to and engage Brazil, particularly as a fellow member of BRICS and G-20.

In a brief summary, since the beginning of the twenty-first century, Russia and the Latin American countries have signed many agreements on cooperation in various areas. A solid legal framework for cooperation had been created. Still, these agreements remained mostly formal.

The Russian Foreign Policy Concept in 2013 and 2016 (during the third and fourth terms of President Putin) assigned Latin America an important and even increasing role in Russia's foreign policy. This positive attitude was in part due to the general deterioration of Russia's relations with the United States and the European Union and the beginning of a real confrontation between Moscow and the West, driven in part by the Ukrainian and Syrian conflicts.

In the context of the Ukrainian crisis, Russia gained political support from several Latin American countries. Of the eleven states that voted against the United Nations' resolution (supported by the United States and Western countries) condemning the Crimea referendum after Russia invaded the peninsula, four were Bolivia, Venezuela, Cuba, and Nicaragua. This vote was not surprising given the anti-Western position of these governments. In addition to these states, Argentina, Brazil, Uruguay, Ecuador, and many others abstained from voting. The BRICS countries for some time did not openly condemn Russia's activities in and around Ukraine (DeLuca, 2016). None of the Latin American countries joined the Western sanctions against Russia.

In the summer of 2014, when the United States, the European Union, and a number of other countries either cut or seriously curtailed their contacts with Russia, Putin visited Latin America and met with officials in Cuba, Nicaragua, Brazil, and Argentina. He had a joint meeting in Buenos Aires with the leaders of Argentina, Uruguay, Bolivia, and Venezuela. That visit symbolically indicated Russia's return to the region in a manner that seemingly challenged the United States' dominant role. The media in Moscow highlighted photo-ops and announcements of new partnership agreements (Ellis, 2016). Relations with Brazil, Venezuela, Argentina, Cuba, and Ecuador were described as strategic partnerships. Energy, space technology, aviation, and automotive industries became the priority areas of economic and trade cooperation between Russia and these five countries.

Russia made considerable efforts to improve relations with Cuba. By the end of the Cold War Moscow had agreed, as you may remember, to write off 90 percent of the debt (over $35 billion) that Cuba had accumulated back in the 1980s. There has been a surge in trade and economic relations, as well as in military cooperation. For the first time in a long period Cuba and Russia have been considering the implementation of several specific economic projects. Russia also helped Argentina complete the construction of a nuclear power plant. Argentina and Russia publicized the signing of several new deals worth $3 billion. These have been mostly energy deals, including oil exploration by the Russian giant Gazprom, building of a new nuclear reactor in the Atucha complex near Buenos Aires, and Russian companies' participation in the construction of the Argentine hydroelectric facility Chihuido-2.

The area of arms sales and military engagement is one of the principal features of Russia's activities in Latin America. Most of the Russian arms sales supply the Latin American countries' air force and navy. Nicaragua received military equipment for the army. Russia sold large quantities of weapons and military equipment to Bolivarian Alliance states including Bolivia, Cuba, Ecuador, Nicaragua, Venezuela, and several Caribbean nations. Russia signed a $528 million deal to sell twenty-four Mi-171 transport helicopters to Peru, and Russia will build a maintenance center to service these helicopters. Russia also signed a deal with Argentina to sell twelve Su-24 Fencer combat aircraft. The Russian-Brazilian military cooperation is also underway. Overall, the military-technical cooperation with the countries of Latin America has been around $14.5 billion since the early 2000s (DeLuca, 2016). It is likely to have increased by the time you read these pages.

Moscow played a limited yet important role in training military and police forces in several Latin American countries that purchased weapons from Moscow. Russia is considering expanding its financial assistance to these states. There have been joint naval maneuvers with Venezuela. Moscow has established an antidrug training center in Nicaragua, thus in some ways challenging the United States' role in long-term antinarcotics policies in the region (DeLuca, 2016). Russia and Nicaragua agreed that Russia would provide security for the proposed **Nicaragua Canal** between the Pacific Ocean and the Caribbean Sea (the project is underwritten by mostly Chinese companies).

Following the sanctions against Russia launched in 2014 Moscow made persistent efforts to compensate for the economic difficulties by exploring possibilities in Latin America. Yet despite all the intentions on both sides no significant breakthrough in trade immediately happened. Supplies of power generation equipment continued. In 2017 about a quarter of power-generating units in Latin America have been either of Soviet or Russian origin.

Russian policy in Latin America over recent years also focused on the Russian-speaking communities there, which first appeared in the nineteenth and twentieth centuries and have continued to grow. Kirill, the Patriarch of the Russian Orthodox Church, visited Latin America in 2016. In Havana he met with Pope Francis (this was the first meeting of the two churches at the highest level since 1068) and also visited Paraguay and Brazil.

Russia's strategies in Latin America

After the 1990s Russia continued an active foreign-policy strategy in Latin America. This strategy is based on several strategic goals. Overall, Russia is trying to undermine the US-led liberal international order and Washington's authority in Latin America; enhance Putin's domestic legitimacy in the eyes of Latin American governments; and promote specific Russian commercial, military, and energy interests. Russia approached its relations with Latin America from at least three key positions (Gurganus, 2018; Yakovlev, 2013).

First, to repeat, Russia for years now has been trying to act in the international arena as a global power, not just a regional actor. Therefore even the physical remoteness of Latin America does not prevent Moscow from actively seeking to develop relations with most countries there. Russia sees them primarily as partners and attaches great importance to the development of not only bilateral but also multilateral relations with the countries of Latin America. Unlike the Soviet Union in the past, Russia views international organizations as an opportunity to build and strengthen a new polycentric world. Russia since 1992 had already accumulated important experience in dealing with Latin America, the experience on which Moscow was hoping to build new international agreements. Many Latin American politicians too appeared to want to develop better ties with Moscow. They believed that their continent had finally ceased to be perceived as a "backyard" of the United States and that Latin America should look for new economic opportunities and political partners. Russia also justifies its policies as a response to an assertive (often called "intrusive") policy of the United States in South and Central America. All in all, Russia, according to its foreign policy doctrine, cannot afford to be simply a regional power and should cooperate with its immediate neighbors as well as with more distant regions, such as Latin America (Gurganus, 2018).

The second position is economic. Russia focuses on mutual trade and investments. Since the late 1990s several Latin American countries, such as Brazil and Argentina, have experienced a period of rapid economic growth, which made them very attractive economic partners. After the West imposed its sanctions in 2014, Russia considered its trade relations with Latin America as a major area (in addition to others) of its foreign economic activity. Among the areas where economic cooperation between Russia and the Latin American countries has been successful are the power generation sector and the arms trade. Although a number of Latin

American countries are exporters of oil and gas, they cooperate in the area of new methods and technologies related to geological exploration and extraction. There is cooperation in nuclear power engineering. Nevertheless, the share of Latin American countries in Russia's foreign trade has remained relatively low, within the range of a few percentage points compared to the overall volume of Russia's global trade. Russian goods have not attracted much attention from Latin American consumers. There is very strong competition from the United States, the European Union, and especially China. Moreover, in 2015–2016 the volume of mutual trade actually decreased as a result of the economic crisis in Russia.

The third position is political. Russian policy in Latin America, as Moscow states, is nonideological. The Kremlin does not openly support left-wing parties, though it tends to agree with their anti-Western and anti-American leanings. Russia, in general terms, distinguishes among clusters of countries in Latin America based on their own foreign policy. One cluster includes the states that are most critical of the United States and its role in international affairs: Cuba, Bolivia, Nicaragua, and Venezuela. The economic "giants" such as Brazil, Mexico, Argentina, and Chile are in the second cluster, which is not openly anti-American or anti-Western. However, either a pro- or anti-American course in any country's foreign policy is subject to change, as political leaders and governments may come and go while you read these pages (see Map 11.1).

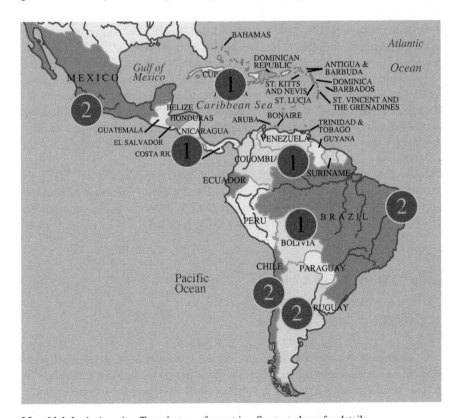

Map 11.1 Latin America: Two clusters of countries. See text above for details.

Obstacles and difficulties

Although Russia has been able to achieve some successes in the Latin American direction of its foreign policy in the twenty-first century, Moscow's positions there are not very strong. In 2015–2018 a number of factors have appeared that weakened its influence.

First of all, one factor is connected to the situation in Russia. The slowdown in the Russian economy led to a reduction in foreign trade turnover, including in Latin America where its volume decreased significantly. The Latin American countries did not join the Western sanctions, but, in practice, almost all of them have refrained from steps that would complicate their relations with the United States and the European Union. This applies to both state and private capital, which work with Russia with a careful eye to a possible Washington reaction. In its turn, the United States' activity in Latin America is growing. Notable in this respect was President Obama's visit to Cuba (2016), which was the first visit by a US president for several decades. The Trump administration in Washington, despite its lukewarm relations with Cuba, has made promises to rework and improve its trade ties with most Latin American countries. In economic terms, China considerably outpaces Russia in Latin America – the volume of its trade with Latin America is almost twelve times as large as Russia's.

Important changes are also taking place in Latin American countries themselves. The impeachment of President Dilma Rousseff did not lead to qualitative changes in foreign policy, but the shift of Brazil – the continent's largest country – to the right could not help but exert a serious influence on domestic politics in Latin America in general. The slide in oil prices in the world market led to complete economic chaos and an acute internal conflict in Venezuela, which had to reduce financial assistance to a number of other Latin American countries. This was one of the reasons why Cuba, Nicaragua, and some other countries set a course for improving relations with the United States.

Nevertheless, despite the impact of outside factors, Latin America will no doubt continue to be an important area in Russia's foreign policy. To advance Russian objectives Moscow will likely to use various tools to influence public opinion and decision-makers in Latin American countries (Gurganus, 2018).

Russia's strategies in Africa

Early years

In the nineteenth century the Russian Empire maintained good relations with Ethiopia, the only African country that remained independent. Most Ethiopians at that time were Orthodox Christians, and this could have been an important factor explaining Russia's attention to this country.

Soviet leaders did not have much interest in Africa for a long time. All their attempts to build communist parties in Africa were unsuccessful. After Stalin's death in 1953 new leaders in Moscow supported various nationalist groups fighting for independence of their territories. Several states in Africa in the 1960s–1980s, including Angola, Mozambique, Ethiopia, Guinea, and Benin, chose socialism, thus becoming Moscow's allies in the Cold War. The USSR offered them economic, military, and other assistance. Thousands of African students studied at Soviet universities.

The USSR and the West always supported different sides in practically all of the armed conflicts that broke out in various parts of Africa during the Cold War. In the second half of the 1980s Soviet policy in Africa changed to become mostly nonideological. Russia's strategic interests in Africa in the 1990s were insignificant. Yet Russia was becoming more active in the twenty-first century.

Main features of Russia's foreign policy in Africa

Putin was the first Russian or Soviet leader to pay an official visit to a number of African countries. On the other hand, Africa is placed last among the list of regional directions in the Foreign Policy Concepts of Russia (2013, 2016).

In Africa Russia first seeks to demonstrate its global position and status in a multipolar world. Moscow pays particular attention to the Republic of South Africa – the country belonging to both G20 and the BRICS. Russia maintains contacts with the African Union and some other pan-African organizations and keeps good relations with Angola, Mozambique, and some other former allies of the USSR. Such relations are in part rooted in the fact that a considerable number of politicians, government bureaucrats, engineers, teachers, doctors, and military officers of these countries graduated from Soviet universities thirty and forty years ago and still keep in personal contact with their Russian counterparts. No African country has joined the Western sanctions against Russia. However, only Zimbabwe and Sudan formally recognized the incorporation of Crimea into Russia.

Second, Russia pays attention to Africa in the context of international security. Unlike in many other regions, confrontation with the West or competition with China are almost absent here. Russia hopes to see a peaceful settlement of military conflicts and takes part in UN peacekeeping missions. In 2017 a limited number of the Russian military and police force (about one hundred people) were deployed as UN peacekeepers in South Sudan, Western Sahara, the Democratic Republic of the Congo, Liberia, and Côte d'Ivoire (*Izvestia*, 2017). Russian diplomats (along with their colleagues from other countries) mediated the settlement of the conflict in Sudan, which resulted in the appearance of a new sovereign state, South Sudan. Moscow is concerned with the activities of terrorist organizations in sub-Saharan Africa. The Russian navy also participated in the patrolling of the waters near the Horn of Africa, to keep pirates in check (The Week, 2010).

Third, Russia moved its economic relations with African countries from an ideological to mostly a market basis in the 1990s. In the twenty-first century such relations are developing mainly in the same direction as those with Latin American countries (i.e., energy, mining, and arms). The Russian government has annulled the large loans given to many African countries in the Soviet period. Russia signed the Trade Agreement or an Agreement on Economic and Technical Cooperation with a number of African states. The main trading partners are the Republic of South Africa, Angola, and Nigeria; however, the share of each of them in Russia's foreign trade does not exceed 0.2 percent. The main attention is paid to the energy sector, as Russia aspires to be the biggest supplier of oil and gas as well as to influence the development of the energy industry on a larger scale. Russian companies invest in geological exploration on the continent. Significant attention is paid to extraction and processing of diamonds. Russia supplies arms to fifteen countries of sub-Saharan and Southern Africa, though in significantly smaller volumes than in Soviet times. Russia has increased its presence in the Central African Republic. Moscow provided military consultants and other specialists to help the government fight insurgents and secure the country's uranium mines. Tourism to Africa is developing, but slowly. For example, around ten thousand Russian tourists visit Kenya every year, which has become the most attractive country for tourism. Yet Russian-African contacts in the fields of science, education, and culture remain limited. In 2018 Putin called for a Russian-African summit to discuss new ways of economic and political cooperation.

In sum, Russia has not yet achieved any notable success on the African continent; on the other hand, Russia does not have any acute or lingering problems to deal with there either. Time may change this status quo.

Conclusion

Overall, over the past thirty years the Russian Federation has been trying to realize a more active and efficient policy in the Asia Pacific region, compared to the days of the Soviet Union. Not only did Russia manage to significantly increase the scope of its bilateral relations with the countries of the region, but it also built those relations with a host of pragmatic goals in mind. More importantly, Russia gradually began to be involved in the multilateral ties and economic integration processes in the region. Unlike the Soviet Union during the Cold War, Russia now places greater emphasis on the economic aspects of cooperation rather than on military ones.

Yet Russia's role in this region still remains quite limited. As a result of a number of factors, both internal and external, the economic potential of Siberia and the far east with their resources and investment opportunities is not sufficiently utilized. Some of the obstacles are Russia's own business practices, the lack of reliable infrastructures (accessible roads, communications, etc.), and regulatory uncertainties. Most western countries were able to overcome the period of severe economic and financial challenges that began in 2008. Russia, on the other hand, entered a phase of economic and financial difficulties. Its own domestic factors, the relatively low oil prices, and the Western economic sanctions all have contributed to Russia's problems. Despite repeated statements about Russia's pivot to the East (Russia will continue to pay a great deal of attention to the Asia-Pacific region for both political and economic reasons), the Western, Euro-Atlantic vector still plays a major role in Russian foreign policy.

Russia continues to pursue a bigger, more important role in Latin America. In part, the search for this new role is based on Russia's increased assertiveness in many international areas and in many other regions. On the other hand, President Obama's policies (2008–2016) in Africa and Latin America could have created a sense of political "vacuum," which led several countries such as Russia to search for a new, more assertive, role in the global world (DeLuca, 2016). On the one hand, the administration in Washington that took power in 2017 was set to reverse these developments and pursued a more robust course of action in Central and South America. On the other hand, with Washington's active engagement or without, Russia, according to Moscow's vision of international relations, has been seriously considering the development of the powerful Latin American "pole" in a multipolar world as a new economic and political reality of the twenty-first century.

In any case, Russia is likely to continue strengthening its old ties with several long-term partners, as well as maintaining its active search for new strategic partners and new markets in Latin America. In Russia's view, Latin America is a valuable partner that shares a mutual desire to reduce the dependency on the West and look to a multipolar world. Trade and economic relations, despite generally favorable conditions, have remained limited so far. Whether Russia and its partners can reverse these negative tendencies depends on numerous factors. Some of them are global; others are based on Russia's decisions. In strategic terms, Russia's motivation to develop relations with Africa will remain strong, yet the practical opportunities are likely to be limited.

Summary

- For almost the entire history of Russia the eastern, Asian, direction of its foreign policy was only secondary to the preeminence of the Western one.
- The first Russian explorers set foot on the Pacific shore of Eurasia in the seventeenth century. However, it took another two centuries for Russia to turn into a significant Pacific power. Its influence diminished after the Russo-Japanese war of 1904–1905.
- After seizing power in 1917 the Bolsheviks were active in Asia. In 1921 procommunist forces with the help of Soviet troops seized power in Mongolia. Moscow provided assistance to the Chinese communists fighting in the civil war against the government of Chiang Kai-shek.
- During the Cold War the US-Soviet geopolitical rivalry greatly influenced international relations in the Asia-Pacific region. Yet other ideological and geopolitical factors are important in our discussion of Russia's foreign policy. The Soviet Union created efficient economic and political ties with many nonaligned countries.

- From the late 1980s the Pacific East of Russia was no longer seen as largely a military outpost but rather as an economic region that could engage in a productive international cooperation.
- Russia sees its policy in the Asia-Pacific region as based on building nonideological, pragmatic relations with all countries. Russia is striving for different, deeper and more efficient forms of integration in the region. The Kremlin also maintains that the balance of power in the global world is changing from the West to the Asia-Pacific region.
- Russia's relations with the countries of the region went through several overlapping stages. Each stage indicated Russia's growing interest in regional cooperation as well as in political and economic integration.
- In 2001 Russia, China, and a few other states formed the Shanghai Cooperation Organization (SCO).
- Russia's ruling elites believe that Russia needs to shape its eastern policy not only with a hope of developing bilateral and multilateral relations but also with a vision of a changing world order.
- Russia did not support the Trans-Pacific Partnership – a trade agreement among twelve nations to lower trade barriers and establish new rules of economic interaction among the countries. Moscow argued that this agreement would benefit Washington but not other countries.
- Russia was acting somewhat cautiously toward the Latin American states during their historic war for independence in the nineteenth century. During the 1920s–1930s the newly formed Soviet Union attempted to establish and give financial support to communist parties across the Latin American countries. On the other hand, Moscow also pursued good relations with most Latin American governments, which were not particularly sympathetic toward communists.
- During the Cold War Moscow provided military and economic assistance to Cuba up to the middle of the 1980s. Cuba coordinated its foreign policy with the Soviet Union. In some other areas Havana also acted quite independently, at times even ignoring Moscow in its decisions.
- After the 1990s Russia continued, with some exceptions, a nonideological foreign policy strategy in Latin America. This strategy was based mostly on pragmatic goals.
- These days Russia tries to act as a global power, not just a regional actor. Even the physical remoteness of Latin America does not prevent Moscow from actively developing relations with most countries there and trying to see them primarily as partners.
- Russian policy in Latin America, as Moscow states, tends to be nonideological. The Kremlin does not openly support left-wing parties, yet it tends to agree with their anti-Western and anti-American leanings.
- Since the beginning of the twenty-first century Russia and the Latin American countries have signed many agreements on cooperation in various areas. A solid legal framework for cooperation has been created. Still, these agreements have remained mostly formal.

- Moscow played a limited yet important role in training military and police forces in several Latin American countries that purchased weapons from Moscow.
- Soviet leaders did not have much interest in Africa for a long time. Several states in Africa in the 1960s–1980s, including Angola, Mozambique, Ethiopia, Guinea, and Benin, chose socialism, thus becoming Moscow's allies in the Cold War.
- In Africa Russia seeks to demonstrate its global position and status in a multipolar world. Russia pays some attention to Africa in the context of international security. Russia moved its economic relations with African countries from an ideological to a market basis in the 1990s.

Glossary

Nicaragua Canal Proposed passage between the Pacific Ocean and the Caribbean Sea; the project is mostly underwritten by Chinese companies.
Northern Territories The disputed islands (belonging to Russia but claimed by Japan) in the southern part of the Kuril Islands chain.
"Power triangle" Metaphor coined in the 1990s to describe the political and economic relations among Russia, India, and China.
Trans-Pacific Partnership A trade agreement among twelve nations to lower trade barriers and establish new rules of economic interaction among countries.
Trans-Siberian Railroad A massive project that early in the twentieth century allowed people to move by train across all of Eurasia.

Review questions

1. What is the essence of Japan's problem with the *Northern Territories*?
2. What are the key features of US policy in the Asia-Pacific region? Name the main periods of Russia's policy in the Asia-Pacific.
3. Cuba in the 1960s and 1970s exercised substantial influence over the Kremlin's foreign policy. How and why?
4. Russia approached its relations with Latin America from at least three key positions. Describe them.
5. Which countries are the main partners of Russia in Africa? What were the main features of Russian politics in Africa in the early twenty-first century?

Conclusion

The Russian Federation as a state was born in December 1991. The old Soviet Union was formally gone. Russia, which once had assumed the role of the superpower during the Cold War, suddenly found itself struggling for survival. The new country was expected to change. It was looking for a new identity. It was building new policies, domestic and foreign. From a historical viewpoint the period from the early 1990s to today has been incredibly short. Yet these years have been filled with remarkable and dramatic events that have only few parallels in Russian or even world history. These were the years of adjustment and confusion, great hopes and big disappointments, rising confidence and growing worries about the future. Even the country's past was rewritten and re-evaluated multiple times. You only imagine how many opinions and theories keep emerging about Russia's future.

Russia is back... Or is it?

Russia went through a great historic aftershock in the 1990s. The country and its people have lived through an unprecedented economic downturn and hyperinflation, trailed by the 1993 constitutional crisis. President Yeltsin used military force to disband the parliament inherited from the Soviet era. The country's economic troubles continued. The populist and left-wing opposition won the legislative elections of 1993 and 1995. The lingering, devastating war in Chechnya became a painful thorn in the nation's psyche. A demoralizing financial crisis in 1998 had a profound and sobering effect on the entire country. Yeltsin lost his effectiveness as a leader. After a few unsuccessful attempts to choose an heir, he transferred power to an unknown colonel, Vladimir Putin. The country was seemingly pleased with the choice of president in 2000 when Putin won his first election. A former KGB officer who later became a government official, Putin was young, hard-working, resilient, and relentless.

Russia in the early 2000s was showing the signs of a steady economic growth. High oil prices and a mixture of government-controlled and free-market policies were helpful in boosting Russia's robust economic rise. In foreign policy Russia became more confident and predictable. It was developing solid relations with its close neighbors and distant acquaintances. One national party – United Russia – has become dominant in the country's multiparty political system. Putin smoothly "transferred" his presidential power to Dmitry Medvedev in 2008. Medvedev returned the presidential chair back to Putin, who accepted this pre-planned gesture and won the elections in 2012 and again in 2018.

In general terms, the political restructuring in Russia as a state over the past thirty years was a transition to a democratic rule. Yet the type of democracy that has been built in Russia is full of ambiguities. The country moved from totalitarian Soviet regime to authoritarian forms with some elements of democracy. According to the Constitution, Russia has three independent branches of government. However, the executive power is disproportionately strong, and it has been getting even stronger as additional amendments and presidential decrees are passed every year. Russia as a country has accepted an increasingly personal form of political rule. It is everywhere. The highest authority is President Putin. He has the support of most ordinary citizens. With a few exceptions, Russian media is on his side. Competition and contention do exist in Russia but only in frameworks allowed by Kremlin. The opposition is weak, fragmented, and disorganized. The country lacks new, nationally recognized political leaders.

New political leaders have to be accepted by the Kremlin. If they are not, expect relentless character attacks against them from the government and the media. From the legal point of view, Russia today offers to its citizens a full spectrum of political liberties. However, the government has developed an effective system of regulating free speech, free assembly, and other civil rights by selectively allowing meaningless dissent and bullying the meaningful opposition. Political self-censorship has become a necessary habit in scores of columnists, bloggers, and reporters working for Russia's mainstream media (mostly financially controlled by the federal government). In such a political atmosphere, the outbursts of nationalism, chauvinism, anti-Western rhetoric, sexism, and homophobia do not usually face public resistance. Many Russians tend not to be concerned about political freedoms. Surveys show that almost half of those surveyed support censorship in the media and the Internet (Goncharov, 2017). Yet, most Russians worry about the social and economic problems of their country and do not hesitate to criticize the government for its failures in those areas. Almost 30 percent of people (age 18 to 24) would like to leave the country for good (WCIOM, 2018).

Back in the 1990s, during the transition period, Russia first embraced economic liberalism. Yet in the past twenty years illiberal economic policies prevailed. They are a mixture of authoritarian methods of management coupled with the selective acceptance of free-market principles. Some economic forecasts related to Russia have been encouraging, especially in the first decade of the century. For example, the average rate of economic growth in Russia was around 7 percent. However, the global financial and economic crisis of 2008–2012 and its aftermath slowed the growth and triggered a recession. Russia seemed to have survived the crisis; yet the recovery did not look sustainable. A key problem was that Russia continued to rely too much on its energy resources at the expense of other economic sectors. The economy today depends heavily on oil and gas exports. If energy prices are low, federal revenues will be low too. As a result, the average size of wages and pensions in Russia is still far behind that of most Western countries. The per capita GDP in Russia is four times lower than in the United Kingdom and five times lower than in the United States (IMF, 2018).

Russia remains a vast welfare state. Most people, especially the middle and lower classes, are overwhelmingly dependent on the authorities. Political psychologists show that this collective reliance of people in a country on somebody else's power sustains a culture of dependency. This dependency becomes a fertile ground in which to encourage and generate public support for those already in power. People become accustomed to believing that only the few powerful leaders could protect them from life's dangers and endless challenges (Svolik, 2012). The more enemies appear in the media or social networks – enemies real or imaginary – the more important and irreplaceable the national leaders become. This phenomenon has important implications in foreign policy.

Russia's direction of foreign policy

With the ending of the Cold War, in the late 1980s, the world had seemingly buried the old fears and mutual prejudices. Russia as an international actor was ready to rewrite its old, outdated script for its new foreign policy. In the 1990s Moscow dropped ideology as a factor in diplomacy and declared a transition to a pragmatic approach. This transition was anxious, complicated, and somewhat disappointing. Seeking a new place in the global world and pursuing an increasingly assertive foreign policy, Russia grew stronger and more confident by the late 1990s. At the same time, tensions between Moscow and many other countries, predominantly in the West, have grown. Domestic ideological and political causes as well as international events (and the way Russia sees them) have contributed to these increased tensions (Lavrov, 2011). Russia claims that the worsening of relations was totally the fault of the West (Putin, 2007; 2013). Most Western experts disagreed (Haas, 2018; Cohen, 2009; Kuchins, 2007). The question remains: why did this lingering confrontation occur? If Moscow's policies played a role in these tensions, was it mostly a clever political move or a strategic blunder? The answer requires further discussion.

First, witnessing the rapid weakening of the West as the financial and economic "core" of the world and seeing the rise of the Asian economies, Moscow had to make a choice in answering a historic question: which economic and political model to follow? Having been affected by the global financial and economic crisis that started in 2008, Moscow projected itself as a participant of a "new" developing economic and political order. Russian leaders believed that the center of this order was emerging in Eurasia, especially in China. The Eurasian "pivot" and the pursuit of various forms of Eurasian integration was a clear sign of a change in Moscow's foreign policy strategies after 2012. Moscow has chosen a model based on authoritarian capitalism, thus giving up on liberal economic models. Has Russia miscalculated these global developments and trends? If not, the Eurasian "pivot" or Russia's capitalist and political system should bring strategic benefits to the country and soon. Yet what if the expected benefits do not materialize?

Second, Moscow's strong criticism of the West's global policies has encouraged and thus strengthened conservative ideological opposition within Russia. It is mostly anti-Western, antiliberal, and nationalistic. Many Russian military and security officials have had a hard time coping with the country's status as an ex-superpower and never have planned to accept the diminishing role of their country. In addition, most people in Russia had very little experience with liberal values, especially with individual liberties. To many Russians the words, "freedom" and "democracy" turned out to be empty declamations – often associated with unfilled promises. Many people, unfortunately, associated freedom with permissiveness and democracy with demagoguery. The anti-Western sentiment across Russia was not only a response to international developments but also a reflection of Russia's acceptance of authoritarianism.

Third, the Kremlin has developed a genuine interest in maintaining and perpetuating the belief in the foreign enemies who continuously harass Russia. These enemies are Western countries in general and the United States in particular. History shows that upholding a lasting image of a foreign enemy helps authorities to preserve their country's national unity and rally people around the government (at least for a time). However, such conformational (as they are seen by the West) foreign policy attitudes only add to tensions. Russia and its leaders are constantly scorned and ridiculed by the Western conservative and liberal media alike (which is, ironically, one of few areas of consent in partisan Western politics). Do these images and attitudes help in restoring trust between Russia and the rest of the word?

Fourth, Russia's assertiveness and ambitiousness as an international player can also be a byproduct of the strategic "vacuum" emerging in many world regions after 2008. In the regions where the influence of the United States and the West diminished in the twenty-first century, the influence of other powers (such as China, Iran, and of course Russia) has been growing. Syria is just one of the examples. And Russia's assertiveness has been also rising due to disagreements between Moscow and most other countries (especially in the West) about a range of international developments. How will the changing tone of strategic arguments coming from Washington DC affect the relations between Russia and the West? Which arguments and actions today and in the future could address Russia's frustrations?

Russia's frustrations

In the twenty-first century most democratic countries have maintained a very critical view of Russian domestic and foreign policy. The policy at home has been seen as increasingly authoritarian and antidemocratic; foreign policy has been criticized as aggressive and expansionist. Moscow has entirely dismissed these criticisms. Russian leaders attribute the worsening of their relations with the United States and Western Europe exclusively to Western policies. The message coming from the Kremlin is straightforward: if Western powers had chosen a different foreign policy in the past, then the relations between the countries would have been different. For most experts studying Russia and working in the field of international relations the situation was increasingly dichotomous. It seemed like there were two types of reality: one was constructed in Moscow; the other was designed in Western capitals. In this book we have introduced both views and critically discussed the view dominant in Moscow. In sum, what were Russia's grievances?

- America and Europe should not have supported Bosnian Muslims in the ethnic conflict in the former Yugoslavia in 1992–1996. Washington and NATO should not have bombed Serbia, which had fought for its own territorial integrity in 1999. The West should not have granted independence to Kosovo by annexing a part of Serbia's sovereign territory.
- NATO should have halted its eastward expansion beginning in 1996.
- America should not have invaded Iraq in 2003. Other Western countries, including the United Kingdom, should not have supported Washington in this aggressive and unjust war.
- The United States and the European Union should not have sponsored antigovernment protests and meddled in the elections in Ukraine in 2004–2005. (The West rejected these accusations as totally groundless.)
- Washington and its European allies should not have supported Georgia in its military conflict with Russia in 2008 over South Ossetia and Abkhazia.
- The West should not have been recklessly one-sided and extremely forceful in supporting the rebels in Libya in 2011, who killed Gaddafi, Libya's leader.
- The West should not have to attempted to remove the legitimate Syrian president, Assad, from power and should not have supported the armed opposition to his government.
- The United States and its allies should not have imposed sanctions against Russia for its attempt to restore "historical justice" (Moscow's label) in Ukraine in 2014 and later (the de facto annexation of Crimea in the West's terms).
- The West should not have interfered in Russia's domestic affairs by passing anti-Russian laws, imposing sanctions on its business and political leaders, recruiting and directing the activities of anti-Russian nongovernment organizations, and toying with Russian political opposition.

Russia's "wish list"

What should be done, in Russia's view, to design a new type of international relations? What will it take to build a reliable foundation for the improvement of Moscow's relations with the United States and the West? Moscow claims that it is ready;

Moscow's leaders insist that it is up to Washington and its allies to make the right decisions. The most important steps, both strategic and specific, from Russia's standpoint, should include:

- American and European leaders should accept the reality of the new and rising multipolar (polycentric, in Russia's vocabulary) world. Not only should such recognition materialize in their declarations or scholarly papers (of which there are plenty), but new practical steps and specific policies must follow. The result of these policies should be the increased role of international institutions such as the United Nations.
- Washington must stop using violence in its foreign policy and turn to peaceful, multilateral solutions to international conflicts.
- NATO must halt its eastward expansion; in particular, Ukraine and Georgia must never become NATO members.
- All political and economic sanctions against Russia should be lifted and a fair compensation to Russia granted.
- The West should accept Crimea as a part of Russia and diplomatically assist Russia and other conflicting sides in resolving the crisis in the eastern part of Ukraine.
- The West should discontinue the activities of nongovernmental organizations working in Russia and halt their attempts to influence political institutions and public opinion in Russia.
- The West must unconditionally accept Russia as a sovereign state with its own political institutions, traditions, and political culture.

Implications for Western policies

Any country's foreign policy depends on the specific contexts in which these policies take place. There are the domestic contexts (such as elections, public opinion, or institutions) and international contexts (such as tensions, conflicts, and their resolutions). Personal factors – such as the individuals in office or the country's elites' views of the world and the way they define their country's national interest – play a role, too. As we have learned in this book, Russian political leaders and foreign policy experts often see their country and international relations differently from the view from London, Paris, Tallinn, Tokyo, or Washington. Can the international experts and politicians be so "wrong" and their Russian counterparts so "correct" in their judgments about international politics?

Those who study Russia are not unified in their views either. Some experts outside Russia look at this country as a foe, as a hostile and unpredictable power, which should be treated with extreme caution and approached with vigilance. They say that Russia cannot be trusted so long as the current government is in place there. Moscow should be resisted.

Others see Russia as a predictable competitor, yet not a foe; thus Moscow, in this view, can be and should be engaged bilaterally as well as globally, albeit in selected areas. Russia, according to this assessment, cannot be trusted; yet it can be respected and contained.

Yet others, although they are in minority, have a completely different view; they downplay the disagreements with Moscow and accept its grievances; they accuse Washington and other key player of expansionist policies. In addition, they accuse the West and its allies of making serious policy blunders vis-à-vis Russia. They accentuate the immediate and potential benefits from engaging Russia; they do not necessarily admire Moscow's policies; they tend to see Russia mostly as a key global actor and a valuable partner.

In light of these arguments, which policy options could Western countries, including the United States, the United Kingdom, and Japan, exercise in the foreseeable future (assuming that there are no sudden and dramatic changes within Russia and globally)? Consider the following scenarios.

The first scenario. Forecast: Disagreements between Russia and the West will increase; mutual criticisms, taunting, scorning, and even episodic hostile actions (as both sides would interpret them) will continue. Russia will interfere in areas that affect the United States' key interests or the strategic interests of its partners and allies, including the Middle East, Africa, Latin America, or the Pacific. Moscow will continue meddling – using cyber-trolling and direct Internet attacks – in the political process in key Western countries, especially in the United States and the European Union. Using a vast propaganda machine, Russia will create a "parallel reality" of facts to sway the views of its own citizens as well as those of the global community in favour of Russia. Policies:

- Neither Washington nor its partners or allies need to engage Russia politically while these unfriendly actions and tensions are in place.
- Russia should be kept increasingly isolated and remain under the pressure of comprehensive international restrictions and even new sanctions.
- The West must continue denouncing Russia's domestic policies – such as the curbing of political freedoms and restraining democratic organizations and institutions.
- Russia's foreign policy should be judged on its merits and not on denials, declarations, and promises.
- Russia's military ambitions should be checked. The US military should demonstrate its strength to Russia. NATO's new strategy should be implemented to further contain Russia; NATO's eastward enlargement should continue and include Georgia and, possibly, Ukraine. Moldova could become the next candidate too.

The second scenario. Forecast: Although disagreements and even tensions with Russia will continue for some time, cooperation with Russia will be possible. The Kremlin leaders will continue their confrontational policies as well as accusations against the West. However, Russia's economic problems and political setbacks in several international areas will persuade Russian authorities that cooperation with the United States and its allies could bring mutual benefits. A few Western (and emerging) populist leaders could also engage Russia – out of their pragmatic economic and political interests at home. Policies:

- Cooperation between Russia and the European Union and the United States (including their allies) will be limited to areas such as trade, educational exchanges, nuclear nonproliferation, and antiterrorist policies.
- Some sanctions imposed on Moscow could be eased, and even lifted, should Russia cooperate with the West and change its policies in some areas, such as in Syria or Ukraine.
- The West should continue to be critical of Russia's domestic civil rights record unless some improvements in this area take place.
- NATO's further enlargement should be reevaluated and, if necessary postponed, based on Moscow's behavior.

The third scenario. Forecast: Some strategic disagreements with Russia will remain. However, in many economic, political, and social areas, the West and Russia will actively engage each other. Russia will re-evaluate its "pivot" toward Asia and will re-engage Europe and the United States. All sides will pursue and at the same time balance mutual interests. They will try to disregard most of the differences. These improvements will also be possible in part because of the political "thaw" in Moscow emerging in the form of a series of political reforms and new social policies. At the same time, public opinion in the West will take a more positive turn toward Russia because of Moscow's changing behavior. Policies:

- The United States first and then the European Union should reach an agreement with Russia regarding the status of Crimea. The West should compromise with Ukraine and appease Moscow.
- Economic sanctions against Russia will be scaled back or even lifted altogether. Russia will re-join G8.
- Parties on both sides (such as the European Union and Russia) will offer deals and reach mutual compromises in several areas including Syria. In a similar fashion, NATO and Moscow can together address several lingering regional conflicts including the Palestinian problem.
- Moscow and Washington will start a series of negotiations about drastically reducing nuclear weapons, means of their delivery, and anti-missile systems.
- Due to Moscow's improving civil rights record, the West can offer cooperation in a wider range of policies and activities, including culture and education.
- NATO's eastward growth will stop.

The fourth scenario. Forecast: Practically all disagreements will be addressed. Russia will be actively engaged, along with the United Kingdom, the United States, France, Germany, Japan, and China as an equal player in global affairs. Though some political and ideological differences will remain, the West will not use them to pressure Moscow. Moscow will stop its organized media campaign against the West. Washington and its allies will emphasize the importance of negotiations in areas of mutual interest and develop partnerships in these fields. NATO's presence near Russia's border could be scaled back; its global role should be re-evaluated to acknowledge Moscow's position. Policies:

- Moscow will start negotiating its new political status in the European Union and NATO.
- Russia and the United States will reach a comprehensive agreement on reducing and even eliminating certain kinds of nuclear weapons.
- Moscow together with other world capitals, including Washington and London, will reach and enforce comprehensive agreements on Syria, Yemen, and Afghanistan.
- Russia will negotiate and achieve visa-free travel between Russia and the United States, the United Kingdom, and the European Union.
- As a result of these policies, a new wave of investments will boost Russia's economy as well as stock markets globally.

When we speculate about these scenarios, we should take many things into consideration. The West is not as united as it was during Cold War years. The United States, the European Union, and Japan have their own particular relations with Russia and sometimes play their own games. The very important factor is China. If Russian-Western relations become worse, the likelihood of Russia-China rapprochement will increase.

Each of these general scenarios can be detailed based on specific contexts, circumstances of the day, or decisions made by individual political leaders. Many variables within these contexts are evolving and increasingly interconnected. The West is likely to continue the debates about the essence of liberal democracy and the policies to sustain it. China plays an increasingly assertive role in international politics and in its ability to impact Russia. Many variables are simply unknown. What we do know is that Russia, as a political player, an energy supplier, a nuclear power, and a cultural hub, will remain a major player in global affairs in the twenty-first century. Will it be feared and criticized or appreciated and embraced? The key to the answer is in the direction of development Russia will choose. The time is now.

References

A

AAP (2017). "Donald Trump withdraws US from Trans-Pacific Partnership." https://au.news.yahoo.com/world/a/34253419/donald-trump-withdraws-us-from-trans-pacific-partnership/#page1 (accessed June 3, 2017).

AFP (2015). "France Says Egypt To Buy Mistral Warship" *Agence France-Presse*. https://www.defensenews.com/pentagon/2015/09/23/france-says-egypt-to-buy-mistral-warships/ (accessed July 30, 2018).

Albertazzi, D., and McDonnell, D. (2008). *Twenty-First Century Populism: The Spectre of Western European Democracy*. New York and London: Palgrave Macmillan.

Alekseev V., Alekseeva E., Zubkov K., Poberezhnikov I. ed. (2004) *Rossiya v geopoliticheskoj i civilizacionnoj dinamike. XVI–XX veka* [Asian Russia in geopolitical and civilizational dynamics. XVI-XX century]. Moscow: Science.

Al Jazeera (2018). "Syria: 'Russian' warplanes bomb rebel-held Idlib, dozens dead." https://www.aljazeera.com/news/2018/06/syria-russian-warplanes-bomb-rebel-held-idlib-dozens-dead-180608085726432.html.

Amnesty International. 2018. Annual Reports. https://www.amnestyusa.org/search/EStonia/ (Accessed May 2, 2018).

B

Bahry, D., and Silver, B. D. (1990). "Soviet citizen participation on the eve of democratization." *American Political Science Review*, 84(3), pp. 821–47.

Bastrykin, A. I. (2008). Interview with the First Deputy of the Prosecutor General of the Russian Federation, March 25. http://www.sledcomproc.ru/smi/543/ (accessed November 11, 2009).

Bastrykin, A.I. (2015). An interview with *Rossiyskaya Gazeta*, July 24. https://bit.ly/2vInVuo (accessed August 12, 2018).

BBC (2013). BBC World Service Poll. http://bit.ly/2qRKlnQ.

BBC News (2016). "India, Russia sign new defense deals." http://www.bbc.com/news/world-asia-india-20834910 (accessed June 3, 2017).

BBC Russian Service (2017). "Levada Center: Almost Half of Russians Support the Death Penalty." https://www.bbc.com/russian/news-38897247 (accessed July 19, 2018).

Beinart, P. (2018). "Trump Is Preparing for a New Cold War." *The Atlantic*, February 28.https://www.theatlantic.com/international/archive/2018/02/trump-is-preparing-for-a-new-cold-war/554384/ (accessed June 8, 2018).

Bianchini, Stefano (2017). *Liquid Nationalism and State Partitions in Europe*. Northampton, UK: Edward Elgar Publishing.

Bieleń S., Khudoley K., and Romanova T., eds. (2012) *Otnosheniya Rossii s Evrosoyuzom* [The relations between Russia and the European Union]. Saint-Petersburg: SPbSU.

Blair, Tony (2016). Quoted in *Guardian*, July 6. https://www.theguardian.com/uk-news/2016/jul/06/tony-blair-deliberately-exaggerated-threat-from-iraq-chilcot-report-war-inquiry (accessed March 8, 2018).

Blake, Aaron (2017). "The 11 most important lines from the new intelligence report on Russia's hacking." *Washington Post*, January 6. https://wapo.st/2tGn3F (accessed March 8, 2018).

Bolkhovitinov, N. (1991). *Russia Discovers America (1732–1799)* [Rossiya Otkryvaet Ameriku]. Moscow: Nauka.

Borah, Rupakjyoti. (2011). "BRICS: The New Great Game." *ISN Insights*. June 23. http://bit.ly/12QmLUU (accessed July 19, 2018).

Borovik, Artyom (1990). The Hidden War: A Russian Journalist's Account of the Soviet War in Afghanistan. New York: Grove Press.

Borshchevskaya, Anna (2014). "On Russia's growing involvement in Iraq." *The Hill*, July 1. http://thehill.com/blogs/pundits-blog/defense/211024-on-russias-growing-involvement-in-iraq (accessed June 3, 2017).

Bottomore, T. (1993). *Elites and Society* (2nd edn.). London: Routledge.

Brown, Archie (1997). *The Gorbachev Factor*. New York: Oxford University Press.

Brownlee, Jason (2007). *Authoritarianism in an Age of Democratization*. New York: Cambridge University Press.

Brzezinski, Z. (1980). "An interview." *The Soldiers of God*. CNN Series: Cold War. Online at: http://www.imdb.com/title/tt1282644/ (accessed June 3, 2017).

Budapest Memorandum (1994). The Budapest Memorandum on Security Assurances. 5 December. http://www.pircenter.org/media/content/files/12/13943175580.pdf (accessed August 14, 2018).

Bump, Philip (2018). "Timeline: How Russian trolls allegedly tried to throw the 2016 election to Trump." *Washington Post*, February 16.https://wapo.st/2vK5ndq (accessed August 14, 2018).

C

Carnaghan, E. (2008). *Out of Order: Russian Political Values in an Imperfect World*. University Park, PA: Penn State University Press.

Census (2010). Russian Federation – All-Russian Population Census 2010 http://catalog.ihsn.org/index.php/catalog/4215 (accessed August 1, 2018).

Chernyaev, A. (2000). *My Six Years With Gorbachev*. University Park, PA: Penn State University Press.

Chronology of Bilateral Relations (2015). *Online Report: Delegation of the European Union to Russia*. http://eeas.europa.eu/delegations/russia/eu_russia/chronology/index_en.htm (accessed June 3, 2018).

Clover, Charles (2018). "China land grab on Lake Baikal raises Russian ire." *Financial Times*, January 4.https://www.ft.com/content/3106345c-f05e-11e7-b220-857e26d1aca4 (accessed July 31, 2018).

Clover, C. (2012). "Clinton vows to thwart new Soviet Union." *Financial Times*, December 6. http://www.ft.com/cms/s/0/a5b15b14-3fcf-11e2-9f71-00144feabdc0.html#axzz4AAgBqLUd (accessed June 3, 2017).

CNBC (2013a). "What's at stake for Russians in Syria." Online Report. http://www.cnbc.com/id/101004539 (accessed June 3, 2017).

CNBC (2013b). "Ukraine leader seeks cash at Kremlin to fend off crisis." Online Report. http://www.cnbc.com/2013/12/17/ukraine-leader-seeks-cash-at-kremlin-to-fend-off-crisis.html (accessed June 3, 2017).

CNN (2011a). "Putin points to U.S. role in Gadhafi's killing." Online Report. http://www.cnn.com/2011/12/15/world/europe/russia-putin-libya/ (accessed June 3, 2017).

CNN (2011b). "World leaders react to news of bin Laden's death." Online Report. http://www.cnn.com/2011/WORLD/asiapcf/05/02/bin.laden.world.reacts/ (accessed June 3, 2017).

Cohen, A. (2009) "Russia and Eurasia: A realistic policy agenda for the Obama administration." Paper by the *Heritage Foundation*, March 27. http://www.heritage.org/Research/RussiaandEurasia/sr0049.cfm (accessed November 11, 2018).

Cohen, A. (2012). "Congressional hearing highlights the need to pass Magnitsky PNTR to Russia." *The Foundry*, June 22. http://blog.heritage.org/2012/06/22/congressional-hearing-high-lights-the-need-to-pass-magnitskypntr-to-russia/ (accessed June 3, 2017).

Collins, N. (2007). *Through Dark Days and White Nights: Four Decades Observing a Changing Russia*. Washington, DC: Scarith.

Concept of the Foreign Policy of the Russian Federation (2013). The Ministry of Foreign Affairs of the Russian Federation. https://bit.ly/2agNI1B (accessed August 11, 2018).

Concept of the Foreign Policy of the Russian Federation (2016). The Ministry of Foreign Affairs of the Russian Federation. https://bit.ly/2qb0l5Z (accessed August 11, 2018).

Conquest, R. (1986). *Harvest of Sorrow: Soviet Collectivization and the Terror-Famine*. New York: Oxford University Press.

CSR Report (2012). "Society and authority during a political crisis" [Obshestvo I vlast' v uslovijah politicheskogo krizisa]. Report of the Center of Strategic Research. Moscow http://www.csr.ru/2009-04-23-10-40-41/365-2012-05-23-10-54-10 (accessed March 31, 2018).

D

Declaration (2002). *Moscow Declaration on New Strategic Relationship between the Russian Federation and the United States*, May 24. http://bit.ly/2qLCEjT (accessed June 3, 2017).

Decree of the President of Russian Federation (1996). *On the coordinating role of the Ministry of Foreign Affairs of the Russian Federation in carrying out a single foreign policy of the Russian Federation* No. 375, March 12.

DeLuca, Derek (2016). "Russian influence grows in Latin America." *American Thinker*, January 28. http://bit.ly/2rpNoqO (accessed June 3, 2018).

Dettmer, Jamie (2018). "Turkey's Erdogan Says He's Ready to Risk Confrontation with US." *Voice of America, 27 January,* https://www.voanews.com/a/ergodan-says-he-is-ready-to-risk-confrontation-with-us/4227613.html (accessed August 11, 2018).

Diamond, Jeremy. (2016). "Russian hacking and the 2016 election: What you need to know." *CNN Politics.* http://www.cnn.com/2016/12/12/politics/russian-hack-donald-trump-2016-election/ (accessed August 14, 2018).

Dobrynin, A. (1995). *In Confidence: Moscow's Ambassador to America's Six Cold War Presidents (1962–1986).* New York: Random House.

Dobrynin, A. (1997). *Sugubo Doveritelno* [Very Confidentially]. Moscow: Avtor.

Donaldson, Robert and Nogee, Joseph (1998). *The Foreign Policy of Russia: Changing Systems, Enduring Interests.* New York: M. E. Sharpe, 1998.

Dubin, B. (2008). An interview. *Novaia Gazeta*, 46, June 30, pp. 6, 7.

Dubin, Boris (2012). "The Myth of the Russian 'Unique Path' and Public Opinion." In L. Johnson and S. White (eds.). *Waiting for Reform under Putin and Medvedev.* New York: Palgrave.

Dudley, Robert, and Shiraev, Eric. (2008). *Counting Every Vote: The Most Contentious Elections in US History.* Dulles, Virginia: Potomac Books

Dye, Thomas (2001). *Top Down Policymaking.* Washington, DC: CQ Press.

E

Eder, T., and Huotari, M. (2016). "Moscow's failed pivot to China." *Foreign Affairs.* https://www.foreignaffairs.com/articles/china/2016-04-17/moscow-s-failed-pivot-china (accessed June 3, 2017).

Egypt Today (2018). "Egypt's exports to Russia increase 35% in 2017." https://bit.ly/2Bolumc (accessed August 14, 2018).

Ellis, R.E. (2016). "Russian influence in Latin America." *The Cipher Brief*, January 5. https://www.thecipherbrief.com/article/russian-influence-latin-america (accessed June 3, 2017).

Erlichman, V. V. (2004). *Poteri Narodonaseleniya v 20 Veke* [Population loss in the 20th century]. Moscow: Russkaya Panorama.

Etzioni, Emital (2014). *The New Normal: Finding a Balance between Individual Rights and the Common Good.* Piscataway, NJ: Transaction.

European Commission (2009). *Energy Dialogue EU – Russia. The Tenth Progress Report*. November, pp. 4–6. https://ec.europa.eu/energy/sites/ener/files/documents/2011_eu-russia_energy_relations.pdf (accessed June 3, 2017).

Evans, Malcolm. (ed.). (2014). *International Law*. New York: Oxford University Press.

F

Foust, J. (2015). "NASA says no plans for ISS replacement with Russia." *Space News*, March 28. http://spacenews.com/nasa-says-no-plans-for-iss-replacement-with-russia/ (accessed June 3, 2017).

Freedman, L. (2018). "Putin's New Cod War." *New Statesman*, March 14. https://www.newstatesman.com/politics/uk/2018/03/putin-s-new-cold-war (accessed July 3, 2018).

Freedom House (2007). *Reports*. https://freedomhouse.org/reports.

Freedom House (2018). *Reports*. https://freedomhouse.org/reports.

G

Gaidar, Y. (2007). *Collapse of an Empire: Lessons of Modern Russia*. Washington, DC: Brookings Institution.

Gatman-Golutvina, O. V. (2000). *Byurokratija ili Oligarkija?* Moscow: The Russian Academy of Diplomatic Service.

Gessen, M. (2012). *The Man without a Face*. New York: Riverhead Books.

Glad, Betty, and Shiraev, Eric (eds.) (1999). *The Russian Transformation*. New York: St. Martin's Press.

Gleason, Gregory. (2006) "The Uzbek Expulsion of U.S. Forces and Realignment in Central Asia." *Problems of Post-Communism*, 53(2), pp. 49–60.

Gleijeses, Piero (2003). *Conflicting Missions: Havana, Washington, and Africa, 1959–1976*. Chapel Hill, NC: University of North Carolina Press.

Global Edge (2018) *Russia: Trade Statistics*. http://globaledge.msu.edu/countries/russia/tradestats (accessed June 23, 2018).

Goldgeier, James (1999). *Not Whether but When: The U.S. Decision to Enlarge NATO*. Washington, DC: Brookings.

Golz, A. (2007). "Rossiyskaya Imperiya i Rossiyski Militarism" [Russian Empire and Russian Militarism], in I. M. Kliamkin (ed.), *Posle imperii*. Moscow: Fond Liberal'naia missiia.

Goncharov, Stepan (2017). "Kostyl Cenzuru" [The Crutches of Censorship]. *Inliberty*. http://old.inliberty.ru/blog/2577-Kostyl-cenzury (accessed August 12, 2018).

Gorbachev, M. (1985). "Interview with Time Magazine." *Pravda*, September, 1–2, p. 1.Gorbachev, M. (1996). *Memoirs* (1st edn.). New York: Doubleday.

Gorbachev M. (2006) *Ponyat' perestrojku ... Pochemu ehto vazhno sejchas* [Understanding perestroika ... Why it matters now]. Moscow: Alpina Business Books.

Gorbachev, M., and Mlynar, Z. (1994). *Conversations with Gorbachev on Perestroika, the Prague Spring, and the Crossroads of Socialism*. New York: Columbia University Press.

Gozman, L., and Etkind, A. (1992). *The Psychology of Post-Totalitarianism in Russia*. London: Centre for Research into Communist Economies.

Green, M. (2015). "Putin Speeches before the National Assembly: A Quantitative Analysis." Unpublished Manuscript.

Gretskiy, I. (2010). *Vneshnepoliticheskie Faktory Prezidentskih Vyborov 2004 Goda v Ukraine* [The External Factors in 2004 Presidential Elections in Ukraine]. Saint Petersburg: SPbSU.

Gretskiy, I., Treshchenkov, E., and Golubev, K. (2014). "Russia's Perceptions and Misperceptions of the EU Eastern Partnership." *Communist and Post-Communist Studies*, 47 (3–4), pp. 145–65.

Grigoriev, Leonid (2006). "How Russia's energy superpower status can bring supersecurity and superstability." Interview with Leonid Grigoriev. http://en.civilg8.ru/2054.php (accessed June 3, 2017).

Grossman, V. (1970). *Vse techet* [Everything flows]. Frankfurt: Posev.

Group of Seven (2015). *Council on Foreign Relations Backgrounders*. http://www.cfr.org/international-organizations-and-alliances/group-seven-g7/p32957 (accessed March 31, 2018).

Grunt, V., Kertman, G., Pavlova, T., Patrushev, S., and Khlopin, A. (1996). "Rossiyskaya Povsed-nevnost I Politicheskaya Kultura: Problemy Obnovleniya" [Russia's everyday life and political culture: Problems of renovation]. *Polis*, 4, pp. 56–72.

Guardian (2016). March 14. https://www.theguardian.com/world/2016/mar/14/russias-mili-tary-action-in-syria-timeline (accessed March 31, 2018).

Gubuev, Alexander (2017). "Shelkovyj Put v Nikuda" [The Silk Road to nowhere]. *Vedo-mosti*, May 14. https://www.vedomosti.ru/opinion/articles/2017/05/15/689763-shelkovii-put (accessed June 3, 2017).

Gudkov, L. (2008). An interview. *Novaia Gazeta*, 40, June 5, pp. 12, 13.

Gudkov, L. (2012). "The Nature and Function of 'Putinism'." In L. Johnson and S. White (eds.), *Waiting for Reform under Putin and Medvedev*. New York: Palgrave Macmillan.

Gudkov, L. (2014). "This is not Conservatism. It's A Neurotic Reaction." *Levada.ru*, February 26. https://www.levada.ru/2014/02/26/eto-ne-konservatizm-eto-nevroticheskaya-reaktsiya/ (accessed July 5, 2018).

Gurganus, Julia (2018). "Russia: Playing a Geopolitical Game in Latin America." *Carnegie Endowment*, May 3. https://carnegieendowment.org/2018/05/03/russia-playing-geopoliti-cal-game-in-latin-america-pub-76228 (accessed August 12, 2018).

H

Haas, R. (2014). *Foreign Policy Begins at Home: The Case for Putting America's House in Order*. New York: Basic Books.

Haas, R. (2018). *Cold War II*. Council of Foreign Relations, February, 3. https://www.cfr.org/article/cold-war-ii. (accessed August 12, 2018).

Hale, H (2011). "Hybrid Regimes: When Democracy and Autocracy Mix." In Nathan Brown (ed.), *Dynamics of Democratization: Dictatorship, Development, and Diffusion*. Baltimore, MD: Johns Hopkins University Press.

Hameed, Saif (2016). "Russia boosts ties with Iraq in challenge to U.S. influence." *Reuters*, February 11. http://www.reuters.com/article/us-mideast-crisis-iraq-russia-idUSKCN0VK288 (accessed June 3, 2017).

Hess, Maximilian (2018). "China Has Decided Russia Is Too Risky an Investment." *Financial Times*, May 16. https://foreignpolicy.com/2018/05/16/china-has-decided-russia-is-too-risky-an-investment/ (accessed August 12, 2018).

Hiro, Dilip. (2010). *After Empire: The Birth of a Multipolar World*. New York: Nation Books.

Hopkirk, P. (1992). *The Great Game: The Struggle for Empire in Central Asia*. New York: Kod-ansha America.

Hosking, G. A. (1992) *The First Socialist Society: A History of the Soviet Union from Within* (2nd edn.). Boston, MA: Harvard University Press.

I

IEA (2017). International Energy Agency. https://www.iea.org/ (accessed June 3, 2017).

IMF (2018). International Monetary Fund. http://www.imf.org/external/research/index.aspx (accessed March 31, 2018).

INF (1987). *The Treaty between the United States of America and the Union of Soviet Socialist Republics on the Elimination of Their Intermediate-Range and Shorter-Range Missiles*. U.S. Department of State. http://www.state.gov/www/global/arms/treaties/inf1.html#treaty (accessed June 3, 2017).

Isaev, B., and Baranov, N. (2009). *Politicheskie otnoshenija I politicheskij process v sovermennoj Rossii*. St. Petersburg: Piter.

Ivanyan, E. A. (2001a). *Entsiklopedia possijsko-amerikansih otnoshenij* [An encyclopedia of Rus-sian-American relations]. Moscow: Mezhdunarodnye Otnoshenija.

Ivanyan, E. A. (2001b). "Iz sitorii: Rossija I SSHA – soyuzniki, partner, ili protivniki?" [From history: Russia and the USA – allies, partners, or opponents?] *USA and Canada*, 12, pp. 25–39.

Izvestia (2017). February 23. https://iz.ru/news/666713 (accessed March 31, 2018).

J

Jamal, Umair (2016). "Russia wants to de-hyphenate India and Pakistan: Should Delhi worry?" *The Diplomat*, September 27. http://thediplomat.com/2016/09/russia-wants-to-de-hyphenate-india-and-pakistan-should-delhi-worry/ (accessed June 3, 2017).

JF (Jamestown Foundation) (1999). "Russia tangles with France over visit by Chechen official." *Monitor*, 5 (213). https://jamestown.org/program/russia-tangles-with-france-over-visit-by-chechen-official/ (accessed June 3, 2017).

K

Kaplan, R. (2016). "Eurasia's coming anarchy: The risk of China and Russia's weakness." *Foreign Affairs*. https://www.foreignaffairs.com/articles/china/2016-02-15/eurasias-coming-anarchy (accessed June 3, 2017).

Katz, M. (1991). *The USSR and Marxist Revolutions in the Third World*. New York: Cambridge University Press.

Khoury, Jack (2018). "In Moscow, Hamas Officials Say Russia Promised to Oppose U.S. Peace Plan." *Haaretz*. https://www.haaretz.com/middle-east-news/palestinians/.premium-hamas-officials-russia-promised-to-oppose-u-s-peace-plan-1.6213186 (accessed August 12, 2018).

Khudoley, Konstantin (2006). "The evolution of views of the Russian elite on foreign policy at the turn of the XXI century." In Yuri Akimov and Dmitri Katsy (eds.), *Post-Cold War Challenges to International Relations*. St. Petersburg: St. Petersburg State University Press, pp. 156–171.

Khudoley K. (2013). "Sovetizaciya baltijskih gosudarstv letom 1940 goda i ee posledstviya [The Sovietization of the Baltic States in the summer of 1940 and its consequences]. Vestnik SPbSU, *Political Science: International Relations*, 6(1), pp. 94–110.

Khudoley K. (2016a). "The Baltic Sea Region and Increasing International Tension." *Baltic Region*, 8(1), pp. 4–16.

Khudoley, Konstantin (2016b). "Russia and the European Union: A Present Rift and Chances for Future Reconciliation." *Stosunki Międzynarodowe – International Relations* (Warsaw University Press), 52(2), pp. 195–213.

Khudoley, Konstantin (2016c). "Russian Foreign Policy in The Pacific Region: 1985–2015." In Aleksandra Jarczewska and Jacub Zajączkowski, (eds.), *Region Azji i Pacyfiku w Latach 1985–2015*. Warsaw, Poland: Wydawnictwo Naukowe Scholar, pp. 253–273.

Khudoley, Konstantin (2017a). "The Evolution of the Idea of World Revolution in Soviet Politics (The Epoch of the Comintern and Socialism in One Country)." *Vestnik SPbSU. Political Science. International Relations*, 10(2), pp. 145–65.

Khudoley, K. (2017b) "Russia and the U.S.: The Way Forward." *Russia in Global Affairs*, 15(4), pp. 118–129.

Khudoley, K. K. (2018) "Evolyuciya Idei Mirovoj Revolyucii v Politike Sovetskogo Soyuza (Pod'em i Raspad Mirovoj Sistemy Socializma) [The Evolution of the Idea of World Revolution in Soviet Politics; The Rise and the Collapse of the World System of Socialism]. *Vestnik SPbSU. Political Science. International Relations*, 11(1), pp. 53–85.

King, C. (2008). "The five-day war: Managing Moscow after the Georgia crisis." *Foreign Affairs*, November/December,2 (11).

Kirchick, James (2017). *The End of Europe: Dictators, Demagogues and the Coming Dark Age*. New Heaven, CT: Yale University Press.

Kogan, Pavel (2016). "Russia-Turkey relations: Rapprochement on Russian terms." *Defense News*, August 31. http://www.defensenews.com/articles/russia-turkey-relations-rapprochement-on-russian-terms (accessed June 3, 2017).

Korshunov, Y. L. (1995). "Vooruzhennyj nejtralitet Rossii na more v period bor'by SSHA za nezavisiomst" [An armed neutrality of Russia during the period of the America's war for independence], *USA: Economics, Politics, and Ideology*, 7.

Kort, M. (2006). *The Soviet Colossus: History and Aftermath*. New York: M.E. Sharpe.

Kozyrev, Andrei (1995). *Preobrazhenie* [Transfiguration]. Moscow: Mezhdunarodnye Otnoshenija.

Krivosheev, G.F. (2001). "Rossiya I SSSR v Voynah 20 Veka" [Russia and the USSR in 20th-century wars]. http://www.soldat.ru/doc/casualties/book/ (accessed November 11, 2009).

Kuchins, A. (2007). "Alternative futures for Russia to 2017." Report of the Russia and Eurasia Program Center for Strategic and International Studies. http://www.csis.org/files/media/csis/pubs/071210-russia_2017-web.pdf (accessed November 11, 2017).

Kurilla, I.I. (2005). *Zaokeanskie partnery: Amerika I Rossiya v 1830–1850e gody* [Overseas partners: America and Russia, 1830–1850]. Volgograd: Volgograd State University).

L

Lanko, Dmitry A. (2013). "The Regional Approach in the Policy of the Russian Federation towards the Republic of Estonia." *Baltic Region,* 5(3, 17), pp. 37–45. doi: 10.5922/2079-8555-2013-3-4.

Lanko, Dmitry, and Dolzenkova, Jekaterina. (2015). "Latvia in the System of European Territorial Security: A View from Inside and from Outside." *Baltic Region,* 7(1, 23), pp. 56–66, doi: 10.5922/2079-8555-2015-1-4.

Lantsova I. (2013) *Gosudarstva Korejskogo poluostrova v mezhdunarodnyh otnosheniyah (konec XX – nachalo XXI vv.)* [The States of Korean Peninsula in International Relations (late XX–early XXI centuries]. Saint Petersburg: SPbSU.

Lavrov, S. (2008). Speech of the Russian Foreign Minister at the Institute of International Relations, Moscow, September 1. http://newsru.com/russia/01sep2008/lavrov.html (accessed February 11, 2018).

Lavrov, S. (2011). Foreign Ministers Answers Questions on Three Radio Stations. October 21. http://echo.msk.ru/programs/beseda/819444-echo/ (accessed August 11, 2018).

Legvold, R. (2009). "The Russia file: How to move toward a strategic partnership." *Foreign Affairs,* July/August, pp. 78–93.

Lenin, V. (1916/1969). *Imperialism, the Highest Stage of Capitalism.* Moscow: International Publishing.

Lenin, V. (1917/2006). *The State and Revolution.* Moscow: Kissinger Publishing.

Lenta (2016). "Konstitucionnyj sud zapretil primenjat' v Rossii smertnuyu azn" [The Constitutional Court banned the death penalty in Russia]. *Lenta, November 19,* https://lenta.ru/news/2009/11/19/death/ (accessed June 3, 2017).

Levada (2000). Poll of September 2000. http://www.levada.ru/2000/10/25/26-oktyabrya-2000-goda/.

Levada (2012). Poll of April 13. http://www.levada.ru (accessed March 31, 2018).

Levada (2014). Poll of December 11. https://www.levada.ru/en/2014/11/12/crimea/ (accessed March 31, 2018).

Levada (2015a). Poll of March 27–30. http://www.levada.ru (accessed March 31, 2018).

Levada (2015b). Poll of July 17–20. https://www.levada.ru/2015/07/27/rassledovanie-katastrofy-boinga/ (accessed August 12, 2018).

Levada (2016a) Poll of February 8. http://www.bbc.com/russian/news-38897247 (accessed March 31, 2018).

Levada (2016b) Poll of June 2. https://www.levada.ru/2016/06/02/rossiyane-reshili-kto-im-vragi/ (accessed March 31, 2018).

Levada (2016c) Poll of November 18. http://www.levada.ru/2016/11/18/doverie-smi-i-tsenzura/ (accessed March 31, 2018).

Levada (2016d). Poll of 24–25 July. https://www.levada.ru/2016/07/29/doping-skandal/ (accessed July 7, 2018).

Levada (2017). Various polls. https://www.levada.ru/en/2018/02/02/enemies/ (accessed March 31, 2018).

Levada (2018a). Poll of 23–27 March. https://www.levada.ru/2018/04/10/17896/ (accessed August 12, 2018).

Levada (2018b). Poll of December 1–5, 2017. https://www.levada.ru/2018/01/10/vragi-rossii/ (accessed August 12, 2018).

Levada (2018c). Poll of July 19–25. https://www.levada.ru/2018/08/09/otnoshenie-k-vladimiru-putinu-3/ (accessed August 12, 2018).

Levada (2018d). Poll of January 2018. https://www.levada.ru/2018/08/02/sotsiologi-zafiksirova-li-nailuchshee-otnoshenie-rossiyan-k-ssha-i-es-so-vremen-anneksii-kryma/ (accessed August 12, 2018).

Levada (2018e). Poll of July 18. https://www.levada.ru/2018/08/02/rossiya-i-zapad-3/(accessed August 12, 2018).

Levada (2018f). Poll 19–23 January. https://www.levada.ru/2018/02/12/otnoshenie-k-stranam/ (accessed August 15, 2018).

Levesque, J. (1997). *The Enigma of 1989: The USSR and the Liberation of Eastern Europe*. Berkeley, CA: University of California Press.

Library of Congress (2016). *Russian Federation: Constitutional Court Allows Country to Ignore ECHR Rulings*. http://bit.ly/2s78bAI (accessed June 3, 2017).

Lipkin M. (2016) *Sovetskij Soyuz i Integracionnye Processy v Evrope: Seredina 1940-h – Konec 1960-h Godov* [Soviet Union and integration Processes in Europe: mid-1940s–late 1960s]. Moscow: Russian Foundation for Education and Science.

Lobanov, Vladislav and Kasrprzyk, Eric (2018). "Russia Denies Syrians Asylum." *Human Rights Watch*, 3 July. https://www.hrw.org/news/2018/07/03/russia-denies-syrians-asylum (accessed August 11, 2018).

Lukassen, Okke (2018). In between War and Peace: A Conceptualization of Russian Strategic Deterrence in the Shared Euro-Russian Neighborhood. Paper presented at the Third Annual Tartu Conference on Russian and East European Studies, 10–12 June, University of Tartu, Estonia.

Lukyanov, Fyodor (2016). "Putin's Foreign Policy." *Foreign Affairs*, May/June. https://www.foreignaffairs.com/articles/russia-fsu/2016–04-18/putins-foreign-policy (accessed June 3, 2017).

Lukyanov F., and Miller, A. (2016), *Detachment instead of Confrontation: Post-European Russia in Search of Self-Sufficiency*. https://www.kreisky-forum.org/dataall/Report_Post-European-Russia.pdf (accessed July 31, 2018).

M

MacMillan, Margaret (2003). *Paris 1919: Six Months That Changed the World*. New York: Random House.

MacMillan, M. (2013). *The War That Ended Peace: The Road to 1914*. New York: Random House.

Makarov, V. G., and Khristoforov, V. S. (2006). Novye dannye o dejatel'nosti Amerikansloj administracii pomoshi v Rossii [New data on American administration of the American Relief Administration in Russia]. *Novaja I Novejshaja Istroriya*, 5, pp. 230–43.

Malcolm, N. (1995) "Russian foreign policy decision-making," pp. 23–51 in P. Sherman (ed.), *Russian Foreign Policy Since 1990*. Boulder, CO: Westview Press.

Mamedov, Ruslan (2018). "Will Sadr's victory impact Russia-Iraq relations?" *Al-Monitor*, 27 May https://www.al-monitor.com/pulse/originals/2018/05/iraq-russia-relations-defense-oil-politics-sadr.html (accessed August 17, 2018).

Mankoff J. (2012). *Russian Foreign Policy: The Return of Great Power Politics* (2nd edn.). Lanham, MD: Rowman & Littlefield.

Maslow, Abraham (2007). "Cho nyzhno Rosii v Africe" [What Russia needs in Africa]. *Strategiya Rossii*. http://bit.ly/2rGKe2r (accessed June 3, 2017).

Matlock, J. (2005). *Reagan and Gorbachev: How the Cold War Ended*. New York: Random House.

McFaul, M., and Stoner-Weiss, K. (2008). "The myth of the authoritarian model: How Putin's crackdown holds Russia back." *Foreign Affairs*, January/February, pp. 68–84.

Mearsheimer, John. (2003). *The Tragedy of Great Power Politics*. New York: W. W. Norton & Company.

Mearsheimer, John J. (2014). "Why the Ukraine Crisis is the West's Fault: The Liberal Delusions That Provoked Putin." *Foreign Affairs*, September/October, 93 (5), 77–89.

Medvedev, D. (2009). An interview with NTV, July 26. http://www.newsru.com/russia/26jul2009/tv.html (accessed February 11, 2018).

Mendkovich, Nikita (2011). "Politika Rossii v Afganistane, 2001–2011" [Russian Politics in Afghanistan 2001–2011]. *Perspektivy*. http://bit.ly/2sEGkEN (accessed June 3, 2017).

MH17 Statement (2018). "MH17: The Netherlands and Australia hold Russia responsible." https://www.government.nl/latest/news/2018/05/25/mh17-the-netherlands-and-australia-hold-russia-responsible.

Mikulski, K. I. (ed.) (1995). *Elita Rossii o Nastoyashem I Budushem Strany* [The Russian elite on the country's present and future]. Moscow: Vekhi.

Milani, Abbas (2001). *The Shah*. New York: Palgrave.

Military Doctrine of the Russian Federation (2014). http://thailand.mid.ru/en/military-doctrine-of-the-russian-federation (accessed August 11, 2018).

More, Evan (2018). "Strengthen the U.S.–India Relationship." *National Review*, February 1. https://www.nationalreview.com/2018/02/india-united-states-relations-trade-military-strategy-alliance/. (accessed August 12, 2018).

Morozov, A. (2004). *Diplomatia Putina* [Putin's diplomacy]. St. Petersburg: Izmailovsky Publishing.

Mukherjee, Pranab (2015). "Russia is a dependable partner of India." http://www.news18.com/news/india/pranab-mukherjee-3–989368.html (accessed June 3, 2017).

Mullaney, Gerry, and Buckley, Chris (2017). "China Warns of Arms Race After U.S. Deploys Missile Defense in South Korea" *New York Times*, March 7. https://nyti.ms/2mOexRV (accessed June 3, 2017).

Murray, Charles (2013). *American Exceptionalism: An Experiment in History (Values and Capitalism)*. Washington, DC: AEI Press (accessed June 3, 2017).

N

National Front (2018). The official party's website. http://www.frontnational.com/ (accessed June 3, 2018).

National Security Strategy (2015). *Russian Federation Presidential Edict 683*. http://www.ieee.es/Galerias/fichero/OtrasPublicaciones/Internacional/2016/Russian-National-Security-Strategy-31Dec2015.pdf (accessed March 31, 2018).

Naumkin, Vitaly (2014). Russia, Egypt draw closer. *Al Monitor*, August 13. http://www.al-monitor.com/pulse/originals/2014/08/russia-egypt-putin-sisi-visit-ukraine-palestine.html (accessed June 3, 2017).

Nechepurenko, Ivan (2017). "Kremlin group employing ex-spies is viewed abroad as propaganda mill." *New York Times*, April 20. http://nyti.ms/2qVl6B9 (accessed June 3, 2017).

Nesterova, Y. (2016). "What Does It Mean to Be Conservative in Russia?" *The National Interest*. August 10. http://nationalinterest.org/feature/what-does-it-mean-be-conservative-russia-17312 (accessed July 10, 2018).

New Start Treaty (2010). *The Treaty between the United States of America and the Russian Federation on Measures for the Further Reduction and Limitation of Strategic Offensive Arms*. http://www.state.gov/t/avc/newstart/index.htm (accessed June 3, 2017).

New York Times (2016). September 24. https://www.nytimes.com/2016/09/24/world/middleeast/aleppo-syria-airstrikes.html (accessed March 31, 2018).

Nonini, Donald (ed.) (2007). *The Global Idea of "The Commons."* New York: Berghahn Books.

Novak, Alexander (2017). An interview, March 27. *RT* (Russian international television network). https://russian.rt.com/business/article/372490-arktika-potencial-novak-intervyu (accessed June 3, 2017).

Novaya Gazeta (2012). January 9. https://www.novayagazeta.ru/articles/2012/01/09/47638-v-konstitutsii-ne-dolzhno-byt-mesta-dlya-vozhdya (accessed March 31, 2018).

Nunn-Lugar Program (1991). *Cooperative Threat Reduction with States of Former Soviet Union*. Legal Information Institute. https://www.law.cornell.edu/uscode/text/22/chapter-68A (accessed June 3, 2017).

Nwosu, C. (2015). "What Happened to the BRICS?" *Foreign Policy in Focus*, July 31. https://fpif.org/what-happened-to-the-brics/ (accessed June 30, 2018).

P

Palazhchenko, P. (1997). *My Years with Gorbachev and Shevardnadze: The Memoir of a Soviet Interpreter*. University Park, PA: Pennsylvania State University Press.

Partnership between Russia and Iran (2017). Center to Study Iran and Eurasia. http://russiancouncil.ru/common/upload/RIAC-IRAS-Russia-Iran-Report29.pdf (accessed June 3, 2018).

Pearson, D. E. (1987). *KAL 007: The Cover-Up*. New York: Summit Books.

Perlez, Jane (2014). "China and Russia Reach 30-Year Gas Deal." *New York Times*, May 21. http://www.nytimes.com/2014/05/22/world/asia/china-russia-gas-deal.html?_r=0 (accessed June 3, 2017).

Peskov, Dmitry (2017). Interfax, March 3. http://www.interfax.ru/russia/556130. (accessed June 3, 2017).

Pipes, R. (1984). *Survival Is Not Enough*. New York: Simon Schuster.

Popova, O. V. (2004). "Conservative Values in Russian People's Stereotypes of Politics, Consciousness and Behavior." http://anthropology.ru/ru/person/popova-ov. (accessed June 23, 2018).

Pulipaka, Sanjay (2016). "Russia's new approach to Pakistan: All about arms sales." *The Diplomat*. http://thediplomat.com/2016/09/russias-new-approach-to-pakistan-all-about-arms-sales/ (accessed June 3, 2017).

Putin, V. (2007). *Putin's Prepared Remarks at 43rd Munich Conference on Security Policy*. http://www.washingtonpost.com/wp-dyn/content/article/2007/02/12/AR2007021200555.html (accessed June 3, 2017).

Putin, V. (2011). *A New Integration Project for Eurasia: The Future in the Making*. Permanent Mission of the Russian Federation to the European Union. https://russiaeu.ru/en (accessed June 3, 2017).

Putin, V. (2012a). Speech before the State Duma, April 11. http://www.rg.ru/2012/04/11/putin-otchet.html (accessed March 31, 2018).

Putin, V. (2012b). "Rossiya I Menjayushisja Mir" [Russia and a changing world]. *Moscow News*, February 27. http://mn.ru/politics/20120227/312306749.html (accessed March 31, 2018).

Putin, V. (2012c). A meeting with managers and editors of television, radio, and print media, January 18. http://premier.gov.ru/events/news/17798/ (accessed March 31, 2018).

Putin, V. (2013). "A Plea for Caution from Russia." *New York Times*, September 11. https://nyti.ms/2OK3yEh (accessed August 15, 2018).

Putin, V. (2014). "Russia Does Not Want to Isolate Itself," Comments Made to the Discussion Club Valdai. http://tass.ru/politika/1531106.

Putin, V. (2018a). Presidential Address to the Federal Assembly. http://en.kremlin.ru/events/president/news/56957 (accessed July 4, 2018).

Putin, V. (2018b). Putin, Macron discuss implementation of joint initiative on humanitarian aid to Syria. http://tass.com/politics/1014340. (accessed July 22, 2018).

Putin, V. (2018c). Meeting of BRICS leaders with delegation heads from invited states. http://en.kremlin.ru/events/president/news/58116 (accessed July 30, 2018).

R

Rabinovich, Itmar (2016). "The Russia-US relations in the Middle East: A five-year projection." Carnegie Endowment for International Peace. http://carnegieendowment.org/2016/04/05/russian-u.s.-relationship-in-middle-east-five-year-projection-pub-63243 (accessed June 3, 2017).

Rahr, A. (2000). *Wladimir Putin: Der "Deutsche" im Kreml*. Darmstadt, Germany: Universtas.

Reuters (2016). "Iran deploys Russian-made S-300 missiles at its Fordow nuclear site: TV." August 29. http://www.reuters.com/article/us-iran-missiles-fordow-idUSKCN1140YD (accessed June 3, 2017).

Reuters (2017). "Russia, China block U.N. sanctions on Syria over gas attacks." February 28. http://www.reuters.com/article/us-mideast-crisis-syria-chemicalweapons-idUSKBN167232 (accessed June 3, 2017).

Reuters (2018). "Kremlin Rejects Blame for MH17 Downing, Says Distrusts Dutch Findings." https://www.usnews.com/news/world/articles/2018-05-25/kremlin-rejects-blame-for-mh17-downing-says-distrusts-dutch-findings (accessed July 11, 2018).

Rey, Marie-Pierre (2004). "Europe Is Our Common Home: A Study of Gorbachev's Diplomatic Concept." *Cold War History* 4(2): 33–65.

RIA (2014). "The Customs Union is studying possibilities for a free trade zone with Egypt." https://ria.ru/economy/20140812/1019750247.html (accessed June 3, 2017).

RIA (2015). "Iran will receive a $5bln credit." https://ria.ru/world/20151112/1319239219.html (accessed June 3, 2017).

Rivera, D. W., and Rivera, S. W. (2009). "Yeltsin, Putin, and Clinton: Presidential leadership and Russian democratization in comparative perspective." *Perspectives on Politics*, 7, 3, September, pp. 591–610.

10.1080/09668136.2016.1159664Romanova, Tatiana. (2016). "Sanctions and the Future of EU-Russian economic relations." *Europe-Asia Studies*, 4, pp. 774–796. doi: 10.1080/09668136.2016.1159664.

Rosenfielde, Steven (2016). *The Kremlin Strikes Back: Russia and the West after Crimea's Annexation.* New York: Cambridge University Press.

Rossijskaya Gazeta (2015). July 14. https://in.rbth.com/author/Rossiyskaya%20Gazeta (accessed June 3, 2017).

Rosstat (2017). Russian Federation State Statistics Service. http://www.gks.ru/wps/wcm/connect/rosstat_main/rosstat/en/main/ (accessed June 3, 2017).

Roxburgh, A. (2012). *The Strongman.* New York: I. B. Tauris.

Rozoff, Rick (2009). *The Shanghai Cooperation Organization: Prospects for a Multipolar World.* Canada: Center for Global Research (accessed June 3, 2017).

RT (2012). *New Era in Russia-US Trade Relations: Obama Scraps Jackson-Vanik Amendment.* https://www.rt.com/business/obama-scraps-jackson-vanik-518/ (accessed June 3, 2017).

Ruble, B. (1990). *Leningrad: Shaping a Soviet City.* Berkeley, CA: University of California Press.

Rupnik, Jacques (1989). "The Empire Breaks UP". *The New Republic*, February 20, pp. 22–24.

S

Saakashvili, M. (2018). "When Russia Invaded Georgia." *Wall Street Journal*, 7 August. https://www.wsj.com/articles/when-russia-invaded-georgia-1533682576.

Sabennikova, I. V. (2002). *Rossiyskaya Emigraciya (1917–1939)* [Russian emigration, 1917–1939). Tver: Federal Archive Service (accessed June 3, 2017).

Sadri, Houman A. (2014) "*Eurasian Economic Union (Eeu): A Good Idea or a Russian Takeover?*" *Rivista di Studi Politici Internazionali*, Vol. 81, No. 4 (324) (OTTOBRE-DICEMBRE 2014), pp. 553–561

Sajalia, Nana (2018). "Georgia Mulls Expedited NATO Membership Strategy." *Voice of America*, March 8, https://www.voanews.com/a/georgia-mulls-expedited-nato-membership-strategy/4286612.html (accessed June 8, 2018).

Sakwa, R. (1993). *Russian Politics and Society.* London: Routledge.

Sestanovich, S. (2008). "What has Moscow done? Rebuilding U.S.–Russian relations." *Foreign Affairs*, November/December, pp. 12–28.

Sharma, Rajeev (2012). "Kudankulam and more: Why Putin's India visit was a hit." *Firstpost*. http://www.firstpost.com/world/kudankulam-and-more-why-putins-india-visit-was-a-hit-568504.html (accessed June 3, 2017).

Sheehy, G. (1990). *The Man Who Changed the World.* New York: HarperCollins.

Shiraev, E., and Bastrykin, A. (1988). *Moda, Kumiry, I Sobstevennoe Ya* [Fashion, idols, and the self]. Leningrad: Lenizdat.

Shiraev, E., and Sobel, R. (2006). *People and Their Opinions.* New York: Pearson.

Shiraev, E., and Sobel, R. (2019). *Public Opinion.* New York: Rowman and Littlefield.

Shiraev, E., and Terrio, D. (2003). "Russian decision-making regarding Bosnia: Indifferent public and feuding elites." In R. Sobel and E. Shiraev (eds.), *International Public Opinion and the Bosnia Crisis.* Lexington, MD: Rowman & Littlefield.

Shiraev, E., and Zubok, V. (2000). *Anti-Americanism in Russia: From Stalin to Putin.* New York: Palgrave Macmillan.

Shiraev, E., and Zubok, V. (2016). *International Relations* (2nd edn.). New York: Oxford University Press.

Shlapentokh, V. (2014). "Putin's destruction of the common vocabulary with the West hurts the Russian-American relations." https://shlapentokh.wordpress.com/ (accessed March 31, 2018).

Shlapentokh, V. (2015). *Putin as a threat to the USA and the West.* https://shlapentokh.wordpress.com/ (accessed March 31, 2018).

Shlapentokh, V., Shiraev, E., and Carroll, E. (2008). *The Soviet Union: Internal and External Perspectives on Soviet Society.* New York: Palgrave Macmillan.

Shlapentokh, V., Woods, J., and Shiraev, E. (2005). *America: Sovereign Defender or a Cowboy Nation?* London: Ashgate.

Shleifer, A., and Treisman, D. (2004). "A normal country." *Foreign Affairs*, March/April, pp. 20–38.

Shpotov, B. M. (2015). "Sovetsko-Amerikanskie Economchskie Svjazi, 1920–1930" [Soviet-American economic ties, 1920–1930]. *Economic History*, 1, pp. 69–74.

Shtepa, Vadim (2018). "Why human rights in Russia are different from the rights in Europe?" *Inosmi.ru.* https://inosmi.ru/politic/20180118/241216572.html.

Simes, D. (2007). "Losing Russia: The costs of renewed confrontation," *Foreign Affairs*, November/December, pp. 36–52.

Smeltz, Dina, Daalder, Ivo, Friedhoff, Karl, and Craig Kafura (2016). *America in the Age of Uncertainty*. Chicago, IL: Chicago Council on Global Affairs.

Smeltz, Dina, Wojtowicz, Lily, and Goncharov, Stepan (2018). "Despite Last Year's Expectations, Public Senses Strains in US-Russia Relations." Chicago Council on Global Affairs, 7 February. https://www.thechicagocouncil.org/publication/despite-last-years-expectations-publics-sense-strains-us-russia-relations (accessed August 13, 2018).

Smeltz, Dina, Wojtowicz, Lily, Volkov, Denis, and Goncharov, Stepan (2018). "US-Russia Experts Paint a Dim Picture of Bilateral Relations before Summit" Chicago Council on Global Affairs. 12 July. https://www.thechicagocouncil.org/publication/us-russia-experts-paint-dim-picture-bilateral-relations-summit (accessed August 7, 2018).

Smolchenko, A. (2014). "China, Russia seek 'international justice', agree currency swap line." AFP News. http://bit.ly/2rTLvEc (accessed June 3, 2017).

Sobel, R., and Shiraev, E. (2003). *International Public Opinion and the Bosnia Crisis*. Lexington, MD: Rowman & Littlefield.

Stalin, Joseph (1952). *Economic Problems of Socialism in the USSR*. http://marx2mao.com/Stalin/EPS52.pdf (accessed: August 7, 2018).

START (1991). Strategic Arms Reduction Treaty. http://www.state.gov/www/global/arms/starthtm/start/start1.html (accessed March 31, 2018).

State, The (1989) "Gorbachev reveals Soviet defense budget." *The State,* May 31.

Strategy 2020. (2012). "A new model of growth—new social policy" [Strategiya-2020: Novaya model rosta – novaja social'naja politika] http://2020strategy.ru/documents/32710234.html.

Svolik, Milan (2012). *The Politics of Authoritarian Rule (Cambridge Studies in Comparative Politics)*. New York: Cambridge University Press.

T

Talbott, Strobe (2003). *The Russia Hand*. New York: Random House.

TASS (2016a). *Russia's Defense Ministry Establishes Arctic Strategic Command*. December 1. http://tass.com/russia/764428 (accessed March 31, 2018).

TASS (2016b). *Levada Center: Russians Have Worsened Their Attitudes toward the USA, Turkey, and Ukraine, and No Longer Want to Join the EU*. June 2, HYPERLINK http://tass.ru/obschestvo/3333320 (accessed March 31, 2018).

TASS (2018). *Putin, Macron discuss implementation of joint initiative on humanitarian aid to Syria*. July 21. http://tass.com/politics/1014340 (accessed August 12, 2018).

Torkunov A.V. (2000) *Zagadochnaya Vojna: Korejskij Konflikt* (1950–1953) [Mysterious war: the Korean Conflict (1950–1953)]. Moscow: Russian Political Encyclopedia.

Treisman, D. (1999–2000). "Russia 2000: After Yeltsin comes ... Yeltsin." *Foreign Policy*, Winter. www.foreignpolicy.com (accessed November 11, 2009).

Trenin, Dmitri (2002). *The End of Eurasia: Russia on the Border between Geopolitics and Globalization*. Washington, DC: Carnegie Endowment for International Peace. 2002.

Trenin, D. (2017). "Russia's Evolving Grand Eurasia Strategy: Will It Work?" *Carnegie Moscow Center.* July 20. http://carnegie.ru/2017/07/20/russia-s-evolving-grand-eurasia-strategy-will-it-work-pub-71588 (accessed July 9, 2018).

Treschenkov E. (2013) "Ot Vostochnyh Sosedej k Vostochnym Partneram. Respublika Belarus', Respublika Moldova i Ukraina v Fokuse Politiki Sosedstva Evropejskogo Soyuza (2002–2012)"

[From Eastern Neighbours to the Eastern Partners. The Republic of Belarus, the Republic of Moldova and Ukraine in Focus of the European Union Neighbourhood Policy (2002–2012].. Saint Petersburg.

Treschenkov E. (2014) "Evropejskaya i Evrazijskaya Modeli Integracii: Predely Soizmerimosti" [European and Eurasian models of integration: Limits of comparability]. *World Economy and International Relations*, 5. pp. 31–41.

Trofimov, Yaroslav (2018). Why Russia's Middle East Gamble Has a Limited Payoff. *Wall Street Journal,* June 21. https://www.wsj.com/articles/why-russias-middle-east-gamble-has-a-limited-payoff-1529573402.

Tsygankov, Andrei (2016). *Russia's Foreign Policy: Change and Continuity in National Identity.* Lanham, MD: Rowman and Littlefield.

The Week (2010). "Russian navy 'sent Somali pirates to their death'." May 12. https://bit.ly/2Ky2xRg (accessed July 8, 2018).

U

Ukraine Freedom Support Act (2014). *Chapter 96A – Ukraine Freedom Support.* http://uscode.house.gov/view.xhtml?path=/prelim@title22/chapter96A&edition=prelim (accessed March 31, 2018).

UN (2009). *Oceans and Law of the Sea: The United Nations.* http://www.un.org/depts/los/clcs_new/submissions_files/submission_rus.htm (accessed March 31, 2018).

UN (2018). Office of the High Commissioner, Report on the human rights situation in Ukraine. https://www.ohchr.org/Documents/Countries/UA/ReportUkraineFev-May2018_EN.pdf (accessed July 8, 2018).

UN Comtrade Database (2018) *United Nations International Trade Statistics* Database. https://comtrade.un.org/ (accessed August 12, 2018).

V

Vice, M. (2017). "Publics Worldwide Unfavorable toward Putin, Russia." *Pew Research Center,* August 16. http://www.pewglobal.org/2017/08/16/publics-worldwide-unfavorable-toward-putin-russia/ (accessed July 7, 2018).

W

Walker, Shaun (2016). "How the world views the US elections, from Israel to North Korea." *Guardian*, October 31. https://www.theguardian.com/us-news/2016/oct/31/world-opinion-us-election-russia-china-mexico-europe (accessed March 31, 2018).

Walt, S. (2005). "Taming American power." *Foreign Affairs*, September/October, pp. 105–20.

Waltz, Kenneth. (2010). *Theory of International Politics.* Long Grove, IL: Waveland Press.

WCIOM (2009a). Poll of February 20. http://wciom.ru (accessed March 31, 2018).

WCIOM (2009b). Poll of May 6. http://wciom.ru (accessed March 31, 2018).

WCIOM (2018). Poll of July 2. http://wciom.ru (accessed July 2, 2018).

Weitz, R. (2011). "China-Russia relations and the United States: At a turning point?" *Rianovosti,* April 14, 2011.

Weitz, R. (2016). "Why China Snubs Russia Arms." *The Diplomat.* http://thediplomat.com/2010/04/why-china-snubs-russian-arms/ (accessed March 31, 2018).

Westad, O. A. (2018). "Has a New Cold War Really Begun?" *Foreign Affairs*, March 27.

Willets, Peter. (1983). *The Non-Aligned Movement: The Origins of a Third World Alliance.* London, UK: Pinter Publishing. https://www.foreignaffairs.com/articles/china/2018–03-27/has-new-cold-war-really-begun (accessed July 8, 2018).

Wilson, A. (2014). *Ukraine Crisis: What It Means for the West.* New Haven, CT: Yale University Press.

Withnall, Adam (2018). "China's Xi declares Putin his 'best, most intimate friend' as Russia looks to the East for allies." *Independent,* 8 June. *https://ind.pn/2MOKVyr* (accessed August 17, 2018).

WTO (2012). Press Release. "WTO membership rises to 157 with the entry of Russia and Vanuatu." https://www.wto.org/english/news_e/pres12_e/pr671_e.htm (accessed July 31, 2018).

X

Xi Jinping (2016). Quoted in *Guardian*, June 25. https://www.theguardian.com/world/2016/jun/26/friends-forever-xi-talks-up-chinas-ties-with-russia-during-putin-trade-trip   (accessed March 31, 2018).

Y

Yafeng Xia, Zhihua Shen (2015). *Mao and the Sino–Soviet Partnership, 1945–1959: A New History.* New York: Lexington Books.

Yaffa, Joshua (2016). "Russia's View of the Election Hacks: Denials, Amusement, Comeuppance." *New Yorker*, December 20. http://www.newyorker.com/news/news-desk/russias-view-of-the-election-hacks-denials-amusement-comeuppance (accessed March 31, 2018).

Yakovlev, Pyotr (2013). "Rossiya i Latinsaya Amerika na traektorii vzaimnogo sblizhenija"[Russia and Latin America on the trajectory of mutual convergence]. *Perspectives*, December 11. http://bit.ly/2rGSijT (accessed March 31, 2018).

Yakunin, V. (2018). *The Treacherous Path: An Insider's Account of Modern Russia.* London: Biteback.

Yasin, Yevgeny (2017). *Prizhevetsja li democratija v Rosii?* [Will democracy survive in Russia?]. Moscow: Litres.

Yeltsin, B. (1994). *Zapiski Presidenta.* Moscow: Ogonjok.

Yeltsin, B. (2000). *Midnight Diaries.* New York: Public Affairs.

Ying, Fu (2016). "How China Sees Russia." *Foreign Affairs*, January/February. https://www.foreignaffairs.com/articles/china/2015–12-14/how-china-sees-russia (accessed March 31, 2018).

Yuejin, Wang, and Na, Zhang (2008). "Russia: Is it a new investment opportunity for China?" *Zhongguo Jingji Shibao Online*, September 23. http://libguides.asu.edu/pres/fbis (accessed March 31, 2018).

Z

Zakaria, Fareed. (2008). *The Post-American World.* New York: W. W. Norton.

Zaslavsky, Victor. (2004). *Class Cleansing: The Massacre at Katyn.* New York: Telos Press Publishing.

Zhuravleva, V. I. (2012). *Ponimanie Rossii v SSHA: Obrazy I mify, 1881–1914* [Understanding Russia in the USA: Images and myths, 1881–1914]. Moscow: RGGU.

Zubok, Vladislav, and Pleshakov, Constantinne. (1997). *Inside the Kremlin's Cold War.* Cambridge, MA: Harvard University Press.

Zubok, Vladislav (2007). *A Failed Empire: The Soviet Union in the Cold War from Stalin to Gorbachev.* Chapel Hill, NC: University of North Carolina Press.

Index

Printed by Printforce, the Netherlands